INTRODUCTION TO REFERENCE WORK

VOLUME II *Reference Services and Reference Processes*

INTRODUCTION TO REFERENCE WORK

Volume II **Reference Services and Reference Processes**

Seventh Edition

William A. Katz
State University of New York at Albany

The McGraw-Hill Companies, Inc.
New York   St. Louis   San Francisco   Auckland
Bogotá   Caracas   Lisbon   London
Madrid   Mexico City   Milan   Montreal   New Delhi
San Juan   Singapore   Sydney   Tokyo   Toronto

McGraw-Hill

*A Division of The **McGraw·Hill** Companies*

INTRODUCTION TO REFERENCE WORK, Volume II
Reference Services and Reference Processes

Copyright © 1997, 1992, 1987, 1982, 1978, 1974, 1969 by The McGraw-Hill Companies, Inc. All rights reserved. Printed in the United States of America. Except as permitted under the United States Copyright Act of 1976, no part of this publication may be reproduced or distributed in any form or by any means, or stored in a data base or retrieval system, without the prior written permission of the publisher.

4 5 6 7 8 9 DOC DOC 9 0 9

ISBN 0-07-034278-4

This book was set in Baskerville by ComCom, Inc.
The editors were Ronda S. Angel and Bill McLane;
the production supervisor was Leroy A. Young.
The cover was designed by Christopher Brady.
The cover illustration was done by Gregory E. Stadnyk.
R. R. Donnelley & Sons Company was printer and binder.

Katz, William A., 1934–
    Introduction to reference work / William A. Katz — 7th ed.
        p.   cm.
    Includes bibliographical references (p.) and index.
    ISBN 0-07-034277-6 (v. 1). — ISBN 0-07-034278-4 (v. 2)
    1. Reference services (Libraries) 2. Reference books–
–Bibliography.   I. Title
Z711.K32 1997   96–1741
025.52—dc20   CIP

ABOUT THE AUTHOR

WILLIAM A. KATZ is a professor at the School of Information Science and Policy, State University of New York at Albany. He was a librarian at the King County (Washington) Library for four years and worked in the editorial department of the American Library Association. He received his Ph.D. from the University of Chicago and has been the editor of *RQ*, the journal of the Reference and Adult Services Division of the American Library Association, and the *Journal of Education for Librarianship*. Professor Katz is now editor of *The Reference Librarian*, a quarterly devoted to issues in modern reference and information services, and *The Acquisitions Librarian*, concerned with collection development. He is the editor of *Magazines for Libraries* and has compiled a second edition of *The Columbia Granger's Guide to Poetry Anthologies*. He is editor of a series on the history of the book for Scarecrow Press including his *A History of Book Illustration* and *Dahl's History of the Book*. Presently, he is writing a cultural history of reference books.

To Janet and Greg

CONTENTS

Preface   **xiii**

PART I   INTRODUCTION

1 *Reference Service and the Community*   **3**
     Gathering Information   **9**
     Library Reference Profile   **13**
     Information Superglut   **16**
     Special Groups Served   **19**
     Information and Nonlibrary Users   **21**
     Telephone Service   **23**
     Suggested Reading   **24**

PART II   LIBRARIES AND THE WIRING OF AMERICA

2 *The Age of Electronic Information*   **29**
     Information Sources   **31**
     Electronic Fun and Games Data   **33**
     Evaluation of Electronic Databases   **39**

Copyright   **46**

Desktop Publishing   **49**

Information Broker   **52**

Death of the Book   **54**

Suggested Reading   **56**

3   **Networks and Reference Services**   **59**

Supernetworks   **61**

World as Library   **64**

Bibliographical Networks   **65**

Regional and State Networks   **73**

Vendors and Networks   **77**

Consumer Networks   **80**

Television and the Computer   **83**

Suggested Reading   **86**

4   **The Internet and Reference Services**   **89**

Internet and Reference Services   **94**

Key Terms   **98**

Access and Searching   **107**

Cost and Management   **110**

Evaluation   **112**

Conclusion   **114**

Suggested Reading   **116**

5   **Document Delivery and Interlibrary Loan**   **119**

Electronic Full Texts   **120**

Document Delivery   **124**

Off-Site Document Delivery   **132**

Evaluation of Document Delivery   **138**

Interlibrary Loan (ILL)   **142**

The Electronic Book   **146**

Microform   **148**

Suggested Reading   **149**

PART III INTERVIEW AND SEARCH

6	*The Reference Interview*	**153**
	Who Needs an Answer?	**157**
	Reference Librarian as Mediator	**162**
	The Reference Interview—Step by Step	**165**
	Interview Problems	**169**
	Interviewing Techniques	1**72**
	Suggested Reading	**176**
7	*Rules of the Search*	**179**
	Search Strategy	**181**
	The Search and Problem Solving	**183**
	Translation of the Question	**186**
	Access Language of the Information System	**190**
	Rules of the Game	**192**
	The Answer	**194**
	Librarian as Mediator	**196**
	Suggested Reading	**199**
8	*Computerized Reference Searches*	**201**
	The Search	**205**
	Expert Searching	**210**
	Future Searching Patterns	**217**
	Suggested Reading	**218**

PART IV INSTRUCTION AND POLICIES

9	*Bibliographical Instruction*	**223**
	Basic Approaches	**227**
	Electronic Databases and Instruction	**229**
	Instruction Evaluation	**232**
	Suggested Reading	**235**

10   *Reference Service Policies and Evaluation*   **237**

Ethics and the Reference Librarian   **239**

Question of Fees   **247**

Collection Evaluation   **248**

Weeding   **251**

Evaluation of Reference Services   **254**

Evaluation Methods   **256**

Evaluative Techniques and Methods   **258**

Evaluating Librarians   **263**

Suggested Reading   **266**

Index   **269**

PREFACE

The goal of *Introduction to Reference Work* Volume II, *Reference Services and Reference Processes*, is to give the reader a more thorough overview and a broader understanding of the possibilities of reference services than could be encompassed in Volume I, *Basic Information Sources*. This second volume introduces the reader to the more sophisticated, imaginative, and, some think, more interesting aspects of the complete reference process. Another purpose is to indicate the ongoing and important changes and developments in information technologies.

NEW TO THIS EDITION

Almost everything in this edition is new, not simply revised from the sixth edition. The decision was necessary because of new technologies and the evolution in the practice and theory of reference services. In the sixth edition, for example, there was a single chapter on networks. In this edition there are two chapters in a section given over to the subject, as well as related chapters on the Internet and on document delivery.

The information highway, and its many off- and on-ramps, is in the process of global construction. If today there is an Internet, tomorrow there will be numerous versions of the famous network. If today the network is primarily employed in finding data, tomorrow it may be the key to searching all reference materials in full text. Networking will bring reference works to the home and, in the process, is likely to change the professional duties of the reference librarian. All of this is discussed in detail in Chapters 2 through 5.

A primary problem in any text of this type is the rapid change in information delivery. It is pointless, for example, to explain in detail how to reach point "c" and "d" on the Internet. Tomorrow the points of reference, the methods, will have changed with new networks, new hardware, and new software. Conversely, it is important to recognize the far-reaching implications of networking, if not the specifics of how to find this or that bit of datum. And it is to that purpose the second section was written, as well as most of the remainder of this second volume.

The second volume is a pragmatic, practical approach to information sources and theory. Basic developments are covered and explained. The footnotes and "Suggested Reading" sections guide those who wish to explore further. Leaders and followers in research and information science are responsible for much of what is revolutionary in reference services today. There are other courses, other places where information science can be considered in depth; all that can be done here is to hint at the joy of the intellectual fields open to the information scientist and researcher.

PLAN OF THE BOOK

The text opens with a discussion of traditional and new reference services in the community. Here the word *community* embraces almost every situation from the typical middle-class public library to the library serving the special needs of equally special groups of users. Problems and possible solutions are considered, especially in terms of limitations of budget and the new technologies. Enough is offered to suggest, if only in the broadest way, the people a librarian serves and hopes to serve. What was Chapter 2 in the previous text is now incorporated, although almost entirely rewritten, in the present Chapter 1.

The second chapter is entirely new to this text. It represents an overview of the electronic library today—and what it is likely to look like in the next few years. The status of the reference librarian in this new age is considered as is the place of the average person seeking information. Enough background information is presented to help the beginner make sense out of today's changing library and equal changes in an information society.

The section, "Libraries and the Wiring of America" continues with the Internet and related information channels. The importance of document delivery and interlibrary loan in future reference service is another major theme.

The third large section is devoted to chapters on the reference interview and various methods of searching. Here the primary focus is on the role of the librarian as mediator, as the person who filters out the useful information for the hapless or even well-informed client. Given this role, the searching process changes. Attention is given primarily to the search for content rather than technology. It is the author's contention that whether the required data are on a CD-ROM, online, in print, or part of a multimedia disc the important factor is what it contains or does not contain. The technologies which carry the message are important and today's reference librarian must be as familiar with computers and software as the databases themselves. Instruction and aid in using computers will become more and more a daily part of reference services.

The fourth and final section, "Instruction and Policies," contains two chapters. Beginning with the pros and cons of bibliographical and computer instruction, the section moves on to a consideration of reference service policies and methods of evaluation.

Students and teachers alike should be aware that much of the material covered in this book is updated, argued, and dutifully considered in several basic journals. *RQ,* the official voice of reference librarians of the American Library Association, excels in its coverage of the topics considered here. *Library Journal,* while more general, now offers excellent and timely articles on the new technology and its influence on librarians. Numerous features in *The Wilson Library Bulletin,* and particularly Jim Rettig's running document on new reference works, make the journal a necessary part of every reference librarian's reading. *The Reference Librarian,* edited by the author of this text, publishes specific discussions of single topics in each issue. These range from online reference services, to personnel, to problems of evaluation. And, not to be missed, is the nicely edited, always useful, and sometimes downright inspirational *Reference Services Review.* There are other journals in addition to these basic ones, of course. Many from *College & Research Libraries* to *Computers in Libraries* to *Online* are found in the footnotes and in the "Suggested Reading" section at the end of each chapter. Knowledge of the rapid changes in the field is not easily acquired. One must keep up to survive; a painless method of doing just that is to read current issues of these journals.

Thanks are due to the reviewers of this book: Eileen Abels, University of Maryland; Bahal El-Hadidy, University of South Florida; Ellen Getleson, University of Pittsburgh; Doug Raeber, University of Missouri; and Antonio Rodriguez-Buckingham, University of Mississippi. Thanks are also due to the editors of this volume, Bill McLane and particularly Ronda Angel whose diligence and imagination have vastly improved this edition. Thanks also to the indexer.

William A. Katz

INTRODUCTION TO REFERENCE WORK

VOLUME II *Reference Services and Reference Processes*

PART I
INTRODUCTION

CHAPTER ONE
REFERENCE SERVICE AND THE
COMMUNITY

Studies of the American way of life agree on three points: (1) Society is be-coming more stratified, more polarized, with the rich and the poor, the ed-ucated and uneducated wider apart than in any time in our history. (2) Limited cognitive skills are associated with lack of proper education, lack of information, and a myriad of social problems. (3) In a period of increasing stratification by income and ability, the library and other educational institutions may act as a bridge between the entrenched social poles.

Out of masses of statistical data, a truism is constant: The more income, education, and stability, the more likely an individual will turn to a library for information, education, and recreation. As the income-education-stability level rises in a community, so does library use. Conversely, in many urban areas where income, education, and stability are low, the library is usually underfinanced and underused. The paradox is obvious: The more people need a library, if only to gain information about better jobs and education, the less it is fiscally prepared or relevant to the community. The division between the information rich and information poor seems to be increasing.

The liberal economist John Kenneth Galbraith sums up the situation: "We have a modern reserve army of the masses consisting of the poverty-stricken population in the central cities. . . . There must be opportunity for es-cape from the underclass. . . . Nothing else is so important [as education]. . . . There is in our time no well-educated literate population that is poor, and there is no illiterate population that is other than poor."[1] A conservative scholar, Kevin Philips, underlines the situation: "The problems include a growing gap

[1]"The Good Society Has No Underclass," *The Guardian Weekly*, February 6, 1994, p. 23.

in income between the top fifth and the bottom fifth, as well as rising rates of poverty among children and the increased need of people for health and unemployment insurance increases."[2] Whether to help bridge the chasm between the poor, the rich, and the suburban middle class (where by 1996 the majority of Americans live) is a decision the public, the school, and to a lesser extent the academic libraries must make. That decision depends as much upon the attitude of the community served as the librarian setting the policy.

Library Role

The primary role of the library is educational. Traditionally, this has been the attitude, if not always the realization, of library reference librarians. It is a view shared by the American public which believes that an important role of a library is as an education center and research center. An average of 85 percent of Americans see the public library as: (1) an educational support for students of all ages (88 percent); (2) a learning center for adult independent learners (85 percent); (3) a discovery and learning center for preschool children (83 percent). The other role of the library as "a recreational reading center of popular materials and best-sellers" was down the list (under 45 percent).[3]

The library exists to serve the community. No one will argue with that platitude, although almost everyone has a somewhat different definition of *community*. People accept that the public library serves the public, and the school and academic libraries serve students and teachers. Beyond these generalizations, it is necessary to look at America as a community in terms of income, education, and interests. This type of broad profile is helpful in defining the local community in order to understand who the library serves—and does not serve. Major demographic trends include:

1. In terms of income (mid-1990s), 30 percent of American families make under $20,000 a year, and of the one-third, 13 percent makes $10,000 or less.[4] At the other extreme, 10 percent of American families have more than $100,000, with 2 percent making over $200,000 a year. Slightly over 50 percent, or what some term the "middle class," are in the $20,000 to $75,000 bracket. That 50 percent is divided into 14 percent from $20,000 to $30,000; 20 percent from $30,000 to $50,000; and 16 percent from $50,000 to $75,000.[5]

---

[2]How Is America . . . ? *The New York Times*, December 25, 1992, p. 12E.

[3]*The Bowker Annual* (New York: R. R. Bowker, 1994), pp. 430–431. A Gallup poll is quoted.

[4]*The Statistical Abstract of the United States.* Washington, DC: U.S. Government Printing Office. Various 1990s issues consulted.

[5]U.S. Treasury Department Office of Tax Analysis (figures printed in *The New York Times*, December 25, 1994, p. E1). Within large urban areas, such as New York City, the differences are even more marked. The median annual income of the poorest fifth in New York, for example, is $21,602 as compared with $175,000 for the richest fifth. *The New York Times*, April 17, 1995, pp. A1, D4, reported that the inequality in wealth in the United States is now greater than in any of the Western rich nations.

2. With respect to education, 24.2 percent of Americans now have a college degree, as compared with 7.7 percent in 1960. Another 25.1 percent (ages 25 to 64) list themselves as having had "some college." To use another comparison, in recent years about 2.2 million freshmen enroll each autumn, whereas some 1.1 million seniors graduate each spring. Approximately 70 to 75 percent have graduated from high school as compared with 40 percent in 1960.

3. The average SAT (Scholastic Assessment Test) score has dropped since 1965 from 466 to 424 in verbal aptitude; and 492 to 466 in mathematics.

4. Figures vary from a high of 50 percent to a low of 2 or 3 percent, but a vast number of Americans are illiterate, or border on being so. No one can say with authority how many adults are functionally illiterate, but the most widely held estimate is that from 23 to 27 million people, nearly 10 percent of the nation's population, cannot read and write well enough to meet the basic requirements of everyday life. At the current rate of decline, something like 2 million people each year are added to the illiteracy pool.[6]

Books—Computers—Reading

Americans seem to be less and less involved with information, but the sales of books, magazines, and computers have increased. The statistics are impressive in terms of volume. Related data in regard to demographics (who, for example, is buying all those books, all those computers) have yet to be analyzed.

1. Total book sales have increased from $10.5 billion in 1970 to close to $17 billion in 1995. And the amount spent on newspapers and magazines for the same time span has almost doubled. Comparatively, by the mid-1990s the amount spent on video and audio equipment and personal computers stands at $71 billion as compared with $8.8 billion in 1970.

The Book Industry Study Group, in 1995, issued a report on book trends which indicates that Americans continue to spend considerable money on books each year. The 1995 average was $79.22, compared with $56.35 for recorded music and $72.97 for home videos. In 1997 it is estimated the amount will jump to $93.91 and in 1999 to $107.19. Total book sales in 1997 will be about $27.5 billion and $33 billion in 1999 as compared with $23.8 billion in 1994. At the same time the number of printed books sold will be about the same because with electronic publishing more books will go digital. Spending increases because of rising costs of books, not necessarily because more people purchase printed titles.

2. A Gallup poll indicates that on average Americans spend about 6 percent of their leisure time reading—and this includes newspapers and magazines

[6]*The New York Times*, September 9, 1993, pp. 1, 22. This is a summary of the U.S. Department of Education report, based on a sampling among 26,000 Americans. It follows the same department's by now famous study, "A Nation at Risk," released in 1983. Things have not improved.

as well as books and gazing at computer screens. Comparatively, out of an average of about 5.5 hours of leisure, about one-third of that time is given over to television.[7] In terms of expenditures for reading, about two-thirds is for magazines and newspapers, while another third goes to reference works and general books.

3. Basic reference materials in the home have decreased considerably since a 1971 study. Then it was found that close to 40 percent of all nine-year-olds said their families had newspapers, books, magazines, and encyclopedias at home. By 1995 the figure had dropped to 30 percent—and is still dropping.

4. Computers, with possible reference materials available (particularly on CD-ROM and through consumer networks such as Prodigy), are found in some 33 million homes. The number increases each month, each year, and is expected to reach at least 50 million by the late 1990s. Only about one-tenth use the computer for what might be called reference. At the same time, the new technologies, from CD-ROMs to online searches, have helped increase the number of people *expecting* library reference services. There are more requests on how to use the technologies than on how to locate data. The catch is that most of the computers and related items in a library are used by people who always go to the library.

5. In the early 1980s, there were wide reports of a decrease in student reading, writing, and science skills. A long-standing argument has gone on ever since about what is to be done, if anything. By the mid-1990s the overall picture could be found in various studies and reports from the U.S. Department of Education. The primary points: (*a*) Students spend more time watching television than reading. (*b*) Those who do read show a marked lack of proficiency in understanding what is read. (*c*) Only 2 percent of eleventh-graders write well enough to meet national goals. Summarizing the role of young people on the information highway Secretary of Education Richard Reily commented: "Holding our own in the information age is simply not good enough. It just doesn't cut it any more. . . . Virtually all 13 and 17 year old's can read, write, add, subtract and count their change. But as one moves up the scale toward slightly more complicated tasks, student success fall off rapidly.[8]

6. In the early 1990s a group of University of Pennsylvania students surveyed 3119 undergraduates at their campus and at seven other Ivy League colleges. Half the students were unable to (*a*) name their home state senators and (*b*) name the Speaker of the House. One-third did not know the name of England's prime minister or that Alan Greenspan was the chairman of the Federal

[7]Gallup data based on a survey of 6000 Americans aged sixteen and older conducted June 1990 through June 1992. *The New York Times*, May 9, 1993, p. 2E.

[8]"U.S. Students Are Found Gaining Only in Science," *The New York Times*, August 18, 1994, p. A14; April 28, 1995, p. A18.

Reserve Board. And 11 percent had no idea that Thomas Jefferson wrote the Declaration of Independence.[9]

Library Users

American use of public libraries has increased steadily over the past two or three decades. Today nearly 54 percent of adults report using a public library. The figure jumps to two-thirds of eighteen- to twenty-four-year-olds. Most of these are from the middle classes in terms of economic and educational advantages.

School and academic libraries have a specific audience, with more attention given to students than to teachers or administrators. Public libraries may spend as much time with children and teenagers as school libraries, but tend to divide their efforts between them and adults.

Highly correlated with income and educational levels, public library use drops dramatically for those with less than a high school education. In this group, only 17 percent of the adults go to a public library. If 70 percent of adults with incomes over $75,000 a year use the library, only about 35 percent of those with incomes under $20,000 visit the library.[10] There are other reasons for this condition, not the least of which is illiteracy, or virtual illiteracy. Someone who can hardly read or write is not likely to turn to a library.

Library Finance

How influential can a library be in a given community? The answer, of course, relies on numerous factors and variables. Something, again, can be learned by statistics.[11]

1. Statistically, there are some 9050 public libraries in the United States with about 1500 urban and country libraries reporting an additional 7000 or so branches. Close to one-half the public libraries (about 45 percent) have budgets of under $50,000 a year. Nearly 37 percent spend between $50,000 and $399,000. Only about 20 percent—or about 1800 libraries—have funding over $400,000. Close to 70 percent of the population is served by only about 950 libraries, primarily in urban and closely aligned suburban communities.

[9]"Big Gaps . . . ," *The New York Times,* April 18, 1993, p. 12. The interviews were interested in other related matters. While two-thirds of the students claimed they read a daily newspaper, only half said they watched television news.

[10]Jim Scheppke, "Who's Using the Public Library?" *Library Journal,* October 15, 1994. This is a report of a 1991 survey by the National Center for Education Statistics.

[11]Data are from *The Bowker Annual* (New York: R. R. Bowker, 1994), pp. 131–plus. Most of the figures represent 1991 data released in 1993. Nevertheless the proportionate figures, give or take for inflation and tax tables, remain much the same over the decades. See, too, *The Whole Library Handbook 2* (Chicago: American Library Association, 1995, pp. 2–58) for even more detailed statistics.

2. Americans spend from $4 per capita to $100 per capita for public library support in various communities. The national average is $16 per capita.

3. There are some 3280 academic libraries, with 488 of the institutions offering doctoral degrees. The 488 take close to 60 percent of all funding, although the 488 represent only about 15 percent of the total number. The same 488 institutions have about 60 percent of all books held in academic libraries. They account for 50 percent of all professional libraries employed. Again, most of the 488 are located in wealthy or relatively wealthy areas and are privately endowed. At the same time, some 50 percent of academic libraries have only enough to sustain minimum services, minimum staff, and certainly a minimum stake in new technologies.

4. Statistics for school libraries (or media centers) are not as precise. Still, if one considers the public library and academic library comparisons fairly standard, it is safe to state that only about 15 to 20 percent of school libraries are adequately financed.

In all types of libraries the future is far from bright. Government, both national and local, is cutting back on educational monetary support. This comes at a time when the new, expensive technologies demand even more investment than in the past.

Conclusion

Considering all the variables, there is little evidence that the age of information has arrived, at least for most Americans. The average member of a library community is better educated, but seems to be no wiser. Illiteracy continues to grow. Book and computer sales are up, but even more so is the popularity of television. Pessimists see a "dumbing" of America. Reference librarians must soldier on in the considered belief of service. How that service is defined depends on the librarian and the community served, but, to return to Galbraith's earlier quotation, many believe that "in the good society there must not be a deprived and excluded underclass."

Constantly in contact with a public anxious to find answers to particular questions, no matter how simple or how complex, the average reference librarian has a rarified view of the actual and potential library public just considered. Libraries concerned with the finer points of information science, as well as government and business closely tied to information potential, are sometimes out of touch with what is going on among the majority. Understandably, the focus of the journals, from *Library Journal* and *Internet World* to *College & Research Libraries* and *RQ*, is on the information researcher. This group is only a small part of the population—probably no more than 1 or 2 percent, although a much larger percentage are casual users of general reference services.

Perspective is needed. This is not easy to achieve. There are many conflicting statistics, studies, and surveys about information and Americans. Also, the reference librarian may argue that perspective is not necessary. There is hardly enough money, personnel, or time to serve the information literate, to say nothing of the illiterates or those less than interested in reference services. Others would argue that librarians must reach out for a public, must, like a corporation, constantly seek new users or be lost. Raw numbers of users often determine how much funding the library receives. There is, too, the social argument. Libraries, and particularly school and public libraries, have a mission in the education of Americans. This is especially true of the reference section.

GATHERING INFORMATION

How information is used, and particularly by different individuals from different educational, economic, and cultural backgrounds, is too rarely addressed. In the larger context of reference services it becomes imperative to understand who uses information and how it is gathered. The importance of this is underlined with each new database, with each new full-text service, with each new network. There are simply too many data. Someone has to be able to mediate between them and the user. This cannot be done until one appreciates not only the information sources, but also the individual seeker of data[12]

The librarian is concerned with the ability to access what is needed for X or Y query. Access in turn implies an understanding of the information process. Such a literate person "must be able to recognize when information is needed and have the ability to locate, evaluate and use effectively the needed information. . . . Ultimately information-literate people are those who have learned how to learn."[13]

Packaging Information

The steps in the creation and packaging of information may be traced in various ways. While not everyone will agree with this or that analysis, a general overview of the different communication packages is possible. The information, or message, goes through three phases before its eventual publication in some traditional reference form, such as a book or periodical article. These phases are: (1) the origin of the message, (2) the informal communication of the message, and (3) the formal communication of the message.

Even with e-mail, Listserv, and other forms of communication over a computer, the basic pattern of information packaging remains the same. What differs is the amount of control by a second or third party. This may be nonexistent, say, on the Internet, but of major importance for a book publisher.

[12]See "Real Time and Real Life Connections," *Library Journal*, February 15, 1994, p. 113, for a brief discussion of this major consideration.

[13]Stephen Foster, "Information Literacy," *American Libraries*, April 1993, p. 344.

Phase 1—Origin of the Message

The message originates when the individual author begins to think about his or her next novel and puts the thoughts on paper. Or it can originate when the inventor developing a better mousetrap is working on the project with six other mousetrap experts. Each is thinking, exploring, and experimenting, but none has yet arrived at the final version—the polished fiction or the decisive way to catch a mouse.

The same process goes on when one undertakes the common task of writing a paper for a class. First there has to be an idea for the paper, even if it is only a suggestion from a teacher, a friend, reading, television, and so forth. The *idea generation* may be the most difficult phase, although the consequent efficient solving of the problem posed by the idea offers another major challenge—deciding how the idea is to be implemented by research and eventually modified for the purpose of the paper. Still, those who have struggled with the innovative process itself recognize the difficulty of phase 1 of the communication process.

The formality, even some say the thought behind the origin of the message, may disappear with the computer and e-mail. On the other hand, even the most informal chatter does require some consideration. The difference here is that e-mail and its many cousins may or may not be a formal way of communication. It is important to distinguish, say, the quick response to a message of love from a plea from a student or researcher for a detailed analysis of drinking water.

Phase 2—Informal Communication of the Message

Once the message is conceived, how is it passed on? Librarians are familiar with the formal method of communication, the translation into the printed word. They are equally familiar with informal channels, but, as will be shown, rarely use them in reference situations.

The information in phase 2 of the communications chain may be labeled in many ways but, essentially, it is the familiar inside information, or "inside dope." Knowledge of this information may give the receiver a certain status from knowing something few others know, or it may help the receiver in an instrumental way by supplying evidence for a decision—a decision regarding whether to go ahead on this or that experiment, business deal, or research project, or whether to modify the experiment or project. The content of the informal message varies, but the transmission process is somewhat the same in all disciplines:

1. Informal channels of transmission:

    a. Face-to-face discussion with colleagues and those interested in the project.

      b. Discussion through the computer, telephone, or private corre-
spondence.

      c. Drafts of manuscripts to be circulated among friends and col-
leagues—by mail, computer, and so on.

      d. Discussion at meetings and seminars.

  2. Semiformal channels of transmission:

      a. Works in progress. A communicator may report the current sta-
tus of the project. In the case of the author of the novel, this communication may be totally informal and may be picked up from
a variety of sources, from *Publishers Weekly* to *The New York Review
of Books;* that is, a note may appear to the effect that Y author's
next novel is finished. In the case of the mousetrap consortium,
there may be a formal outlet for the communication such as a series in a journal that reports works under way by X and Y scientists.

      b. Semipublished studies. If one accepts "semipublished" in the sense
that the work has not been offered for general circulation but is in
a printed form, this would include computer printouts. There are
several online services, such as FINDEX, which focuses on abstract
research reports, studies, and surveys otherwise not published. In
fact, many scientific and social science reports, studies, and talks
can be found online for many months, if not years, before they are
formally published.

What is peculiar about both the informal and semiformal channels of
transmission indicated here is that generally the information packages are not
available to libraries. "Generally" is used advisedly because online services make
many of these relatively inaccessible forms part of the reference process. Also,
the alert reference librarian may tap into the semiformal levels of transmission
when those are committed in some form to print—works in progress are often
parts of journals and books; reports that are unclassified and not private are indexed and abstracted, and many are available to librarians; dissertations are generally available by means of well-organized indexing.

However, this merely skims the surface, tapping only the obvious aspects
of the semiformal channels of communication. Much more is needed in terms
of bibliographical control of traditional print and nonprint materials.

Phase 3—Formal Communication of the Message

Time passes, and the communication chain is completed. In terms of our model,
this means that the communicator's message has been codified, having been
transmitted formally in a format that may range from an online journal article
to a book. The time from gestation of an idea until the publication of a report

or journal article varies with individuals and disciplines. However, in most disciplines this is usually two to three or more years.

It is generally only when the chain is complete that the reference library comes into play by (1) acquiring and organizing the message in whatever form it may take; (2) acquiring the necessary indexes, abstracts, bibliographies, and cataloging to gain ready access to the message; and (3) organizing the reference system in such a way that the message may be retrieved with a minimum of effort and a maximum of relevancy for the user.

The communication packages in phase 3 include the standard resources found in any reference situation. They are listed here in the general order of most current, next most current, and so forth.

1. Databases, particularly those updated hourly or daily.

2. Reports (printed and other, including computer e-mail, tapes, and televised news shows and news events).

3. Periodicals, the timeliness of which increases when they are published as discs or tapes and are available online.

4. Indexing and abstracting services—databases are usually, though not always, available faster than printed versions.

5. Annual reviews and state-of-the-art reports.

6. Bibliographical reviews.

7. Books.

8. Encyclopedia summaries.

9. Almost any other resource in print or in nonprint form, that is, textbooks, conference proceedings, the library catalog, audiovisual materials, and so on.

Library Access to Communications Forms

The guides to this morass of information become increasingly scarce as one moves from published to semipublished sources. Internet, for example, is a jungle when it comes to discovering a particular piece of unpublished information, especially if the data retrieval is not within the experience of the searcher. In fact, some information is extremely hard to come by because it is private (office memoranda, for example) or has never been indexed, abstracted, or otherwise made available. Totally unpublished material has little chance of circulation except at a computer terminal, in conversations, conferences, meetings, and the like, where one might learn about, and sometimes even view, the materials.

What is needed are effective access and retrieval systems which will make it easier to acquire, control, and access records. The records available should include not just those in libraries, but others as well—as long, of course, as they are available to the public, as limited as the public may be. A method of discrimination and evaluation must be built into these devices to eliminate the records that need not be maintained. To date we are closer to a system of acquisitions and control than we are to devising a means of evaluation. It is likely that for generations to come the essential task of the librarian will be the establishment and implementation of standards in information storage.

Another major consideration is the highly international nature of information. It is increasingly the case that the well-informed draw upon data from all over the world, not simply the country of origin. True, most of the time the information has to be in English, but everyone from U.S. industrialists and scientists to European technicians and businesspeople understand a language that is a key to modern markets and products. This is not to argue against knowing a foreign language, but only to admit a basic weakness of most Americans from all professions. The development of the European Community, with a population of over 350 million and a gross national product exceeding that of the United States, gives the librarian more opportunity for information channels.

LIBRARY REFERENCE PROFILE

Despite the dismal state of the American "community" and the financial condition of libraries, there is hope. When one turns to those who use libraries for reference assistance, one becomes more optimistic. There have been countless studies of various types of reference users and libraries, studies which are valuable in understanding how information is matched with the needs of the individual. Several generalities have emerged, and some of them are outlined here.

The average client study is based on demographics, that is, an evaluation of education, age, occupation, economic status, and so forth. Often the study is balanced with such variables as the size of the library collection, the education of the staff, the distance of the user from the library, and so on.

Another type of patron study considers communication patterns and such things as how and why the reference section is used, and why one person may prefer periodicals to books or databases. Several conclusions have emerged:

1. People have different patterns of behavior when they are seeking information, at least information other than the ready-reference variety. Although libraries may separate information into the classical divisions, such as the humanities and science, and their subdivisions, people rarely seek information within those specific, logical areas.

2. Few people seek information as an end in itself; rather, it is used to help trigger decision making or to enhance understanding of the immediate environment or the world. Most clients want the information. They are not interested in how it is obtained.

3. The average patron does not contact the reference librarian. Signs indicating where to get the right type of help, and an understanding among staff about directing an individual to a reference librarian, are helpful in improving information communication.

4. Where the library has one or more computer terminals for public use, the user is more likely to look to a librarian for assistance. It is vital for users to understand that such assistance is freely available.

5. Despite the mass of material on communication and information, the general public still knows too little about these specialized fields. The average person copes with a glut of information from radio, television, newspapers, and magazines very simply. Most often, the public does not hear, view, or read—it ignores. When information is "received," the receiver may:

a. Accept it, that is, use it as a means of reinforcing existing opinion; or reject it because it challenges existing opinion. A characteristic verbal response is often "I know that," or else, "I didn't know that."

b. Add it to memory without allowing it to make any real impression. Verbally, the response would be "Yes," or "Oh, I see," or simply, "O.K., I understand."

c. Use it to answer a latent question, that is, "the information may be pictured as connecting two previously isolated elements of knowledge." Here the person would say, "Oh, that explains things."

d. In some cases, the person accepts the new information and uses it to transform an opinion or an idea. Verbally it would be expressed: "That does change matters" or "That alters my position."

6. Information may be graded in terms of potential value to users. For example, a finding in an otherwise undistinguished article may trip the thought processes of one researcher, who is then led into a completely new approach to a problem. There are many relationships among information sources, and there is no valid way to determine what is or is not valuable for all people at all times and in all places.

7. The successful decision makers are those who are able to acquire and process information quickly, no matter what type of situation they happen to be in. The ability to acquire and process information is very difficult to achieve. Reference librarians should see their primary function as one of assisting in this important processing operation. Inability to separate knowledge, facts, and understanding from the masses of data often results in what one author has come to call *information anxiety*. Anxiety can reach the nervous breakdown stage when the average layperson (or student) is confronted with technical material from almost any field.

8. It is harder and harder for experts to understand even what other experts are saying. Using a scale from plus 50 to minus 50, the vocabulary of the more technical fields ranks close to 50. Popular magazines and newspapers would be between 0 and 10. A boy chatting with a cow would be about *minus* 50. Some laypeople feel more at home with the cow. Reference librarians must be comfortable with cows and with vocabularies in the plus 50 bracket. More important they must be able to interpret to laypeople what the experts are about.

The "Invisible College"

How do most people collect the information they need to make a decision or simply to answer some persistent query? Most often the answer is found by the researcher in the so-called invisible college, and by the layperson at the "back fence." Although more analysis has been made of the phenomenon of the "invisible college" than of the "back fence," there seem to be similarities in both approaches.

Several studies indicate that the procedures in information gathering are common to us all.

1. The first and possibly the single best source of information for both laypeople and subject experts is conversation with a friend who knows the subject matter. Lacking someone next door or in the next room, the curious individual may turn to a personal computer, pick up the telephone, or even write a letter to the expert.

Most research on the "invisible college" has been limited to the scientific community, but the few profiles available of other information seekers confirm the general pattern followed by scientists. When scientists, social scientists, and those involved with the humanities are asked to list their information sources, all note that informal personal contact is valuable. When asked the method most often employed for locating a reference, all include personal recommendation, although in different orders of importance. Social contact at conferences and meetings is also cited as valuable for information gathering.

2. Thanks in good part to the Internet, and low-cost communication by e-mail, today's "invisible college" is most likely to be through a network channel. Where heretofore one might chat on a phone, now one talks person to person over the Internet, or uses a Listserv or the ubiquitous Usenet discussion group. Meetings are arranged without benefit of conferences; and papers and findings are exchanged without print publication. In effect, the computer network may have made the "invisible college" all too visible in that privacy can be short-circuited and, where at one time it was a one-to-one conversation, now it can turn with intent or not into a one to a thousand discussion.

3. A third source of informal information may be the personal library of books, periodicals, newspaper clippings, or like material. These days an individual is likely to have numerous reference sources on CD-ROMs or downloaded on personal discs.

4. Should the personal library fail, the user is then forced to turn to the formal library and perhaps even ask a reference librarian for assistance. The librarian is likely, through networks, to have access to data which may or may not be in either the personal or institutional library. A growing number, too, turn to sometimes less than reliable data on the Internet and World Wide Web.

The common denominator of these various approaches is convenience and ease. Most people turn first to what they can find with the least amount of effort, with or without a computer. Many are willing to sacrifice an in-depth article available in a library for a quick, possibly shallow, answer from a friend, or an online or CD-ROM database. Parallel studies show that user expectations are highest for the formal library—although this may be the last place one goes—and lowest for the personal library.

Selective Dissemination of Information (SDI)

Selected dissemination of information, or SDI, is a term commonly employed in the computer-assisted search, and is a way of saying that once a day, once a week, or once a month, the librarian searches the available new literature and prepares a bibliography of materials likely to be of interest to a particular person. For example, if X client is involved with hospital administration, the librarian would search databases likely to give the latest information on the topic. The computer printout is then sent to the client or it may be sent electronically to the user's computer or to an organizational computer to which the user has access. In this way the material is "selected" from the latest periodical indexes, that is, databases, and the "information" is "disseminated" to the user.

SDI can be done almost automatically. A search is made each time a database is updated or new databases are added. OCLC's Article First and Contents First can be programmed to indicate articles of interest to users. The key search words or phrases are built into the standing search. The user mentioned above, for example, is notified each month how many citations are available for "hospital administration." The client can then modify the request (if there are too many or too few citations) and receive an updated printout of the citations or abstracts. There are scores of similar services which make SDI, once it is set up for an individual, an easy-to-follow program.

INFORMATION SUPERGLUT

What is the single biggest problem concerning information today? There is too much of it.

It is that simple, and it is the topic of countless articles, discussions, books, and even television programs. Some call it *information overload,* others label it *information anxiety,* and still others consider it an *abundance of garbage.*

The problem is twofold: (1) Does the public, general or specialized, really want or need all the new or rehashed data? (2) Does the public really need still another technology to speed along the mass of material to the person at breakfast time who can hardly get through the front page of a newspaper much less another conference speech or a journal article? A serious error in today's reflections about information science is the sometimes unconscious and unconscionable assumption that the more information available, the better off the society. Total undifferentiated access to information can well enslave the poor user.

The Librarian's Response

How does the reference librarian solve the problem of too much information? One solution, and the most pressing, involves efforts to find the money, shelf space, technology, and staff to cope with the overload. There are other half solutions. There is no perfect answer.

As a result of tight budgets, the administrative response to too much information has been to cut back on periodicals, limit book purchases, hold down staff development, and do just about anything else that will work while not totally destroying the library service.

From time to time the suggestion is made that people write less, publish less. Extensive studies have been made which end with the predictable answer: "We don't need all those mediocre to poor articles, books, or electronic publications." Fine to say, but how does one stop the publication? How does one stop the tide?

Eventually the market serves as a check on the amount of data about. Software producers as well as print textbook publishers and CD-ROM distributors have an understandable urge to issue more and more. But the demand is finite, particularly for repetitious information. The lack of buyers will sooner or later check the flood of information.

Reference Librarian as Information Mediator

One major, significant answer to the problem is for the reference librarian to serve as an information mediator, to determine what is useful, what is needed, and what can be rejected. As an information mediator, the reference librarian of today is ensured a major role in the information society of tomorrow. Where once the librarian was a useful individual, tomorrow, as mediator, he or she will be absolutely necessary.

Librarians, might consider the mass of information a blessing because, if nothing else, it (1) increases the chances of finding the best, current, precise answer(s) and (2) it encourages the layperson to think of the librarian as an individual trained to cope with the overload.

In the past the reference librarian has had the opposite concern. Never quite certain that the user was receiving enough information about a given question, the tendency was to give as much as was available and let the user select and choose. Thanks to information overload this formula today is one that can lead only to disaster and a frustration for most users. Specialists, of course, may still want "all" that is available, but they are rare.

Common sense dictates that the professional reference librarian command and control information. The ability to determine what is good, bad, or indifferent for a given individual with a given question is at the heart of the matter. In its broadest context it is one exercised almost every day by the librarian. For example, how does one select just the right periodical, or the best article from among 120,000 to 140,000 journals now being published? Which of the 40,000 to 50,000 books issued each year in America can be of help to a particular reader? Should the baffled high school senior turn to the CD-ROM Readers' Guide, or rely on a more specialized service to find current data on hunger in America?

The reference librarian *selects what is relevant* and thereby helps tame the information giant.

Beyond exclusion and inclusion of information, the librarian must deal with what is at hand and, furthermore, what can be had at the computer terminal. So, while it is important to wage war on too much information by careful selection, the second weapon in the battle is an understanding and appreciation of individual information needs. This assumes that the librarian has certain capabilities when fielding questions:

1. An understanding of what the individual client requires. In most cases the librarian must have an appreciation of the research process. How does one move from an unqualified mass of data to a particular fact or group of facts which, in turn, may be employed to solve a larger problem?

2. An understanding that most people with questions not only have a query about the information itself, but also are often working blindly toward a thesis which they may or may not fully understand. This hit-and-miss aspect of research is evident in such problems as attempting to (*a*) pinpoint the solution to juvenile crime; (*b*) appreciate the contribution of Henry James to the class novel; or (*c*) solve the meaning of the expanding universe.

The individual moves from the general to the particular and hopes for assistance from the librarian. Examples include a frustrated carpenter who needs all information available for construction of a garage roof and does not want everything on the subject of carpentry and certainly not a history of garages; or a high school student searching for material on "democracy versus socialism," where the librarian must narrow the query and select a minimum amount of material to meet the time limits and educational background of the student.

The role of librarian as mediator, as evaluator and friend of the user, is an important one. It is the professional duty of the librarian to pick and choose, to select what is needed for the specific user for a specific situation.

SPECIAL GROUPS SERVED

There is a major problem with any discussion of library service to special groups. As long as "special" is read to mean the middle and upper classes, all is well. As soon as the label is used as a disguise for the underclass, there can be disagreement. The argument goes that the underfinanced library has no business trying to solve gigantic social problems such as illiteracy and promote outreach programs for the poor. It is a logical value judgment about the mission of the library and librarian. Others, including this author, grant that these are terrible problems, but they believe the role of the library is to serve all, not just the few. In this text, the library is seen as a social as well as an information service. The two, particularly at the public library level, are inseparable. Even the reader who rejects this assumption should at least know there are millions of nonlibrary users out there, as well as clients who need special attention. And that is what this section is about, argument or no.

Multicultural Groups

There are various ways to designate groups that are composed of other than white, middle-class, "average" users of the library. The descriptions of these groups vary—such as disadvantaged or underprivileged. It is impossible, and unwise, to lump all members of the groups under a single name. Whatever they are called, the majority of their members unfortunately represent nonusers of library services today.

Primarily, there are two large groups in the category of the disadvantaged. The first is composed of those lacking necessary education. The second, which may be a part of the first, is the poor and includes many ethnic minorities: African Americans, Hispanics, Native Americans, and so forth.

While not all members of minority groups are underprivileged, enough are to identify them as part of the larger, deprived group. In any case, and whatever the descriptor, the disadvantaged include both adults and youngsters, both city and country dwellers.

In providing reference services for ethnic minorities, several factors must be considered: (1) Foreign language materials, particularly the basic reference works, for example, encyclopedias, dictionaries, geographical sources, and so on, should be part of acquisitions whenever possible. (2) Members of the reference staff should be familiar with the language(s) of the ethnic groups. (3) Community information files should be tailored to the needs of these groups. (4) Maximum effort should be made to reach these groups through information and referral centers, publicity, and so forth. The use of television, radio, and door-to-door canvasing are effective tools here. (5) Including local members of prominent minorities and ethnic groups on the staff is an obvious benefit.

It is necessary to pay close attention to cultural differences simply as matters of sensitivity, courtesy, or diplomacy. Give it any name, but the name of the game is success at answering questions, and any barrier, cultural or otherwise, that stands in the way of that goal is to be routed out and overcome.

In a national report, a major suggestion was made about library service to racial-ethnic groups:

> A library could begin by identifying the significant service populations of its community based on race, gender, age, education level, size of household, or any of the other demographic characteristics reported in these surveys. For each of these significant service populations (for example, African-American households with preschoolers), the library could then identify the roles that are reported in these surveys to be most important to the respondents who represent the service population. . . . A library could then develop a tentative set of roles for its community that could be tested by a small community survey, or by interviews with representatives of its various service populations, or by town meetings, or by any other method appropriate to local conditions or resource.[14]

Multiculturalism—the Debate

In his far from favorable book on multiculturalism, Richard Bernstein, a *New York Times* reporter, demonstrates that the phenomenon he deplores is on the rise. A search of NEXIS in 1981 showed the words multiculture and multiculturalism 40 times; but by 1992 the terms appeared more than 2000 times, or a fiftyfold increase in just eleven years. A related term in the literature, "politi-

[14] *The Bowker Annual.* New York: R. R. Bowker, 1994, p. 431. See also the second edition of the American Library Association's *The Whole Library Handbook 2* (Chicago: American Library Association, 1995; Chapter 6, Special Populations, pp. 332–353), in which the other than traditional white middle-class users of libraries are considered in terms of library services. Groups discussed, as well as collection and selection policies of materials for said groups, include: African Americans, Hispanics, Native Americans, illiterates, the elderly, and prisoners. Each group varies in number and importance in terms of the library, but each group is made up of deserving individuals who are the real concern of the reference librarian. "Groups" are handy and sometimes useful slots, particularly when deciding cultural and language-interest reference works to buy or to pass over, but they are no more than reminders that everyone is not the same. The obvious danger of such categorization is stereotyping. An African American with a print impairment may be no different than a white middle-class American with the same problems. Conversely an elderly Hispanic whose English is shaky may be a great intellectual, and still have problems with English-language reference works. It comes to this—every member of a community or group must be treated separately and, eventually, as an individual. (Note: After the March of One Million in Washington, D.C., in the fall of 1995, numerous leaders called for a return to the descriptor "Black" instead of "African-American." In this text the latter term is used as it seems, at least for the present, more prevalent.)

cally correct" was evident seven times in 1991, but by 1992 the author found 5007 appearances.[15] No matter how one stands on what these words imply, there is no denial of their importance in the American vocabulary—both to the right and to the left.

The argument is rarely over the basic principles of multiculturalism but rather concerns how far to go and what to do to, as a cliché puts it, "level the playing ground."

Multicultural reference service is part of a long tradition of equal service for everyone. The benefits of attention to the area is that it focuses, or refocuses, the need for services not only to Caucasian Americans, but to African Americans and Hispanic Americans (to name the three largest groups).

The Handicapped

Reference services for the disabled follow national moves to give the disabled vital access to formerly restrictive surroundings. Librarians have focused their attention not only on materials, but on physical access to library facilities. Most important, they are offering reference assistance which helps the individual gain an understanding of educational, medical, social, and related programs. Services can be offered either directly or through an intermediary working with the disabled.

Some of the services the library might offer the handicapped include a referral center for volunteer readers and a space set aside where handicapped patrons can work with librarians and with specialized materials and equipment.

. . . And

There are other types of librarians serving other types of people. Prison libraries, for example, have existed since the latter part of the eighteenth century. (Here is one case where one wishes that success could be measured by a decrease in the audience, but that is another matter.) The Library Standards for Adult Correctional Institutions see the prison library as a method of habilitating and integrating the offender into society. However, there are problems, not the least of which is finding professional librarians for the posts.

INFORMATION AND NONLIBRARY USERS

Most people in the United States function without a reference library. Between friends, the mass media, and experience and intuition, they make decisions

---

[15]Richard Bernstein, *Dictatorship of Virtue* (New York: Alfred A. Knopf, 1994). For another, pragmatic side to multiculturism see the 1994 report by the National Center for History and Schools, "National Standards for United States History. . . ." This is the second guidebook on how to teach history in grades 5 through 12.

which do not require reference use. For them, the library is primarily a place to find fiction or to rest for a few minutes. The library simply does not appeal to the average person's notion of an information environment. This is unfortunate, because the very people who desperately need reliable information are unable to cope with the library itself. The nonusers who need it the most are the up-rooted people on the move, the underclass, the chronically poor.

There are major disparities among socioeconomic groups, which are reflected in library use. Some critics see it as an inevitable circle: education and economic security lead to exposure to information, which in turn leads to increased knowledge about self and the community. The poor and undereducated rely on interpersonal communication and organization, usually outside formal channels. If librarians are to reach these people, they must understand the methods of communication and the limited information universe of the information illiterates, who number in the many millions. Librarians are concerned with striking a *balance* between meeting the needs of the information literates and reaching out to the rest of the public who do not, or cannot, use a library.

It is just possible that everyone does not want to have instant access to information. "Very few people anymore want a real superhighway through their neighborhood, and perhaps it will someday be the same with . . ." the information highway.[16] True enough, but at least they must be given the opportunity to accept or reject the highway—and that decision is only possible when there is an adequate reference section to turn to, or to avoid. Hence, the need for I&R (information and referral services).

Information and Referral Services (I&R)

A term frequently seen in connection with reference service at the public library level is *information and referral,* or simply *I&R.* The term comes from the fact that the librarian begins by giving information, but if this is not enough, will refer the person to the proper agency or individual. The referral process may go as far as having the librarian make an appointment with an agency for the individual. There are other terms used to describe this service, such as *community information center.* Essentially, the purpose of this special reference service is to offer the users access to resources that will help them with health, rent, consumer, legal, and similar problems. Libraries can provide free information on such subjects.

Even in the most traditional library, it is now common to (1) call individual experts, including anyone from a local professor to a leader in a local special-interest group, for assistance; (2) provide files, pamphlets, booklists, and so on, which give users information on topics ranging from occupations to local

---

[16]"So Are the Wired," *The New York Times,* October 24, 1993, p. 16.

housing regulations; and (3) provide a place which active groups in the community may identify as an information clearinghouse for their needs.

The "reach out" aspect of I&R is its most important characteristic, and this has been implemented in a number of ways. The most common is the storefront reference center where someone may wander in from a shopping center or a main street in a downtown area to find a helpful reference librarian. I&R is an effort to overcome an inequality attendant on people who do not know that certain information exists and who are therefore unaware of their rights. These rights can range from free school lunches to the minimum wage, and many people forgo what is legally theirs out of pure ignorance.

Another basic problem which I&R tries to solve relates to an individual's inability to understand information in the form that it is presented. This not only includes the illiterate, but many others who are borderline literates, or who simply have a difficult time deciphering legal or social jargon. I&R tries to offer information in various formats that can be understood by the user who has a reading problem.

I&R services are as varied in scope and purpose as the imagination of librarians and the needs of users. A major stumbling block is budget. No matter how willing the librarian or how great the need, without funding, the program is likely to go nowhere. Another requirement is staff involvement: Librarians must be convinced that the course of action is worthwhile and practical.

TELEPHONE SERVICE[17]

Unequal reference service is often given when someone telephones with a query and the librarian drops everything to respond. Understandably, the people waiting at the desk may be less than pleased. There are two ways of overcoming this problem:

1. Install a telephone answering service, which can be done without too much cost, to be used when the librarian is busy. The message: "What is your question(s)?" and "I will get back to you as soon as possible." In this way, the person on the phone feels satisfied and the individual in front of the desk is not overlooked.

2. If the library is large enough, there is a specialized telephone reference service that allows librarians to screen calls. Here the usual process is to identify the question, which usually is no more than a ready-reference problem ("What is the address of X or Y?" "Where can I find information on colleges?" "What is the height of the tallest building in the world?"). If specialized assis-

---

[17]Brian Quinn, "Improving the Quality of Telephone Reference Service," *Reference Services Review*, no. 4, 1995, pp. 39–50. Practical points by a working librarian.

tance is needed or if the answer requires materials beyond those in ready reference, the call is transferred to the regular reference librarian.

Most libraries provide telephone reference service and use many types of reference works, including telephone books. Larger libraries have separate sections for phone reference, usually out of view of the public. The smaller- and medium-sized libraries perform the service from the main desk.

The telephone aspects of reference follow specific procedures. For example, libraries differ in such matters as answering requests by patrons concerning whether the library has a needed book or periodical. Some will look to see if the library owns the item; others will ask the user to come in and check. Should one answer legal or medical questions over the phone? Should the librarian give out city directory information over the phone? These and countless other policy issues must be established if effective service is to be given.

In many libraries a special group of reference works are set aside for telephone service. These vary from place to place, yet inevitably include local directories and telephone books, as well as national works such as *Facts on File* and *Books in Print.* Normally, too, a great deal of emphasis is placed on how-to-do-it types of manuals and handbooks from music and sports to first aid and gardening. The reference sources that are used most often tend to be dictionaries, various almanacs, and local guidebooks.

While the telephone service requires the same basic steps needed when dealing face to face with people at a reference desk, some particular skills are necessary. One must be able to ascertain the nature of the question quickly and be sure it is clearly understood. Interviewing procedures tend to be somewhat less personal than at the desk and yet are even more necessary to master. One must know when to terminate a query, when to call back, and when the question should be referred to another section. As more than one reference librarian has observed, telephone reference service can be a unique type of work that requires specific skills—and certainly much experience.

A model of its kind, the New York Public Library's telephone reference service draws upon 1500 reference works to answer some 1000 calls a day. Staffers can answer most questions without leaving the desk, but when an answer is not readily available they transfer the call to various subject areas within the library. The limitations to the service are those followed by many other libraries: Questions one must be able to answer involve contests, crossword puzzles, or school homework.

SUGGESTED READING

"American Ethnicity: Recent Sources," *The Booklist* (Reference Books Bulletin), November 15, 1994, pp. 619–621. A briefly annotated listing of basic reference sources. Note that once or twice each year, RBB publishes similar listings which serve as excellent sources of books, particularly for small- to medium-sized public and school libraries.

Cassidy, John "Who Killed the Middle Class?" *The New Yorker*, October 16, 1995, pp. 113–124. Drawing upon documented statistical data and opinion, from the president of the Federal Reserve Bank of New York to Robert Reich, the Secretary of Labor, to academic economists and political scientists, the author concludes the middle class is dead. "This is nobody's fault; it is just how capitalism has developed." The conclusion, accepted or not, helps to underline the difficulty libraries now have in gaining economic support. Also, the article goes a long way to explain changes in library users.

D'Elia, George, and Elanor Jo Roger, "Public Library Roles and Patron Uses . . . ," *Public Libraries*, 1994, vol. 33, pp. 135–144. If asked, the majority of African Americans use the library for education and information gathering. And where there are diverse populations this role is the primary one. Recreation plays a larger part in better-off communities. The lesson for the reference librarian should be obvious.

Dorrance, Joan, *Meeting Community Needs*. New York: Neal-Schuman, 1994. Subtitled, *With Job and Career Services*, this is a how-to-do-it manual for those working in job and career information centers operated by public libraries. Practical advice is given on I&R and the need to deliver reference works for those with the greatest requirements.

Elshtain, Jean, *Democracy on Trial*. New York: Basic Books, 1995. A scholarly study of the weakness of democratic institutions in America and the politics of group identity. Weakening of civic ties, according to the University of Chicago professor, means lack of common interests or common ground. All of this adds up to why libraries are important in American life. See, too, the more controversial Christopher Lasch, *The Revolt of the Elites* (New York: W. W. Norton, 1995). These are two of scores of titles that detail the division in American economic, educational, and social areas.

Frum, David, "Welcome, Nouveaux Riches," *The New York Times*, August 14, 1995, p. A11. A senior fellow at the Manhattan Institute analyzes the growing differences in income among the poor, the middle classes, and the extremely rich. He gives useful facts and figures about a "serious new problem," but believes it is more a problem of observation than of reality. A conservative response to complaints about the wide divergence in income.

Jesudason, Melba, "Academic Libraries and Outreach Services," *Reference Services Review*, Winter 1993, pp. 29–36. A study of a less considered aspect of library outreach programs, this explores the need for cooperation between academic and school libraries. Participation in "precollege access programs highlight[s] how collaboration between school and academic libraries helps the town and gown community relationship, and point[s] out how precollege programs help minority students."

Kaestle, Carl, *Literacy in the United States*. New Haven: Yale University Press, 1991. This is an academic study of "readers and reading since 1880" which points up the conflict between statistics and literacy, not only for the second part of the century, but for earlier times.

Katz, Bill, ed., "Reference Service Expertise," *The Reference Librarian*, 1993, no. 40. In his introduction, "Anticipatory Reference Service: The Wave of the Future," Norman Stevens sets the stage for a series of articles that consider current and future developments. These move from an evaluation of CD-ROMs to a consideration of "legal research and the democratic process."

Miller-Lachmann, Lyn, *Global Voices, Global Visions: A Core Collection of Multicultural Books*. New Providence, NJ: R.R. Bowker Co., 1995. The editor of the magazine *Multicultural Review* lists and annotates some 1700 books for adult readers with varying backgrounds and levels of sophistication. Each section is devoted to a particular cultural group. The nonfiction parts include basic reference works.

Rettig, James, "Academic Reference Service," *Wilson Library Bulletin*, May 1993, pp. 53–54. A brief report on a much longer meeting of an institute that had the goal of "rethinking reference." The not surprising consensus was that more had to be done to bring reference services into the technological age and to fulfill the needs of students and faculty.

St. Liver, Evan, "Public Libraries Meet Fiscal Reality Head On," *Library Journal,* January 1995, pp. 44–47. The author's survey shows that librarians are aware that the "period of fiscal conservatism" is likely to continue and that they will have to rely on imaginative methods of overcoming the budget shortfalls. Good statistics, too, on the state of the finances of public libraries in the mid-1990s.

Somerville, Mary, "Global Is Local," *Library Journal,* February 15, 1995, pp. 133–137. The author explains the need to serve recent immigrants, and gives pointers on what the average librarian must know. She makes the argument that "serving immigrants serves all" and the library by so doing meets a historic role in the education of new citizens.

PART II
LIBRARIES AND THE
WIRING OF AMERICA

CHAPTER TWO
THE AGE OF ELECTRONIC
INFORMATION

In less than a decade the electronic library has developed from an idea to a reality. Even the smallest library has access to electronic data. By the mid-1990s all large libraries offer CD-ROM, online searching, and access to the Internet and other electronic information sources. Tape-loaded catalogs offer easy access for basic reference works. Internet is as customary as CD-ROMs, and the online search has become relatively common as an end-user method of securing data. All major libraries are connected through various networks.

Global networking lets the librarian and the user talk to anyone with similar hardware and software across the global community. One may seek information from England to Finland, chat with strangers from France to South Africa, and it is all much cheaper than using the telephone. In its race to cyberspace the Internet looms as an increasingly important factor in reference work.

In this chapter the focus is primarily on CD-ROMs, online systems, and related electronic information matters. Also, a suggestion is given as to various approaches to information outside the library.

The digitalization of books and other formats comes at the right time. Large research libraries simply do not have the space (or the money) for many more volumes of periodicals and books. This is the perfect market for the digital book. "In other words buy our products, liberate hundreds of feet of shelves. . . . With these bonuses, many libraries will see [CD-ROMs and online] as an irresistible purchase."[1]

It is estimated that business alone (not including government and individuals) spends $12 to $14 billion a year searching online and buying CD-

[1]John Sutherland, "When in Rome," *London Review of Books,* June 9, 1994, p. 7.

ROMs. The CD-ROM market is growing, although by 1996 it represented no more than 5 percent of the online profits.

Many experts believe the CD-ROM is little more than an intermediary to something even more spectacular. Technology has methods of storing much more data on discs of the same dimension. Superdensity discs hold up to 10 billion bytes (5 on each side) and eventually will replace the videodisc.

The Thesaurus Linguae Graecae (Irvine: University of California, 1994, $500) is a primary example of how scholars have adopted the new electronic database technology in their research. Basically the CD-ROM contains the full text of 18,400 ancient Greek texts surviving from the period between 800 B.C. Homer and Greek literature and about A.D. 600. Some 12,900 authors are represented. Suitably enough this is modeled on the first print Greek thesaurus by Henri Estienne in 1572 drawn from fewer than 150 Greek authors.

As miraculous as it is to compress information, there is a problem. What's to be done with all the stored data? Who is to say what is useful, what is garbage, and what is in between? "Technology threatens to accelerate this process by offering us the dream/nightmare of a . . . database made up of the totality of all texts. All writers from all times will be waiting there to leap onto your screen at the touch of a key."[2]

Information Society

In advertisement, political speeches, and even classroom situations, one is reminded that this is the age of the information society. More and more computers, telephones, and television sets mean more involvement with information. An example is the effort to improve the common television's picture. High-definition television (HDTV) is now tied into the possibilities of turning the television set into an interactive information source. Digital code, the lingua franca of today's information industry, is part of HDTV. Mastering this technology opens a ramp onto the information highway. Therein lies the political battle that involves every corporation from telephones to computers to software and back again.

Information is considered by many to be a commodity that can be bought, sold, and traded for gain; for example, the U.S. Office of Management and Budget makes the point that information is not a free good, but a resource of sub-

---

[2]Peter Campbell, "Total Knowledge," *London Review of Books*, September 10, 1992, p. 10. Jean Favier, head of France's Bibliotheque Nationale de France, explains that a modern library must conform to "new forms of memorisation. . . . It means we have to accept that civilization now also has a verbal, figurative and electronic memory." The book is no longer the sole medium of interest to libraries, if it ever has been. The electronic age has changed memorization in many ways. Private correspondence is decreasing, but handwritten reports which existed only in the original are now typed and photocopied so there may be 300 or 3000 copies of the original about. "Bold Future for France's Written Heritage," *Guardian Weekly*, September 11, 1994, p. 22.

stantial economic value and should be treated as such. Librarians, long accustomed to thinking of information as public rather than private, are, for the most part, in opposition to the present policies.

The primary questions and issues that have developed parallel to the new dimensions of the information industry include:

1. Is information a free source for all, as it has been in the past? Public libraries were founded on the concept that the poor should be able, theoretically, to have the same access to information as the rich.

2. If no longer free, is information a commodity for sale and, if so, how should the library react to this view of it? Case in point: Some libraries charge, and others do not, for online searches.

3. What is the role of the private and public sectors in information? Some of the databases (such as ERIC) are less expensive because they are sponsored by the government. Is this fair competition with private companies who put out similar, but more expensive, databases? More to the daily point, should the reference services in public and academic libraries continue to be free when private information brokers are trying to make a living from selling the very information that the library is giving away? Is all of this unfair competition by the public sector in the information industry?

INFORMATION SOURCES

According to Carlos Cuadra in his white paper, "The Corporate Memory and the Bottom Line" (Los Angeles: Cuadra Associates, 1994), word processing, e-mail, fax, and other services have accounted for an explosion of documents. In the United States alone, over 100 billion documents are created each year in electronic form. How does one find the specific document? Cuadra offers his own key word software, but this is hardly the real solution. A more likely solution is to have a mediator (librarian, archivist, or whomever) to decide what to retain, what to scrap, and how to store and retrieve what is saved.

Methods of delivering information will become far less important than what to do with the data once they are received. Mediators or "automated information filters" will screen the data, probably by the number of key words in each piece of information. "There is so much to be read . . . that in the next five years the most important advancement for information delivery will come from new ways to sort, judge and eliminate messages before the reader/recipient even opens the mailbox."[3] Meanwhile, the librarian must struggle with too many data,

---

[3]"Computer Books Skyrocket . . . ," *Publishers Weekly,* June 20, 1994, p. 62.

too little money for their purchase or control, and too much technology for comfort.

CD-ROM Publishers and Vendors

There are a half dozen or so leading publishers of CD-ROMs. They are Compton's New Media (part of the Tribune Company and the Chicago Tribune), Broderbund, Microsoft, Simon & Schuster, Time Warner, Addison-Wesley, and Grolier, Inc.

Publishers who have the original printed reference work in digital form find it relatively easy and cost efficient to make the same work available online and on CD-ROMs.[4] For example, *Facts on File* publishes *Native American Multimedia Encyclopedia* on CD-ROM. This is based on four separate print books. The publisher adds sound and animation, but essentially the multimedia product is much the same as the print editions. One can argue that this is an electronic page turner, which offers little more than the books. Convenience seems to be the greatest selling point. Much the same is true of other CD-ROM products. For example, Scribner's has collected several sets on American authors into one CD-ROM: *Scribner Writers' Disc, American Authors*. Gale has married material from its many literary biography and criticism sources, as well as new material, to create *Discovering Authors*, a CD-ROM of the 300 most-studied authors.

By the mid-1990s the line between producers of information and those who made it available to libraries—from print to online services—had blurred. Many databases, such as those produced by The H. W. Wilson Company, are now available from the publisher and a number of sources such as OCLC to DIALOG. It is difficult to say just who does what in the electronic world.

SilverPlatter Information is the vendor and distributor for several of the subject indexes on CD-ROMs discussed in this text. As a trailblazer in the marketing of CD-ROMs, SilverPlatter in 1995 joined information stored online and on disc by initiating Internet access to its databases. The databases are on CD-ROM, but stored at SilverPlatter in a single server. Entry is through Internet: (1) Cost is dictated much as SilverPlatter prices the CD-ROMs, that is, not by search but by gross use. (2) Searching patterns are the same as on the CD-ROM, say of ERIC, available in the library. The new CD-ROM/online crossover system will not be in full operation for several years, but to begin with, MEDLINE and ERIC, among other government-sponsored databases, will be accessed in the new manner.

---

[4]"CD-ROM Reference . . . ," *Library Journal*, April 15, 1993, p. 59. More of a problem is whether to put the product into DOS or Windows or another form of system software. Ideally publishers have versions for all systems.

ELECTRONIC FUN AND GAMES DATA

It is a sobering thought, at least for many reference librarians, that the possible majority of drivers on the information highway seem more involved with stomach-churning thrills than information. Under the heading "What People Really Want on the Net," *Wired* magazine pointed out most respond with "searching reference books," "taking courses," "searching card catalogs," "obtaining government information," and so forth. *In reality* the majority of people use the Net to "date by video, gamble, have role playing interactions, obtain sport statistics," and so on. Near the bottom of the list is "searching reference books, taking courses, and searching card catalogs."[5]

The popularity of e-mail, games, and "role interaction" on the networks, as well as with CD-ROMs, indicates that entertainment by and large outpulls information. For example, a phenomenon of 1995 was the network game *Doom* which permits players (often through Internet) to "stalk each other through marbled hallways, dash through shimmering pools of toxic waste and, of course, rip or blast each other's guts out with a variety of weapons."[6] Also, "it is depressing that so much ingenuity and effort is going into technical innovations which only have a deleterious effect on film's ability to communicate something more than the most primitive of human responses. Fun though it is, the latest technological development . . . confirms how misguided is our age's faith that technical progress can provide a solution to every problem."[7] Free e-mail is now available, and more of it will be offered. How can it be given "free"? The answer is the traditional American one—FreeMark Communications and Juno Online Services, two firms offering free e-mail, finance the venture by advertising that is visible on part of the user's screen.

Popular CD-ROMs

The aim of many commercial publishers is to cut the cost of CD-ROMs and distribute them as freely as music CDs. The purpose is to make CD-ROMs as common as television sets. "Why do I need one?" a popular magazine advertisement asks its readers. "You don't really, but of course, you didn't need a color TV either. . . . You didn't need a VCR until a Blockbuster Video was sprouting up on every other corner." Still, of the over 7000 titles available in 1996, only about 1500 are truly for the retail trade. These include games such as *Where in the World Is Carmen Sandiego?* for children to *Penthouse Interactive* for equally inquisitive adults. Average cost for a commercial CD-ROM is from $25 to $50. Popular reference works, such as electronic encyclopedias, average from $50 to

[5] *Wired*, February 1995, p. 48.
[6] "I Computer, Therefore You Die," *The New York Times*, January 22, 1995, p. E2.
[7] "A Terrifying Experience," *The Spectator*, September 10, 1994, p. 45.

$150.[8] Many libraries are circulating popular CD-ROMs, much as they check out recordings, books, and other forms of information and entertainment.

Multimedia

The key word in discussions of electronic communication is inevitably "interactive." Generally, it is simply a descriptor of an individual pushing a key, clicking a mouse, or making a noise which will bring up a printed message, a voice, or a graphic image. There is much more, but the point is that the individual may command the medium to do everything from spin in space to play a game. Interaction means the user may change the end of the game or story, as well as the characters.

The concept is as old as the first storyteller who called upon the listener to imagine a battle or an individual in love. Even the most superficial book requires interaction on the part of the reader. More involved novels fine-tune the interaction so that one is part of the story and can visualize the characters. Experimental plays and movies let the audience influence the action. Even the technology is relatively old. Video games were invented in the early 1960s.

Multimedia, in the sense of joining text with sound and pictures and being navigable in a nonsequential way, is a broad synonym for "hypertext"—used first by Vannevar Bush in 1945. Hypertext destroys linearity in that the order of chapters and sections is less apparent.

Educational Multimedia

The use of educational CD-ROMs and network multimedia is open to debate, particularly among teachers. On the plus side, many argue that students who may have problems with reading are often able to succeed by using a computer and multimedia. Superior students have a wider variety of choices. It breaks down the hierarchies among texts and students. The student is given more power to make choices. The real test, and one still to be passed or failed by a significantly large group, is whether the multimedia approach is better or worse than print and a teacher.

Amid all the hype and earnest desire to improve education there are questions. Will multimedia depress the desire to read? Partly, this depends on the sophistication of the software. Too much of it is simplistic or just plain dull. Linear presentation disappears and the constant hopping about from word, to picture, to sound, to disconnected paragraphs underlines the student's lack of ability to pay attention.

[8]See *Game & Entertainment on CD-ROM* (Westport, CT: Mecklermedia, 1994 to date, irregular, 195 pp., paperback, $29.95). This lists and annotates some 1500 games and entertainment-related titles. The guide is annotated and arrangement is much the same as found in the same publisher's *CD-ROMs in Print,* which includes most of the entries in this guide.

No one challenges a child's interest in computers. No one doubts that imaginative programming, from showing how a bridge is constructed to how a cow produces milk, is not useful. Still, all of this is canned. It leaves too little space for the child's own imaginative approach, or so the other argument goes.

Virtual Reality[9]

Virtual reality is another, more sophisticated form of multimedia, and precisely what it connotes. One has an experience which is almost (i.e., virtually) real, but not quite. A well-known example is the flight trainer where a pilot is offered the motions, the sounds, even the suggestion of bad weather in a confined space with simulated landings and takeoffs. The wrong move at a precise duplication of an airplane control panel results in a wrecked—or "virtually destroyed"—airplane.

Today's virtual reality consists primarily of games such as a Simon & Schuster's computer program that depicts the *Enterprise* with real photo quality. Somewhat similar to the now retired 3-D movie experience, this and other entertainments usually take the viewer into a closed environment and allow wandering in virtual space. The level of discourse and viewing is promising—but at this point no more than that. Popular virtual reality, with or without a multimedia helmet which projects scenes on goggles, is more experiment than reality. It may happen, but well into the next century.

In a broader, more practical sense virtual reality can be applied to anything that acts as a substitute to physical presence. A good example: Using World Wide Web on the Internet (which allows accessing pictures, sound, and graphics), a conference and trade show in Atlanta was thrown open to anyone with access to the WWW. "Internet users . . . were able to register for the conference, navigate the booths of companies . . . hold spoken conversations with colleagues and sales representatives through microphones attached to their computers, view product demonstrations, gather sales information and take guided tours of company displays, all by pointing and clicking on the computer screen."[10]

---

[9]See *Virtual Reality Marketplace* (Westport, CT: Mecklermedia, 1993 to date, annual). This "complete sourcebook to the virtual reality industry" will give even the casual readers a better idea of the multifaceted aspects of the industry, which in the 1994–1995 edition numbered over 200 companies. Most libraries are more concerned with electronic data than virtual reality, and some say the "virtual library" was dead before it even began; for example, see Cheryl LaGuardia "Virtual Dreams Give Way to Digital Reality," *Library Journal*, October 1, 1995, pp. 42–44.

[10]"A Virtual Trade Show," *The New York Times*, September 13, 1994, p. D4. The catch is that one needs the right technology to make the connection from home, that is, a high-speed connection which few Internet users have. The person showing the equipment must invest at least $12,000 for the software and training, as well as (in this case) $2500 for a listing.

Personal Computer

The primary technology behind mass information and the electronic format is the PC or personal computer. Whether in the library or at home, the terminal is the point of entry for an estimated 30 to 40 million people (and growing). The problem, as more than one critic has observed, is that computers are just now beginning to break free of the hacker mentality.

People still wait for the ultimate personal computer which will not require manuals and memory. This may come sooner than later because "training and supporting users remain a ridiculously large part of the cost of owning business computers."[11] Ease of use, with commands (possibly by voice) such as "Do it for me" will replace the sometimes byzantine patterns of typed orders necessary to gain access to information or, for that matter, master a simple word-processing program.

Microsoft, with its Bob software package, is a step toward the ultimate, everyone-can-use PC. Bob, like its numerous spin-offs, is intended to make it easier for novices by having the user turn to characters who give spoken instructions rather than the older method of memorizing lists of commands.

Developed in the mid-1990s, IBM's speech recognition technologies allow speech commands for querying reference works and for word processing on CD-ROMs. Some 1000 active words are recognized from a base of over 20,000 words. Words are added or dropped as one navigates the CD-ROM.[12] The IBM dictation technology allows the speaker to draw from 32,000 words, with a reserve of 100,000 words. Dictating, by speech, at 70 words per minute the user need not touch keys or mouse. The final letter, report, book, and so on can be present for a given format as required. "IBM's system should help bring the power of the personal computer to those who can't type or are intimidated by arcane commands. So if you're looking to get rid of that keyboard, just perk up."[13]

Compton's New Media is working with IBM to use the voice recognition method to operate multimedia CD-ROMs. Here a user of any age could speak into a computer and give commands. For example, users might navigate *Compton's Interactive Encyclopedia* by voice, calling up different screens and requesting information from the text or by matching a picture of a bird to its distinctive call. The next step is technology that will permit the user to dictate notes about research in the encyclopedia on a "scratch pad" area in the computer's memory.

---

[11]"When Will Computers Behave Like People?" *The New York Times,* January 1, 1995, p. 8.

[12]For just under $1000 the user obtains a software program that requires expert advice to install. As the words are spoken they are shown on the screen in a dictation window. Here you can make any corrections, additions, and so forth. It works fairly well. This is only an indication of what is to come when speech recognition will eventually be a standard feature of new PCs. "IBM's Dictation System," *PC Magazine,* April 12, 1994, p. 28.

[13]"The Voice of Progress," *Discover,* October 1994, p. 67.

Handheld Electronic Books

In 1991 Sony introduced the "data discman" which measures 10 by 5 inches and weighs under 2 pounds. It is a reader for miniature discs which can hold a little more than one-third of what is found on a CD-ROM. A 26-character keyboard allows one to operate the disc. By the mid-1990s the cost for this and similar electronic books ran from $150 to $600. Discs cost from $30 to $130 or more.

The advantage of the machine is that it may be carried about and used as a dictionary (e.g., there are discs for Japanese-English/English-Japanese, and so forth) or for playing games. The catch: no printout, a screen which normally can display no more than 30 characters or a 3.8-inch graphic image, and lack of many miniature discs. To date the technology has not caught on with the public, although some see a more sophisticated system as a way of eliminating the printed book. Examples of this include Michelin travel guides which may be purchased on miniature discs; *The American Civil War* with text and illustrations, which is a handheld book costing $29.95; and *The Portable Family Doctor*, another handheld book for $59.95.

Miniature discs are only one approach to the electronic handheld book. Time Warner, Simon & Schuster, Bantam Doubleday Dell Publishing Group Inc., and other major publishers have shown interest in a small, portable device intended for general readers that can display the text and full-color illustrations of books recorded on Smartcards (cards about the size of a credit card with embedded memory chips). Such a device can be produced for approximately $250, and cards that can hold up to 200 books would cost about $40 each.

A handheld book which weighs less than five ounces and can be slipped into a pocket is offered by Franklin Electronic Publishers for $199. A small card, which snaps in and out of the unit, carries the text. *The Merriam-Webster Dictionary* with some 170,000 definitions and *The Video Companion* which catalogs over 6700 video titles searchable by title, cast, theme, topic, and critic ratings are on another card. The cards are from $80 to $100 each.

While these have the advantage of being small enough to slip into a pocket, they are cumbersome and time-consuming to operate. Certainly for reference purposes they are a total loss, and not recommended. Individuals may find them mildly useful.

On the other hand, the handheld reader which is employed as an individual's "personal organizer" has it points. Here one puts diary, calculator, and address book into a single computerized package. More expensive units allow almost laptop computer operations, but they tend to be larger than the average handheld machine. Aside from this use, as well as for leisurely games and fun, the handheld disc player is not really a reference work. Libraries in every case would be better off with an equivalent book or CD-ROMs.[14]

[14]"An Electronic Books Player: Not Ready for Prime Time," *Consumer Reports*, November 1992, p. 685. In this brief article the death knell was sounded for most such books by America's leading con-

Beyond the Glitz

There are a few indications of what the new media, or interactive media, could be in the next decade. Consider, for example, Bob Stein of Voyager Company. He publishes a CD-ROM based on the Pulitzer Prize–winning Maus books by Art Spiegelman. The disc permits "the user to view the story of Nazi cats and Jewish mice while listening to the late Vladek Spiegelman's voice telling his story on tapes made a decade ago. . . . It also incorporates family photographs, storyboards and home movies, along with detailed notes, sketches and original source material from the Holocaust."[15] There are similar examples from many companies, but none to date has produced what one publisher calls the *Citizen Kane* of multimedia.

Critics of popular *online* services point out that they too often reflect mass (poor) taste. Live exchanges of messages, called chats, can also degenerate into meat markets in which any user with a female handle is likely to be asked, "What are you wearing?"

Those with "higher" values turn to a vast number of alternative networks. Such services number their subscribers in the very low thousands with monthly fees from $10 to $20 plus additional charges for Internet use. Each offers e-mail and varying degrees of Internet access. Still, the core appeal is the bulletin board where users post messages on specific topics. A few examples of these esoteric networks from New York City: Echo, about 3500 members, "a cyber salon for downtown intellectuals"; The Well, about 8000 members where the "talk is literate and competitive, as reporters from *Harper's, Time, Newsweek,* and *The Washington Post* weigh in.[16]

There is a downside to the thrills of the new technology. An associate director of addictions at Harvard University Medical School points out that one may become addicted to the online life. "Unlike chats and games, computers are a psycho-stimulant, and a certain segment of the population can develop addictive behavior in response to that stimulant," Dr. Howard Shaffer believes.[17] Signs of loss of control are overuse of e-mail and logging on at odd night hours. Initially, being on line insulates the user while expanding his or her electronic horizons. The transition from real life to life online is easy. The return is

sumer magazine. It ticked off the problems with the format from lack of search methods to tiny keypads. A clue to the lack of success of these, at least in reference work, can be found in any mid-1990s edition of the *Gale Directory of Databases.* Here less than 100 are listed, as compared to over 10,000 listings for CD-ROMs, online, and so forth.

[15]"He's Finding the Fire . . . ," *The New York Times,* July 17, 1994, p. F8.

[16]"Virtual Downtown, Where the Users Are Discriminating," *The New York Times,* January 25, 1995, pp. 25, 38. The modem for Echo: 212/989-8411; for The Well: 718/793-0005 (at prompt, type "Well").

[17]Molly O'Neil, "The Lure and Addiction of Life on Line," *The New York Times,* March 8, 1995, p. C1.

difficult. Part of the excitement, the addiction, is the clublike atmosphere with specific rites and shared technical experiences. How prevalent is this type of addiction? No one knows, except the addiction grows as more and more computers are introduced into homes, businesses, and, yes, libraries.

EVALUATION OF ELECTRONIC DATABASES[18]

In a review of a CD-ROM, J. Douville of *Choice* makes the essential point about all electronic titles: "As with any new product, the best way to become accustomed to its possibilities is to explore it, using as many of the system's features as possible. This reviewer did just that, and found some of the CD-ROM's features better than others; other users will have different experiences."[19]

Unfortunately, few librarians have the time (or even the review disc) to adequately evaluate electronic databases. For the most part they depend upon reviews and the experience of other librarians. Reviews such as the cogent notes by Cheryl LaGuardia in *Library Journal* are plentiful. "Electronic Media" is a regular feature of the "Reference" section in *Choice* and another American Library Association publication for reference librarians, *RQ,* regularly reviews databases in the "RQ Sources" review section. Then there are countless CD-ROM journals and online publications with reviews. See *Magazines for Libraries* for annotated reviews of the reviews.

There are not many compilations of the "best" databases. Several are discussed in the first volume of this text, e.g., Patrick Dewey's *303 CD-ROMs to Use in Your Library* (Chicago: American Library Association, 1995); and Stella Bentley's "Reference Resources for the Digital Age" *Library Journal*, August 1995, pp. 45–48. Also: Mike O'Leary's *The Online 100* (Wilton, CT: Pemberton Press, 1995). The college library director offers the leading databases under broad subject categories—current events, social sciences, technology, and so on—with about one to two pages of information about each database. The list is well constructed and a reliable guide, although no one will agree with all choices. See, too, the same publisher's related guides: Carole Lane's *Naked in Cyberspace: How to Find Personal Information Online;* and Reva Basch's *Secrets of the Super Searchers.*

Basic Points

As noted in the first volume of this text, the basic evaluation of information sources is much the same whether they are in print or in electronic format. The

---

[18]A practical guide to evaluation with precisely the details needed is Gail Dickinson's *Selection and Evaluation of Electronic Resources* (Englewood, CO: Libraries Unlimited, 1993). See, too, Reva Basch, *Quality and Value in Information Services* (London: Ashgate Publishing, 1994).

[19]*Choice*, April 1994, p. 1280.

primary concern is threefold and true to all sources: (1) What is the content? How much or how little of the subject is covered, and for what period of time? (2) What is the primary purpose of the source—to educate, inform, entertain? (3) Who is the audience—the child, the adult, the specialist? Beyond basics, these are questions that are applicable to almost any form of electronic database.

Essentially the librarian must have the same knowledge of the database as the printed version, although there are more details to remember. One, after all, can look at the printed *Psychological Abstracts* and, through trial and error, discover the pattern of presentation. Online or on CD-ROM that is possible but more difficult. The searcher must first know

1. Which years are covered. Most machine-readable records go back only four to ten years, whereas the printed version begins with the first issue of ten, twenty, or even fifty years ago.

2. How often the database is updated—daily, weekly, or quarterly.

3. The subjects and subtopics covered, and what related fields are likely to be a concern to the service.

4. The type of documents—from periodicals and reports to books and proceedings—included or excluded and, to be sure, the years covered. One should know, too, what is indexed or not indexed completely.

5. Whether a thesaurus is available containing a controlled vocabulary, and how frequently the thesaurus (or word list) is updated.

6. The types of concepts to search for when there is no thesaurus and the vocabulary is uncontrolled.

7. The relationship between the controlled and uncontrolled vocabularies where the database allows for both.

8. The codes or keys that may be used to shorten the search.

Given the complexity of such organization and content, it is understandable why so much energy and effort is put into guides to databases and their use.

Beyond this there are particular questions that must be asked about each database:

1. How much does one database overlap another in its coverage? For example, in a study it was found that in one service 29 percent of the articles cited were duplicated in another database.

2. Does the database provide only citations, or does it include abstracts? Usually the database duplicates what is offered in the hard copy version. However, for reasons of economy, most databases allow the user to reject (or accept) the abstract printout.

3. The level of accuracy and reliability is of primary importance. Does the database include what it claims, or only, for example, selectively index and abstract certain documents? How often is duplication evident? Are there errors in citations, spelling, and so forth?

4. How effective are the access points that are provided? One would like to know the best access terms (subject, titles, abstracts, key words, codes, etc.) for a particular service. Also, one may compare similar services, although at this point the quality and type of indexing vary so much from service to service that a valid comparison is difficult.

5. Does the publisher provide a "hot line" so searchers can call for assistance with difficult searches? Does the publisher send out a newsletter or other periodic update to inform users of changes? Does the publisher provide the means for users to suggest changes or to make complaints about features of the databases?

Evaluative queries regarding the technical aspects of the access and retrieval process are important. These range from the type of terminal to the format of the printout. Such questions are too technical for a beginning text, but the reader should at least be aware of their place in evaluation.

CD-ROM Evaluation

The CD-ROM offers a few distinct problems and questions of evaluation. Otherwise the same evaluative techniques used for other forms of electronic databases are employed to judge CD-ROMs.

1. A problem with CD-ROM is that it is quickly dated. A 1995 check shows that about 50 percent are updated only quarterly, whereas about 25 percent may be updated biannually or only once a year. Weekly and monthly updates are usually confined to business and science. Some more general titles such as *Books in Print Plus* are issued every month. In time this is likely to change. One can see frequent updates for all of the CD-ROMs.

2. There are numerous versions (and software) for the same index or abstracting service. For example, there are at least six, if not more, versions of ERIC in this form. MEDLINE (produced by the National Library of Medicine) can be obtained from over 10 different publishers or vendors. The duplication is common with almost all frequently used services. Given this, the librarian must ask which of the firms offer the best search software.

As each organization that sells CD-ROM tends to have its own different software, it is important to find a publisher who has more than one CD-ROM offering, who, in fact, offers a number of related databases that employ the same search patterns. The question: If X publisher issues Y number of CD-ROM discs, can they all be searched with the same software? Generally the answer is yes, and that is why libraries prefer the CD-ROMs issued from firms such as

R. R. Bowker, The H. W. Wilson Company, OCLC, EBSCO, SilverPlatter, and Information Access Company.

3. Then comes cost evaluation. If one firm seems to be offering the same service for less, investigate all the possibilities before deciding.

4. Networking of CD-ROM is common; for example, The H. W. Wilson Company's online/CD-ROM services can be accessed at multiple workstations. Several users may now access the same CD-ROM on a local area network. Information Access Company offers similar possibilities for its indexes. The difficulty is that there is always an added charge of several hundred to several thousand dollars for more workstations.

5. Presentation of information. While improving with each month, the CD-ROM for interactive use (as an encyclopedia, dictionary, or whatever) can be frustrating. The animation, films, and pictures are often of only passable quality, sometimes worse than the average television picture. Where type is used, it is often blurred and the resolution is not as good as on the printed page. On the other hand, there is promise of video and film clips and stills of much better quality than now found even in finely printed books.

Online Evaluation

Searching online presents certain specific evaluative problems.

In determining which network, vendor, or provider to use the librarian should ask several basic questions: (1) What type of telephone access is available, and how much will it cost for otherwise long-distance connections? (2) Is there a surcharge for faster modems, that is, speeds over 14,400 bits per second? (3) Is the interface easy to understand, easy to use? (4) How difficult is it to connect the specific online database? Is it available 24 hours a day, or for how long? (5) How safe is the password, that is, can it be used by others without permission? (6) Is there support at the end of a telephone line—just in case something goes wrong?

(7) The interface software should be judged in terms of how easy or difficult, sophisticated or elementary it is to fish information out of the database. Today most systems allow for the beginner and the expert in that they offer a choice of interfaces that are extremely slow and easy to follow (for amateurs) or a single interface that requires a thorough knowledge of electronic searching (for experts). DIALOG online, for example, allows the user to go step by step through a menu of suggestions or, for the expert who wants to short-circuit the beginner's steps, to enter specific commands.

Beyond these important generalizations, one will want to know such things as whether or not commands may be abbreviated, types of truncation, use of combining sets, how one searches by subject or free text, and so forth. Much of this is technical and revealed only by actual use of the database; but a diligent reading of background material will be most helpful.

Guides

If an electronic database requires a manual of 50 pages or more, which is not always that unusual, either it is a splendid example of sophisticated searching possibilities or a confusion of impossibilities. Unfortunately, too many tend to be the latter, and resemble nothing so much as the typical VCR guide or the how-to-do-it book which comes with a desktop computer. Length is not the only quick evaluative check of database guides. There are others:

1. *Jargon.* The guide should be in language comprehensible to the average layperson. While "interface" and "media toolbar" may be plain English to hackers, they are meaningless to beginners. Also, anyone who requires jargon to explain the operation of a CD-ROM is likely to have a product beyond the reach of the person to whom it is directed.

2. *Tutorial programs.* The directions should be straightforward. Few people want to march through a tutorial program that will train them in every aspect of searching.

3. *Illustrations.* Illustrations, graphs, charts, and the like are useful as long as they (1) can be understood without reference to another manual and (2) are not repeating everything on the disc itself, usually as part of the menu.

4. *Well-written directions.* Finally, the overall set of directions should be logical, well written, and easy to understand. Again, "easy to understand" by the beginner, not by the dedicated computer fan.

Where the library relies on electronic searches and, particularly, CD-ROM searches that are made by laypersons, the use of a manual should not be necessary. Enough information should be given in a precise, clear way on the screen to allow even the rank beginner to make at least a basic search. "End-user workstations in libraries should not require the user to spend valuable research time memorizing codes and being trained in the principles of information storage and retrieval. Instead of studying . . . documentation, the end-user would rather spend time browsing, to get a feel for the database's content, and to find, by serendipity or through her own patent genius, the kind of juicy hits that she wasn't even sure would exist."[20]

[20]John Marcus, "Wilson Business Abstracts on CD-ROM . . . ," *Database,* June 1994, p. 54. Well-prepared guides are, of course, a great help and should be encouraged. A basic evaluative question: Are there supporting printed, online, CD-ROM, and so on aids which will answer questions about content, software, and the like in an easy-to-understand, thorough fashion? Does the vendor or publisher offer free time online to practice and evaluate? Does the CD-ROM publisher offer user support, advice on necessary hardware, installation help, and the like?

Cost[21]

An information CD-ROM is typically priced from around $395 to $1500, with some running in the multiple thousands of dollars. Costs are coming down, particularly for libraries, but reference works in print or in electronic format have always been, and will continue to be, expensive because of the limited market. The prices contrast with popular encyclopedias and collections of novels on CD-ROMs. These can be sold in the many thousands if not millions for much less.

What follows are pricing policies for 1995 to 1996 among a few vendors and publishers. These will change, but they at least indicate the lack of common ground and the desire, apparently, to confuse. With changes, pricing may or may not be easier to understand, but odds are cost estimates will continue to baffle, no matter how revised.

Every publisher, vendor, software firm, or CD-ROM distributor has bizarre, often difficult-to-follow prices. The H. W. Wilson Company is a good example as of 1996: (1) *Online:* If one subscribes to the *Readers' Guide* print version, the online cost is $43 to $50. Nonprint subscribers pay $50 to $60 an hour. But it is not that simple since there are various "packages" that raise or lower the rates depending on which one the library purchases. Then there is the 50 cents online charge and the same cost offline to print out a citation or abstract. And to add to the complication, rates are higher or lower with different vendors such as OCLC or FirstSearch and CDP (formerly BRS) online. (2) *CD-ROM:* Here the quarterly CD-ROM update costs a flat $1995 from the publisher. Based on a school year, public libraries may get the same service for $995 with a monthly update, or only $395 for a quarterly version. How then can the publisher justify a double, even triple, cost for a CD-ROM that comes out only quarterly? The answer: With the higher cost one gets unlimited access to *Readers' Guide* online, which is updated twice a week. But wait—the SilverPlatter Company offers the same CD-ROM version, but monthly instead of quarterly, for $2294. Fine, but this does not give one access online. Given one more variable, it is little wonder librarians have such a difficult time trying to settle on the best electronic format for their library.

Note, too, The H. W. Wilson Company, like most others, has an extra charge for "networking," that is, in a library where the same disc is being used by several users. This is $2868 as compared to $2294 for the single-user version.

---

[21]"The single worst habit of the information industry is not providing open information on prices." From "Me Consumer—You, Vendor," *Information Today,* March 1994, p. 7. In 1994 DIALOG Information Systems, for example, began basing its fees on the number of people within a corporation who are authorized to read documents downloaded from DIALOG. "With a $2 document it would cost $6 for up to 25 people to have access to the document through the corporate archive (in the company computer). The client would pay $8 for permission to send electronic copies directly to 25 people." This avoids copyright law problems, but depends on the honesty of the user in counting copies and suggests cost planning to baffle an accountant. *The New York Times,* April 6, 1994, p. D5.

Network considerations become a major headache, and that is why many librarians favor online or the loading of a given index available on magnetic tape into their own system.

Costs vary, depending as much on the skill of the searcher as the format. Online, where speed and accuracy are essential, at SUNY-Albany in 1995 the least expensive search was on the government database ERIC (average about 15 cents per hit). The average cost for commercial databases was between 40 and 50 cents. Among the most expensive: *Science Citation Index* at $4.51 per search and *Dissertation Abstracts* at $2.52. The most costly: *Statistical Masters Index* at $11.93.

The alternatives to the so much per minute and per printout taximeter approach to pricing online information include:

1. Subscription plans (from OCLC and DIALOG to Dow Jones Prodigy and CompuServe) vary: (*a*) There is a flat subscription price at so much per month for up to 5, 10, 15 hours, and so forth, with a surcharge after the "free" hours. (*b*) The subscription is based on past use over a year. If after a year more is used, the subscription goes up; if less is used the subscription goes down.[22]

Flat fees have become increasingly popular because they tend to be lower and are easy to calculate. The usual procedure is that the library pays for a set number of searches. The more searches the lower the flat fee. The H. W. Wilson Company, OCLC's FirstSearch, and several governmental databases such as ERIC rely on a flat fee.

2. SilverPlatter, the large CD-ROM vendor, offers the use of its CD-ROMs online at a subscription rate. (Normally, of course, the library has the CD-ROM and pays for its use in the library.) Available on Internet, a limited number of CD-ROMs (from ERIC to *Criminal Justice Abstracts*) can be tapped from a server at SilverPlatter's Norwood, Massachusetts, headquarters. Prices match those the library would pay for taking possession of the CD-ROM and using it in the library.

3. The subscription rate approach has modifications. The most popular rate system is called site licensing. Defined as locally loaded tape leases, or access to remotely stored tapes, CD-ROMs, and other electronic databases, site licenses have increased dramatically in the mid-1990s. A library, for example, may lease a database for a few thousand dollars or spend anywhere from $20,000 to $30,000 (1996 figures) for access to several full text databases which may be accessed at various times in the library or throughout the campus or community. Information Access Company is one of several firms which offers site licenses.

[22]On OCLC FirstSearch the subscription runs from a minimum of $6500 a year (which limits search to about a dozen databases) to $100,000 for 20 or more users enjoying all of the databases. In addition there are blocks of searches which range from 90 cents per search in blocks of 500 searches to a low of 50 cents in blocks of over 40,000 searches.

The future will probably see elimination of time charges. Instead, there will be (*a*) a group of databases for a flat fee, no matter how often used; and (*b*) additional services paid above and beyond the basic subscription fee—a pricing structure similar to the one used for cable television.

Finally, but not last, get a copy of the contract on specifics of what is or is not provided for CD-ROMs and online. Check the specifics from cost of one user at a CD-ROM terminal or a dozen users for backup when the program(s) is down.

COPYRIGHT

Laypersons understand vaguely that a copyright or patent protects the originator of a work. For example, it assures an author of exclusive rights to a novel or scientific treatise. Under most (but not all) circumstances the author must be paid each time the novel is purchased or the article is faxed or photocopied. However, because of exceptions and gray areas, understanding copyright law has developed into one of the great mysteries of modern times. It truly takes an expert to fathom its various aspects.[23] For example, when the new Library of France opened in Paris, some 300,000 documents were available both in print and in electronic format. All had to be used in the building because of publishers' concerns over copyright.

Who owns the rights to reproduce articles online or on a CD-ROM, or another electronic form? The person or corporation who owns the copyright of the article is the usual answer. Problems arise when a free-lance writer, who has been paid *x* dollars for an article, demands royalties when the piece is used on a CD-ROM, online, and so on. The publisher claims the *x* dollars gave the publisher full rights to the article. The writer's claim, "Yes, but only when printed in the magazine." Outside the magazine format, the writer should receive royalties. Although this is fought by some publishers, the common approach today is to give the writer an extra one-time amount for future electronic use of work. (Magazines, for example, whose articles appear on America Online give free-lance writers $100 for each article, above and beyond what they received for publication in a magazine.)

In the midst of the confusion the librarian continues to offer public access to data from the author's novel or article. Perhaps this is acceptable, but when is there a limit to how many photocopies one can make of an article, a book, a chapter, or whatever? When and how is the author paid or recognized for such use? While the U.S. Copyright Revision Act of 1976 is clear about authors'

---

[23]"Cox on Copyright," *Against the Grain*, November 1994, p. 12. This is an excellent, easy-to-understand, brief overview of the present copyright law and modern telecommunications problems.

rights, Section 107 concerning "fair use" is vague.[24] Fair use is a method of defining what someone may do with a copy of an article, or a page out of a book, or a video recording, and so on, without violating the rights of the copyright holder or author. In general, one is free to photocopy an article as long as the copy is not put to commercial use, but is used for research, scholarship, teaching, and so forth.

Section 108 of the copyright law concerns photocopying in libraries and interlibrary loan. Essentially, it says that copying is legal as long as it is done without a profit motive. Beyond that there are problems: (1) It is legal for the library to make up to 10 copies of an article for students to read in the reserve section of the library. (2) It is *not* legal to store an article in the library electronic data file in anticipation of future use. This assumes systematic commercial copying, and requires that the copyright owner be paid. The key is the verb "to transfer." Information transferred from a printed or electronic source to the single user's file is legal. But to transmit the article to a library server for future use is not legal. (3) Books may be borrowed, but only if the book cannot be purchased at a reasonable price. That is, almost any book in a current edition of *Books in Print* should not be sent on interlibrary loan. While this protects the publishers and the authors, it does raise sticky problems. Some librarians conveniently overlook the rules, others pay for the periodical articles, and still others may claim that an interlibrary loan from a library within a system does not infringe on the copyright law.

Texaco Corporation violated copyright laws when it allowed its library to photocopy whole articles from journals and distribute them around the country. The court ruled the action was "archival" in that the company was collecting articles for future use as in (2) above.[25]

Studies show the copyright law has not had much effect on libraries. The average library is not likely to request an article, book, or report more than once. The chance of a periodical article or of a single periodical being requested on interlibrary loan more than once is largely accidental. One may also interpret broadly the section on books, particularly since it is stipulated that the book must be sold at a "fair price." This is not to say the copyright law is not an important consideration and one of much interest to librarians but it has not had real (as opposed to theoretical) influence on the activities of the majority of libraries.

---

[24]The U.S. Copyright Revision Act of 1976, as well as several international acts, is complex. For reference teachers, librarians, and writers the determination of what is "fair use" of a journal article, document, book, and the like from a copyrighted work is the stumbling block. While there are general rules, more complex cases seem to be settled case by case.

[25]"Texaco Pays $1 M to Settle Copyright Case," *Library Journal,* June 15, 1995, p. 14. The settlement raises many questions, still to be answered, about for-profit versus nonprofit use in libraries. See, too, "Court Sharply Limits the Photocopying of Scientific Articles," *The New York Times,* October 30, 1994, p. 43.

Copyright Fees

Copyright fees may be paid in a number of ways:

1. Through the Copyright Clearance Center (established in 1977) where a certain sum is set for each article that is copied. This is paid to the copyright owner. Numerous periodical and book publishers are registered at the nonprofit center, but almost as many are not. Be that as it may, it has proven to be one way of simplifying the problem of who owes what to whom.

2. Ordering articles from document delivery services which build in royalties to authors and publishers in their fee for the copyright work. These services have arranged licensing fees from the individual publishers.

3. Licensing of CD-ROMs or online databases by the publisher or vendor. The license then sets the rights as to what may be copied, if anything, and how. Most licenses, for example, forbid the user to use the data to create a new database, printed work, and so forth. On the other hand, DIALOG's ERA is an automatic copyright payment system whereby a certain amount is charged for copyright material online.

4. The library can exercise its "fair use" option to pay no fee, and pass on the little or no cost per copy to the user. Under law the commercial service is obligated to collect and pay the copyright holder some royalty fee, *"but* libraries are permitted to make fair use of material without collecting or paying a royalty fee. This is not meant to discourage patrons from using a commercial service. But in fact libraries have an advantage over commercial services: We can beat them at their own game. . . . The computer, if used wisely, gives us unprecedented opportunities to advance the Jeffersonian vision of an informed, prosperous, and free citizenry."[26]

Copyright in the Electronic Age

Networks provide major questions for copyright experts. How can multimedia—using both new and older works—meet the rights of copyright owners of only a small part of, say, a multimedia CD-ROM? Is the present copyright law a feasible way to govern computer networks? Most important: Can copyright be enforced online? On the Internet it is possible for anyone to use a service called "anonymous remailer," and send copyrighted material to thousands of places online without being identified. Why would one want to pay for copyrighted books, magazines, reports, and so forth? Today, quite literally, those with access to a computer network can avoid copyright protection. The ease of infringement is made even more so by the lack of any method of enforcement. (The FBI and other enforcement agencies do monitor bulletin boards and reg-

---

[26]Scott Bennett, "The Copyright Challenger," *Library Journal,* November 15, 1994, p. 37.

ularly arrest notorious copyright infringers. While this discourages organized groups, it is no protection against the single teenager.)

The answer to all of this is threefold. First, the copyright laws will be rewritten and constantly updated. Second, major copyright violation in the past, present, and future is done for profit by professional criminals, not by librarians. Third, the photocopying machine, the fax, and the computer laser printer open the way for individuals to avoid copyright, but they are hardly important players in the game. "Each of us can now perform widespread copyright infringement without getting caught, if we're careful. However, none of this will make a hair's breadth of difference. We may eventually see a societal move away from information hoarding, but it will not happen because copyright law does not work."[27]

Others are not so sure. They claim that copyright law, at least as we have known it, will not work with the new information electronic age. The United States Congress to the European Commission are studying methods of implementing copyright to meet the challenge of networks. Familiar restrictive terms are suggested, but then comes the inevitable question: "How can these laws be enforced when more than 30 million people can move copyrighted material over the globe in a matter of seconds?" So far there is no convincing answer, although methods are slowly being developed to compensate authors, composers, publishers, and so on. A solution will come, but as one critic puts it: "Information is a vast lake. All of us dip into it, and millions of us contribute to it, by the tankerful or the teaspoonful. If we try to account for every drop, and fight over the ownership of this or that gallon, all but the lawyers will drown in the flood."[28]

DESKTOP PUBLISHING

Although reading printed matter (such as a magazine or book) online has proved less than popular, the use of the computer to publish print books and magazines has taken hold. The same steps are employed as in electronic publishing, except the end product is a printed work.

The mimeograph machine, followed by photocopying, revolutionized what has come to be known as "desktop publishing." For the first time an individual was able to "print" a pamphlet, magazine, or book at home. Distribution remained (and remains) a problem, but author-editor no longer had to depend on expensive typesetting and printing equipment. Today desktop publishing is linked to computer, word processing, and software programs.

[27]Lance Ross, "The Emperor's Clothes Still Fit Just Fine," *Wired*, February 1995, p. 1. See also Carol Risher and Laura Gasaway, "The Great Copyright Debate," *Library Journal*, November 15, 1994, pp. 34–37. The authors conclude, as do many others, that the present copyright act may need some change, but is basically suitable for the electronic age and its problems.

[28]Jim McCue, "Who Cares about Dickens' Heirs?" *The Spectator*, February 25, 1995, p. 24.

Thanks to scores of software programs, anyone can now generate and combine text and graphics at a computer keyboard. Pages may be arranged in almost any form. They are then printed on a laser printer, bound, and mailed. A more sophisticated, as well as expensive, process is to use the laser printed pages as camera-ready copy. This is then the basis for lithography or printing on a large system. To a reader the desktop publication appears no different than one done by standard production methods. An editor has the ability to publish a magazine or book which, in appearance, may be even better than one pulled from a million-dollar printing press.

Everything from creative layouts and incorporation of various typefaces and artwork into a page is possible. More important, money and time are saved. Expensive, individually typeset pages are no longer required. The result is evident in many places, but particularly in the rapid growth of small presses. There are now 6000 or more of these across the United States publishing, usually at a desk top, everything from one-page political tracts to how-to-do-it books, poetry, and fiction.

Other Publishing Possibilities

What one technology gives, another takes away. Consider, for example, the limited possibilities of CD-ROMs for the small press publisher. The high cost of preparing and producing CD-ROMs makes it an unlikely place for small publishers or self-publishing. It is estimated that $800,000 to $1.5 million are required to have a successful CD-ROM product, often with nearly half of that going to marketing and promotion. The result is that CD-ROM publishing, like book publishing, is controlled by a dozen or so publishers. The decline of the small and independent publisher is likely to be more marked in CD-ROM publishing than in print.

At the same time, many more avenues for small publishers are opened up by networks, and particularly the Internet. Here there is almost total freedom to publish what one wishes and has the time and patience to prepare. Overhead is small, and there are few technological barriers to publishing, say, a poem or a book of poems online. The drawback is lack of control and, for many, lack of profit. This is not to say a whole new method of publishing is not open to the same people who brought the small press to the world, but it is going to take time before it becomes as popular, as well known.

A computer, linked to a network, can produce a completely digital journal, newsletter, or magazine. There is no true estimate as to how many such titles are available, say on Internet, but they cover the globe. Most are described as "e-magazines." Some are free and pay their way by generating other work for the people who produce them. For example, *Tidbits* out of Seattle is a weekly newsletter for Macintosh users. It is free and distributed in 46 countries with a circulation estimated at over 100,000. The newsletter has generated offers of journalism work for its founder, and later a book contract.

There are problems. Some simply recirculate articles they did not write as their own, or more often use the e-magazine title as a setting for advertisements, press releases, and other types of publicity. Standards vary, although paying subscribers tend to be much more discriminating.

Electronic Journal

More and more reference works, and particularly indexes, directories, and "not to be read cover to cover" books are available electronically. Ideally, journals will be published in the same way, but there are problems that are symptomatic of the difficulty of moving from print to digital format. Problems, which are bound to be overcome in the next decade or so, include: (1) Most researchers and teachers who contribute to journals prefer the old-fashioned tried-and-true print copy because (as of today) it is more prestigious. A nicely printed journal is physical evidence of publication that can be stored and displayed. Also, citation indexing and circulation figures indicate the relative importance of the print journal and, by implication, the importance of the contributor's paper. In time, when more writers are accustomed to electronic databases (and those who evaluate them), this stumbling block may be removed. (2) Editorial standards, or so it is argued, disappear when the author can go directly online with an article. There is no one between the contributor and the reader. Actually, for an acknowledged online journal this is not true in that no matter what the format there is an editor, and often a board of referees, to check the article before it is available in any format. Still, the feeling persists that producing writer-to-reader material electronically destroys the editorial superstructure that protects high standards. (3) Cost of the electronic format is usually much lower than print, but here the assumption is that all potential readers have invested in PCs or have free access to PCs and other hardware and software.

Despite doubts and drawbacks to the electronic online journal, few question that in the decade or so ahead, many, if not most, standard and sometimes little read scholarly journals will be converted to this format. The savings in trees alone is a fine argument. The journals, when properly edited, will be reliable and considerably more current than the present print versions. The obvious advantage to the scholar who is able to search across a wide range of journals, instead of through the full text of only one or two journals at a table, is impressive. From the library point of view there is a tremendous saving in space, binding, cataloging, and the like. As teachers become familiar with the new format, electronic journals will be as prestigious as their print cousins. Overall cost will be lower for publisher, library, and individual. Eventually copyright problems will be solved. The publisher is likely to agree to an annual sale to a library or individual, such as a subscription, and then let the journal be used online as it is in libraries today.

With that, though, it should be understood that more popular journals and magazines will retain the print format. As with the printed book, the magazine with a circulation of over 20,000 or so—and well into the millions—is simply easier and more commercial to publish in print. And the print version reaches many, many more readers. The major hurdle is how to attract advertising dollars to online mgazines. With no promise of the success of the printed magazine, the online title is less than attractive to necessary advertisers. It is a problem that Madison Avenue has yet to solve.

Periodicals on CD-ROM

Texts of current periodicals are, for the most part, preferable online. Conversely, for storage purposes the CD-ROM format is ideal, and is likely to replace microform. It can be less expensive, easier to handle, easier to access, and generally preferable to other formats. An example: *The New England Journal of Medicine* from January 1989 through December 1991 is available for $295 on a CD-ROM. This is full image in that not only text, but also every table and illustration, is included on the single disc, and the text may be searched word by word.

While the medical journal is typical of CD-ROM use in libraries, the same format has wider application (particularly with multimedia) in the popular arena. *CD-Romance,* a monthly magazine, features more than 300 single women and men who present themselves in 100 minutes of multimedia with details about their interests and hobbies. The interactive disc allows the subscriber to enter his or her personal likes and dislikes and the CD-ROM "drops" names on the month's disc of those who are most suitable. To make contact, each lonely heart is provided with a confidential box number or an e-mail address. The market seems large since about 25 percent of Americans are single.

INFORMATION BROKER

The information broker is a private individual or organization that sells the type of reference information that is free from libraries. There are two basic types of private information services.

1. The information broker, or search service, tends to deal with specific questions and problems. The paid response includes citations and documents which will aid the user in the solution of the problem. The documents are screened, and only those thought to be of benefit are presented.

2. The consultant, who may have one or more information brokers in his or her employ, goes a step further and not only validates, but also evaluates, the information. Recommendations for action are made based upon the documents.

The specialists do many things, but essentially they act as consultants, advising the paying client about the course to take based on the best sources of information. This usually means that the broker takes the question and does extensive research which provides a list of citations or the actual information required. The search will be manual or online, or a combination of both. For example, a client may want to know the advisability of opening or expanding a business which sells X products. The information broker will identify information sources that will help identify trends in the area of X products, show strategic planning for development, and even provide market forecasts. This may be done by providing citations, that is, a bibliography, but more likely it will be a written report.

Today there are information brokers across almost all the United States and the Canadian provinces. The actual number of for-profit information organizations is somewhere between 1500 and 2000, of which the majority are one- or two-person operations. Only a few, probably no more than two dozen, employ more than three or four professional people.[29] Each maintains its own unique fee structure, although billing tends to be based upon (1) the time spent on the question or project by the organization, (2) direct costs from photocopying to online searches, and (3) miscellaneous costs, from typing and phone calls to travel. The broker may itemize the bill, or simply charge a flat fee normally set before the project begins.

The information broker came into existence for many reasons, but the primary one was the failure of the library to meet the information needs of some parts of the public. Perhaps "failure" is not the right word, because librarians consciously do not provide certain types of services either because of lack of funds and personnel, or simply because of tradition. It tends to be more the former than the latter.

Of particular interest to librarians is the opportunity to turn to an alternative career as an information broker. This can be done, and is done most often by starting up one's own operation or, for experience, joining a larger firm. There are several possible leads: (1) "Alternative Career Directions for Librarians," is a pamphlet available from the American Library Association in Chicago; (2) *Burwell Directory of Information Brokers* (1960 West, Suite 214, Houston, TX 77068; tel.: 713-537-9051; fax 713-537-8332) is a directory that is up-

---

[29]The best known and largest of these is Find SVP, a commercial document delivery service that earns $16 million a year and employs 157 people. The French owner of Find SVP is simply SVP. See "Answers to Almost Any Question, For a Price," *The New York Times,* July 1, 1991, p. D8.

dated bimonthly. (3) *Association of Independent Information Professionals* (38 Bunker-hill Dr., Huntington, NY 11743) is a group of some 500 independent information professionals. They publish a newsletter and a directory.[30]

One response to the competition or threat of the information industry impinging on traditional reference services is for the library to develop its own private fee-based information model. Here the librarians perform many of the duties of the information broker, but with an essential break with the past—there is a charge. This does not simply mean charging for an online search, but sometimes using the fee structure for detailed studies and reports.

One may argue that this competes with what should be a private type of operation and discriminates against the user who can't pay for such in-depth services. Conversely, if the library does not offer such services there is a good chance that support from the business community will dwindle.

There are now some 250 to 300 libraries in the United States and Canada that offer fee-based services. This includes everything from rapid document delivery to translation services and, of course, individual research and reference assistance. University and college libraries make up the greatest number of such services.[31]

A useful guide to fee-based systems in libraries is compiled and produced by the staff of the County of Los Angeles Public Library in cooperation with the Fee-Based Information Centers in Academic Libraries. This is *The Fiscal Directory of Fee-Based Information Services in Libraries* (Norwalk, CA: FYI/County of Los Angeles Public Library, 1988 to date, biennial). The mid-1990s' edition has listings of close to 250 fee-based information services in about 150 academic and some 50 public as well as about 50 special libraries. Arrangement is alphabetical by name of library and there are a good half dozen indexes, including one to subject specializations. Each service and its fee are clearly designated.

DEATH OF THE BOOK[32]

What is going to happen to the printed book?

If it is a basic reference work, and particularly one which is a listing and updated regularly—such as an index, bibliography, directory, and the like—it

---

[30]For additional sources see "Using Information Skills in Nonlibrary Settings," *The Bowker Annual* (New York: R. R. Bowker, 1994), pp. 380–383.

[31]It should be understood that fees charged to businesses are one thing, but fees charged to the average user are another. The former is debatable, but just. The latter is a constant source of discussion. See Wendy Smith, "Fee-Based Services, Are They Worth It?" *Library Journal*, June 15, 1993, pp. 40–43.

[32]Michael Gorman, "The Season of the Learned," *Library Journal*, February 15, 1994, pp. 130–131. This is a good summary of the reason so many technocrats and bureaucrats are anxious to replace the printed book with other forms.

will be bypassed by electronic substitutes. At the end of the century electronic reference works will have virtually replaced conventional print sources.[33] Whether or not they replace standard texts, from biographical and ready-reference sources to encyclopedias, remains to be seen. Ideally, of course, *all* reference works should be in electronic form for searching. But that is going to take time and technology beyond 2001.

This hardly means the death of the book. Books, after all, are used only marginally for reference. Thoughtful novels, from the classics to modern-day winners of National Book Awards to Nobel Prizes, are not yet being read electronically. Printed books are still preferable.

Although for over a quarter of a century the dire warning about the "death of the book" has been heard, it has not happened. If anything, there are more books published today than ever before—some 45,000 to 50,000 in the United States and about 80,000 in England. Books grow in strength, particularly as one is offered the alternative of a blinking computer screen or an awkward and expensive miniature reader. One does not have to be sentimental or unrealistic to pronounce the book far from dead. In fact with every electronic development, the book flourishes. As one English critic puts it: "A book is still the best vehicle. . . . If you wish to project a person or a story into the electronic stratosphere, you still do what you have always done. You write words, chop down trees and call in the heirs of Caxton. . . . Nothing fuels the rocket of publicity like a book. It is compact, private, portable and attractive."[34] And it is relatively cheap. Periodicals such as the popular *Wired* and *NewMedia* publish countless articles which agree and demonstrate that "text" is important. Someday, to be sure, the book will be replaced by another form, but it does not look as if it will be today's electronic substitute.

The More Things Change . . .

The more things change, the more they remain the same. Despite the late Marshall McLuhan's dictum that "the medium is the message," content in reference services remains the primary consideration.[35] The message may be transmitted

---

[33]Ironically, it is equally likely that many of today's technologies will be replaced. For example, in the decade ahead there is every indication that online searching will replace the temporary CD-ROM stopgap measure. The CD-ROM is a technology that is reliable, easy to use, and almost impossible to pirate. But it is an information device which is nearing the end of its life. New systems of networking will undermine the whole notion of site-restricted materials on which retail distribution of the database is founded.

[34]Simon Jenkins, "Centre Point," *The Spectator*, October 8, 1994, p. 38.

[35]McLuhan, of course, is right when one considers "television," "film," "radio," and so on as usually being more important than what is said and seen over the media. In many homes listening and watching are governed by the medium rather than the content. The quotation is from his *Understanding Media* (New York: McGraw-Hill, 1964), Chapter 1. It is the chapter title.

over a back fence, handwritten, or fired over a computer network. What it says is the important matter. Someone looking for a street address, the moon, or the meaning of life is likely to be more involved with the answer than the technology of how it is received.

SUGGESTED READING

Auletta, Ken, "The Magic Box," *The New Yorker,* April 11, 1994, pp. 40–45. The famous critic explains how Time Warner hopes to employ family TV (rather than a PC) for information, and more particularly for entertainment. The home First Service Network will ask the user to pay from $20 and up for movies on demand, news, shopping, and so forth. The question remains whether this type of interactive television is economically viable and whether this, after all, is what the information highway amounts to for most of the population.

Berreby, David, "Get on Line for Plato's Cave," *The New York Times,* June 25, 1995, p. E5. A summary of backlash against computers, Internet, and the notion that "information" is all. Information is the current obsession, and the "digital revolution is based on the idea that things as disparate as love letters, Hollywood movies, and Beethoven's Fifth Symphony can all be broken down into the digital code."

Book Industry Trends. New York: Book Industry Study Group, 1994. The 1994 issue covers the years 1988 to 1993, that is, gives statistics which are firm up to 1994. The compilers speculate on book production for much of the remainder of the century. Publishing, library acquisitions, and related matters are covered.

Bruwelheide, Janis, *The Copyright Primer for Librarians and Educators,* 2d ed. Chicago: American Library Association, 1995. The second edition includes valuable material on "the electronic environment and digital issues" as well as the Internet, multimedia, and so forth. The 100 pages give easy-to-follow information on how to handle copyright problems in the library. A first choice for librarians.

Dillon, Patrick, and David Leonard, *Multimedia Technology from A to Z.* Phoenix, AZ: Oryx Press, 1994. This is by way of a dictionary and explanation of multimedia jargon. As such it is useful to anyone who wanders outside a specific library and tries to understand the rapidly developing technical language of multimedia.

"Evaluating Electronic Resources," *Choice,* April 1995, pp. 1236–1261. This is an excellent point-by-point evaluative guide with a superior reading list for further study of evaluation. The latter feature makes it particularly valuable in that many of the sources will remain meaningful.

Gabbard, Ralph, "Recent Literature Shows Accelerated Growth in Hypermedia Tools," *Reference Services Review,* Summer 1994, pp. 31–40. An annotated bibliography takes into account trends in CD-ROMs and the Internet. A good deal of the information is technical.

Gasaway, Laura, and Sarah Wiant, *Libraries and Copyright.* New York: Special Libraries Association, 1994. Subtitled, *A Guide to Copyright Law in the 1990s,* this is a one-stop publication for practical advice on library copyright problems. Particularly useful is the section on the new technologies from Wide Area Networks to Internet.

Landow, George, *Hypertext.* Baltimore: Johns Hopkins University Press, 1992. A history of the form from Vannevar Bush's first article "As We May Think" (*Atlantic Monthly,* June 1946) on hypertext to the present. Along the way the author explores the various ways hypertext is employed and is likely to be used.

Nunberg, Geoffrey, ed. *The Future of the Book*. Berkeley, CA: University California Press, 1966. A series of popular papers, including an "Afterword" by Umberto Eco on the role of the new technology in the future of the book. All contributors are enthusiastic about digital data, but they see the new media raising critical issues about the act of reading and the nature of discourse.

Rheingold, Howard, *The Virtual Community*. London: Secker & Warburg, 1994, 325 pp. This is both an informative and a winsome exploration of the history of networking and its numerous public characters.

Richardson, John, *Knowledge Based Systems for General Reference Work*. San Diego: Academics, 1995. In the confusing array of claims for knowledge-based systems, here is a voice of sanity and considered thought. Reference materials, reference methods, and particular traits of the users and the reference librarians make up the ideal knowledge-based system. The analysis of such a system and its many cousins makes this a valuable guide—particularly for those new to the field.

Sherman, Barry, *Glimpses of Heaven, Visions of Hell*. London: Hodder and Stroughton, 1993. This is one of the better overviews of "virtual reality and its implications." Today the major missing element in this mechanical world is tactile. Physical contact has yet to be realized or even poorly simulated.

Slatalla, Michelle, and Joshua Quittner, *Masters of Deception*. New York: HarperCollins, 1995. Subtitled *The Gang that Ruled Cyberspace* this concerns kids who, at an early age, learned to program inexpensive computers to master the art of hacking. Eventually, the hackers formed a "gang" whose goal was to break into top-secret computer programs. Despite a code of ethics that forbid either profit from or bringing about crashes, the gang was sentenced to jail for conspiracy. The government ended up looking more nervous than understanding. A marvelous read.

Williams, Wilda, "You Can Take Your MLS out of the Library," *Library Journal*, November 14, 1994, pp. 43–45. A discussion of alternatives to the lack of employment in many libraries. Hints are given, too, about where to find additional information on an important professional subject.

CHAPTER THREE
NETWORKS AND REFERENCE
SERVICES

Networks are a major theme of the 1990s. They are important as carriers on the information highway. They link libraries, individuals, and organizations, making it possible to send information to a friend down the block or to a hospital halfway around the globe. In all the enthusiasm, an observer wisely notes: "If a network brings about a more efficient flow of information, greater contact between persons, better understanding and greater knowledge then it will have succeeded. Failure to establish the real quality guidelines for networks, whether for document supply or any other purpose, does less than justice to their capabilities and achievements."[1]

Hardly a day goes by that the newspaper or television station does not have a report on networks. For example, a federal program to support the development of advanced computer networks is seen as essential to the nation's half trillion dollar information technology industry. The National Academy of Sciences and the National Center for Supercomputer Applications call for massively parallel computers and advanced networks. A new class of distribution information systems is being considered which will make it possible to manipulate large databases across the country and the world. The NREN (National Research and Educational Network) reports efforts to link educational institutions and specialized research centers. An enhanced educational network will be a stage for the study of the possible effects of a national-international educational system on teaching and education.

---

[1]Graham Cornish, "Europe Divided or United?" *Libri*, 1994, no. 1, pp. 74–75.

Networks and Libraries

Designed originally to bring free reading to users, the public library depended almost entirely upon local financial support. It gained or lost strength depending upon that support. In time, state, regional, and federal aid expanded the financial base and expanded the boundaries of service. With electronic networking many of these boundaries will disappear. At a library computer terminal one may draw information from the whole world.

Networking may create a library without walls, but the librarian, as pointed out numerous times in this text, serves as the mediator between the masses of information and the individual. The professional librarian is the guide on the information highway who directs the individual to what is needed. Furthermore, the librarian instructs the individual on how to find data at home or in the library. In a world of rapidly changing technology, this role alone would justify the librarian. Of course, it is much more than that. For one thing the network assumption considers only information in electronic format. The library remains the single place to turn for books, periodicals, and, yes, the expensive electronic CD-ROMs and other yet to be marketed information packages.

Types of Networks

An electronic network, and that is today's most common use of the term "network," consists of two or more servers, that is, computers linked together to share files, e-mail, games, and anything else that can be exchanged. Networking is made possible because a series of computers are linked to a similar "protocol," that is, a common language and standard for exchanging data. The ultimate goal is to tie personal computers to local or international networks, with the ability to communicate in a single language. Today it is more like the Tower of Babel.

A complete internetworking system is made up of switching equipment and software. Ethernet, for example, is a technical standard that allows personal computers in companies around the world to use networks. Specialized computers, or "hubs," are used to control larger networks. "Routers" connect several networks or can segment large networks into smaller ones. Database vendors offer "gateways," or access, to systems of other vendors, publishers, networks, and so forth. For example, the Easynet gateway offers a single method of searching and gaining access to DIALOG, Data-Star, NewsNet, and so on.

There are two basic types of networks, commercial and nonprofit. One processes information while the other communicates the data to the user. Some systems are a combination of both. Beyond that there are main divisions:

1. *Bibliographical networks or utilities,* such as the ubiquitous OCLC. This is tied, in turn, to (*a*) regional or state networks linking libraries and their holdings, and (*b*) community networks which serve to link two or more libraries to one another in an immediate urban or county area. All are nonprofit.

2. *Information processing vendors* such as DIALOG where the information is sent to the individual or to the specific library. Closely related are (*a*) the consumer networks such as Prodigy which process information for the average individual; and (*b*) the new CD-ROM networks which make available CD-ROMs, not individually, but collectively over a network. All are for profit.

The future of local and regional networks, as well as national and international systems, depends on how long it takes to integrate and develop the information superhighway, or, as many librarians now prefer to call it, the national information infrastructure. Close cooperation, if not amalgamation and merger, will be the pattern of state, regional, and local networks over the next decade.

Networks and Sharing

A network is traditionally a group of libraries tied together by mutual interest, a fax machine, an online database, and a cataloging system. The average librarian thinks of networking in terms of sharing. It is a formal arrangement whereby several libraries or other organizations engage in a common pattern or exchange of information, materials, services, or all three for some functional purpose.

There are some variations: (1) The American Library Association recognizes a group of libraries as being a network only when they have central management and programs. (2) A *library consortium* is usually a synonym for networks, but can also be confined to acquisitions and selections of materials. A consortium is probably limited by subject, geographical location, size of the library, and so forth. (3) Other terms, with slightly different connotations but essentially representing a network, include federated systems and cooperative systems.

SUPERNETWORKS

No one is sure about the form or even the technologies of the next decade's networks. Everyone knows they are in place and functioning. The question is how networks can be improved and brought into the daily lives of more Americans.

The potential of a superhighway carrying data at thousands of times the speed of today's systems is often compared with the development of railroads, telegraph lines, and interstate highways. Each revolutionized the flow of goods and information. Each enriched the nation and the individual. It is a familiar pattern. There are countless other possibilities on the on- and off-ramps of the information superhighway. New information industries will develop, and the complexity of the task will challenge thousands of new workers. Ideally, individual lives will be enriched and made safer.

Someone who wants a paragraph or a small library of articles and books could tap into the resources of the global network, or superlibrary. Taken a step further, the same individual's health records could be checked by a doctor in Europe and a faraway specialist might suggest what steps the local physician should take. Computer monitors could be used for conferences among groups, or for comparison of experimental data among engineers. On the lighter side, any movie ever made could be called up for the couch potato's television screen. That same spud would be at home because all of his or her work with the boss, customers, and suppliers is carried on over a computer.

Cyber

In his science fiction novel, *Necromancer* (1984), William Gibson first defined *cyberspace* as a network of people becoming one with computers. The term developed to mean the place where hackers converse. It is now an umbrella term for anyone or anything connected with networks. As an integral part of cybernetics, networks have become synonymous with the term which is more used than well defined. A pub in London, where one can get Russian drinks, is called "Cyberia."[2]

Marshall McLuhan foresaw that information networks would tie the world together into a "global village." Today the village has other names such as "virtual communities" or "electronic communities." Here one may conference with individuals or groups through the computer. For example, a user may want to know about working as a reference librarian abroad and puts out a request to the community of librarians with the same interest. Detailed or short reports on opportunities, drawbacks, experiences, and so forth are received from librarians in foreign places. A nuclear scientist might pass reports over the Internet to researchers in Japan, England, and New York State and, in turn, receive reports back from this particular electronic community.

Cyberspace, as a postmodern term for reducing everything to an electronic impulse, does and does not exist. It *does* exist when employed loosely as a synonym for network or a working tool such as the computer or a CD-ROM player deck, as well as for databases and related digital information sources. When cyberspace is used as a synonym for "virtual reality," as it often is in science fiction chatter and over the many computer networks, it does *not* exist. Thousands,

[2]William Safire, "Cyberlingo," *The New York Times Magazine,* November 20, 1994, pp. 32–34. According to *Webster's Third New International Dictionary* (Springfield, MA: 1995) "cybernetics" is the "comparative study of the automatic control system formed by the nervous system and brain and by mechanical-electrical communicating systems and devices (as computers and thermostats)." Transpose "network" for "system" and the current use is clear.

of course, use it as a given for an environment of games and fun where many users set up a simulated world. A computerized version of Dungeons and Dragons is often referred to as action taking place in cyberspace.

Network Implications

In discussing the wider implications of the worldwide information superhighway, several comments regularly surface. (1) It represents the most significant change in communication since Gutenberg invented a press and movable type in the mid-fifteenth century. (2) Time and space are shrunk to zero. In a second all of the world's experts in any given subject area can be located, as it were, in one room. (3) One can now be thousands or more miles from a laboratory, business office, or classroom without being intellectually isolated. (4) Collaborative efforts on a world scale are now possible because of rapid, almost instant, communication of twists and turns in research. (5) As it breaks geographical and time barriers, the computer network hammers away at social and professional roadblocks. Theoretically, at least, no one because of rank, position, wealth, or education has to wait for information until someone else sees fit to have it published. Data once confined and held up by journals and journal editors are out there floating around seconds after their appearance on the networks.

Networks present basic questions:

1. Who owns what, and how is ownership to be maintained when information crosses the world in seconds? There is the matter of "fair use" and royalties and, well, just about anything of concern in copyright.

2. How does one preserve electronic data, at least that which is used and generated for only a brief time? A simple example: the personal letter which is a valuable source of information for everyone from corporations to social historians. Can e-mail communications be "trapped" like typed or handwritten letters?

3. Who is to control the means of transmitting the information? This is an explosive social, political, and ethical issue. Should a national resource as important as health care and scientific research be developed and controlled by the government or by private interests?

4. Internet is inexpensive and, for many on college campuses and in business or government, free. As advertisers become more involved and as Internet becomes more business oriented, is information going to be the next giant commodity to be sold on a worldwide marketplace only to those able to buy? Will everyone have equal and universal access to this information?

5. Cyberliteracy, or computer literacy, is important if people are to make full use of the information highway. Who is going to be educated, who is going to be left behind? Are there going to be as many cyber illiterates as there are now text illiterates in the United States—in the world? Lack of this kind of literacy will simply widen the gap between the haves and the have-nots.

At the day-to-day reference services level, several major questions about networks have yet to be answered: (1) What is done best at the national, state, or local level? The plethora of networks—from state networks to Internet and OCLC—blurs the lines of discernment. (2) Who is responsible for what? (3) Will the access to such networks improve, make the flow of information from institution Y or Y to individual P more efficient and speedier? (4) Does access to such a network affect either the amount or the quality of research, particularly at the graduate level? The same question might be asked of teaching aids from the earliest grades through a four-year college. (5) Finally, what does it cost, and how efficient is it in the information exchange process? Is the expense worth the end results? Most of these questions have yet to be answered, at least in a definitive fashion. Conversely, individuals will gladly tell anyone who will listen how helpful networks are to their quest for information.

The problems associated with the information superhighway offer an opportunity for the reference librarian. Faster and more efficient ways of delivering information require considerable expert navigation. The reference librarian is that navigator.

WORLD AS LIBRARY

Thanks to networks, electronic databases, and digitalization of information (from books and periodicals to reports and sound and motion pictures), a library is no longer a library unto itself. The world is the library. A great library is no longer the one with a million or two volumes. Today it provides services to allow users to make the maximum use of information available hundreds or thousands of miles away.

What will be and, in fact, what are the duties of the reference librarian in the world library, in the electronic age of information?

1. As always the primary duty is to answer questions, although now, because of wider access to information, both the query and the response are likely to be complex.

2. The reference librarian continues to be a mediator between the individual and information, but in a more refined way. A few years ago, the librarian pointed out the value of one or two citations in *The Readers' Guide to Periodical Literature*. Today the librarian indicates to the user what index would be best, how index formats (print, magnetic tape, CD-ROM, online, and so on) differ, where to find the index, how to locate the citations, and, often, how to search the electronic database. In an unlimited sea of resources, the librarian is the navigator who indicates to the user where to find what in the shortest amount of time.

3. Instruction in searching electronic databases, in finding one's way through the various networks, is a major duty. Even librarians who hesitate to support the old-fashioned bibliographical instruction realize the importance of making information available to those who want and who need instruction.

4. Knowledge management, in the acquisition, labeling, and storage of data—as well as skills in locating elusive facts on one or more networks—is a major professional duty.

5. In sophisticated situations, the reference librarian is part of the research team which may be seeking answers to everything from the key to cancer to the best transportation system to high-definition television.

Librarians attempting to meet the challenge of the new approaches to networking hold meetings and publish reports on every aspect of the network situation. Findings include what every librarian who works with electronic information sources knows: (*a*) The more the average user knows about electronic databases, the more use he or she wants to make of them, with the resulting higher costs for the library. This also leads to a stress on hard-pressed staff. (*b*) Moving back and forth from the print to the electronic reference work not only is a stress, but also requires considerable skills in estimating costs and the place of the new technologies. (*c*) Security and privacy on networks are growing problems, particularly with easy availability of e-mail and bulletin boards. To meet this, many encourage a "firewall" system of computers to monitor the flow of messages in a network.

BIBLIOGRAPHICAL NETWORKS

Essentially, a bibliographical network (or *bibliographical utility,* as it is sometimes called) puts a massive national-international catalog at the fingertips of the librarian. The librarian may locate 30 to 50 million books and a comparable number of periodicals, reports, recordings, and so forth. Over the past years the size of the international catalog(s) has been increasing. By the turn of the century it is quite possible that bibliographical networks will give access to virtually all information in the world.

Bibliographical utilities such as OCLC and RLIN are nonprofit networks that cross state and national lines. They are managed in a variety of ways and provide services in many different forms. Still, there are certain basic functions they all perform. The reference librarian uses such utilities to be able to quickly answer four basic types of questions:

1. *The bibliographical query.* One is able to gain complete information about a given book, journal, recording, or other type of library material.

2. *The verification query.* One can determine the proper spelling of an author's name, the name of the publisher, the date the book was published, the number of pages, and so forth.

3. *The location query.* The system indicates which libraries have the material. There is usually also a method of requesting the wanted title on interlibrary loan.

4. *Database access.* Through OCLC, RLIN, and company, one may search indexes online or on CD-ROMs. Unlike bibliographical services, this is not a unique service. Librarians have a choice of using, for example, OCLC or DIALOG or Prodigy or a group of numerous vendors.

Other uses of the bibliographical network system made by reference services include:

1. Finding specific titles in a series.

2. Locating a subject either by the first word of a title or by use of a full-subject search.

3. Providing a complete bibliography of a writer's work.

4. Finding a title with only partial or incorrect information, that is, one really needs only the author's correct last name and the correct first word of a title. Even if the remaining information is incorrect, one is still able to find what is needed. Example: If with this given information, "Hank James, Portrait of a Lad," one enters instead "Jame," and "Port," the correct author and title will emerge: Henry James, *Portrait of a Lady.*

5. Finding government documents otherwise difficult to locate.

6. Locating information on periodicals, music, maps, and other material.

7. Frequently, although not always, finding the birth and death dates of an author, musician, and so on.

8. Searching for a writer using the correct name established by the name-authority file.

9. Locating information quickly on various editions, reprints, and places of publication. The latter may be important when the work is, for instance, first issued in England and then reprinted in the United States under another title.

Major Bibliographical Networks

The most direct, easy-to-understand bibliographical network is the one that gives easy access to another library's catalog. This type of network is growing and is found at both the local and national levels.

Internet is an example of an informal organization of academic, research, and government libraries. The core data are the catalogs of each. One gets online and taps the catalog of, say, the University of California, Purdue University, or Boston University. Each catalog is searched separately. It can be an inefficient way to find a needed periodical or book. Beyond that, one may find unique items, develop and assess collections, compare holdings, and so forth. The Internet connects a group of local, regional, and national networks in such a way as to suggest a new approach to bibliographical reference queries.

At a formal level, and one that offers countless approaches to data, there are two major bibliographical networks or utilities. These are OCLC and RLIN. Briefly these may be described as follows.

OCLC

Located in Dublin, Ohio, OCLC (Online Computer Library Center) has the greatest membership of all the bibliographical networks. By 1996 the number, from all types and sizes of libraries, was over 18,000 in 52 countries throughout the world, although most are in the United States and Canada. The system supports a growing database of over 30 million books, films, reports, monographs, and so forth. The titles are derived from the online-merged catalogs of the member libraries.

OCLC grows each year, month, and day. Approximately 2 million records a year are added. MARC tapes[3] are at the heart of the OCLC system. OCLC also includes the important original cataloging of members and holdings of all major government libraries. In an average year the system carries close to 50 million interlibrary loan requests. As the publicity for the networks says, "Select one of our detailed record displays, and you'll find holdings information. . . . It's like opening a card catalog to nearly 60,000 libraries at once."

Only rarely is it impossible to find what is needed on OCLC. When that does happen, the desired information is probably so esoteric (such as the morning prayers, printed, of the Tibetan monks) that an answer will be found only on RLIN, or a similar database which includes highly specialized information.[4]

In addition to being a giant bibliography and catalog, OCLC has three basic reference services: (1) FirstSearch, with between 50 and 60 reference databases. It is so constructed that, by means of menus, the layperson may search the databases with relative ease. In addition to being able to search OCLC itself (WorldCat) the user may browse through numerous indexes, including all

---

[3]MARC (machine-readable cataloging) is discussed in the first volume, but it will be recalled that it is a database that covers much the same material found in the *National Union Catalog* from 1968 to date, and supplied weekly by the Library of Congress.

[4]In addition to books, one finds pretty much what is on the MARC tapes: computer data files, computer programs, films, periodicals (but not individual articles), manuscripts, maps, musical scores, newspapers (but not individual articles), slides, sound recordings, and videotapes. For an overview of how OCLC may be used to search nonbook items, see Joseph Palmer, "Obtainability of Specialized Subject Videos Found with OCLC's EPIC," *RQ* Fall 1993, pp. 101–109.

of those put online by The H. W. Wilson Company. ArticleFirst and ContentsFirst offer easy access and content alert to some 15,000 journals. Also, there is an electronic document ordering system in place. (2) EPIC is pretty much the same as FirstSearch. The difference is that EPIC offers a more sophisticated searching system. Also, it is an easy key to the most used of all the OCLC databases, the Online Union Catalog. (3) Only in the beginning stages, and now more experimental than useful, "Electronic Journals Online," or EJO, is an effort to offer users full text, with illustrations of a rigorous, peer-reviewed group of journals. To date there are only a handful of scientific journals available. Also, through cooperation with UMI, certain indexes such as ABI/Inform offer full text of many of the items indexed. (4) Other services, and the number grows as the system develops, include easy access to Internet (NetFirst) and the Web (Web Access). The access includes full explanations of how to gain certain types of needed materials. Along with the Web come full text and images.

Access to OCLC

Access to OCLC is available in several ways: (1) directly to the OCLC Online Union Catalog database; (2) through Internet to the same database, or to WorldCat, a part of FirstSearch. In the mid-1990s more than 70 percent of the users accessed the main bibliographical information through WorldCat on FirstSearch; this is the favorite approach of people working from their homes, too; (3) through various regional networks such as the State University of New York OCLC Library Network (which services all the campuses in the statewide system) or NELINET (New England Library Information Network). Each one of these systems has various services.

OCLC offers CD-ROM discs made up of subsets from the main database, or about 3 million of the most frequently used records, depending on which set is employed. All the basic records are updated quarterly. This is workable for small libraries, but of limited use to those with larger acquisitions.

Another cost-cutting measure, at least for some retrospective records, is offered by OCLC's Search CD450. The CD-ROMs are sold in five subject areas: general reference, agriculture, education, arts and humanities, and science and technology. Each set offers access to OCLC records in these areas and, furthermore, adds basic indexes. For example, the education package (for $1095) includes OCLC records in education as well as current and retrospective ERIC discs. The ERIC discs are updated quarterly, whereas the OCLC records unit is updated monthly.

Another example is *Music Library: Musical Sound Recordings*. This annual CD-ROM disc for $350 contains over 400,000 bibliographical records of recordings from compact discs and LPs to cassettes. The system allows the user to search quickly for all work by a particular artist, types of music, versions of a particular song, and so forth.

Searching FirstSearch

In searching OCLC's FirstSearch WorldCat, it is essential to recognize, as on any database, the scope and purpose of the reference work. (An overall view of the database and basic search techniques is usually available by simply typing "help.") The scope is more than 30 million records of books, computer files, films, journals, maps, newspapers, slides, and so forth. The heart of this is the National Union Catalog's MARC augmented by holdings of member libraries as reflected in the OCLC Online Union Catalog.

The purpose is to make available to reference librarians, catalogers, and others what is available, in general, and in over 8000 libraries, in particular. Thus if a user is trying to find the book *Information for a New Age* she or he might look to WorldCat for the name of the author, publisher, and so on. At the same time the user might find which library, including her or his own, has or does not have the title. And, of course, full details about the book will be given in the record.

Each record indicates whether the parent library has the item when the library symbol is part of that record. At the end of the record the symbols for libraries that do have the book appear, if the book is not owned by the parent library. Librarians inevitably know their own record symbols and those of heavily used libraries about the country. For those who cannot recall the meaning of the symbol, one simply types in "h" and the three-letter symbol for a full explanation of the symbol.

On WorldCat as on most OCLC, and, for that matter, other bibliographical databases, one enters certain key words to search by: subject, author, title, accession number, government document number, content notes, place of publication, publisher, and a half dozen other points of entry.[5] Where too much material turns up, as for example in searching the work of Hemingway or material on drugs and children, then one may "limit" the search by asking only for books in a given language (e.g., English or German); by years of publication (in a single year, in or after a given year, in or before a given year, or in or between two years); and finally by type, that is, limit the search to books, serials, maps, recordings, and so forth.

Searching FirstSearch, and similar services, is not always that simple because the software is not all that clear. One example: On first sight one is given the option of searching by subject, that is, "su:" on FirstSearch's WorldCat. This search is by individual words, but is too broad for most purposes. If one reads on in the directions, or calls up the added directions on the screen, it is revealed

---

[5]As of 1995, no boolean logic "or" for searching and no truncation were available. Also, FirstSearch only allows downloading five records at a time to diskette.

that a specific search of a subject requires "sh=." This approach is considerably more useful than the much explained "su." But it requires some knowledge of the database to even appreciate its availability.

RLIN

Located in Mountain View, California, RLIN (Research Libraries Information Network) is the upmarket bibliographical network. In addition to the records of the "ivy league" universities, it includes the major research centers such as The New York Public Library and the California State Library. Membership is limited to only the largest of systems.

The records include the "standards," that is, MARC tapes, National Library of Medicine holdings, bibliographical records of the Government Printing Office, and so forth. While the membership is limited, the actual number of records is over 25 million in 365 languages.

The small homogeneous membership has two things in common: (1) huge collections of materials, often with esoteric data; (2) comparatively large staffs in reference, acquisitions, and cataloging. The assumption of some librarians is that the larger research libraries are more careful about their cataloging and that therefore the RLIN cataloging entries are more precise than found in other networks. This is not the case. Analysis reveals no statistically significant differences in accuracy or fullness between OCLC and RLIN cataloging.

The RLIN equivalent to the OCLC WorldCat is called the RLIN Bibliographic File or BIB. This represents all the bibliographical material on RLIN, including records from a wide assortment of museums; historical societies; law, medical, and art libraries; and the like. (These, as noted, give RLIN the advantage of holding records of such limited interest, at least for many, that they are not found on OCLC, and are unique to RLIN.)

While RLIN has nothing as ambitious as OCLC's FirstSearch, it does offer a somewhat similar, limited service—CitaDel. This has about a dozen databases, although one or two are rather unusual, such as Index to Foreign Legal Periodicals and Inside Information. The latter is the table of contents of more than 12,000 frequently requested journals held at The British Library. Used in conjunction with OCLC's ContentsFirst, little of importance, at least in English, will be missed. RLIN plans to expand its service, but it is unlikely it will ever rival in scope the OCLC network.

Many librarians prefer the searching methods offered by RLIN. For one thing they include boolean logic, not found (at least by the mid-1990s) on OCLC. There are numerous points of entry, too, not offered by its competitor. And the limitation search possibilities are much more useful than in other services.

Ideally, and often this in the case in larger libraries, the library will have access to both RLIN and OCLC. Over the Internet and related networks some universities and research and business organizations make these systems available at home. Most people, however, tend to save money (although certainly neither time nor effort) by searching individual library catalogs through the Internet or other networks.

Cost

RLIN and OCLC have different methods of charging for services. These change constantly and are likely to be different in the next few years. Still, the patterns are much the same.

OCLC charges libraries flat fees. The library buys blocks of 500 or more searches. The more searches purchased, the lower the individual search cost; for example, in 1996, 500 searches cost about 90 cents per search; while 80,000 cost about half that amount, or 45 cents per search.[6] Another approach, useful for only the largest of libraries, is to pay a flat fee for unlimited searches in a single year. Either way, the charge covers all connect-hour time displays of data. Where the search EPIC is employed the charge is about $95 per connect hour, as well as $2.50 for full record.

RLIN, which tends to be more expensive than OCLC, has its own unique charging system. For example, they offer all libraries, not simply large research institutions, savings on cataloging. As a 1995 advertisement for RLIN explains: "We're offering you *full* MARC records for copying cataloging using communication paths you *already* have in place. No large up-front costs. No dedicated equipment. No tapes to load. No waiting. $200 gets you started reducing cataloging costs with RLIN record transfer. How does it work? Simple. You search RLIN over the Internet and then use FTP (File Transfer Protocol) to transfer MARC records for local reuse—immediately."

Libraries paid a fixed annual fee for each of CitaDel's databases. Fees vary with the size of the library and how much the databases are to be used. Files range in price from a low of about $2000 a year to a high of $21,000; but most are in the $7000 to $12,000 range.

It is important to stress that costs presented here are only tentative. Different pricing systems seem to appear each month or so, and certainly costs can

---

[6]The flat fee is only one approach. There are many others. The OCLC charges vary and include equipment and its maintenance. Then, too, there are telecommunications charges. If contacted through a regional network, there are annual dues of $500 to about $2000. Actual cataloging costs are added and vary from $1 or so to less than a penny an item, depending on the volume of cataloging. If an average is possible, at this writing it would cost about $2400 per terminal per year, but this is exclusive of other charges. All dollar figures are estimated averages as costs vary with the library and usage time. The expense is not inconsiderable, although when balanced against savings in cataloging, interlibrary loan, and reference, they are much less than the old-fashioned approach to these services.

expect to go lower as more and more individuals and libraries employ OCLC and its various offerings.

After OCLC and RLIN

Although OCLC and RLIN dominate the national and international library world in terms of both coverage and use, there are auxiliary bibliographical networks employed by libraries in the immediate region and larger libraries looking for special services.

The leading bibliographical networks outside OCLC and RLIN include:

1. CARL Corporation, a Knight-Ridder owned and managed system which was begun in 1988 as a for-profit spin-off of the Colorado Alliance of Research Libraries. The sale to Knight-Ridder (which also owns DIALOG) in 1995 put this network in the peculiar position of being a for-profit system in a group of networks that are otherwise cooperative and generally not for profit.

The system includes the basic bibliographical data found on OCLC and RLIN and in addition, some indexes, including *ERIC, Magazine Index, Facts on File*, and so forth. The primary "outsider" use of CARL is the UnCover system which offers almost immediate access to the text of some 20,000 journals held by CARL members from 1988. As with OCLC the service updates daily a listing of tables of contents from which articles may be chosen. Also a key word search is possible. When an article(s) has been chosen it can be delivered electronically or in other forms to the user for a relatively low fee.

2. WLN (Western Library Network), located in Olympia, Washington, provides computer services to over 370 libraries in Washington, Arizona, Alaska, Idaho, Oregon, and Montana. A division of the Washington State Library, WLN has a database of close to 8 million records, which is much smaller than either OCLC or RLIN. The records represent what is available on MARC tapes and from the subscribing member libraries. The records cover books, periodicals, audiovisual materials, and instructional materials. The emphasis is on English-language works, and about 5000 records are added to the file each week.

3. MELVYL (University of California) is available on Internet and the University of California online facility. It has over 8 million books, 1 million periodicals, and other materials available from the various University of California centers as well as Stanford and several other private schools.

The OPAC Directory (Westport, CT: Mecklermedia, 1993 to date, annual) offers a state-by-state listing of online public access catalogs and, where available, databases. This gives users a key to access virtually every major network and catalog in the United States. A typical entry includes the name of the institution, the number of volumes and number of titles, subject strengths, personnel, system data (along with the practical and technical aspects of networking).

REGIONAL AND STATE NETWORKS[7]

Beyond CARL, WLN, and a few other large networks there are smaller and less ambitious systems. The regional network, which may be only a handful of libraries in the immediate area or spread out over several states, is important to reference librarians. This type of network differs from the bibliographical utility in that it has many purposes, not simply bibliographical services.

There are different methods of defining and determining what a regional network is: (1) It acts as a broker for bibliographical utility services (such as OCLC) directly or indirectly to libraries within the group. (2) It provides training and skills in services not likely to be found in member libraries. This may range from building union lists to assisting with financial problems. (3) It is of no particular size, although this is not much of a test, as networks may have as few as a half dozen or more than 3000 members. (4) It has a small staff which may include only one or two employees or as many as 50.

In 1993 an amalgam of 17 regional networks was founded as the Alliance of Library Networks. The 17 represent 9500 libraries and information centers throughout the nation. The alliance formulated several key goals. The goals are indicative of the hopes and the actions of regional libraries, both in an alliance and working by themselves:

- Strengthen the capabilities of alliance partners to provide high-quality, cost-effective services and support to member libraries and information centers;

- Contribute to the development and evolution of a sound, equitable information infrastructure in North America;

- Sustain and enhance a strong partnership with OCLC and other suppliers through cooperation for the benefit of member libraries;

- Collaborate in arranging joint agreements that will enable alliance partners to provide member libraries and information centers with the greatest value per dollar spent through economies of scale and through concerted negotiations with suppliers; and

- Develop and carry out joint operating and research programs for the benefit of member libraries and information centers.[8]

Regional Networks

The number of regional networks crossing state lines are limited. They tend to be of assistance to reference people in that they make available shared cataloging (usually through OCLC or RLIN), lower rates for online searching through DI-

---

[7]For a complete list of the local "networks, consortia, and other cooperative library organizations," state by state, city by city, see *American Library Directory* (New York: R. R. Bowker, annual). Each listing includes a brief description of the activities of the organization.

[8]*Library Journal*, October 1, 1993, p. 26.

ALOG and other vendors, better interlibrary loan systems, and technical help with any of numerous problems. Among such better-known networks:

AMIGOS (a Texas system) has over 150 members.

CAPCON is a multiregional library system with 130 member libraries in Washington, DC, Maryland, and Virginia.

FEDLINK has about 1200 libraries and information centers contracting with information from the Library of Congress.

MLC (Michigan Library Consortium) has over 300 libraries.

OHIONET serves the needs of well over 200 academic, public, and special libraries in the Ohio area.

SOLINET (Southeastern Library Information Network) is one of the largest of the systems, with a membership of 724 libraries.

Network members use a turnkey computer system to cooperate with one another and to facilitate interlibrary loans. Examples of this type of networking can be found in most systems listed above.

The networks appoint managers whose staffs make most of the day-to-day arrangements for service. Each member of the system has a voice in governing, and there are regular meetings to discuss problems.

Nonreference services vary, too, but they generally include: (1) Arranging contracts with the major bibliographical utilities, and in so doing, acting as a director in negotiating terms between the utilities and the individual members of the regional network. (2) Holding down the cost of services made possible by a large membership base. (3) Providing for the training of librarians and consulting with libraries that wish to modify existing database services. (4) Arranging new services for members and developing those services at the local, regional, and national levels. (5) Determining the authorized control of records for the members and improving circulation and acquisitions databases. (6) Helping members change or even drop bibliographical brokers who serve the local system.

State Networks

The earliest networks, for everything from interlibrary loan to cataloging, were organized at a state level. Many of these continue as a middle unit between libraries and national and international networks. And several, such as CARL (Colorado Alliance for Research Libraries) and the Washington Library Network (WLN) and the California Library Authority for Systems and Services (CLASS), go beyond state service to regional and even national importance. They link cooperative collection development to interlibrary loan and resource sharing, as well as national information networks. Oklahoma, for example, has launched a close to $4.5 million project to link 38 rural hospitals through a single high-speed network. Doctors in the various hospitals around the state may share x-rays and other medical documents and images.

Statewide networks are cost savers, particularly among universities and larger public research libraries. The purpose is to cut duplications of low-use materials so the individual libraries can expand collections of much-used items as well as more esoteric titles that will be used across the network. For example, libraries on primary campuses of the State University of New York, as well as the libraries in the City University of New York system, share catalogs, indexes, and other commercial databases. This means one may search basic databases at the various campuses, although the primary home of the service is at one center; for example, SUNY-Buffalo provides both PsycInfo and ERIC, while CUNY provides Newspaper Abstracts. Delivery service, with a two-day turnaround, is available for articles and books located in and through the network.

A typical pattern of state reference networking connects the smaller libraries in the state to the central state library. When a person has a question the local librarian cannot answer (usually because of lack of materials), the reference librarian sends the request to the central network headquarters by teletype, fax, telephone, or in writing. If the request is not clear, the central service may talk with the librarian or the patron. Today the service is likely to involve a computerized system giving access to databases. Thus the individual may receive (1) simple citations, (2) citations and annotations, and (3) in rarer cases, the documents and articles themselves.

The New York State Education and Research Network (NYSER Net) is an example of a superior, ongoing state network. Funded at about $12 million a year, it literally offers electronic gateways for libraries throughout New York State. A five-year plan will see a hundredfold increase in the network's technological ability to carry information. Working jointly with telecommunications companies, the founders of the network have set up services which range from access to online databases and library catalogs to a ramp onto the Internet.

Local Area Networks (LANs)

The local area network, or LAN, is normally located in an urban center which draws upon the resources of libraries within a larger governing unit, such as a county. LAN differs from other networks in that the members are literally neighbors. Most are within walking or driving distance from one another. This establishes what some call a "natural information network."

The locals rely upon one another for advice and assistance in all aspects of management and reference services. There may be mutual pooling of funds for a given project or service or monthly meetings to discuss current problems.

Normally the librarians serve the same type of audience and meet much the same needs.

The electronic LAN usually links a half dozen to hundreds of computer workstations in a university, business, or government organization. The server (or servers) which feeds the workstations is usually a large computer. There are, as well, CD-ROM towers, faxes, modems, and gateways to OCLC, Internet, and other networks. Depending on the extent of the network, the cost for an initial LAN may be from $25,000 to well over $250,000. The bill is as large as the service.

Electronic local area networks, complete with access to Internet, and other sources of databases are a much heralded feature of modern university life. The terminals are scattered throughout the campus. They may be in an individual teacher's office, a dormitory, a classroom, or, of course, the library. In a way, it is like connecting telephones throughout the campus to a central operator, but in this case the central operator is the library computer.

In an ideal situation, a professor may work from a personal computer (in office or home) and be linked to the campuswide LAN. She or he searches the library catalog and finds several items and then instructs the library to send them to her or his office. Two of the books are not owned by the library and the professor files an order requesting that the books be purchased. Another title is not in the local catalog, but can be obtained on interlibrary loan from Princeton. The request is placed, perhaps through Internet. An article in a magazine held only by the University of Michigan is ordered by telefacsimile transmission.

While the electronic aspects of the LAN are dramatic, the administrative purposes are more usual. Most activities occur by informal arrangements, usually at the local level, without any sharing on a regional or statewide basis. Typical business includes:

1. Informal meetings between public and school librarians to address mutual concerns

2. Exchange of lists of collection holdings

3. Joint compilation of community resources

4. Joint material evaluation, selection, acquisitions, and processing programs

5. Placement of public library book catalogs in school libraries

6. Reciprocal borrowing and lending of materials

7. Provision of the public library with school curriculum guides and units of instruction

8. In-service programs designed around topics of mutual interest and concern

9. Production facilities for materials

10. Preparation of union lists or catalogs

11. Access to specialized and computerized databases

12. Joint film cooperatives

Community Networks

Community networks, unlike the conventional library network, are places where people may look for employment listings, participate in political discussions, use e-mail, and a number of other things associated with the more mundane activities of Internet fans. A Listserv (Communet) is available on Internet which gives tips and information on such community efforts.

Free-nets, sponsored and financed by local governments, are another type of community network. They may give access to Internet. They will not open up all the Internet features, particularly the costly ones, but they do afford basic services such as e-mail. The only expense for the user is a phone connection.

The Buffalo Free-Net in Buffalo, New York, is an example of a system that not only accesses Internet, but also gives information of local interest from public library holdings to cultural calendars. The Buffalo Free-Net is a volunteer group of librarians, students, and residents who are typical of a grassroots effort to keep the information freeway free. While limited in scope, the network is determined to offer a community such things as job service listings and educational programs. Similar services are available in Westchester and Danbury, both in Connecticut, as well as in other parts of the United States.[9]

VENDORS AND NETWORKS

Networks, as noted, are of two primary types—commercial and nonprofit. The latter includes OCLC and much of the Internet coverage. The former includes vendors from DIALOG to Prodigy. Libraries draw on both types. Confusion arises in that the database vendor may be one and the same as the database publisher (e.g., The H. W. Wilson Company, which publishes and distributes databases over its own network, as well as produces and sells CD-ROMs). There are approximately 3000 producer-publishers of online and CD-ROM databases in the mid-1990s. The number grows each year. Many of these make up the more than 1800 vendors who network their databases.

Vendors provide the means of networking the databases to libraries and to individuals. Also, they distribute CD-ROMs and other data in electronic for-

[9]"Information Freeway?" *The New York Times*, August 4, 1994, pp. B1, B6.

mat. Aside from distribution, their primary and, in fact, major contribution is the search engine, the mainframe or server computer, the storage capacity and related hardware and software which make it possible to use the electronic databases.

While there are well over 1800 vendors, only a handful, as in American publishing, control most of the business. The big five or six (the consumer networks such as CompuServe aside) would include: DIALOG, the best-known online service with hundreds of much-used databases, particularly abstracting and indexing services. (DIALOG retained its name online, but in early 1995 the company name changed from DIALOG Information Service to its new owner's name, i.e., Knight-Ridder Information, Inc.) CDP (formerly BRS) specializes in scientific and medical databases as does ORBIT-QUESTEL and DATA-STAR of England. WilsonLine is the network of The H. W. Wilson Company and fields many of the popular general indexes.

The primary vendors of full-text databases include Mead-Data Central (NEXIS, LEXIS); Dow Jones News/Retrieval; and, again, DIALOG which took over the major full-text firm, VUTEXT, as well as the document delivery, CARL.

As "gateways" to databases they share importance in a library with the aforementioned OCLC, RLIN, and numerous regional networks that offer several of the same valuable services.

If at one time the librarian had only a single gateway to a given number of types of information databases, today there are numerous access points. This prompts the questions: Which is best? Which is most efficient? Which is more economical? Unfortunately, there is no single answer. There are too many variables. Each library must determine for itself the best access route. The librarian must be at least familiar with the major on-ramps to information.

Vendor Database Guides

The main vendors have their own guides to individual databases. They are often issued in the form of loose-leaf notebooks which allow the users to add or delete pages as the databases are updated. Arranged by file number, each of the database summaries offers similar information. The outline for each description includes: (1) database summary sheet with sample record; (2) subject searching options; (3) code-searching instructions; (4) limiting capabilities, if any; (5) output formats; (6) sortability options, if any; (7) search aids available; and (8) document retrieval, if available. Each vendor also has a newsletter in which information on individual databases is included. The various vendors offer specific search guides for both the beginner and the expert. They give basic information as well as more sophisticated hints on searching.

The vendors offer much the same information online. A click of the mouse or a key pressed will turn up a screen full of similar data. Also, they show the connecting links between various databases.

Costs

Similar to the bibliographical utilities, commercial services have complex methods of computing costs to users. Until the mid-1990s the rate structure, and the one used throughout this text to indicate relative cost, was based on so much per connect minute, plus so much more for citation, and so forth. The exact rate per minute varies from database to database. Government services, such as ERIC, are relatively inexpensive, while private efforts from, say, Dow Jones News/Retrieval may run into the hundreds of dollars for an hour of information; for example, ChemSearch is $354 per hour.[10]

By the mid-1990s everyone, including Dow Jones, realized that mass use of the commercial online services would be impossible without a more equitable (equally easy-to-understand) rate schedule. Dow Jones, for one, eliminated connect-time pricing and switched to view-time pricing. This so-called information pricing is based on what appears on the computer screen, not on how long it takes to find the data or the time of day the search is made. At the same time Dow Jones offers flat subscription fees for given services; for example, for $500 a month one has unlimited access to business and other databases. At the end of three months, the company looks at the bill and decides whether the charge has to be changed. Every six months, based on usage, the flat fee is reset. DIALOG and other vendors have reduced and simplified their charges, using a system of price tiers from about $15 to $120 per hour.

Again, all these charge plans are based on use by libraries, government, and business. The consumer networks, such as CompuServe, have much more simplified, much less costly, plans in place for the average user. Even these, though, can be expensive.

The real question facing all network-for-profit vendors is, What price level will the traffic (literally in this case) stand? The other questions are: How can one increase the traffic, lower the prices, and retain a profit? How can the vendors compete with the virtually free services on the Internet? How can network databases compete with CD-ROMs and other lower-priced information packages?

CD-ROM Wide-Area Networks

In an effort not to be bypassed by online databases that are easier to use and less expensive, CD-ROM vendors and producers now offer wide-area network

---

[10]Providers of information through the commercial networks receive various amounts, but on average they are from 10 to 20 percent of the connect-time charges, no matter how they are compiled. Microsoft claims to pay considerably more for these services.

alternatives to the single CD-ROM–player-user approach. SilverPlatter, for example, has a system whereby one may use all of their CD-ROMs, which they load into their own computer, just as one would use a regular network or the services of a vendor. The company gives the library the choice of either leasing the single CD-ROM or gaining access to it over an electronic network.

Other companies offer much the same alternative. The Information Access Company integrates all of their CD-ROMs in a server. The system gives access to all the IAC databases, from *Magazine Index Plus* to the various full-text resources (i.e., ASAP). Access is provided through Internet, CARL, and other networks. The user is able to search any of the indexes needed. The company has variations on a theme, which are described as database site licenses. These allow the library to load the databases locally into the library electronic catalog (OPAC), or into a systemwide network to which the library belongs. There are other approaches, as well.

CONSUMER NETWORKS

The so-called growth area of networking is the promise of the consumer network. Information companies are racing to provide new services and win new customers. Generally, the consumer networks are of limited use or value for daily reference work. At the same time, the reference librarian should understand what they are about, and how they are used. Also, in libraries without funds for electronic information services these, at least, offer a beginning. Furthermore, most services now open the Internet to easy use, which may be sufficient for a library to consider one or two such services.

All the consumer networks have several things in common. (1) They are directed to laypersons with little or no knowledge of the finer points of networking and searching databases. The search mechanisms rely on simplicity. (Librarians and seasoned online users complain that they are too simple and too time-consuming for searches.) (2) They all offer limited access to Internet and an easy path to e-mail, usually through the Internet. (3) Information on everything from the current weather to travel and convenient places to shop is available. Still, the greatest use of the service is to play games and to search for entertainment, if only on one of the hundreds of bulletin boards that cover animals to Zen. (4) The object is to wire American homes for new paths to information and, more important, new paths into homes for advertisers. All the services are built around some form of advertising. More than any other, Prodigy fills this business need. Almost every screen has an ad that takes up one-quarter to one-third of the space. Granted one can bypass them quickly, but they are hard to ignore.

"I subscribed to online consumer services such as Prodigy and was amazed to see how much information we typically associate with libraries that is available to consumers in their homes for less than a monthly cable subscription. . . . Many consumer magazines are on these systems, along with lots of travel information, the full text of the Bible, movie guides and extensive investment information."[11] Several of the networks have information suitable for, and directed to, children.

While contents differ from each network to the next, most tend to have an encyclopedia, usually the *Academic American* (i.e., without the pictures and none of the bells and whistles found on a CD-ROM version). Mobil travel guides, restaurant surveys, Dow Jones data, and fact books of various types are available. The magazines, again without pictures or graphs, include *Consumer Reports, Omni, Time, Newsweek,* and a few more specialized titles. America Online is best for magazines, while CompuServe has a strong list of newspapers. Still, none of the networks even comes close to the minimum offering in magazines found in most libraries. They do better with newspapers and with some reference works, such as indexes.

Cost is a major factor or roadblock in the development of consumer networks. The problem is that unless prices for the services fall below $10 a month, the market will be limited to relatively slow growth. The basic use fee for five hours at the computer averages $10. After that, the various services charge $2.95 to $25 per additional hour of use. It hardly takes a math expert to figure that a wild child can soon run up a pocket-wrenching monthly bill.

Another difficulty, or challenge, is that three or four companies (Prodigy, CompuServe, America Online, Microsoft) control most of the network consumer services. In trying to reach everybody, like large television networks, they overlook special needs—needs which can be met by equally small consumer networks. For example, Transom of Manhattan is directed to eighteen- to thirty-four-year-old users who watch MTV and look to Transom for electronic forums in areas of their interests, as well as information about music, audio, cars, and related matters.

Primary Consumer Networks[12]

The leading service in the United States, America Online of Vienna, Virginia, claims to have about 3 million subscribers. It is among the easiest of the systems for the layperson to use. Cost is low: $9.95 a month, and after 5 hours, $2.95

---

[11]Sandy Whiteley, "This Year in Electronic Publishing," *The Booklist* (Reference Books Bulletin), May 15, 1994, p. 1704. This section of the magazine is one of the best places to turn for current information on CD-ROMs, as well as the latest offerings of networks.

[12]"The Best Way to Go," *PC Computing*, September 1994, p. 163. This is one of countless evaluations of such services. Here CompuServe was thought best for offering access to more information files but, of course, at a cost, as well as having the greatest number of useable downloadable files and technical support for use. America Online is rated best for its e-mail service, pricing structure, and access to current news, sports, travel, stock quotes, and so forth.

per hour. There is a beginning ten or so hours of free online time. The user is offered a large selection of magazine articles as well as pieces from *The New York Times*. Although America Online offers entry to Internet, by late 1995, early 1996, it was exploring an independent network for Internet access. This service is independent of the main consumer network. It offers Usenet with some 6000 different discussion groups.[13] Negative points: In the past it has tended to be beset by problems of overloading, busy lines, and crashing. It is often difficult, if not impossible, to get through to anyone with either a phone or the computer. Downloading time is slow (as of 1995 about 9600 bits per second).

CompuServe (Columbus, OH: H & R Block) with about 2 million users has the richest reference sources among its competitors. There are over 1000 different databases available, many of which are of assistance to professional and business people as well as the average consumer. (The possibilities require a good manual such as *Using CompuServe* by Jill Ellsworth.) True, it has its share of bulletin boards and games, but the emphasis is on information. The rate of $9.95 a month is for unlimited basic use (weather, sports, travel, etc.) However, it costs from $5 to $25 an hour for information databases and even more for "premium" services. There is access to Internet which will expand in the years ahead, primarily because in 1994 CompuServe purchased Spry, Inc.,a large purveyor of Internet software. One click and one is into Internet over CompuServe. It is one of the easiest of the consumer services to use for this purpose.

Microsoft Network (known as MSN), started by the company of the same name, began operations in mid-1995. It offers all the same benefits of the other commercial networks from e-mail to bulletin boards. Beyond that, the network promises to be different because: (1) Windows 95, a Microsoft software expected to sell up to 45 million copies (as compared to about 6 million subscribers to the other networks), will make it an easy-to-use network service. A single click of the mouse and the software will open 35 countries in 20 languages with a single local call.[14] (2) It has the ability to receive graphics faster at a lower cost than now possible with other services. (3) It provides full access to Internet services. Estimates are that by 1996 to 1997, there will be 9 million users of MSN, making it the leader in the field.

Prodigy of White Plains, New York, is jointly owned by Sears Roebuck and IBM. It has about 1 million users. It provides limited, although one of the better, connections to the Internet. It offers the usual entries into information about current sports, news, financial services, and the like. Fees average $14.95

---

[13]One of the most popular areas on America Online is the "chat" arena. Here one is encouraged to adopt pseudonyms, representing either gender, to carry on "conversations" of a personal, sex fantasy.

[14]The problem in the mid-1990s with most systems is that the user has to switch between the computer's operating mode and the network application software. The Microsoft network promises to end this by bringing the two together.

per month with unlimited use of the basic services. Prodigy was among the first of the consumer networks to offer access to Internet, and by mid-1995 claimed to have over one-half million users. The firm introduced, too, Multimedia Mail which allows users to imbed pictures and sound into their e-mail.

Other consumer networkst in the same league as the leading four or five are: (1) Delphi, owned by Rupert Murdoch's News Corporation is the fourth largest of the group, and by the mid-1990s was beginning to make plans to compete head-on with the other networks. (2) Genie, owned by General Electric Information Service, is last among the consumer networks. (3) Eworld, Apple Computer's online information service. As a connect to Internet it has about 100,000 subscribers who, of course, all own Apple MacIntosh products. It is growing and many think it will be among the top four commercial networks by the end of the decade.

Given the communications green light in the mid-1990s, the various telephone companies are sure to enter into the consumer network business. AT&T's Interchange, for example, offers full-time Internet service, as well as a few standard network services. Here AT&T is pioneering the idea of a flat fee, much as for cable television. The flat fee will be offered to those who use consumer networks more than x hours a month. The charge method for infrequent users will continue to be by the hour.

TELEVISION AND THE COMPUTER

Computers which depend on visual and audio messages as opposed to textual materials suggest possibilities. If today's television is for the couch potato, tomorrow's will allow the individual to manipulate images and sound, to master a different, yet to be defined, kind of literacy.

Is the world ready for the empowered couch potato? There are billions of dollars rushing down the digital highway in quest of the average television viewer's interest and dollars. The trick will be to make the television easy to operate interactively for entertainment and shopping. There are 93 million households in the United States, each with at least one television set. Close to 65 percent have cable. Most are willing to have 500 stations piped into the living rooms. Why order a computer or a CD-ROM player when virtually the same results can be obtained with a cable and the existing television? Granted, it may not be as sophisticated as the average PC, but eventually it will work for shopping or ordering a ticket, movie, lunch, and so on.

Potential interactive television systems are one response to the reluctance of Americans to purchase computers to gain access to consumer networks. In operation, or planned for the rest of the decade, these systems offer two popular services: video on demand and home shopping. Beyond the two favored interactive services, Time Warner is prepared to offer a rotating television carousel which will allow viewers to select specific actions beyond movies and shopping. These are to include games, news, and other basic information services.

A Time Warner system in the mid-1990s includes such things as *The News Exchange*, which permits the user to watch *NBC Nightly News* or CNN newscasts as many times as they want at any time of day or night.[15] Much of this technology is now a reality. Time Warner wishes to harness it for profit. Thus the average family will be billed $25 a month for interactive television, plus costs. The costs can run up to an average of $100 a month, for example, through watching a half dozen first-run films. The question is not so much the technology, but whether or not the public is willing to pay for such services.

Teletext

Time Warner is following in the steps of a well-developed system in Europe. This is teletext, a method of transmitting text alongside the standard television signal to be decoded by special equipment added to the ordinary television set. Developed by the BBC in 1972, it has shown little promise in England. Conversely, as Minitel it is an important part of person-to-person, home-to-home communication in France and parts of Europe.

Minitel allows the distributor to send a limited amount of information directly to the user's television set. A handheld decoder is employed to turn to the menu of what is available and, subsequently, to turn to the pages that have the data. The information is made up of sets of specialized documents, often updated, which cover everything from train and airplane schedules to lists of restaurants and theater offerings. The hard of hearing benefit with subtitles. The new Bibliothèque Nationale in Paris accepts book reservations entered through any of the country's 6 million Minitel terminals. The system has the advantage of being relatively easy to use and equally low priced. The system is interactive. The user can both receive and send messages. This single feature allows the user to do everything from order groceries to pay bills.

Health Net is an example of an American interactive television information service. The Princeton firm has a computerized database of text and videos on health topics for laypersons. Cartoonlike faces (child, man, woman, elderly person) are shown along the bottom of the television screen. Viewers with a special remote control device select from those which are of interest. The woman's face as a choice brings lists of items to the screen from nutrition to cancer. Choosing cancer brings informational videos that describe disease causes, symptoms, complications, and treatments. Technically, the Health Net—like other interactive services—is loaded into a centrally situated video service computer and viewers download what they need from the server. The total is brought into the

---

[15]"Time Warner's Ordinary People Plug Interactive TV," *The New York Times*, December 18, 1994, p. F9.

home by one of a dozen cable services from Time Warner to Bell Atlantic. The ultimate in this interactive television service (a decade or so away) would be for the viewer at home to show on a two-way camera an injury or symptom that could be analyzed by a doctor or a nurse for a telediagnosis.

Videoconferencing

Videoconferencing has been about for over a decade, but only in the mid-1990s did it begin to show promise as a viable communications technology. The system is employed by anyone trying to avoid the high cost of travel and a meeting in an expensive conference hall. Apple's Quicktime Conferencing, for example, not only allows two computer users to view each other's faces as they speak, but has space on the screen for a document on which both might be working simultaneously. Each makes notes the other can see while cutting and pasting the document.

Videoconferencing is now more satisfactory because of the added dimension of multimedia. Until the mid-1990s the problem was the inability to send material over a network at high enough speeds to make its application at a meeting useful. Thanks to several new software and hardware additions this seems to be on the edge of being solved.[16] A so-called media server which answers the problem of speed has opened up a new, but growing, $2 billion networking industry.

Meanwhile, doctors are using the combination of interactive television and electronic data in what is known as *telemedicine*. For example, a radiologist can study the results of an MRI (magnetic resonance imaging) thousands of miles from the hospital in which the imaging was done. The images are beamed from Montana to New York by way of satellite as a series of numbers. The New York radiologist then examines the images and makes recommendations.

The system is also opening up a new era in education. A teacher can stand in one room and beam the lecture to a room hundreds or thousands of miles away. Interactive television allows questions and answers between the distant teacher and the students. Students in Boston or Paris can take part in a seminar originating in London or New York. The possibilities for the third world are as exciting as they are promising.

The Winner

"By the turn of the century . . . all TVs will behave more like computers and all computers will start to act more like fabulous TVs you can talk to."[17]

<hr>

[16]For comments on one such program, see "A Multimedia Networking Challenge," *The New York Times*, September 14, 1994, p. D7.

[17]"The Wide . . . Word of CD-ROM," *Family Life*, March/April 1994, p. 58.

Nevertheless there is a feeling, if not an entire consensus, that for interactive applications the personal computer *will defeat television*. New computers can run videos with a resolution far superior to television. Some computer terminals access cable television for shows, games, and interactive entertainment such as assuming the role of a character in a drama and thereby directing its plot and ending.

The ultimate resolution is a wedding of computer and television. What is now the computer screen will be used equally as a television screen, and vice versa. The end result? No one knows, but some have a sense of more entertainment, more commercials, less information.

While the future of technology is uncertain, Americans remain ever optimistic: "Somehow the technology that's due tomorrow always seems far more profound and revolutionary than the high tech products that arrived today. . . . The panorama of almost all new technology that's visible for the next 20 years is foreshortened in common perception as if it were all about to happen immediately."[18]

SUGGESTED READING

Auletta, Ken, "The Magic Box," *The New Yorker*, November 11, 1994, pp. 40–45. An analysis of how Time Warner, as well as competitors, is testing futuristic visions of matching computers and television sets, particularly for shopping and entertainment. The real question, "How much interaction do Americans really want?"

Bane, Adele, and William Milheim, "Internet Insights: How Academics Are Using the Internet," *Computers in Libraries*, February 1995, pp. 32–36. Educators are using the Internet as much as laypeople. E-mail is the first choice, followed by discussion groups, net news, and the use of electronic journals. Respondents were enthusiastic, calling Internet the best source of information in their field.

Burrow, Gale, and Linda Gunter, "The CD-ROM Network . . . ," *Reference Services Review*, Summer 1994, pp. 7–14. This, as the subtitle indicates, is the network at "the Claremont College; implementation, instruction, and remote access." The article is clear, and most useful as it takes what, for many, is theory and shows application.

"College Libraries and Cooperation Grants," *Library-Hi-Tech*, 1994, no. 1. The issue is given over to projects that demonstrate aspects of networking and electronic databases. Retrieval effectiveness is considered as well as common problems.

Hapgood, Fred "The Media Lab at 10," *Wired*, November, 1995, pp. 142, 145, 196–210. The MIT Media Laboratory opened in 1985. Ten years later, what has it accomplished? The author explores the good and the bad points about an organization dedicated to exploring the future of technology in society. See, too, the following article, an interview with the Media Lab's founder, Nicholas Negroponte, pp. 146–148.

Harasim, Linda, *Global Networks*. Cambridge, MA: MIT Press, 1994. A collection of papers that both describe and evaluate the global networks. The arguments are all here about the best technology, the best use, the best ethical code, and so forth. A good overview of questions that are not likely to change (or be resolved) for years to come.

[18]Nicholas Wade, "Method and Madness," *The New York Times Magazine*, January 16, 1994, p. 14.

"It's Hot and Heavy on Cyberse Front," *The New York Times,* March 26, 1995, pp. 1, 34. A discussion of the major concern of many parents—the amount of unrestricted eroticism and pornography on the Internet and, particularly, over the World Wide Web.

Kohl, David, "OhioLink," *Reference Services Review,* Summer 1994, pp. 27–29. Considered by many to be "North America's most interesting experiments in automation," the Ohio network is explained in this article. Made up of the leading Ohio academic institutions, the network provides "a virtual library of 20 million volumes" plus many other important resources.

Maule, R. William, "Smart Valley Infrastructure," *Internet Research,* Summer 1994, pp. 48–58. A discussion of a commercial regional information network in northern California's Silicon Valley. The effort joins public and private networks for interactive use. Much of the information is applicable in other areas of the country and world. The author stresses the need of the local regional systems to have access to other networks including Internet.

McClure, Charles, "Network Literacy," *Information Technology and Libraries,* June 1994, pp. 115–125. An excellent survey of the past, present, and future situations with information and network literacy. The importance of such literacy is stressed and supported with a winning argument and a set of facts. See, too, the same author's "So What Are the Impacts of Networking on Academic Institutions?" *Internet Research,* Summer 1994, pp. 2–6. See, too, the author's *The National Research and Education Network* (NREN) (Norwood, NJ: Ablex, 1991).

Molin, Sandra R., "Campuswide Access to OCLC's FirstSearch: A Study of Use at The University of Minnesota," *Reference Services Review,* 1994, no. 1, pp. 21–28. A clear explanation of OCLC's FirstSearch. The evaluation tends to be on the side of a given university, but many of the data and techniques are applicable to evaluation elsewhere.

Polly, Jean, and Steve Cisler, "Community Networks," *Library Journal,* June 15, 1994, pp. 22–24. The authors examine possibilities on the Internet and give background on the various types of community networks. More important they indicate the role libraries may play in the use and development of such networks.

Resource Sharing and Information Networks. Binghamton, NY: Haworth Press, 1981 to date, semiannual. This journal offers a running account of practical information on networks of all types. As the title suggests, there is an ongoing interest in problems of collection development and document distribution. A recent issue featured "Campus-wide Information System," a piece on automation of Idaho's libraries, the usual "News Notes, and some 25 pages of reviews of books and software.

Stone, Allucquere Rosanne, *The War of Desire and Technology at the Close of the Mechanical Age.* Cambridge, MA: The MIT Press, 1995. A polished author with excellent style explores the ethical issues behind the information network. Most people are blind to the implications of a society where an individual can sit alone in a room, hour after hour, day after day, year after year, and ride back and forth on the information highway. Not Ms. Stone. An impressive—and frightening—anaylsis.

Tenopir, Carol, "Knight-Ridder's Shopping Spree," *Library Journal,* December 1995, pp. 34–35. What does it mean when a large conglomerate takes over the largest information database vendor in the world? Add to that the takeover of a bibliographical network (CARL), and it adds up to, well, what? The author is optimistic that it spells good news for librarians. Others are not so sure.

CHAPTER FOUR
THE INTERNET AND REFERENCE SERVICES

The largest, most impressive network of them all is the Internet, or Net. It is described in almost as many ways as there are users, for example, "a vast ocean of information resource," "the backbone of the information highway," "the network of networks," or "the on-ramp to information."

It "just grew" from the early 1970s. No one is quite certain of its dimensions, possibilities, or even numbers and types of user. Essentially, as the descriptor implies, it is a net which links laptop to server to mainframe computers throughout the world. It has both databases and linkage capacities. In time it may be superseded, replaced, modified, or simply given another name, but the Internet is unique in that it has shown the way to true, international networking. Internet, no matter its fate, is a major accomplishment by not one, but by hundreds of thousands of individuals. It is the confident, happy face of a brave new world.[1]

---

[1]This chapter is an overview. It is not an instruction package on how to use the Net, at least in terms of specific commands. Software changes, as do approaches to finding information, but the overall purpose and content remain much the same. A cottage publishing industry has been built around Internet. There are countless guides in print to navigating the network. One of the best: Ed Krol's *The Whole Internet: User's Guide and Catalog* (Sebastopol, CA: O'Reilly, 1992 to date, irregular). See, too, Martin Courtois, "How to Find Information Using Internet Gophers," *Online*, November/December 1994, pp. 14–25. A superior overview of how the Internet is employed in reference services will be found in *The Reference Librarian* (1994, no. 41/42): "Librarians on the Internet: Impact on Reference Services." The two dozen articles are by working librarians. Editor Robin Kinder is a reference librarian at Smith College.

 Library Journal runs a regular column on the Internet, as do numerous other library-oriented periodicals. These are favored by reference librarians in that they address practical, daily problems from methods of connection to use of Internet in particular situations.

Internet for most people is synonymous with entertainment. This is made even more so by the World Wide Web, which essentially adds pictures, sound, and other hypertext features to the Net. Commercial entertainment interests play a major part in the development of Internet and possibly its replacement. Rupert Murdoch's newspapers match his satellite programming in numbers of people reached worldwide. Time Warner's cable systems and periodicals are as well-known as the home shopping services. Telephone companies and television concerns do battle over who is going to "wire" the typical American (worldwide) home. Microsoft is organizing software to connect cable operations and consumers for everything from films to banking and shopping.[2]

Statistics vary widely as to how many people are on the Net, but the usual broad guess is from 30 to 40 million, and growing at the rate of about 1 million every month to six months. In early 1996 a third of American households had a computer, compared to one in seven households in Europe. The Internet connects 10,000 to 20,000 individual networks worldwide. There are an estimated 200,000 to 250,000 different bulletin boards, or discussion groups, on the Net. Most use e-mail to talk to one another. Viewed as a viable industry, estimates are that the Net generates about $10 billion a year. This includes the infrastructure, hardware, software, online services, as well as people employed. In comparison, publishing in the United States alone is a $15 to $18 billion annual industry.

Despite guesses and informal surveys, it was not until late 1995 that the first major survey of Internet was taken by a reliable organization. The survey, conducted by Nielsen Media Research for Commerce Net (a consortium of businesses for promoting electronic commerce), found: (1) An estimated 24 million adults—10.8 percent of the combined population of the United States and Canada age 16 and over—use the Net. (2) The majority of users are male, highly educated, and affluent. However, the number of women users is growing, and by the end of 1995 it was found that about one third of the users are women. (3) Close to 70 percent of these users are on the Net at work, while another 30 to 40 percent use the Net or online services at home. Only 4 to 7 percent of users are in school. (4) Within any 24 hours the majority are using the Net for Web access (5 million), followed by e-mail (4.5 million), and discussion groups (2.5 million). An insignificant minority employ the Net and the Web for what might be called reference-informational purposes.[3]

---

[2]By early 1995 the first radio station on the Internet appeared. The Internet Multicasting Company of Washington, DC, is a nonprofit group broadcasting 24 hours a day, including audio broadcasts from the House and Senate. Sophisticated and expensive hardware and software are necessary to receive the computer bits heard through the computer's loudspeakers.

[3]"On the Net. Another Survey of Internet Users Is Out, and This One has Statistical Credibility," *The New York Times*, October 30, 1993, p. D5. Even this study can be questioned. Guesses vary from a low of 3 million Net users to a high of over 40 million. Much depends on who is quoting the data and for what purpose. As of late 1995, the Nielsen study reported here seems the most realistic. But only a few days before, *The Times* published the results of another survey, indicating the confusion

These hard data are important for libraries because they give some perspective to the ways real users make use of the Net and the Web. More importantly, perhaps, the statistics are of value to business and advertising decisions. The primary questions in 1996 for business are whether the Net will become a mass media consideration, or whether it will be used by an impressive, yet in terms of other media, minority audiences.

A study in 1993 to 1994 shows that approximately 21 percent of public libraries are on the Internet. Actually, in small libraries the percentage is lower—about 13 percent—while 95 percent of large libraries have the service. Less than 15 percent of the latter offer public access to terminals, primarily because of the cost involved. Most public libraries use the Internet to access various bibliographical databases. By 1996 many of the medium to large public libraries have made the Internet available for entertainment purposes as well.

Academic libraries have a much higher percentage of uses. Close to 80 percent of university and college libraries offer Internet access. The figure is 100 percent for medium to large libraries with research programs.[4]

The wide gain of Internet popularity is due to many factors, not the least of which include: (1) Low-cost terminals, printers, modems, and so forth, which brings the technology to the middle classes. (2) Virtually free access for students, teachers, businesspeople, government employees, and laypersons who use libraries. (Organizations pay the access bill.) (3) The advent of the World Wide Web and other types of software, making it easy for people to find disparate fragments of information through hypertext. Easy access, easy use spells more use. (4) E-mail, or electronic mail, as important to 30 to 50 million people as the telephone or the fax machine. Business and private computer networks use e-mail through the Net. (5) Peer pressure, helped a bit by mass advertisements, making it as fashionable to have access to the Net as to own the latest high-fidelity equipment or television "theater" site. Almost by accident a complex system provided

---

over the number of people on the Net. A computer book publisher (O'Reilly & Associates) found that 5.8 million American adults are connected directly to the Internet. Another 3.8 million use the Internet through a commercial online service such as America Online. The O'Reilly research found that 67 percent of those with direct Internet access are male and over half are between the ages of 18 and 34. "Who Uses Internet?" *The New York Times*, September 27, 1995, p. D2. A study of 60,000 computer users found that participants in the study spent an average of 20 hours a week online. "Most Go On Line at Home," *The New York Times*, October 22, 1995, p. D6.

According to the results of a poll published in *Time* magazine (September 5, 1994, p. 20), "there is a dearth of women in cyberspace, with 95% of Internet users being male and only 5% female. The survey also chronicles Internet users by age, with the largest group (29%) aged 21–25, the next largest (27%), 26–30 years old, followed by 31–35 (17%), 36–40 (11%), 41–50 (8%), 16–20 (6%), and over 50 (2%)." *Library Journal*, October 1, 1994, p. 13.

[4]The study was made by the U.S. National Commission on Libraries, and is reported in *Library Journal*, June 1, 1994, pp. 16–17. No one is sure how many school libraries are involved, but to date the number appears to be insignificant—more for a lack of money for hardware than interest.

individuals with what one expert calls a "a new social space . . . informal public life."[5]

Internet History

Connecting the traditional military-industrial-academic complex, the Internet developed and grew in the 1990s because it was based on the convergence of technology (computers and phone lines) and social need (i.e., you pass on or answer my message and I will pass on or answer your message). What began as Pentagon technology developed into connectors for government administration, then turned to linking business and industry for conferencing, and to networking production-line schedules. Along the way the academic community joined to pass on and download research data as well as open each other's catalogs and archives. Not far behind, the information business joined the link with everything from reference works and newspapers to indexes. Paralleling this were thousands of individuals and interest groups who widened the Net into an everyperson's communication system.

Behind the backs of officials and planners, and with only accidental aid from the government and corporations, the Internet has become the universal and common information highway spanning the world. True, it lacks a board of directors, it seems to lack any planning or programmers, but on the wild frontier the diligent searcher may find almost any bit of information needed.[6]

Because of its accidental growth, the Internet was the only large-scale communication system that sold itself rather than selling an audience. The Internet has become so popular that people flock to it without being urged. Despite great animosity to commercial encroachment on the Net, the scene is changing rapidly. By 1996 advertisements of every type were on the network, particularly when used with the multimedia World Wide Web. The Net in the mid-1990s remains an audience-driven system, but the advertiser is not far behind.

[5]The appeal of the Internet, for many, is that it is "tribal." People long to talk one with the other or join the tribe, or so the theory goes, through their PCs. The Net is often a metaphor in social writing for the totally dependent individual, that is, a return to the womb, the dismissal of the physical world for the electronic world, and so forth. See some of this conjecture in Howard Rheingold's *The Virtual Community* (London: Secker & Warburg, 1994).

[6]The advice-referee body for Internet and other government network plans is The National Information Infrastructure Advisory Council. It was organized by the Department of Commerce to make policy recommendations. It is made up of laypersons and experts as well as a few politicians. Also, The National Research and Educational Network (NREN) was established by the federal government in 1991 to offer assistance in development and extension of U.S. communications technology. It has been (by 1995) virtually eclipsed by other administrative groups. At the same time it remains a valuable, highly used network in its own right.

Advertising, Mass Media, and the Net

The Net and the Web originated as information highways for people in quest of useful data. By the mid-1990s advertising began constructing ramps to the highway, and by the turn of the century it promises to turn the Web into a freeway for advertisers and customers. Information and advertising may travel together, but more skeptical persons see the time when the Net, once free from commercial interests, will become simply another spoke in the mass media. Precisely what this means for working reference librarians remains to be seen.[7]

While advertising was considered bad form in the early days of Internet and the Web, today commercial interests have moved in with hopes of turning the Net into another television. This time it is interactive, that is to say, on the Net or Web the user can make queries or place orders and get responses and confirmation from the computer. Home pages contain specialized types of advertising for everything from bank accounts to plugs for politicians. Games and other forms of electronic entertainment proliferate along with accompanying advertisements which bring the games to the user for "free." Other examples are the more than a dozen insurance companies which offer information and services at a central site on the Web. Anyone shopping for an insurance policy can get specific information and make comparisons of costs and benefits. Purchasing a policy is possible. Participating companies pay $2.50 to $10 each time a consumer uses the service.

Examples of so-called interactive advertising on the Net include: (1) A soft drink company learns about customers and potential customers by asking for personal information (from name and occupation to tastes in food) from thousands of Net users. To the surprise of the company, a good 80 percent of the users furnished the information which was not only used by the company, but by others who had access to the data. (2) The Web allows the user to call up full screen advertisements which may call for personal information about the user. (3) Pioneers in advertising see the day when ads may be tailored to particular viewers on interactive television. At the break in a program, for example, the television will know whether to show an ad which appeals to a 19-year-old man or an 80-year-old woman. (4) A teenager watching a movie may see a sweater, dress, or whatever on one of the actors. A touch of the interactive television button and information is given on how and where to order the given sweater, dress, and so forth.

---

[7]By the mid-1990s, the Internet and the Web had become primarily a commercial highway for everyone from fast food advertisers to software companies from Microsoft to Netscape. Colorful, moving advertisements will soon appear as a fixed frame in a computer screen while the user seeks information in other frames. Some imagine the time when advertisements will be as prevalent on the Net as on television.

Internet Hazards

Like the famous Monty Python shapeless blancmange pudding which gobbled up everything in sight, from Scotspeople to tennis players, Internet is equally formless, and just as hungry. The inexperienced can be swallowed by hours and hours of fruitless searching.[8] Quests that begin logically enough may end in cyberspace. There may be too many, or too few, data. Internet performs or helps to carry out three primary missions: (1) interactive discussion (e-mail); (2) massive index to everything from collections of periodical articles to an inventory of pictures in the Vatican; (3) FTP (file transfer protocol) to transfer a file from one computer at X or Y university to another computer's memory in P or Q agency. Files can be moved from anywhere to anywhere, although sometimes security and cost are involved.

Along the way a misstep may call up the painting where an index is required, or a lonesome librarian's message where a bulletin is needed. Worse, the sea of information may render less than nothing, no matter how long one fishes. Another headache, particularly on World Wide Web, is the slowness of transferring images and text. Sometimes there is such a traffic jam it might be easier to find a book with the answer, and twice as fast. Even when things are moving with relative ease, it is slow, slow, slow.

If the librarian is to avoid the greedy electronic blancmange, three steps are necessary: (1) There must be specific avenue(s) of access which reduce the opportunities for both error and time loss. (2) There must be complete knowledge of the field(s) of interest one is attempting to navigate. And (3) there must be constant vigilance with reference to new additions and methods of searching the Net. "It's awfully hard to keep up just with the products," the father of the Internet revealed in an interview. "I spend my weekends hacking around, configuring Internet software. And it's not easy."[9]

INTERNET AND REFERENCE SERVICES

The obvious problems with using Internet for reference services are twofold. While the depth and type of information on Internet are impressive, the information is badly organized and takes time to locate—so much time, in fact, that it may be less expensive and certainly more efficient to use a commercial online

---

[8]Millions of words are spilled each year in an effort to explain, map, and otherwise chart the ubiquitous Internet. While everyone agrees it exists, most are at a loss to define it accurately. Two of the more "winning" explanations were offered in *Internet World* (May 1993, p. 14). The Net "is more of a biological phenomenon, more like slime mold, growing without anyone in charge." "The network is a bucket of tinker toys, a smorgasbord of possibilities and tools."

[9]Vinto Cerf, quoted in "For Father of the Internet . . . ," *The New York Times,* September 25, 1994, p. F4.

vendor who offers direct access to a specific information source. Although there is software to search Internet, the organization sometimes baffles even the most skilled professional searcher. Now and again the Internet is useful for ready-reference work but as of now there are so many other faster, easier ways of finding answers that Internet can be more trouble than it is worth.

With that, though, it should be added quickly that Internet is becoming easier to use. If the technology is not all that it might be for ready-reference work, for the quick answer, it is well worth the effort to gain material for search and research questions.

Two major questions to be answered over the next decade concern Internet and reference librarians. First, how can Internet (or its successor, cousin, or other relatives) be employed by the reference librarian to help the nontechnical, often non-Internet-involved individual find what is required? Second, how can the librarian assist in access to and gain of specific bits of information (from graphics to sound bites) for the individual who wishes to access the Internet in the library?

Internet definitely has a place in the nitty-gritty area of answering questions, but it is a distinct place. In view of the resources made available it is primarily employed for in-depth research questions and, at the other extreme, entertainment. The researcher, for example, searches the world's libraries for information on Coleridge. The average student or person off the street is likely to be more involved with an e-mail pal.

Library users of the Internet are at home or in the library itself. In either case the library must have the hardware and software to navigate the network. More important it must be in a position to instruct the user in helping find what is needed or find the information for the user without the user knowing anything about the Internet; that is, in view of the skills required, it may be wise to have reference librarians retrieve the document.

The Reference Link

While Internet (through e-mail, Listservs, newsgroups, etc.) "may provide a link for solving reference problems or learning of new reference resources, it is wise to occasionally take stock of such electronic endeavors and consider what is being gained in terms of professional development, and when the activities are keeping higher priorities from being accomplished."[10]

The basic concern about the Internet and reference services is summarized by a working librarian: "Making the most of [Internet] is a time consuming endeavor. Not only must we track the sources on the Internet, but we bear

[10]Karen Diaz, "Librarians on the Internet," *The Reference Librarian*, 1994, no. 41/42, p. 7.

the same responsibility for evaluating them as we do for any reference source. The Internet has made our jobs easier in some ways, but has created new workloads for us in others."[11]

In the physical sciences, virtually "every major type of printed information source normally found in a reference collection can also be located on the Internet."[12] It is important to stress "type" because a few specific, highly valued reference titles may not be on the Internet, may be available only in print or, more likely, only on CD-ROM. This is particularly true of almost everything published before 1985.

An equal number of well-known reference titles are online. These are accessed through DIALOG and other vendors at a relatively high cost. "While the Internet does not usually offer free versions of the major online databases available from commercial vendors . . . there are valuable indexing services at low or no cost available that can be very useful in a physical sciences reference collection."[13]

This raises the real question: Is it worth the effort to try and end run with Internet around a commercial service in order to save money? The time and effort involved may more than cancel out the speed and efficiency with which one, for a fee, finds the same answer on, say, DIALOG. (Note, too, that DIALOG and almost all other online information services may be accessed through the Internet, although this has nothing to do with searching or fees, which remain the same.) Conversely, (1) a trained librarian who knows an area of the Internet can search it for the required information as fast or even faster than by using a commercial service; (2) much, much more important, there are resources on the Internet found nowhere else and these are open to the alert librarian.

Another major question which is just beginning to emerge is the problem of authority. How accurate or authoritative are the sources on the Net? It is not clear, for example, that a query about a Postal Service decision to issue stamps honoring comics is answered by: (*a*) the Postal Service; (*b*) an expert on the Postal Service; (*c*) an article about the Postal Service in an identified, reliable source; (*d*) or, and this too, is often the case, simply an opinion by someone browsing or surfing on the Net. Anyone who has a minimum of research skills can easily separate out opinion, garbage, and whims from authority, reliable facts, and relevancy; but few Americans have those skills. The user can, if he or she is skilled, separate out what is needed and useful, but lacking an editor or a filter, the Net promises to flood the world with as much idle talk as solid information.

[11]Susan Starr, "Evaluating Physical Science Reference Sources on the Internet," *The Reference Librarian*, 1994, no. 41/42, pp. 262, 273.

[12]Ibid., p. 262.

[13]Ibid., p. 265.

Guides

Print: Gale Guide to Internet. Detroit, MI: Gale Research Inc., 1995, 600 pp. $95.
No electronic format.

In the style of many Gale reference works, this lists and annotates about 2000 databases available on the Internet. Plans are to update the directory each year. The number of databases will grow. Each entry includes the name of the database and a description of content. Advice is given on how to access and retrieve information. Fees, producers, related databases, and the like round out each entry. Arrangement is alphabetical by name. There is a detailed subject index which, according to the publisher, "employs more than 4,000 terms and cross references." In addition there are numerous other indexes to organizations, hosts, and the like. Of particular value to librarians—a specialized Gopher appendix which gives the names and access paths to specialized sites. This is arranged by subject. See, too, the current bibliography and brief, yet useful, glossary of key terms.

In a more general way one finds information on the Internet in almost any library periodical, including standards like *Online* and *Database* to the more popular *Computers in Libraries.* Then, too, there are now a number of magazines devoted exclusively to the Internet, for example, *Internet World* (1991 to date, monthly, Westport, CT: Mecklermedia.) This monthly has a wide variety of primarily popular articles and guides to Internet and other networks.

For further suggestions about guides, books, directories, and so forth concerning Internet see the "Suggested Reading" at the close of this chapter.

Mediator-Teacher

High-speed, efficient globalwide networks are the key to reference services in the decades ahead. The role of the reference librarian in this new and ever-changing environment is both traditional and innovative. As in the past the reference librarian must find answers to questions and will use the Internet and related networks for that purpose. Now the difference is that more emphasis must be placed on scanning the whole world for what is needed in numerous formats. Also, because of the vast area of possibilities the librarian must, as mediator, be able to pick what is precisely needed.

Equally important to these modified traditional roles is the innovative place of the library in the community. It must be where users will find the latest electronic and printed resources for gaining information. More important, it must be where users can turn for current, accurate, and friendly help in mastering their own navigational routes on the information highway. Librarians must not only promote the Internet, they must police it and map it for users.

The real role of the library with Internet may be relatively simple—offer Internet facilities, with instructions where required, and the hardware and software to people who use the library. School and public libraries should offer Mosaic (or its equivalent) to dazzled students. Let the kids (and the adults, too) organize their own networks, participate in other networks, and become involved both in the library and at home.

The vital question for librarians is where to find the funds to connect the superhighway with schools, libraries, and other centers that are badly underfinanced and unable to even keep up with print materials. Even large, relatively well-financed libraries are torn between spending more and more on electronic networks and less and less on printed sources from journals to books that are easier to understand and used more often.

KEY TERMS

The Internet is not always easy to understand or to use. "Nobody cares what the ISMAP function of WWW is, or whether it is implemented in HTML or HTTP. All they care about is that if they click on the left side of the picture, they'll get one document, and if they click on the right side they'll get another."[14] This is a challenge for reference librarians who may spend part of their time instructing people in the use of particular aspects of the Internet.

The Internet, like most networks, has a vocabulary all its own to describe vital functions. A few of the more important follow:

BBS (Bulletin Board Services). The BBS are points of discussion on almost every topic under the sun. Sponsors include individuals, companies, government groups, and so forth. A large number are free, others have minimal charges. There are two basic types of bulletin boards, and for these see Listserv and Usenet.

The ubiquitous bulletin board is a synonym on Internet for personal communication. Bulletin boards may be accessed in dozens of methods. Their appeal and why there are an estimated 10 to 15 million users each year are found in their ease of use. (Much of the software is now part of a standard PC.) Find the wanted number, pick a topic of interest, and send and receive messages at your convenience. The messages, and particularly the responses, are readable in sequence by others with access to the same bulletin board(s). All can be downloaded for little or no charge. And users usually can transfer their own files to a particular bulletin board.

[14]Peter Deutsch, "The Ten Commandments of the Internet," *Internet World*, September 1994, p. 98. What follows are some of the major terms. There are, to the confusion of all, hundreds of other descriptors which may or may not be explained on the modem screen. See the far from complete, yet helpful: *Dictionary of Computer Words*. rev. ed. New York: Houghton Mifflin Co., 1995. There are a half dozen or more equally good dictionaries in this area.

There are approximately 100,000-plus public access bulletin boards in the United States. In comparison, there were no more than 4000 in the mid-1980s. Most of the boards are open to three or four areas: (1) Information is first. This ranges from notes on the weather to The Federal Whistleblower's BBS, run by the House Government Operations Committee, which lets callers leave anonymous tips on abuse in government. The Bird Info Network helps with birdwatching, while Dartmouth College's Dante Project reports on the latest research on Dante's *Divine Comedy*. (2) The second most often used are news groups dedicated to conversation and news about hobbies and vocations. (3) Games are another large category followed, probably, by (4) "adult only" groups, which field dates, send nude images, and allow uncensored chats.

At another level there are company bulletin boards and home pages which far outstrip in number and use the public points. Approximately 150,000 such boards are in daily operation by Eastman Kodak to Blue Cross and Blue Shield. These are used for everything from doctors dialing in claims to 24-hour customer service lines, where clients can get information, leave messages, or place orders. The biggest use is for communication among office employers and employees.

Bulletin board size may be measured in numerous ways, but a sure indication is the number of phone lines to the board, that is, the number of access points. Usually only one or two lines are in place, but if the board becomes popular it can grow. Large services have up to 250 lines or more, and many (such as Exec-PC) offer so many services and so many data that they are closer to consumer networks than bulletin boards.

There are several companies that sell operating programs—both for companies and for private use—to set up bulletin boards. Their gross is in the millions, but nowhere near the profits of the telephone companies that provide the lines. Extra line installations alone bring in an added $800 million or more a year.

Reference service use: Numerous governments (both federal and local) provide current information on the boards that is useful in reference work to find the latest about X or Y activities. For example: (1) United States Government Department of Commerce's Economic Bulletin Board (EBB) contains 20 different major subject areas with updates daily of some 2000 files. Trade data to action by the Treasury are reported. It is part of the University of Michigan program.[15] (2) Bulletin Board for Libraries (BUBL) is a United Kingdom–based board. This serves as a current source of information on networks and networking for librarians as well as a service for news, current contents sources, job openings, meeting information, and so forth. Access point is through JANET.[16]

[15]Keith Morgan, "Economic and Statistical Information on the Internet," *The Reference Librarian*, 1994, no. 41/42, pp. 65–80.

[16]Jo Kibbee, "A Virtual Library for Librarians," *The Reference Librarian*, 1994, no. 41/42, pp. 99–107.

Listserv. This is a descriptor of the more than 4000 discussion groups scattered throughout the United States and the world. One subscribes to a particular subject Listserv. These differ from Usenet news groups in that the user must formally subscribe to a Listserv and the data are sent directly to that individual through e-mail. (*See* Usenet, below.) Listserv tends to encourage ongoing e-mail from interested members. One replies to an individual, or more likely sends a question, answer, or discussion point to all the subscribers.

In a survey of how this was used among reference librarians, it was found that almost all read the Listserv daily, although only about 37 percent post "often or sometimes." The majority rarely post. "On the other hand 10% of respondents respond to queries often."[17]

The service is considered important for various reasons, although a prevailing one is that "It helps keep me current and gives me a support group."

"Lists" or "Listserv lists" or discussion groups join people with like interests in an ongoing exchange of information.[18] One joins a list (or subscribes) and then sends and receives messages and data from other members. It can be one to one, although generally by definition the list presupposes a question or problem and responses by all members of the group. The conversation goes on until something else comes up or the subject is dead. Topic Listservs are as numerous as members. They may range from reference services to news from China to the delights of being a vegetarian. The lists become more or less personal, depending on the type and number of people involved.

Reference service use: (1) Stumpers-L is a Listserv whereby a librarian may pose a question that is difficult to answer and ask those who are part of the Listserv to suggest answers and sources. (2) Internet Hunt is a monthly Listserv which gives more time and sometimes more energy to seeking answers to more involved queries. (3) BL-L is a discussion, question, answer service for those involved with bibliographical instruction. (4) LibRef-L is a general point of discussion for all types of reference problems in as many types of libraries. (5) The possibilities of such service for pressing research questions has been realized by the National Library of Medicine. The librarians there are able to respond to questions within the day. There are several divisions of the service on the Net. (6) First-

---

[17]Donna Cromer and Mary Johnson, "The Impact of the Internet on Communications among Reference Librarians," *The Reference Librarian,* 1994, no. 41/42, p. 145. The authors discuss two Listservs briefly: Public Access Computer Forum (Pacs-L) which offers some 7000 users information on electronic communication; and BI-L which gives information to about 2000 subscribers and bibliographical instruction in its broadest meaning.

[18]A list of lists is available from various Internet services. The list expands each day, which makes print versions almost immediately dated. Be that as it may, major lists and indications of types will be found in most popular guides to the Internet. *The Clearinghouse for Subject-Oriented Internet Review,* compiled by the School of Information and Library Studies at the University of Michigan, provides a source about subject-oriented Listserv databases and other resources. Addresses are available online and in a number of commercial magazines from the most popular, *Boardwatch Magazine,* to titles like *BBS Caller's Digest* and *Computer Shopper.*

Search-L is a list maintained by OCLC for users of its reference service. The file has the usual news articles, but is of great value to librarians in that it carries searching tips and suggestions of how to use the service. (7) Soc.Libraries.Talk is a general point of communication for librarians involved with information in general, and certain issues in particular. For example, a sender might inform recipients of government actions in regard to libraries or other issues of public policy.

Other examples of practical aspects of Listservs for reference librarians will be found in Ellen Berne's alphabetical listing of Internet sources useful in answering ready-reference queries.[19] Compiled for the Eastern Massachusetts Regional Library System, it can be used in any part of North America. The list, which printed out runs to well over 30 pages, begins with Adoption, African-Americans, and Age-Law and ends with Women Prisoners and Zip Codes. The resources are all on Internet, that is, on a database that can be reached over the Net, usually through World Wide Net, Gopher, or Telnet. A typical entry with a citation reads: Diet. "Dietary fat & cancer," gopher to zeus. esusda. gov/Fed/USDA and other/Food labelling/Dietary fat."

Aside from the format of the bibliography, the list has several features unique to electronic databases. First, it can be updated, added to, and corrected almost at will. The compiler points out that this single list must "be a living, breathing document. You are encouraged to share your discoveries with others by sending additions, corrections, and changes to the compiler." Second, it is a one-stop reference source in that "only full-text sources/data suitable for ready reference are included." In other words, having a citation one does not have to dig out the book, periodical, document, and so forth. It is all on the PC monitor. Not so unique and a welcome feature for working libraries are the subject headings. They are based on those used in *The Readers' Guide to Periodical Literature*.

Usenet News Groups. This is a vast collection of individuals interested in as many subjects as there are interests. The software is free and there are over 200,000 sites. Approximately 7 to 10 million people use these sites, or about 30 percent of the total traffic on Internet. Single articles are sent to the user's host computer. These may comprise many pages or a single line. In a typical two-week period close to 1 million articles flow over the Net. Each Usenet bulletin board, discussion, or newsgroup (they are described variously) has from a dozen to thousands of members.

Responses go to a server or mainframe computer rather than to the individual; one then goes online with the computer to gain the latest Usenet information. This differs from Listserv not only in the way messages are received,

[19]Ellen Berne (Director, The Winsor School Library, Boston, MA 02215), "Using the Internet for Ready Reference," *Internet*, November 1994 (eberne@al. mec. mass. edu.).

but also in another important way—it tends to be more popular, more general, than Listserv. A basic problem is that, like cable television, there are only a certain number of news groups available to the individual user. At the present no one access point opens up all the news groups.

There are thousands of subjects from sex and social issues to computers and the arts. Within each primary hierarchy there may be hundreds, if not thousands, of groups. These can be subdivided by narrow interests and geographically. Many systems are in conjunction with Usenet FNews (Fast News Reader), which offers a vehicle for reading and/or posting articles.

All systems carrying Usenet are like photocopying machines in that the original message is logged into the host computer and a duplicate is sent to a group of connect systems, and on from there to the individual's screen. "It doesn't take long to realize that a system where anyone can publish ("pos," in Usenet parlance) anything results in an unbelievable flood. . . . There are a variety of solutions. . . . A person or group of people act as newspaper editors, moderating the flow of information . . . if the article is approved . . . it is posted by the moderator."[20]

Reference service use: As with Listservs, the reference librarian may turn to Usenet for help with a given question. This query may be from a user, or concern some interest of the librarian—professional or otherwise. Usenet is frequently employed by researchers for helpful tips and information on subject areas. Here the reference librarian may assist in finding the required boards, or in placing messages for the user. There are numerous ways to turn the Usenet to reference services. The "catch" is that it can be relatively expensive, and it may take more time and effort than the average user is willing to expend.[21]

E-Mail (Electronic Mail). The most popular aspect of the Internet is that it offers everyone an easy, efficient, inexpensive method of exchanging ideas.[22] Needless to add, it is used as much for idle chatter as for intellectual pursuits.

Ahead of word processing, bulletin boards, information databases, and even games, e-mail has become the favored use of Internet and other computer networks. It is as addictive as television, or, if you will, reading. Why is it so su-

[20]Dave Taylor, "Usenet . . . ," *Internet World,* November/December 1994, p. 28.

[21]Andrew Kanton, "Learning the Ropes: A Usenet Style Guide," *Internet World,* November/December 1994, pp. 24–25. A group of related articles (to p. 42) follow. See also Jean Polly and Steve Cisler, "Usenet for Librarians," *Library Journal,* September 15, 1994, pp. 31–32; Larry Gainor and Erin Foster, "Usenet and the Library," *Reference Services Review,* Fall 1993, pp. 7–14.

[22]Among the public, Internet is best known as a conduit for electronic mail (e-mail or email). Various guides to e-mail addresses of the famous and the rich are available, a sure indication that the system has arrived. The joy of receiving letters rather than phone calls for e-mail is stressed by Vivan Gornick ("Letters Are Acts of Faith," *The New York Times Book Review,* July 31, 1994). See, too, letters in response to the article in the *Book Review,* August 28, 1994.

perior to telephone calls, regular letters, and so on? There are as many answers as users, but most agree: (1) It allows rapid transfer of a document or a personal note from one computer to another over a network, or series of networks. (2) There can be almost instant response by the person to whom the message was sent. (3) Regardless of time zones and national boundaries, e-mail can be received and read at any time. (4) If the cost of the hardware is discounted, the expense of e-mail is less than postal mail—and, of course, costs nothing to those fortunate enough to be tied to an institutional account.[23] (5) Unless the message(s) is printed, it saves trees.

Business is now using the Net as a fast way of communicating, a type of 800 number on e-mail. Internet is used in parallel with telephones, fax machines, and telex to reach people quickly. Employers stay in touch with salespeople, customers, and suppliers regardless of distance or time zones. As of mid-1996 there were slightly over 20,000 commercial designations with an Internet address, and about 1400 are added each month.

There are drawbacks to e-mail: (1) There are few ways of ensuring privacy, or at least the same privacy as a posted letter. (2) Mixed passwords, mailing lists, and poor commands may result in sending the letter to the wrong address. (3) Artificial illiteracy results because speed is an advantage and many people do not proofread their messages. (4) "Flaming" is the tendency for otherwise reasonable people to send rude, vulgar, or intemperate messages to friends and strangers alike. (5) Anonymous mail—including unwanted advertisements—can flood your e-mail address. (6) Similarly, the so-called "cc"—that is, carbon copies of material sent to one person—can create messages for hundreds of friends and strangers.

The worst problem with e-mail deserves its own paragraph, and a question. Just how much time does the individual have to filter out and read through daily e-mail deliveries? An average person with an average number of interests calling for e-mail will receive about 20 messages a day. Hundreds can flood the computer when a specific query is put out, or a name is on dozens of subject lists. E-mail can be the "sorcerer's apprentice" of the electronic network.

Reference service use: (1) Primarily, e-mail provides the ramp onto numerous Internet services such as Listserv. A query or statement to Listserv through e-mail is distributed to all those who belong to the particular list. Responses are then sent, again through e-mail, to the particular address of the individual with an inquiry. (2) Those with questions may use e-mail to send the query to the reference desk. This allows the reference librarian time to answer the question and respond. The patron does not have to wait on the phone, or for a fax or letter. (3) The Clinton administration became the first to accept e-mail from the public and to take the next step and disseminate its own documents over the Inter-

---

[23]Lacking free access to Internet, many people use commercial services—from America Online to Prodigy—to transmit their e-mail.

net and other networks. (On CompuServe the Presidential Discussion Forum is among the 10 busiest of the service's 250 bulletin boards.) (4) E-mail allows instant exchange of ideas and in a sense publication. Moreover, as e-mail contributions and commentary appear side by side they mimic a primary function of journal publication: validation by peer review. (5) Subject-specific "clipping" services are available—at a price—on most of the consumer networks such as CompuServe and Genie. The user types in specific key words and each day or week the service searches for articles from their resources that have the key words. The results are printed offline.

Gopher and Veronica.[24] The Gopher is equivalent to access to the holdings (often in full text) of an estimated 1500 to 2000 worldwide academic libraries and institutions. It is possible with some, but not all, Gopher sites to retrieve the document. For example, one can download archives of historical interest from Mississippi State University or music data from the University of Wisconsin at Parkside.

Searching by menu, the computer can either access a local database or a remote database. Gopher returns either another menu full of choices, the document needed, or another database to search. Thanks to the hierarchical menu system for searching, Gopher is relatively easy to use. The problem is lack of standardization among the Gopher members.

The Gopher is a useful guide to who has what type of information, but can fail when data are needed outside the immediate, often local, jurisdiction of the X or Y Gopher. And even when one is dead on, accuracy in locating material depends on using the right key words to tie in with the particular Gopher titles or various menus. Once the user has navigated a number of Gopher servers it becomes obvious that differences and similarities exist. Some are logical, others are erratic.

Most reference librarians use Veronica for finding Gopher resources. It serves the purpose of searching at once all the Gopher servers, or about 7000 national and international databases. Veronica is used to search the various Gophers for particular items and particular formats. Veronica (developed at the University of Nevada) is a wide search tool which allows one, by way of key words, to seek likely Gopher titles and directories for a particular subject. A menu indicates Gopher sources for the topic. Also, it establishes almost immediate access to the data. Boolean logic may be employed for more refined searches. The search takes items from varying sites to create a menu of matches for the subject (key words) sought. Then one locates the Gopher site for a given search re-

[24]Gopher was so named after the team mascot of the University of Minnesota where it was developed. For a detailed study of the Gopher system see Peggy Seiden and Karen Nuckolls, "Developing a Campus-Wide Information System," *The Reference Librarian*, 1994, no. 41/42, pp. 275–296. See, too, Christopher Brown, "Creating Automated Bibliographies . . . ," *Database*, February 1994, pp. 670–671. The author discusses a few of the major catalogs available through Internet.

THE INTERNET AND REFERENCE SERVICES

THE INTERNET AND REFERENCE SERVICES   **105**

sult line. Problem: Veronica can be a long way around to find a topic. Many times, too, there is too much undifferentiated information revealed.

With that: (1) Veronica searches only listed terms in Gopher menus, and not key words. There are no approaches possible by controlled vocabulary, subject headings, abstracts, or other indexing aids. (2) Boolean logic may be used with most of the Gophers, but not all. (3) Form restrictions are possible on most Gophers, that is, one can restrict to directories and Telnet sessions, with added restrictions by subject. (4) There are numerous other applications of Veronica. The problem is that there are all too few Veronica servers, and these are often busy. The best time to search is early or late in the day.

Even with Veronica it is no easy matter to locate specific bits of information on the Internet. What is needed is an overall searching tool which will make accessible precision points of interest. Meanwhile, the librarian must learn to cope with online catalogs, directories, and aids that are less than satisfactory.

One of the more useful Internet/Gopher features is the "bookmark" which literally sets off for future use a part of the particular Gopher. (One simply types an "a" to add a part; and a "v" brings up the bookmark. A "d" deletes the bookmark.) The advantage of all of this is that while it may have taken a half dozen steps to reach the required information, it requires only a single letter to see it again and again and again. A subtle touch is that the capital "A" selects the whole menu (i.e., the current screen) while the lower case "a" selects an individual entry.

Reference service use: Gopher is a central point for answering (given time and patience) many reference questions. Sample Gophers:

1. Library of Congress Marvel gives access to government information and the Library of Congress Information System (Locis) which allow entry into many titles, including the National Union Catalog.

2. University of Southern California Jewels indicates other Gophers by subject.

3. University of Michigan Clearinghouse for subject-oriented Internet resource guides provides lists and guides of various detail and length which give Internet addresses and descriptions of resources for selected topics from the social sciences and music to government information.

4. Rice University Rice Info, a campuswide information system, has a subject approach to data from astronomy to jobs to weather.

Frequently Asked Question (FAQ). This is a feature found in numerous networks and databases and serves two purposes. First, it introduces basic questions (and answers) about the system; and second, in discussion groups (i.e., bulletin boards, Usenet, Listservs, etc.) it serves to help beginners with subjects experienced users already know.

Reference service use: (1) There are thousands of bulletin boards from which to select likely and useful articles. When a subject(s) has been selected, the reference librarian should ask for the "frequently asked question" (FAQ). (2) The problem, more so than with other Internet data, is the authority of the responses. This has to be evaluated by the individual librarian. Generally, the FAQs have been mediated by the principal organizer of the questions. In addition, the librarian may check the authorship of the query and answer—at least where known. (3) By limiting service to groups that have moderators to filter out the garbage, the library has some protection against a flood of data.

Other Access Points

Acting as super catalogs or directories, there are a number of other services that help one find specific data in the Internet web of information. The primary aids:

1. ARCHIE (derived from "archive") was developed at McGill University. It is software that is part of thousands of computer databases. It permits the user to search the whole of the Internet for public files that can be copied on the individual's own PC, that is, allows file transfer protocol. The user enters key words and ARCHIE searches for these in the database(s) as one would search for key words in an electronic database index. The catch is that the user must know what host computer to turn to, such as homer% telnet archie. rutgers.edu; or telnet archie. sura. net etc.. Also, search by key words, while the key to success, is a somewhat crude method compared to more sophisticated search software.

2. WAIS (wide area information server) allows the user to look for various databases (from the Britannica to abstracting services) by using specific key words to locate documents. WAIS gives access to about 500 to 600 databases.

There are other key words often found in current use of Internet in libraries. Among these:

BITNET is a well-known network, begun in 1981, which links research institutions, primarily in the eastern United States. It is used for Listservs, among other things, but is likely to be retired.

JANET (Joint Academic Network) is an English-based network designed specifically for academics. It accesses online library catalogs and various information services, and maintains the BUBL (Bulletin Board for Libraries). In many ways it is similar to the American BITNET.

TELNET is the command, often embedded in the software, which connects one computer's database to one or thousands of terminals. It is synonymous with "logging on" to a system.

Internet Web Guides

A growing number of software companies are publishing guides to logical use of Internet and The World Wide Web. One of the best known is the Netscape Communications Company's "Navigator." This service makes it possible to jump from Web site to Web site in an orderly fashion when in quest of a particular subject.

Software such as "Navigator" is essential to making order out of the chaotic Internet and Web. There are, for example, over 100,000 sites on the Web, and the number continues to grow each month. The obvious problem is how to locate specific bits of information, entertainment news, or discussion groups in the various sites. "Navigator" is only one of numerous solutions. Other guides are available from various companies with names such as "Yahoo," "Excite," "Lycos," and "WebCrawler."

The importance of such guides is apparent to veteran Web and Net "surfers," as well as to potential advertisers. Eventually thousands of businesses will have Web site, and obviously it is important those sites may be reached and searched with ease.

ACCESS AND SEARCHING[25]

Synonymous with anarchy and apparent total disorganization, Internet can be a problem for librarians who are accustomed to orderly arrangement and access to information. A logical response to the librarian blancmange might be to simply give the user a spoon, that is, a simple, direct method of searching. This is never likely to happen because the quantity of information is so vast that refinement, both in subject and quality, is needed. And refinement spells something more than simply typing in, or asking vocally for, say, how to make a blancmange. Given the amount of data available—text, visual, and sound—one might literally be swallowed up by the gross amount of material in the pudding. Also, does one really need an Internet, an information highway, when a simple, printed recipe from a nineteenth-century cookbook, easily located on a library shelf, might be considerably more useful?

Technical connecting to the Internet requires a terminal, software (usually part of the existing system available to library-university-organizational users), and a minimum 14,400 bit-per-second modem. With that one may em-

[25]There are scores, if not hundreds, of books, pamphlets, and directives on using the Internet. (See "Suggested Reading" at the end of this chapter.) Most of these are directed to what is available and how it can be accessed.

The actual connection is relatively simple. A password is needed, as on all networks. This may be built into a free academic or commercial system where Internet connections are constantly used. Here the computer is a dumb terminal which the user uses much as one would use a library catalog online.

bark on a search for conversation, pleasure, and, of course, information.[26] Addresses, access points, or domains (as they are sometimes called) get the user on the ramp to the Internet. These are abbreviations in combination such as edu. (an educational institution) in ny. (New York). This is a companion to the unique address, or Internet number, for each computer on the system.

Most individual users have one to two ways of accessing and paying for the Internet. The first is free and "formal." The service is free because it is part of the perk of working for or attending a university, member company, or government agency. Libraries often make their Internet networks free to users.

The second is the informal "connection," another way of saying "pay," through a consumer online service such as America Online or CompuServe. At a minimum, subscribers can normally send e-mail over the Net and read a limited number of bulletin boards. Another cost-effective method is the use of the country's hundreds of dial-up providers. They provide the individual user a password and an account, and once established, they cost in the area of $25 a month for unlimited use.

Who is the best provider for access to Internet? Part of the answer may depend on charges. Beyond cost, the best thing is to ask the Internet. Here users give candid evaluations of providers as well as advice on other computer-oriented items.[27]

World Wide Web/Mosaic

The World Wide Web (WWW) is the multimedia, hyperlinked system for displaying and organizing Internet information. A Web browser, Mosaic (one of now many methods of using the Web), is the software. World Wide Web is a series of servers on the Internet which enable the user to jump from one database to another. Hypertext permits color photographs, interactive diagrams, sound, video clips, and other multimedia features. The Web is a major access point for Internet information because of its hypertext feature which links like bits of data, no matter where they are located.

A person browsing through a document concerning reference services on the Web will come across one or more highlighted words or phrases related to

[26]Numerous software packages offer access to the Net, for example, Mosaic, Spry's Internet in a Box, and Hooked's Mac are only three of scores or more entry packages. Ongoing evaluative and descriptive reviews of such software will be found in popular computing magazines; see "Sampling the Sites," *Internet World*, December 1995, pp. 38–61. The editors evaluate ten basic Internet connect software packages.

[27]G. R. Notes, *Internet Access Providers* (Westport, CT: Mecklermedia, 1994). This provides information on close to 100 American and Canadian vendors that provide access to Internet. Another 34 are included for the rest of the world. Any issue of the magazine *Internet World* (or similar periodicals) offers scores of advertisements, notes, and even full-length stories on new ways of getting on the Internet. The number of access points increases each day—but always at a fee.

the document being examined. With a few clicks of a mouse, the reader can find information on reference services (and related topics) across the Internet—in other words, bibliographies, library catalogs, indexes, bulletin boards, and so forth. Furthermore, the multimedia feature makes it possible to find not only text, but pictures, video, and sound.

Developed in France in 1989, the Web requires a special connection to the Internet. This is usually provided by universities, large organizations, and anyone offering Internet access. By 1996 most of the major consumer online information services, such as Prodigy and America Online, offered WWW access.

Mosaic is a hypertext program developed at the University of Illinois which permits users to browse the World Wide Web.[28] Multimedia links allow the viewer to jump from one document to another (regardless of where they are located). The winning aspect of the Mosaic system is that it contains graphics, sound, and other multimedia features as well as text. One can view a relatively clear reproduction of a work of art while reading comments about it from another source.

The World Wide Web is one of the fastest growing parts of Internet. The growth is not due entirely to its intellectual possibilities, but rather because the combination of text, sound, and images has a vast appeal for Internet users who have been limited to text only. Also, much of the material is pure entertainment—from jokes and cartoons to games.

Transfer of graphics, art, and sound appears to be a step forward from reading pure text. It has major drawbacks—at least for the present. The user must wait, sometimes for minutes or longer, for the jammed network to send the desired picture. One of the reasons for the slowness is the congestion of popular destinations. Another drawback is the sometimes less than favorable resolution of the pictures.[29]

Reference Service Use. Three examples of how hypertext is employed will show the extent to which this service, given enough time, will be of help to reference librarians:

---

[28]The software was born in the National Center for Supercomputer Applications at the University of Illinois Urbana-Champaign campus in the early 1990s. It was offered free to one and all, and the university estimates that by the mid-1990s about 2.5 million copies of the software are in use, with 50,000 copies being downloaded each month on the Internet. Also, many software groups, including Microsoft, are selling variations on the basic Mosaic theme. Cello is another software often compared favorably with Mosaic and used to access and display the wide range of graphics, sound, animation, video, and text available on the Internet's World Wide Web. By mid-1995 the favored software was the Netscape Communications Corporation's Netscape Navigator. It has pushed aside Mosaic and most other competitors. *The New York Times* reported (March 1, 1995, p. D1) that "On many of the most popular World Wide Web sites, three of every four visitors find their way there using Netscape Navigator.

[29]"What's Wrong with Mosaic?" *Library Journal,* July 1994, pp. 32–33. A brief summary of the system with a rundown of its delights and problems.

1. Images, from sculpture to graphs, are available through the World Wide Web and Internet. The majority are offered through university, museum, and, to a lesser extent, government servers. A few commercial firms offer images. Subject matter is as wide as human interests and moves from fine art and photography to education and astronomy. There are numerous paths to locating files, but the easiest approach is to turn to Mosaic (or its equivalent) which accesses information in Gopher services.

There are several problems, not the least of which is an adequate description of what is stored and what is sought. Exceptions include the well-documented Vatican Library and Renaissance Culture from the Library of Congress and the ArchiGopher at the University of Michigan (which includes such items as images of Hellenic and Byzantine architecture and five Kandinsky paintings). As of early 1996 the images were somewhat limited in number and type, but are sure to develop.[30]

2. Manuscript collections, otherwise unavailable except by personal examination in the library where they are housed, can be accessed by digital images. Using Internet a *Beowulf* scholar can see more details in the 1000-year-old manuscript image than if he or she were to come to London and study the original in the British Library. Why? Because the pages are illuminated from behind by high-intensity fiber-optic light, allowing researchers to see details obscured by fire damage in 1731. The images of the unique manuscript will form the centerpiece of a complete electronic archive of *Beowulf* material. A retrieval system for this collection, as well as for other manuscripts, will follow the familiar pattern of allowing the user to pull up a list of all references in the electronic archive which pertain to a given element.[31]

3. In mid-1995 IBM and the Vatican Library (with over 1.5 million books and 150,000 manuscripts) reached an agreement whereby IBM will put the library's manuscripts and texts in digital form to be available online. The IBM move is an effort to expand into information technology at the text level. In addition to the Vatican Library, the firm has plans for similar arrangements with The New York Public Library, the Los Angeles City Public Library, Indiana University, and several others. Meanwhile, of course, other computer firms are becoming involved with similar digitalization of library materials.

COST AND MANAGEMENT

In 1995 the federal government began turning over to the private sector the operations and maintenance of many of Internet's highways. Specifically, the

---

[30]Jennifer Cox and Mohamed Taleb, "Images on the Internet," *Database*, August 1994, p. 22.

[31]"British Library Pulls *Beowulf* into Hi-Tech Era," *Independent (London)*, February 27, 1994, p. 10.

major guide of the system, the National Science Foundation, is to be phased out. This means the end of almost total financing of the system. How fast the withdrawal will take place remains to be seen.

Nobody really knows what it will cost in the future to use the Internet superhighway. The concept is at a stage where no more than guesses are possible. Today one must go along with existing financial signboards, which indicate that a data highway reaching into as many offices and homes as today's telephone network would cost hundreds of billions of dollars.

Aside from the initial expense of the hardware and basic software, there are the operational expenses. One of the least expensive services, America Online, charges a monthly fee of $9.95, with five free hours. If the online service is used—particularly by children—an average of three hours a day, this leaves about 85 unfree hours a month at about $3.50 an hour. That comes to $9.95 plus $297.50 per month or $3689.40 a year. It can be relatively painless since most services allow you to charge against a credit card number which you put into the system.[32]

Much to the dismay and grief of Internet purists, international business concerns are trying to cash in on the system by offering consumer-for-a-price versions of Internet. Everyone from Ted Turner and his CNN to Telecom companies is considering how to package services and information online. One problem is estimating the potential size of the market for Internet and similar existing and yet-to-be-created online services.

Countering privatization, a coalition of companies, universities, and research organizations is continually exploring ways of making at least government databases available at no cost to the public over Internet. An example is the Internet Multicasting Service, a nonprofit group supported by MIT and Time Inc., among others. The system allows access to the entire patent database as well as text and images from the trademark database and all current Securities and Exchange Commission filings, as well as other government databases. Sponsors argue that the Internet database does not conflict with more refined and immediate information now being sold through commercial online services such as NEXIS and LEXIS.[33] There are various suggestions on how to

---

[32]Aside from the cost of hardware, a user spends "$400 in connection fees a year for access to the Internet, not to mention $350 in telephone charges." Lacking institutional support, a typical user would pay (on average) $15 to $40 a month plus the long distance calls for e-mail, Telnet, and so forth. If standard information databases are employed, the cost goes up and depends on what the vendor or publisher charges for use of the said databases. David Bennahum, "Mr. Gingrich's Cyber-Revolution," *The New York Times,* January 17, 1995, p. A19.

In an effort to tie every student to the Net, the AT&T Corporation in late 1995 announced it will provide $150 million in the next five years to help connect all the nation's public and private elementary and secondary schools to the Internet and other electronic networks. There is a trade-off. The program "would allow AT&T to develop business in schools and display new products to parents." See "AT&T School Offer . . .," *The New York Times,* November 1, 1995, p. D5.

[33]"Group to Widen Access to Federal Data Bases," *The New York Times,* December 23, 1994, p. D2. The group hopes to expand public knowledge about AIDS and help ease the financial burden on

keep the cost down for individuals. One already in place is the continued underwriting of service for members of a school, business, government group, and so forth. Another system for the individual without such support is to charge a flat fee for the service or a fee for each packet of information sent. The third response is to make the Internet, like most other reference works, a free service in the library. Ideally, anyone who walks in off the street should have access to at least the basic Internet services from e-mail to Gopher and bulletin boards. The library, to be sure, will have to absorb the expense.

EVALUATION

By now the reader of this text, and certainly every working librarian, is familiar with the basic techniques of evaluating reference sources—from CD-ROMs and print works to other electronic formats. Generally, the same techniques are applicable to resources on the Internet, particularly when they fit into basic reference categories such as bibliographies, indexes, encyclopedias, almanacs, and so forth.

The problem is when one is asked to evaluate nonedited, noncontrolled, and in a sense nonpublished reference materials. In this gigantic category one must include most e-mail; a good number of one-person journals, newsletters, and unsupervised data; as well as news groups, bulletin boards, and Listservs.

If, at a simple level, the librarian queries a Listserv about a quotation and a response is forthcoming, how accurate is the reply? If the librarian asks for advice on instruction of patrons in the use of CD-ROMs, how good is the advice? If a patron's query concerning medication for a rare orchid plant is put out to a bulletin board, is the return answer(s) to be valued or discarded? And so it goes.

The evaluation of all this grapeshot information depends on two quite simple conditions. First, as anyone knows, can the answer be verified? Did the respondent indicate the source of the data (in print or from an electronic encyclopedia)? If it is a personal opinion, or a personal voucher for fact, the individual who presents it should give qualifications. Second, where there is more than one answer, the librarian must weigh the sources and make a logical determination about which answer is best, and certainly which answer is likely to meet the needs of the person putting the question.

Most important, if the answer falls into the second category (or if any doubt at all exists) the librarian should make this clear to the person with the question. "Here is an educated, probably good answer. The difficulty is that it can't be verified." With that the individual must make his or her own decision.

---

private organizations. The government provides unlimited free access to its AIDS-related electronic databases at the National Library of Medicine. The individual is given a password for free access to databases on a computer.

The added assumption is that the librarian *will know* the source that is used for verification, or will have access to a guide that will evaluate the source. Obviously one may quarrel about what is fact or fiction, what is verifiable and not. A good example of this type of question will be found in almost any issue of the *Guardian Weekly's* "Notes & Queries." A question is put, and readers answer. Some questions with different responses may run for months, for example, "What is the world's only true religion and how do we know?" or "Can anyone confirm that in a field . . . there used to be a sign saying 'Please do not throw stones at this notice'? Are there any other examples of this kind of helpful public information?" On the whole, though, they tend to be one-time questions such as "Is it true that we use only 10 percent of our brain?" Responses are signed, but there is no indication, unless in the answer itself, from whence the reply came.

Evaluation Points

There are specific evaluative points about the Internet, or more precisely complaints. Two among the more common follow:

1. *It is too slow.* This is true, particularly with the introduction of hypertext and multimedia. One solution is more efficient modems able to transmit data at more than 28,000 bits per second. Put another way, the transfer of data will take seconds, not minutes and more. At any rate, the librarian must determine how to speed along the message, and what this will cost. What, too, is the best technological method for gaining such speed?[34] The High Performance Computer Act was passed by Congress and signed into law by the President. It establishes a national communication network, the National Research and Education Network (NREN), capable of transmitting data at one gigabit (1 billion bits) per second or greater by 1996. At this speed one could transfer in one minute high-resolution images of nearly 250 large reference books, or the information content of 5000 such books.

2. *Electronic traffic jams,* increasingly, are becoming a headache, particularly for much-used networks such as Internet. A bulletin board, an electronic gossip sheet, may attract so many users that a wait to view the material may take minutes to even hours. There are numerous technical—and expensive—solutions, but even these may be overwhelmed by the volume of users. The prob-

---

[34]Speed and storage are technical problems made bothersome by the fact that most PCs accept 2400 to 9600 bits per second, but at least 14,400 bits per second are needed for speed of transfer. (In comparison, it take about 2.42 hours to transfer a 2.4-million-bit file with 2400 bits per second and 22 minutes with 14,400 bits per second. At 28,800 modem speed, which is not common, the time is cut to a few minutes.) Dedicated phone lines, rarely available to the average PC user, speed things up; for example, the same file may be transferred in under 6 minutes on a 56,000 bits per second line, or under 12 seconds on an even faster line. Fiber optics will solve much of this problem of imagery and sound, speed and storage, but this is in the future.

lem of data congestion is not new. In fact in 1987 Internet almost collapsed under the burden.[35]

CONCLUSION

In the natural excitement to wire America and the world it may be forgotten that the Internet—and its numerous relatives—is of limited interest to the vast majority of people. In a Times-Mirror survey, approximately one-third of American households report having computers. Only 12 percent have modems. Half that number may dial up a commercial or consumer network such as CompuServe. Internet is used most extensively for e-mail, but only 2 percent of Americans send and receive e-mail over Internet or any other way.[36]

At a conference on electronics in Phoenix, a reporter asked passersby a single question: "Where can I find the on-ramp to the information highway?" No one knew, although several suggested taking a left on X or Y street until one found the ramp.[37] The question is how useful the information highway (and particularly Internet) ever will be to the majority of citizens.

Unquestionably the Internet, or some form of it, will play a major role in American homes. It will be used primarily for entertainment, not hard information. Libraries are for information. Homes are a place to enjoy life. Few, except hard-pressed students and professionals, appreciate enjoyment and information as not mutually exclusive.

The reference librarian will be the key mediator between the average library user and Internet (at least for questions to be answered). In deploring the lack of a ready bibliography-index-directory guide to the Internet, a popular computer magazine underlined the need for trained reference librarians. "You'll have to search for what you want. Searching involves learning and using one of the Internet's search tools . . . or paying someone up to $100 an hour to do it for you. There's no guarantees you'll find what you want either."[38] The magazine was referring to a paid information broker, but this suggests an opportunity for librarians.

[35]Greg Notess, "Understanding Your Access Options," *Online*, September/October 1994, pp. 41–47. A good introduction to the technology of access on Internet. For a detailed discussion see the author's *Internet Access Providers* (Westport, CT: Mecklermedia, 1994).

[36]Times-Mirror Center for the People and The Press, "Who's On-Line?" in *Smart Money*, October 1994, p. 62.

[37]"The Elusive Information Highway," *The New York Times*, September 23, 1994, p. D1. Still, a hard core of technology buffs or Internet surfers is growing in number. A 1995 poll indicated that 70 to 75 percent of this group would be willing to switch off cable television if offered an alternative online, through Internet or another service. Even the 40 percent who are "not eager for new technology" are so discouraged with cable television that they are willing to change. "Interactive Enthusiasts Seen Turning Out Cable," *The New York Times*, March 1, 1995, p. D6.

[38]"Internet," *PC Magazine*, March 15, 1994, p. 118.

Problems to Be Solved

Information glut, information explosion, information flood, no matter what the popular descriptor, it all adds up to saturation. Given the global Internet (along with unlimited e-mail, lists, bulletin boards, and databases), 500 interactive television channels (to order jewelry, play games, and find out the weather in Nome, Alaska), and access to all of the world's books, periodicals, films, videos, and so on, one may safely say that there is more of a threat of too much, rather than too little, information.

Little or no quality control of the information exists. How can one evaluate what is useful, and if so, whether it is authoritative, current, comprehensive, and so forth? Many of the data are ephemeral and the amount is increased by e-mail, discussion groups, Usenet, news groups, and the like. How can one ascertain what is useful, particularly to retain for future use? "The fact is that information is now becoming a form of garbage. We don't know what to do with it, have no control over it, don't know how to get rid of it."[39]

After the Internet

There is a consensus that the Net is only a beginning, an alternative to a much more sophisticated network system to come. Even by the mid-1990s the amount of traffic, the confusion about who has what, and the masses of on- and off-ramps have led to proposed modifications and alternatives. Among the more promising:

1. Sponsored by the government, the National Information Infrastructure (NII) is the network of networks and is forming through approximately 100 financed projects to study replacements and refinements for the Net.

2. The Gigabit Testbred Initiative will melt the glacial speed of Internet with billions of bits-per-second connecting wires.

3. The Multicast Backbone (MBone) is software which will route various types of signals at fascinating speeds.

4. The Asynchronous Transfer Mode (ATM) routes data much faster than Internet, and is still another contender.

5. The Microsoft Network, launched in late 1995, is a unified approach to speed and ease of use which offers to use and tame the Net at the same time. Some believe that, with modifications, it will eventually replace the Internet.

All promise not only speed, but superior sound, pictures, and various hypertext links far in advance of what is now available on the World Wide Web. A truly basic difference, though, will be that the new nets are likely to be charging for anything and everything, while the present Internet, at least for those connected to an institution, is virtually free.

[39]Neil Postman, "Buried in a New Kind of Garbage," *The New York Times*, October 24, 1993, p. 16.

If You Are Sick of All Those Information Revolutions, Press 1

There are those, including librarians, who would agree with Henry David Thoreau's 1849 statement about technology: "We are in great haste to construct a magnetic telegraph from Maine to Texas, but Maine and Texas, it may be, have nothing important to communicate."

Anyone who enjoys a conversation with another individual at table width rather than global distance takes a dim view of the Internet. Human contact, if only over a telephone, is a given of modern society. Rather than bringing us closer together, the computer and networks isolate one from the other. "In the holy names of Education and Progress—important aspects of human interactions are relentlessly devalued."[40] On the other hand, for people who are unable to leave their homes because of some disability, the Internet is a blessing. It opens up a world otherwise closed to them.

In the words of the humorist and observer of the passing scene, Russell Baker, the Internet indicates that to gain information an individual will never have to leave home. The kind of sensory data one gains from contact with other human beings, or with the world of nature, or live performances of music, will disappear. Communicating and playing games, an individual will be able to sit at a computer and dominate the universe. Never again will humans have to go out on a real highway. "You settle down on fiber-optic wires and cruise the information superhighway. . . . The question is whether we will be as desperate for total communication as we once were for television and still are for wheels?"[41]

As Beavis and Butthead put it, the technological revolution may be "cool" or it may "suck." Either way, the librarian is going to be a witness and take part in the wiring of America.[42]

SUGGESTED READING

Abbott, Tony, *Internet's World on Internet.* Westport, CT: Mecklermedia, 1994 to date. Primarily this is an alphabetical listing, with complete Internet information both as to content and access points of Listservs, electronic journals and newsletters, electronic texts, free nets, campuswide information systems, commercial service on the Internet, Usenet news groups, and WAIS accessible databases. While hardly complete, it at least gives a basic listing which will

[40]Clifford Stoll, "The Internet? Bah!" *Newsweek,* February 27, 1995, p. 41.

[41]Russell Baker, "But Will It Fly?" *The New York Times,* January 4, 1994, p. A15.

[42]A 1995 Princeton Survey Research poll indicates the size of the audience for computers and databases: 45 percent of employed office workers and executives say they use a computer each day; 33 percent of the adult public use a computer at home, usually for word processing; 52 to 62 percent of prekindergarten through high school children have computers in the schools while only 15 percent of those same children have computers at home if their parents earn under $20,000. The figure rises to 74 percent for those whose families have incomes of $75,000 or more. *Newsweek,* February 27, 1995, pp. 24–42.

be of help to both librarians and laypersons. There is a good subject index, but no name index. The Usenet is simply a listing by title without annotations, while the WAIS has more information.

Benson, Allen, *The Complete Internet Companion for Librarians*. New York: Neal Schuman, 1995. By and large this is the *best* guide to the Internet for librarians. It offers precise methods of riding the net and of finding specific corners where data on reference services are located. More important, it points out the places where answers may be found to many reference queries. The style is as clear as the book is pragmatic. A first choice for most libraries.

Braun, Eric, *The Internet Directory*. New York: Fawcett Columbine, 1990 to date. This is a frequently updated guide and description of the thousands of Net information addresses—from news groups to commercial databases. There is an excellent index.

Clement, Gail, A Guide to Internet Guides. This is an updated bibliography available on the Internet and a good place to start. Available at Florida International University [gopher: //gopher. fiu. edu.].

Directory of Directories on the Internet. Westport, CT: Meckler, 1993 to date, 175 pp., irregular, paperback, $29.50. A self-explanatory title, this includes various guides. Often updated.

Directory of Electronic Journals, Newsletters, and Academic Discussion Lines. Washington, DC: Association of Research Libraries, 1995. Updated frequently, this is a running account of current Listserves of use to academics and librarians, as well as related newsletters, and so on.

Engle, Mary, et al., *Internet Connections—A Librarian's Guide*, 2d ed. Chicago: American Library Association, 1995. This is a relatively easy-to-follow guide which is directed in good part to reference librarians. The multiple authors explain nicely the confusing acronyms, jargon, and other treacherous ruts of the information on-ramps. The appendix features library-oriented lists and electronic serials.

Kinder, Robin, ed., "Librarians on the Internet—Impact on Reference Services," *The Reference Librarian*, 1994, no. 41/42. Close to 400 pages of articles by working reference librarians on how they use the Internet in daily reference services. As pragmatic as it is objective, the issue is one of the best available concerning the Internet and the specifics of reference service. Also issued as a book by the publisher, Haworth Press.

Klassen, Tim, "Usenet as a Reference Tool," *Reference Services Review*, Summer 1995, pp. 13–16. The author demonstrates how posting difficult-to-answer questions on Usenet news groups can be helpful. He outlines the most useful groups from those concerned with education to "discussion groups on controversial issues." The primary benefit of Usenet is that it pinpoints "a group of subject oriented users." See, too, in the same issue: Theodore Hull, "Reference Services and Electronic Records," pp. 73–78.

Lanier, Don, and Walter Wilkins, "Ready Reference via the Internet," *RQ*, Spring 1994, pp. 359–368. The focus here is on the practical ways of using the Net for reference, and particularly how it is used to find bibliographical information (often through Gopher). The cost and limitations are considered as well. A good bibliography.

Levine, John, and Carol Baroudi, *The Internet for Dummies*. San Mateo, CA: IDG, 1994. The title is self-explanatory and the content supports the boast. This is one of scores of guides, but is better than most because it offers basic, easy-to-understand information. The step-by-step approach is often updated, for example, *More Internet for Dummies*, 1995.

Seabrook, John, "Home on the Net," *The New Yorker*, October 16, 1995, pp. 66–76. The humorous, yet factual, account of how one man set up a home page on the Web in order to draw attention to himself. He uses the home page to meet people.

Seabrook, John, "My First Flame," *The New Yorker*, June 6, 1994, pp. 70–79. A journalist explains the meaning of "flaming" and how he was caught up in the process through e-mail. "Then came the bitter realization that on-liners can behave just as badly as people in the real world—and sometimes worse." A sad short story which is a delight to read.

Stoll, Clifford, *Silicon Snake Oil*. New York: Doubleday, 1995. Subtitled *Second Thoughts on the Information Highway*, this is a book by a computer expert about the pitfalls of the computer age. His misgivings range from the lack of any physical contacts on the Internet, to hustlers who use the Net for everything from advertising to mediocre, not always accurate, information and entertainment. While the book lacks coherence, it more than makes up for this with a necessary, closer look at a less than perfect electronic library.

Winchester, Simon, "An Electronic Sink of Depravity," *The Spectator*, February 4, 1995. The author was "like Newt Gingrich, a starry-eyed admirer of the global information superhighway. Then he discovered alt.sex. . . ." Sex and other aspects of the Internet offer challenges to everyone; for example, "A computer owner in (England) can have easy access to material over the net which would be illegal for him or her to read (elsewhere)."

CHAPTER FIVE
DOCUMENT DELIVERY AND
INTERLIBRARY LOAN

How does the reference librarian secure a document that is not in the library? There are at least three paths:

1. Interlibrary loan is the most popular in libraries today.

2. Order the article from a commercial or bibliographical network-vendor-distributor.[1]

3. The third approach is to request the article online and in some cases actually read the article at the computer terminal. The library has to have access only to the online service. It does not have to own the journal or book or document, that is, have it in the library.

Searching a printed or CD-ROM index, the librarian finds precisely the citation needed to answer a question: the citation to a journal, book, or whatever is in print, or is probably printed out at the computer terminal. After that the steps are traditional. Say, for example, one is looking for a periodical article. If the article is in the library (in print, microform, or CD-ROM) the user makes a photocopy, prints it out, or takes notes. If not in the library, the article is ordered through interlibrary loan (ILL). The nearest, most convenient source of the article is found through the bibliographical networks.

That is the traditional, and still much used, method. Today there are other options. "The new approach emphasizes . . . finding and supplying documents, rather than finding the reference."[2] (1) The full text of the article is available on-

---

[1]"Outsourcing" is the jargon word for the library's ability to draw upon documents, CD-ROMs, and so on from different vendors and different parts of the country and world.

[2]Barbar Quint, "The Mail Order Catalog," *Information Today*, February 1993, p. 7.

line. The citation indicates its whereabouts. The user calls up the article to view on the monitor. It may then be printed out or downloaded, in part or in whole. (2) The full text is available from a commercial or bibliographical network. The user "orders" the required item directly from that source much as one would order it from another library or on interlibrary loan. (3) If available only as an electronic journal or as a book in digital format, the user may view the text at the monitor and download as needed.

ELECTRONIC FULL TEXTS

Electronic full texts means material available other than in print. Normally the data are on a CD-ROM, or are available online, or both. Eventually almost all print, audio, and film, as well as other forms of communication, will be available digitally. The whole of the world's past, present, and even future information will be at a single computer terminal—at home, in the library, or at work. By then the library will be more involved with access and mediation between user and data than with acquisitions. "Libraries will begin to devote more of their budgets, used traditionally for collection development, to document delivery services—both commercial and library consortium based."[3]

The primary role of transmitting documents electronically is of central importance to the future of information access. Although there has been rapid progress in delivering documents through interlibrary loan (ILL) and private concerns, the best route is to supply the reader directly. "The technology now exists to enable large quantities of documents to be transmitted across networks, whether those documents were originally in electronic form or not. . . . The whole future of document supply is intrinsically linked to this issue (of electronic delivery)."[4] The barrier of document to user is not technology, or even copyright and ownership (although a problem). The true barrier is cost. Converting an article from paper to a digital form poses an expense, as does transmitting it over phone lines, along with the cost of hardware and software for both transmission and receiving. This may all add up to $10 to $26 or more.

The next question is Who is going to pay for this service? Most libraries share the cost, but others absorb it all. "The one certainty is that, one way or another, these problems will be resolved and at some time in the future it will be the norm and not the exception to be reading articles such as this in electronic format."[5]

[3]Ronald Leach and Judith Tribble, "Electronic Document Delivery," *The Journal of Academic Librarianship,* January 1993, p. 359.
[4]Cornish Graham, "Europe Divided or United?" *Libri*, 1994, no. 1, p. 72.
[5]J. A. Braid, "Electronic Document Delivery," *Aslib Proceedings,* June 1993, p. 166.

Electronic Sources

Some are confused by the term *electronic document*, assuming this means any journal, newspaper, or newsletter available in electronic format. Actually, there are two versions. The first is available *only* electronically. There is no print equivalent.

The second type, certainly the greatest number, is essentially print material *also* available in an electronic format, that is, either online or on a CD-ROM, magnetic tape, or whatever is digital. The electronic format is another version of the print title. It is not available exclusively online, nor exclusively in print.

A journal that is published only and primarily online can be called a true "electronic journal." While for over a decade there have been countless meetings, papers, and seminars on the subject of electronic journals, little has developed. The guide *On Internet* for 1994 lists only about 400 "electronic journals and newsletters" out of a universe of over 170,000 periodicals alone in print format.[6] And of the 400, the vast majority are low-circulation newsletters primarily available as bulletin boards on Usenet or as Listservs. The "electronic only publications have not been around long enough for us to determine their acceptability. . . . I assume electronic only publications will grow in user acceptance."[7]

The fewer potential readers the more likely a journal will be available *only* online. Conversely, one should never forget that future developments may make the online journal more popular than print or CD-ROM. Whereas the average print journal is months behind, and often out of date before it even appears, the online journal can present articles and news briefs within moments after they are received.

There are two basic types of online journals. The first follows standard patterns of excellence. There is an editor, an editorial board, and a system of checking and double-checking the worth of the material made available. The second, and by far the most prevalent, follows no rules of acceptance. It may be little more than representative of the interest of the editor and friends; or in some cases without an editor and willing to accept any contribution. Is this, then, a journal? Some say no, others are more affirmative. Librarians should avoid references to nonedited journals, particularly those that seem to lack any authority, any control, or for that matter any objective content.

Turning from journals exclusively in electronic format to those that are primarily in print but also offer an electronic format, probably from 3500 to 4500 periodicals are available full text outline. While impressive, this is hardly a dent in the 170,000 or more journals published the world around. One may argue that the periodicals online are the ones most used and most cited, and they should

[6] *On Internet* (Westport, CT: Mecklermedia, 1994), pp. 231–293.

[7] Ruth Orenstein, *Full Text Sources Online* (Needham Heights, MA: BiblioData, 1994), p. vi. See, too, the same author's "How Full Is Full?" *Database*, October 1993, pp. 20–23.

supply 99 percent of needs. Perhaps, but a more serious drawback is the lack of retrospective files. Most online periodicals can be had in full text only from the early 1990s or, at best, mid-1980s. Another drawback is lack of graphics, although this is being overcome with such systems as World Wide Web. Despite problems, the bets are down that most scholarly journals, with limited readership and a need for rapid dissemination of information, are most likely to be available in electronic format in the next ten years. This is particularly true of scientific journals. Popular magazines will be slower to follow the electronic path.

Rapid scanning of print to convert it into online digital format is one reason for the growing popularity of printed journals available online. Another, of course, is that most of the journals before they are printed and distributed are set first at a computer terminal. The resulting disc, tape, or whatever is then used to make the print edition. Publishers now find the same electronic format may be converted to online use. At any rate, recovering costs, increasing circulation, and maintaining quality are now possible online.

A few relatively popular print magazines are available electronically, as well as in print. The real question is whether the successful, often well-known and historically important titles will switch from print to online. The answer is that they will continue in both formats, at least until one or the other proves more popular, more useful to readers.[8]

Newspapers, as described in Chapters 5 and 6 of the first volume of this text, are available in part or in full online. The usual procedure is to highlight primary stories and columns, deleting everything else in the newspaper. Few offer illustrations or, for that matter, advertisements. The advantage is "instant" news. The disadvantage is the inability to turn page after page in quest of something of interest, no matter how briefly reported. The problem for publishers is television. Current news breaks even faster on television than in electronic newspapers.

What Is Full Text?

Full text as a descriptor of the electronic format of a periodical rarely means the complete text as found in the printed version. The descriptor is deceptive in that:

---

[8]Turning to newsstand, coffee-table consumer magazines, *Newsweek* is a typical example of the print-electronic magazine. Published weekly it is available online through NEXIS at various rates, but about $50 per hour. It contains the precise text of the newsstand copy, but lacks any illustrations or advertising. It may be searched, though, by the subject or title of the illustration. Its competitor, *Time*, is available through the same network; also as part of Information Access Company's *Magazine ASAP*, from 1984; directly from the publisher from 1985; and from Dow Jones *The Business Library*, 1983.

On CD-ROM, *Newsweek* becomes *Newsweek Interactive*, a quarterly. Here the publisher has chosen a different approach in that each disc concentrates on a particular subject. News stories, interviews, and most articles of the past three months of issues of the news magazine are included. It costs $100 a year. *Time* has no equivalent on CD-ROM.

(1) Few digitally converted magazines or other printed full-text titles include advertising, letters to the editor, filler matter, corrections, and so forth. (2) Full text may mean only the text, without illustrations;[9] or the text, plus any illustrations—including, sometimes, advertisements—which appear on the page. (3) Some services have "select" full text in that they only use certain articles, and more particularly the ones they have indexed. Often, too, newspapers delete copyrighted syndicated columnists. And almost all services drop brief stories or features.

In Orenstein's study, there was a wide variation on what major publishers of abstracting and indexing services consider as "full."[10] UMI's ABI/Inform includes all articles one column long or more, whereas Predicasts (PROMT) includes only articles of a certain type. Photographs are not found in many of the major services, although some such as ABI/Inform have a reference to what is not found. Letters to the editor, book reviews, and editorials may or may not be included.

The scanned full-image version is preferred by most users, or at least those concerned with "everything" on the page. The drawback, from the point of view of the producer, is that it requires a significant investment in technology. Also the complexity of reproducing graphics makes it necessary for the library or individual to have a high-resolution computer screen and sometimes equally complex hardware and software.

Since the complete full text would require more space, better hardware and software, and higher costs, the average publisher of indexing and abstracting services who offer full text as part of that service prefer the text only, ASCII version. Most reference-oriented CD-ROMs include only the text, not the illustrations. For example, the combination of index and full text offered by EBSCO and Information Access Company includes only the text.

A full image is rare for most online journals. There are exceptions, and there will be more as the World Wide Web and the development of hardware and software for online hypertext become more widespread. Chemical Journals for example is an online service by the American Chemical Society which offers the complete text (with images) of 23 primary journals published by the society. Conversely, Elsevier and John Wiley offer online chemistry journals, but only the text.

Full images are more the rule on CD-ROMs. The same American Chemical Society offers its *Journal*, updated quarterly, with access to tables and graphs. One can search for particular subjects, or click on a document which will bring up the total, full original page of the *Journal*.

---

[9]Where the electronic format includes *only the text*, not the illustrations, advertisements, and other matter, it is known as ASCII formatting. ASCII is the code for only the text, that is, American Standard Code for Information Exchange. It is rarely spelled out.

[10]Orenstein, op. cit., p. vi.

Steps to a Full-Text Document Delivery

When one speaks of full-text document delivery, this is simply another way of saying the necessary information is being delivered in several ways, other than as the conventional printed book or periodical. Up to a point, though, the steps are the same. (1) First there has to be an author(s) of the material. (2) Then there is a publisher, who edits and brings the author's words to the public. (3) The publisher normally issues the work in printed format, but may also wish to lease out the product to a database producer who provides the software so the product may be accessed at a computer screen. (4) The publisher's printed work is then sold directly to the library or, more likely, to a jobber who sells it to the library. Another approach: If electronically converted, the information will be on a CD-ROM or online and the publisher then sells it to the same jobber (who may handle CD-ROMs) or to a vendor such as DIALOG who specializes in online services.

After point (1) there is a possibility that the author may simply put the work on the Internet, offer it for free, and avoid all the subsequent steps. Well, not quite. An arrangement for access has to be made and this usually does involve another party who has a server, or large computer. It is somewhat more involved, say, than simply typing out the meaning of life at a terminal and giving it to the world on Internet, or another network. At any rate, these complications and new byways and highways are the stuff of confusion, delight, and limitless possibilities for document delivery, and more particularly Internet.

DOCUMENT DELIVERY[11]

As one enthusiastic advocate puts it, "The . . . darling among academic and research library options is document delivery. It is . . . becoming the favorite for

---

[11]While "document delivery" is clear enough, it does have more refined meanings. Document delivery, among librarians, primarily means securing an article, book, film, or whatever now owned by the library. The traditional response to the missing item is to request it on interlibrary loan from another library. Usually the item has to be returned.

Document delivery as meant by most people outside the interlibrary loan office means the user retains a copy of whatever is requested. Interlibrary loan may give the user a copy to keep, but in the broader sense the user may borrow X item which must be returned to the library from which it came.

Also, document delivery is usually in the form of a copy of the document, not the document itself, and is supplied by other than the publisher of the original. The supplier may be a periodical vendor (EBSCO) or an online vendor (DIALOG). Nonprofit networks such as OCLC and RLIN may serve as a conduit between the user and the document, but will ultimately be responsible for its supply.

In addition to CD-ROMs, several index-abstracting firms offer local access through tape-load, that is, magnetic tapes are rented to be fitted into the library's local mainframe or server. Many libraries use these tapes and make them available as part of the online catalog. Prices for the tapes vary widely and depend on amount of use, size of library, and so forth.

fulfilling requests for specialized information by individual users."[12] Why all this enthusiasm? The new system allows fast delivery. "Document delivery services are the child of decades of frustration with inadequate collections or slow interlibrary loan systems."[12]

Other elements account for the rapid development of this approach. First, the higher cost of serials has meant many libraries have been forced to cut back subscriptions. Now and then someone wants an article from a journal discontinued from the library holdings. Second, the increased use of electronic databases—often with accompanying full texts online or on a CD-ROM—has encouraged the user to expect almost instant access to materials. Third, the increased use of networks, from Internet to OCLC, opens up avenues to a vast area of information which the library does not have on hand. The material must be ordered, and document delivery is simply more efficient, often even less costly than traditional interlibrary loan. Fourth, staff cuts and reduced operations of ILL offices have made the appeal to commercial suppliers of documents even more appealing. Fifth, the commercial firms take care of such sticky problems as copyright clearance, and the need to have the latest issue of this or that periodical.

The drawbacks to document delivery are obvious: First is the cost. This varies widely with the amount and type of material needed as well as the source from which it is ordered. In 1995 to 1996, if an average can be reached (and this is really impossible because of so many variables), costs average between a low of $6 and a high of $30 per document. Second, most users, and particularly those who have grown accustomed to free (if somewhat slow) interlibrary loan services, balk at paying such high charges for documents. Third, if the library decides not to charge, then it must absorb the high costs in an already tight budget.

The faster the article is sent, or if an article with full illustrations and not simply text is requested, the higher the cost of transmission. Whereas a photocopy by mail may cost no more than a dollar or so for postage, an electronic transmission (with the largest expense being the telephone service line) can run much more. "With some notable exceptions, most users want a fast delivery but are not prepared to pay for it."[13]

Technology

When using a bibliography, index, or whatever, the decision as to which document is needed is made at a computer terminal. The greatest number of documents are specific articles from journals. When X article is required the document must be located. This is done in several ways:

[12]Mounir Khali, "Document Delivery," *Library Journal*, February 1, 1993, p. 43.
[13]Braid, op. cit., p. 162.

1. The logical approach is to combine the process of searching with that of the request. The most advanced method is to simply press a computer terminal key, or click a mouse, which will bring up the article for viewing or make it possible to order it from an outside source or print it out at the terminal. This is possible through numerous DIALOG services as well through hybrid index and document services such as those offered by UMI.

2. Some systems indicate whether the library has or does not have the article, that is, periodical. If it does not have the periodical, the user may automatically place an order—usually routed through the local interlibrary loan system—for the article. The OCLC ILL system is a good example of this approach.

3. Where there is no indication at the terminal of who has what, and it is not found in the library, the usual procedure is to turn to the interlibrary loan office. ILL checks to be certain the needed item is not in the library and then orders the document from a nearby library or a commercial or nonprofit service.

4. Depending on the sophistication of document delivery, when the request order is received at point Y, where it is to be filled, several things may happen: (*a*) Incoming electronic requests are matched automatically with files of, say, periodicals in the library or the document center. (*b*) Once the request is validated, the required item is taken from the shelf and the article is photocopied, faxed, or reproduced in some fashion so it may be sent to the point of request.

Electronic Delivery

Until the advent of rapid transmission of documents as well as means of copying them (from xerox graphic copies to photocopies) document delivery and interlibrary loan were minor considerations in a library. Today they are in the forefront of the information revolution.

Other than print, documents today are supplied electronically on CD-ROMs, magnetic tape, or online. Most of today's "documents" are periodical articles. This section is primarily concerned with periodicals.

There are three paths to securing the document: (1) Hybrid databases (i.e., those which combine the index and the full text of indexed items in one package) are probably the best way out of the dilemma of lack of speed of delivery, lack of enough periodicals available in full electronic text, and, eventually, the high cost of electronic document delivery. UMI, for example, offers a full-text backup on CD-ROMs of a select group of periodicals indexed on its ABI/Inform. (2) The document is independent of any other indexing service and may be ordered from a document delivery service. (3) The document is retrieved, read, and printed or downloaded at an online terminal.

Document delivery directly to the user's computer screen is only beginning. To date, technology has been an obstacle, but the problem is being solved. At the Massachusetts Institute of Technology in the mid-1990s it has been demonstrated that it is possible to send 50 gigabits, or billions of bits, of data over fiber-optic networks. For example, 104 years of *The Wall Street Journal* could be delivered electronically in half a second. The consequences of such speed of delivery have yet to be understood.

Usually, though, delivery requires numerous steps. The document is ordered from an outside source and arrives by fax, electronic printer, mail, and so forth. Ideally, the effort would involve one step. Different types of machines would be able to communicate and allow the computer to control all devices. For example, a document can be ordered from the computer today, but usually comes in at a different fax station. With a network, a fax machine might store the incoming electronic document, rather than printing it out and then be callable at a computer monitor. This requires networking software to link communication devices within the library as well as across the block or across the world. Information operating systems would all be at the command of a single person at a single computer. In the mid-1990s IBM, Novell, and several other companies were working on just such software to link communication equipment.

Hybrid On-Site Databases

In an effort to tie closely the full-text journal to the computer terminal where the user searches an index, several commercial firms offer: (1) The index or indexes for search on a CD-ROM. Note, too, that many of these services offer an alternative—the index on magnetic tape which can be downloaded to the library's existing catalog or automation system. (2) A select group of the journals analyzed on the CD-ROM index in full text, but on another CD-ROM or group of CD-ROMs. The user finds a citation, pushes a key or clicks a mouse, and is then able to examine the full text of the article at the same monitor. If any part, or the whole, is needed, another key, another click, and it can be downloaded or printed out.

UMI, like other systems with full text on CD-ROMs, uses a combination technology of a high-end personal computer, CD-ROM jukebox, and software. When the user sends a request for an article, it is located in the jukebox and routed to the user's high-resolution print server.

On CD-ROM the major vendors and publishers of full-text newspapers and periodicals in this format include EBSCO, Information Access Company, and UMI. UMI with its ProQuest series is by far the leader in full scanned images. UMI uses this format for periodicals found in its index and abstracting services such as ABI/Inform, Periodicals on Disc, and Social Sciences Index-Full Text.

Documents Online

The ability to examine a document at a computer monitor, decide whether it is useful, and then download or print out parts of it then and there is the ideal,

REPRESENTATIVE HYBRID ON-SITE DATABASES

EBSCO (Text Only)

No. of Titles	Database
90	Magazine Articles Summaries Full Text Elite, 1991 to date, $3199
90	Academic Abstracts Full Text Elite, 1984 to date, monthly, $3399
60	Magazine Articles Full Text, Select, 1991 to date, monthly, $2599

Information Access Company's Infotrac (Text Only)

380	Expanded Academic ASAP, 1994 to date, monthly
100	Magazine ASAP, 1989 to date, monthly, $4000
	Online: Also available on NEXIS, CompuServ, CARL, DataStar, 1983 to date, weekly; DIALOG, $60 per hour
400	Business ASAP, 1992 to date, monthly, lease, rate varies
400	Health ASAP, 1989 to date, monthly, lease, rate varies

UMI's Proquest

500	Business Periodicals Global, 1988 to date, monthly, $27,500 (includes sub to ABI/Inform)
100	Magazine Express, 1988 to date, monthly, $3150
280 to 360	General Periodicals on CD-ROM, 1986 to date, monthly, $11,350–$17,625

Note: Site Licenses: These and several other firms offer site licenses, alternatives to on-site databases. The companies lease the library tapes which may be loaded into individual systems. Here prices vary considerably.

still to be universally reached, delivery system. In order to succeed it requires that the majority of periodicals, books, and other forms of communication be in digital form. As indicated, this is far from true in the 1990s. It is a promise for the early part of the next century. The future is suggested by several of today's ongoing document-online-delivery services.

NEXIS online is by far the most ambitious of the various index online full-text services. In addition to newspapers, it offers some 200 full-text periodicals. The databases may be searched as one, that is, the user may look for a term in all the magazine and newspaper indexes at once, or, instead, may select a single newspaper or magazine for a search. Search costs vary. An average search will cost from $40 to $50 and up.

The Dow Jones News Online is an umbrella term for four separate databases, including sports and news. The News World Report offers up-to-the-minute news from the Associated Press wire. As this is updated continuously, it can be considered an ongoing newspaper, and differs from the on-wire service itself in that it extracts only major events. The full text of each article is available.

Dow-Jones News not only covers newspapers but, for investors, offers Tradeline, an international report on over 25,000 equities on some 90 exchanges in 35 countries outside North America.

Dow Jones News/Retrieval—Enhanced/TEXT is a collection of 1800 full-text magazines, newspapers, news wires, and newsletters of interest to investors in support of Dow Jones indexes. One may search the texts of much of the material.

Online the Information Access Company offers full-text special services:

1. Computer ASAP, 150 titles, 1987 to date, weekly; DIALOG, $60 per hour. Also on CompuServe.

2. PROMT, 1972 to date, daily, DIALOG, $90 per hour. Also available on DataStar, NEXIS, and others. This has the full text of a selected group of the 1200 periodicals, reports, and so forth indexed by PROMT, that is, Predicasts. In a more limited form, available on CD-ROM as well ($2500 to $6000).

3. Trade & Industry ASAP, 1983 to date, weekly; DIALOG, $90 per hour. Available, too, on NEXIS and DataStar. Selected full text from 200 business and trade publications. All of these are accessed by citations, that is, subject headings, title words, abstracts, and so on, but *not* by key words in the text itself.

DIALOG, the leading online vendor, offers close to 4 million records indexed and abstracted from its over 400 services. Even at that, only a minority of such services offers full text, and one has to pick and choose. Where full text is available, the material may be ordered and received online. As a consequence this is one of the fastest of the document delivery systems. It is a foretaste of what is likely to be the delivery method of documents in the years ahead. The cost varies widely, depending on the length and type of article or document, but ranges from a low of about $7 to a high of about $22.

DIALOG's DialOrder follows more conventional methods. Here one may order the document from one of many suppliers (indicated with the citation) and it is faxed or mailed to the user at somewhat less cost than the online version.

Newspaper Online

As of 1995 to 1996 there were approximately 200 to 250 American newspapers available online, with the majority available from the vendors DataTimes, Dow Jones News/Retrieval, DIALOG, and Mead Data Centrals' NEXIS. Most of the major papers are available on all of these services. Their major selling point: The text is available before or no later than the print edition hits the street. The drawback is that only text is offered—no pictures, no advertisements, no graphs, and so on. Few vendors offer more than two or three years of the paper, and, at any rate, few were available online before 1990.

There are variations on an economic theme. Anxious for more revenue, several newspapers offer abridged, headline-type editions on consumer networks, for example, *The New York Times* on America Online and the *Los Angeles Times* on Prodigy. Few of these make back issues available in electronic formats. The focus is on today's news.

Few, too, offer search capacity of the text. One must first find the citation in a conventional index and then turn to the full text. It is impossible, at this time, to search for key words in the text of a newspaper story—at least with the majority of online services. This is likely to change in favor of the key word and full-text search.

Charges vary, depending primarily on the speed of access. NEXIS and Dow Jones News/Retrieval, for example, charge from $48 to over $100 per hour, plus a given amount for each line. An average search of *The New York Times* (1995) full text on NEXIS costs about $15. America Online charges $3.50 an hour after the first set number of hours are paid.

Information Access Company provides related full-text titles online: (1) Newswire ASAP, 1985 to date, daily; DIALOG, $60 per hour. This is the complete text of United Press International, plus a dozen specialized and foreign services. (2) Newsletter Database, 1988 to date, daily; DIALOG, $90 per hour. Available, too, on DataStar, Dow Jones News/Retrieval. This is an index to the contents of 600 newsletters published in the area of business and related technologies. The complete text is provided for each of the newsletters.

Inevitably CD-ROM will challenge microfilm as a method of storing the full texts of newspapers. A case in point is DIALOG OnDisc/NEWSPAPERS. A number of metropolitan dailies are offered by the online firm on CD-ROM disc. It is important to stress two elements about this service: (1) The CD-ROMs include only the text, not the index. (2) In order to find information in the DIALOG discs, one must turn to a separate index. This awkward division of text and index is sure to change, and there will be a combination of both on a single disc.

Not too far into the future, newspapers themselves envision when they will bring their own dailies to the house or office. Given the powers of hypertext, the user will be able to have graphics and maps, as well as animation. There may be expanded versions of standard stories in sports and politics, available only electronically and not in the printed version. Experiments continue with the electronic newspaper, but it is slow because of cost and the reluctance of most of the public to accept a paper in this form for casual reading.

Full-Text Online Directories

What magazines, newspapers, newsletters, and newswire copies are available in electronic full text? Two guides discussed earlier in this text are useful. The *Gale*

Directory of Databases indicates the broad databases which include numerous periodicals and newspapers. Unlike several of the other guides described here, *Gale* and *Ulrich's* allow one to find specific titles available through network, vendor, gateway, and so forth. The assumption is that one knows the title of the full-text item. *Ulrich's International Periodical Directory* indicates electronic versions of periodicals. See "Serials Available on CD-ROMs" and "Serials Available Online." The listings are thorough, but the information is brief.

An alphabetical listing of "over 150 local, regional, national and international daily newspapers" which are available online in full text will be found in *Newspapers Online* (Needham Heights, MA: Bibliodata, 1990 to date, 3 yrs). This comes in a loose-leaf binder, with two updates a year. Not only are there data on databases, but for each of the listings one finds detailed editorial policy statements. (This can be useful in and of itself.) Also, important notes on what is included or excluded in "full" text is indicated.

Internet's World on Internet (Westport, CT: Mecklermedia, 1994 to date, irregular) has a section "Electronic Texts, Text Archives, Selected FTP Sites and Internet Resource Guides" as well as "Electronic Journal and Newsletters." By and large the information given for each item, in alphabetical order, is considerably more detailed than in the other guides. There is a full, sometimes detailed description of the online database as well as "how to access" advice.

Bibliodata (Needham Heights, MA) issues *Full Text Sources Online*. This is a semiannual which covers journals, magazines, newspapers, and so on in all subject areas. Access is shown through about 20 major national and international networks and host services. (Note: This is available online as well as Bibliodata Full Text Sources Online.) The 340-page periodical listing is in alphabetical order by title with three to fifteen vendors and networks that give access to the title. The dates of beginning issues are indicated. For example a listing for *Library Trends* shows that four vendors have the journal online from January 1, 1993, to the present. A subject index is added and under "Library/Information Industry," for example, one finds some 50 titles from *Academic* and *Library Computing* to *Worldwide Databases*.

The ARL (Association of Research Libraries) (Washington, DC) has an annual publication, *Directory of Electronic Journals, Newsletters and Academic Discussion Lists*.

The Library Alliance (265 Lexington Avenue, New York, NY 10016) offers *Books & Periodicals Online*. This costs $299, and has been issued annually since 1988. Over 60,000 publications are listed as found in close to 2000 databases. In addition to basic data about the publication, there are indexes by subject and guides to document delivery centers.

Document delivery guides should also: (1) Note when the service begins. Usually the time period is from the mid-1980s to the present. (2) Note when the database is updated. Usually there is a lag period between publication of the printed version and electronic availability. For a daily newspaper this may be 24 to 48 hours. For a weekly magazine it may be two to seven days. (3) Note if it includes only the text or includes both text and illustrations. There should be an indication, too, if advertisements are deleted or maintained. (4) Note if the item is available in full, or if only selected coverage is offered. Selected means many things from choosing only items of subject interest from a periodical to selecting only major news stories and deleting fillers, features, and so forth.

OFF-SITE DOCUMENT DELIVERY

The on-site hybrid databases and the online full texts are close to the ideal; but the primary method of document delivery remains interlibrary loan, dependent on a two- or three-step process. After the document is located, it must be ordered from an off-site source and then sent by that source to the library user. Unlike the on-site methods, this has the major drawback of taking time—from as little as a few hours to up to weeks. It can also be expensive and not entirely reliable.

There are two basic approaches to off-site document delivery. The first is to employ one of the not-for-profit networks for ordering and receiving material, usually from another library. And in this, it is the familiar interlibrary loan system with an electronic twist. The second form is to order the document from a commercial firm or organization. More often than not the two are combined, that is, the network carries the order and a commercial firm (rather than a library) fills the order.

Documents on Bibliographical Networks

The major bibliographical networks offer document supply in support of many of their services. Those considered here are OCLC, CARL, RLIN, BLDSC, and MELVYL. OCLC's ArticleFirst and CARL's UnCover concentrate on locating material by way of key words in the table of contents of from 12,000 to 17,000 periodicals.

Any experienced reference librarian will know that searching tables of contents is a grapeshot approach, and will not, even under the best of circumstances, lead the searcher to material located by regular indexes. Be that as it may, the advantage of ContentsFirst and ArticleFirst and similar services is that they cover so many titles whereas most indexes are limited to 250 to 1500 titles.[14]

---

[14]See, for example, Scott Stebelman, "Analysis of Retrieval Performance . . . ," *College & Research Libraries*, November 1994, pp. 562–567. Using OCLC, UnCover, Faxon Finder, and a local database which gave access to six Wilson indexes he found that a representative subject search turned up two or three times more items when the index was used than when the table of contents systems were employed. "The result of this study demonstrates that a database that includes subject descriptors and a large number of abstracts has the ability to retrieve more dictation than a database that restricts searches to the basic citation fields."

OCLC offers full texts through UMI's ASCII text database. Articles are linked to the FirstSearch indexing and abstracting services. Access is available through both FirstSearch and its twin, EPIC. (EPIC, it will be recalled, is much the same, but with a more sophisticated searching system.) Internet, dedicated lines, dial-up, and so on are other methods of establishing contact. The user may switch from a citation to the full text (i.e., any part or the complete text) where available at the computer keyboard. Key word searching of the text is not available.

The user can have the document sent from UMI or in many cases users request interlibrary loan articles. Users can automatically send requests to the individual library interlibrary loan office. Where neither the full-text online or ILL is used, the library may order the documents from FirstSearch. These are sent by fax or mail. Charges vary, but average about $10.50 per article.

CARL's UnCover system, from Denver, is an example of a regional bibliographical network document delivery system. (Note that this began as a public service which is now private. It was acquired by Knight-Ridder in 1995. The corporation continues to offer the same services, but the fees may change.) It may be accessed in a number of ways, including Internet. There are about 15,000 journals in the UnCover database located in libraries throughout the United States. Tables of contents for searching cover the journals from a wide variety of subject fields. Generally, articles are available only from 1988. The British Library Document Supply Centre is sometimes used as a backup. One may search by key words in the table of contents (personal names, key words, or some subjects assigned to the journal title). Boolean searches are possible. An order may then be placed where the particular article is located. The article is scanned at the library which has the journal, then sent to a mainframe computer in Denver for transmission to the person who requested the information. In some cases the article is stored for future use, but this is not usual. For from $7.50 to $15, an article is faxed directly to the user within 24 hours. (As of the mid-1990s UnCover does not index motion picture, music, or book reviews.)

Many libraries now prefer CARL for it clever management strategy. As of the mid-1990s the system does not charge for bibliographical access to information. Its only charge is for delivery of the wanted document(s). In other words, free bibliographical access is provided in return for the chance to sell faxed document delivery.

RLIN's document delivery is similar to other systems; that is, online ordering of necessary material is possible with several, although not all, of the CitaDel databases. The individual or the library may place the order by interlibrary loan or directly. The user may pay for the service with a credit card; fax or the mails are used for delivery, which takes from 24 to 48 hours on average. If speed is necessary, RLIN offers the user the Internet. Documents, as with OCLC, are available through UMI and the process of ordering, again, follows much the same pattern as OCLC. Here the difference is that RLIN has its own software, ARIEL, for delivery through fax or by mail.[15] Costs are from $9.50 to $17 on average per article.

The British Library Document Supply Centre (BLDSC: Boston Spa, England) is the largest document delivery system in the world. It averages over 3 million requests a year, primarily for interlibrary loan items which range from periodical articles and books to reports and statistical data. There are some 220,000 journals available at the center as well as over 3 million books. In addition to document supply the center offers numerous other services from a journal contents page system to publishing CD-ROM, microforms, and the like.

Beyond the national-international and regional bibliographical networks, some states have their own system of full-text document delivery. An example is the California MELVYL system. Among other services it offers full text of several thousand documents and journals through ABI/Inform (about 500 to 700 business titles); CQ's Washington Alert (full text of bills, hearings, reports, as well as the Congressional Record); and databases from the MELVYL system itself, which provide full text of computer magazines and The Expanded Academic Index (Mags) with articles from 350 general periodicals from the some 1500 indexed. The system is available 24 hours a day, is free to users, and is convenient because the librarian does not have to help a student or teacher find the article in a periodical or document.

Commercial Document Delivery Firms

There are several dozen commercial suppliers of documents, and particularly articles from periodicals. The major document suppliers in the mid-1990s include Adonis, EBSCO, Engineering Information, Information Access Company, Fax Research Services, UMI, and Reed Elsevier. Each has its own peculiar system, but they share in common the ability to deliver in hours or days (depending on how much the library wishes to spend for the added speed) the given document(s) in full text and or in full-text image.

Ordering is usually done in one of two ways: (1) The librarian finds a citation to a wanted article (which is marked with the information concerning full text) that is available, say, from UMI. A click of a mouse and the push of a key send the order on the way for the full article to UMI. It may arrive from UMI in hours by fax or a laser printer, or be sent by mail.

---

[15]Valerie Bennett and Eileen Palmer, "Ariel on the Internet," *Microcomputers for Information Management*, September 1993, pp. 181–193. Ariel is the name of the software employed by RLG for document delivery. It, like similar systems, links the computer terminal with a scanner and a laser printer. The scanner sends the full page, including illustrations and text. This is stored in a computer and sent over a network to the recipient's terminal/monitor for printing and downloading. The software, Ariel, is a system by itself and has nothing to do directly with RLIN, although requests for copies can be sent to RLIN using Ariel.

Where to order the document? Normally the system indicates the source(s). This is particularly true when the document cited is in an index or abstracting service online or on a CD-ROM. UMI's numerous indexes key to the UMI document service, as do the indexes published by Information Access Company. DIALOG, like many vendors and networks, offers DialOrder which gives online access to several commercial document delivery organizations such as ISI's Genuine Article. Then, too, every interlibrary loan office will have detailed information on such matters.

What follows is a representative group of document suppliers, including most of the large organizations. These indicate process, cost, and services, but the readers must realize that all of this can change literally overnight. New technologies, competition, inflation, and so forth alter particulars. What is not changed is the initial ability of the librarian to locate virtually any document.

In the 1990s the name of the corporate game is to supply everything. Once a company delivers information from its own index, it distributes the full-text backup, and offers document delivery. The same publisher-distributor-vendor-network that offers abstracting and indexing services, as well as full texts of periodicals indexed, has direct document services with no particular connection to the indexing services. EBSCO Information Services, for example, is made up of four sections, one of which includes indexed periodicals and another of which is an independent document delivery service. UMI is another major player in this multiple-service system.

A publisher of a print index, almanac, or encyclopedia is not prepared to go online or make a publication available on a CD-ROM unless there is money for the electronic formats. Typically, the Information Access Company (which publishes numerous indexes and full-text services primarily on CD-ROMs) pays a publisher about a 30 percent royalty. Large publishers, to whom IAC must turn in order to improve its services, may receive more than 30 percent.

Print publishers know that they can charge their customer more for electronic access to make up for the revenue loss from splitting the money with an online service. All of this leads to a type of stagnation, because online and CD-ROM may not offer the publisher sales and marketing effort which builds volume—and royalties.[16]

Another approach is for a large publisher of periodicals to avoid the middle person entirely and offer the periodicals directly in electronic format. Here the problem is simplified, but difficulties remain. Why, for example, should a library pay $1000 a year for a subscription when for a flat fee of so much per hour online it can gain four or five articles in that same year for $50? Of course if the service is heavily used the $1000 online and the $1000 in print balance out for the publisher.

[16]Carol Tenopir, "Electronic Access to Periodicals," *Library Journal*, March 1, 1993, p. 55.

Primary Document Distributors

UMI: Advanced Document Delivery System (Ann Arbor, MI) allows the user at any PC with a high-speed modem to view the full text of some 10 million articles. If a decision is made to purchase the article, it may be ordered at the same PC for delivery to the user's laser printer or a fax machine. Cost averages $12 to $20 per article. Delivery can be within four hours or two to five days through the mail. Depending on need and availability, the article(s) may be sent with only the text (ASCII) or full image with text and any graphics, advertisements, and so forth.

UMI: InfoStore is an online service with full information on over 12,500 periodicals. It is available online from UMI and a number of services including OCLC and CDP from $24 to $44 per hour. This too, supports the various UMI indexes, such as ABI/Inform. It allows the searcher to order an article by telephone or fax, using a credit card. The article is identified by a specific UMI number. The average fee is $12.50 per piece. Turnaround time averages four to five days, with a 24-hour (higher-fee) special service.

Information Access Company's InfoTrac Articles or InfoTrac 2000 Delivery System (the name varies) offers approximately 4000 periodicals, newsletters, reports, and the like. The librarian searching any of the IAC indexes locates an article citation. Availability is indicated with the citation. An order is then sent to IAC for the wanted article. The order may be sent at the same computer keyboard at the same moment the citation is located over a "simple central 2000 service." The article is sent through fax or laser printer or by mail. Depending on need and availability the article is returned either in full text or in full-text image of the complete page(s). This, or so says IAC, eliminates the problem of reading full text on a sometimes less than satisfactory, less than high-resolution monitor.

EBSCOdoc from the Ebsco Company (Peabody, MA) offers access to some 30,000 full-text titles. The document is sent in a number of ways. Essentially the company, either through its own supply or through source departments in other places, will deliver most documents within a day to a week.

The Faxon Company (Cambridge, MA), one of the best-known periodical vendors, offers online Faxon Finder. This is similar to CARL and OCLC's ArticleFirst in that it provides the table of contents of more than 12,000 periodicals. There are citations to each of the articles, book reviews, editorials, and whatever happens to be listed in the table of contents. It goes back to 1990 and is updated weekly. It is made available online by the publisher, that is, Faxon Research Services, Inc. Note, too, that there is a CD-ROM version which is published monthly. Documents may be ordered from Faxon as needed through fax, e-mail, and so forth. Turnaround time is about 24 hours. They are delivered by fax, mail, overnight couriers, and over the Internet. Costs: $11 to $20 or more.

Article Express International (Hoboken, NJ) supplies technical documents from two large suppliers in the Netherlands. Their collections contain over 50,000 journals, many not obtainable in North American collections. Standard turnaround time is a week or so, although documents may be delivered through the Internet (at a higher cost) in a matter of 24 hours. Delivery is by fax, mail, ScanFax, courier, and Internet. Costs run from $15 to $35 or more.

In 1995 to 1996, Reed Reference Publishing established Information Marketplace. The company gives users access to documents from over 9000 publishers. More important, it clears the way for access to copyrighted material without extra paperwork or problems. When an order is placed for this or that document or article, a system records and bills the users who may receive the information online, by fax, or as required. Furthermore, Information Marketplace serves as a mediator between the publisher and the users on the Internet, World Wide Web, and related operations.[17]

Institute for Scientific Information (ISI) is the publisher, among other things, of the citation indexes. In support of those indexes the Philadelphia firm offers document delivery through The Genuine Article. Not all periodicals cited are included, but material from well over 6000 periodicals is available from ISI, as is selected material from about another 4000 titles. Articles are ordered directly from ISI, or more likely online through DIALOG, OCLC, or whatever service on which the user happens to find the cited article. And, of course, one can use e-mail, fax, telephone, or other methods of communication.

There are numerous document delivery services from other scientific and technical organizations. For example, Chemical Abstracts (Columbus, OH) supports its abstracting service with the charges for delivery of documents indexed. The cost varies from $10 to $20 and up. One of the largest collections of material is found at the Engineering Societies Libraries (ESL Information Services, New York, NY). Here the engineering and related indexes are supported with document delivery which ranges in cost from $10 to $40 and up.

Variations

Using either CD-ROM or online, several firms now offer limited full-text data. For example, the CD-ROM contains only medical, bird, or computer magazines.

There are other avenues to scientific full text on CD-ROMs. An outstanding example includes ADONIS, with headquarters in the Netherlands

---

[17]Actually, the Folio Corporation operates the Information Marketplace Company, but Folio is part of the Reed Reference Publishing conglomerate which, among other things, owns R. R. Bowker, Mead Data Central's LEXIS/NEXIS, and other worldwide publishing operations. Copyright is cleared through an agreement with the Copyright Clearance Center, a nonprofit organization in Danvers, Massachusetts, which represents the more than 9000 publishers.

and offices in Cambridge, Massachusetts. ADONIS specializes in the distribution of full-text biomedical journals. (Here full text equals the full-page image.) More than 500 titles are available on CD-ROMs which are updated weekly. Hence the library has an ongoing full supply of scientific journals on CDs which are delivered in much the same fashion one would deliver a print subscription. The price, in view of the number of scientific titles, is reasonable: about $15,000 per year. Also, specific articles may be ordered directly from ADONIS when the library does not want to subscribe to a full run of the periodicals.

TULIP, an Elsevier science journal system, differs from several other document delivery approaches and illustrates the direct approach from publisher to library without the middle person. It primarily limits itself to 42 journals published or distributed by Elsevier. The library with a subscription to X or Y Elsevier journal searches the full text and graphical version online, usually over Internet. If the library does not subscribe, for a fee it may subscribe only to the online electronic version, often for less than the printed format; or find a citation in an Elsevier journal in any index and, as with most services, simply order the given article from TULIP. The distributor-publisher offers an insight into the future and costs: "There's a serious question about whether pay-per-use in any form would undermine the whole subscription structure." After all, what sane librarian would dole out hundreds of dollars per journal when he or she could get "piecework for pennies"?[18]

The publisher's problem is how to charge. One way is to have libraries pay a fee covering a set period of time that will allow a reader to browse through the electronic version. It has not been decided how to charge for downloading. In comparison, representative science journals in print cost from $500 to $1000 per year, but the average electronic journal costs a library 20 to 50 percent less.

Electronic journals offer the possibility of publication at minimal cost. The problem is to convince authors, publishers, readers, and those who evaluate the journals of the value of the purely electronic title. To date this has had limited success. Only time and a generation or two of people educated with computers will reveal the real future of the electronic journal.

EVALUATION OF DOCUMENT DELIVERY

Which of the document delivery systems is best? The answer depends on the particular needs of the library, as well as applicable evaluative measures. As of now the document delivery process is in a period of transition, of development and growth. Also, it relies on technological and information process changes which may drastically affect everything from cost and speed of delivery to currency of materials. "The field of electronic document transmission is changing almost daily. . . . The introduction of these document delivery systems can be

---

[18]"Inside Publishing," *Lingua Franca*, November/December 1994, p. 18.

compared to the late 1970s when interlibrary loan messaging systems were introduced by OCLC, RLG, and WLN. Interlibrary loan librarians are still waiting for compatibility among these messaging systems, and are hoping for better compatibility among the new delivery systems."[19]

In selecting a private or not-for-profit document supplier, the evaluative questions are almost self-evident, or certainly self-evident to anyone who has requested a document on interlibrary loan, or worked with interlibrary loans themselves. The questions: What technologies are required to place the request and to accept the document? Expensive hardware can cancel out any benefits. How long does it take the dealer to fill the order for the document, that is, what is the turnaround time? Is copyright compliance met by the dealer? Does the dealer have access to the needed documents, or have them immediately on hand? What subject areas are covered, not covered? Finally, What does all of this cost?

Among a sampling of faculty and graduate students at three Ohio universities (1992–1993) it was found that most respondents acquired at least one copy of an article in a typical month and most, if asked, would be willing to pay to acquire data. The "catch" is that while they were willing to pay $3 to $4 per article, few would pay the average cost of a commercial service, that is, $6 to $30. The timeliness of delivery seems to be of much less interest than the potential cost.[20]

In another study it was found that undergraduates at a small university who were primarily using DIALOG and what was then BRS (now CDP Online), were able to locate useful citations to online documents from about 50 percent to about 70 percent of the time. In the case of NEXIS the success rate fell to 33 percent. The 1242 student requests for articles and the 594 requests by faculty from citations found online could be filled online *only about 3.5 percent of the time.*

Failure was laid to the lack of back files and the availability online of much-used periodicals, and particularly those located in a general index. Only about 33 percent of the articles found in the *Readers' Guide,* for example, were available in full text online. (As might be expected, the closer one comes to specialization the more likely a periodical will be online, e.g., *Business Periodicals Index* has 62 percent of the articles required in the study.)[21]

Interlibrary Loan versus Commercial Services

Commercial vendors claim fast turnaround time. It is not a valid claim, at least for normal transactions. "Rush" can be placed on an order but this costs more.

[19] Mary Jackson, "Document Delivery over the Internet," *Online,* March 1993, p. 21.

[20] Mark Kinnucan, "Demand for Document Delivery," *LISR,* Fall 1993, pp. 355–374.

[21] David Everett, "Too Little, Too Late?" *Online,* March 1993, pp. 22–25.

UMI, for example, will deliver a document slightly faster than the usual request that goes through interlibrary loan offices. An average request for a document, whether through ILL or a commercial vendor, will take from ten days to two weeks to be fulfilled. The commercial service may be a day or so sooner, but, then again, may be equally as many days behind the ILL service.

Comparing four commercial suppliers of documents (UMI Article Clearinghouse, ISI's The Genuine Article, Information on Demand, and The Information Store) with standard interlibrary loan (ILL), Vassar College found that despite all the fuss and advertising, standard ILL compared favorably with private firms. ILL was able to fill 83 percent of the demands compared with slightly more for the commercial suppliers. The average turnaround time for ILL was thirteen days compared to an average of twelve to fifteen days for the private services—and some were even longer, twenty-two to twenty-three days. The greatest difference was cost. An article from ILL averaged about 56 cents. UMI's average: $9.75; while the others ranged up to $20.

The study (1991–1992) concluded that "in most cases the use of commercial document delivery suppliers did not appear to be a more effective or efficient means of obtaining access to articles not available in our library."[22] The commercial delivery was preferable when an item was needed urgently, when high resolution was required for the copy, and when there was a question about copyright.

In an extensive, mid-1990s study comparing traditional ILL with commercial sources of documents, it was found—to the surprise of few reference librarians—that "In most cases the use of commercial document delivery suppliers did not appear to be a more effective or efficient means of obtaining access to articles not available at our library. . . . When items are needed urgently, special ordering from commercial document suppliers with fixed inventories, while expensive, may be worthwhile."[23]

When "rush" or "urgent" is a factor commercial suppliers of documents (at least when online service is available) can be preferable to standard ILL. The result of a limited full-text online document experiment of commercial vendors at the Massachusetts Institute of Technology using, primarily, a small number of periodicals and newspapers indicated the following:

---

[22]Kathleen Kurosman and Barbara Durniak, "Document Delivery: A Comparison of Commercial Document Suppliers and Interlibrary Loan Services," *College & Research Libraries*, March 1994, p. 138. This is one of the few cost/time/convenience studies made of this area, and it is a model for other such research. See, too, Marilyn Roche, *ARL/RLG Interlibrary Loan Cost Study* (Washington, DC: Association of Research Libraries, 1993). This is more specific, but relatively current and a good point of departure for comparison with commercial and bibliographical network systems.

[23]Keith Glavash, "Full Text Retrieval . . . ," *Online*, May 1994, p. 84. The results are supported by another study: *Survey on Access to Full-Text Electronic Periodical Articles* (Washington, DC: Association of Research Libraries, 1994).

1. *Time.* Most documents are delivered within two days. Rush items were received within a day, and were printed online. Hardcopy delivery usually takes a week or more.

2. *Staff time.* Only about 5 minutes was required to place the order. This contrasts with 30 minutes to an hour for normal service processing.

3. *Cost.* An average of $4.15 per document, as contrasted with less than a dollar for the usual photocopy, fax, or mail copy. Also, as new technologies for online delivery are required the real cost is even higher than $4.15. And here may be the major stumbling block: "Full-text retrieval should be used with care if costs are to be recovered by standard fees or if online budgets are restricted . . . full text retrieval is an expensive alternative to traditional hardcopy retrieval."[24] On the plus side, online requires less labor, thus saving money. More important "the proliferation of full text retrieval may allow more libraries access to more materials at a lower cost than outright ownership or traditional interlibrary services."[25]

Questions and Problems

There are several ethical and legal questions regarding storing, digitizing, and making available books and other forms of communication for the individual user. (1) Copyright poses the largest hurdle. Ways will have to be devised to compensate authors and publishers for their distributed material. Methods have to be discovered to overcome "borrowing" without paying for copyright material. (2) If the Library of Congress and large library holdings are made available at a computer, should they be free or should a charge be levied? Some argue taxpayers have paid for the material in the Library of Congress and at other public institutions. Why, then, should they have to pay again, particularly since there is no charge when they visit the Library of Congress, use interlibrary loan, and so on? (3) What privacy protection will be put in place for users who do not want everyone and anyone to know what they are reading, researching, and the like? (4) What universal standards will be applied for storage and access of material— or will every database require different software, different search patterns? (5) What security measures will be put in place to foil hackers, viruses, and other potential system failures? (6) Will everything be censor free?

There is another question about databases with full text: How current is the material? Many newspapers, business services, stock reports, and so on can be viewed online the same minute, hour, or day they are published. Many, in fact, are ahead of the printed version. On the whole, though, there is an average two- or three-week gap between the time X magazine is published in print,

[24]Ibid.
[25]Ibid.

is available on a newsstand, and appears on a coffee table before it is online or on CD-ROM. Some electronic periodicals have a delay of six months to a year, because the publisher does not want to compete with the printed title.

INTERLIBRARY LOAN (ILL)[26]

By and large the oldest, best-known system of moving material from one library to another (whether it be a book, a photocopy of an article, or an e-mail response) is known as *interlibrary loan (ILL)*. The term is self-explanatory, although today "loan" may not be quite that when a document is sent by fax; and "interlibrary" is often more than one library to another library. Still, it is a useful, well-known term for sharing resources.[27]

The benefits of national and international interlibrary loan library networking are numerous: (1) One may secure a book through interlibrary loan from another library in the same community, state, country, or, for that matter, from a library abroad. (2) An elusive magazine article may be secured in the same fashion. Thanks to modern technology one may place the order at a computer terminal and have the needed material within days—if not in minutes, where a fax machine is available. (3) As indicated elsewhere in the text, an individual may sit in her or his home or office and obtain much of the needed material without even going near a library.

Interlibrary loan has two complementary purposes. The first is to aid the researcher in acquiring specialized material from other libraries. The second is to assist the general reader in borrowing material otherwise inaccessible because of lack of complete library resources. The interlibrary loan as a research aid is almost exclusively the charge of college and university libraries. The interlibrary loan as a boon to popular reading, and, to a lesser extent, as a reference tool, is usually a service of public libraries in cooperation with one another or with a state library.

The best-known subsystems for interlibrary loan are those operated by OCLC and RLIN. Somewhat similar services are offered by the other bibliographical utilities.

[26]The North American Interlibrary Loan/Department Delivery (NAILDD) project is an effort to eliminate paperwork and streamline interlibrary loans as well as weld closer links between local and national systems. Out of this has come, too, a different descriptor for interlibrary loan—ISRD, that is, information search, retrieval, and delivery. For details see Mary Jackson, "The NAILDD Project," *Wilson Library Bulletin*, November 1993, pp. 66–68. See other articles by her for an update on the situation.

[27]Networking of resources is another matter, as is agreement to purchase, say, in one subject area while a neighboring library purchases in another area. In this chapter resource sharing is limited to supply of documents.

In addition to supplying the material, a function of interlibrary loan is to supply the user with the material promptly. The user is normally in a hurry, and a common question is "When may I expect to receive X book or Y article?" There is no single answer to the question. The amount of time depends on how close the requesting library is to the source of the book—across town may take only a few hours, whereas across the country may take days or weeks. The actual processing of the request is another factor. Experience indicates that this varies from library to library and a safe guess is from 24 hours (exceptional) to a week (average within a state or regional system) to two or three weeks (average when one has to go beyond the state or region). "Technology, such as OCLC and fax, has speeded [the interlibrary loan] process. Nonetheless, the biggest drawback continues to be the amount of time a patron must wait to receive a document. Even a fax transmission of a photocopied article might mean a wait of several days while all the necessary processing is done at both ends of the transaction."[28]

There are so many variables, so many different people involved in interlibrary loan, that it is impossible to ever accurately answer a question about a particular source of information. According to OCLC calculations, the successful fill rate for an interlibrary loan hovers around 90 percent.

There are three favored ways to make the desired item available. The first is the U.S. mail service. The second, feasible in communities with heavy interlibrary use, is a courier system whereby libraries are visited on a regular schedule. The third is electronic and uses three primary methods: (1) Online, which makes it possible to retrieve the full texts of articles almost immediately; high cost is a factor. (2) Fax, or telefacsimile transfer, has so vastly improved that it is now possible to send documents quickly and at a relatively low cost from library to library over a machine. The process is almost as speedy as full text online. (3) Electronic mail, which allows one to send messages on a computer and avoid the necessity of the mails, telephone calls, and other forms of standard communication.

Finally, and this may be forgotten in the network-technology excitement, one can simply refer an individual to another member library. If the library is near, it is much simpler for the user to read the article or book there than to use any of the above avenues. Thanks to reciprocal borrowing among network libraries, the individual may well take the material home.

When is it legitimate and practical to send a person elsewhere? One must take the person's added effort into consideration, even if it only involves walking or driving to another library. Consideration should also be given to what is fair to the other library, particularly if it is a common practice to send people to that library.

[28]David Everett, "Too Little, Too Late?" *Online*, March 1993, p. 22.

An Association of Research Libraries white paper on interlibrary loan activities serves the useful purpose, among other things, of defining terms and focusing on "the current interlibrary loan environment."[29] While the group finds ILL is functioning well, they believe the "ideal system" would be one where the document would be requested by the user and the request would be automatically sent to a document supplier who, in turn, would send the document directly to the user. This would eliminate the various steps involved with the user first turning to the interlibrary loan office.

An illustration of the interlibrary loan process dependent on high-speed telefacsimile is the National Library of Medicine's DOCLINE. The automated interlibrary loan system has a highly successful record. On average, loan requests are filled either at the NLM or from its member libraries within 48 hours. Document transmission is over the telefacsimile network. Generally the photocopies are acceptable, although from one-quarter to one-third of the time the copy quality is poor enough that retransmission is requested. Typically, the most expensive part of the DOCLINE and similar systems is the telephone charge. The average document transmission cost alone is from $1.50 to $2.00.[30]

Problem or Crisis?

During the 1990s, major university budgets were cut. Something had to go, and in most cases it was serials and other acquisitions from books to films. The result was twofold. The major libraries had less to lend and, in turn, had to borrow more. Patron requests for material they thought was in the library had to be referred to interlibrary loan. Also, the size of the browsing possibilities declined as did the amount of resources.

Tight library budgets, new forms of information, and access to international libraries resulted in increased interlibrary loan and related activity. The Association of Research Libraries, for example, reported that the decade between 1982 and 1992 saw a 108 percent increase by members in borrowing and a 52 percent increase in lending. The information highway, with more of a flow in the borrowing lanes, will continue to see increase in traffic. Each time a new library catalog is open to general scrutiny, for example, a new source is available for interlibrary loan.

Impressive as the volume of interlibrary loans may be, there is one truism. The small- to medium-sized library accounts for receiving most of the interlibrary loans. Large libraries—particularly large research libraries—do less interlibrary loaning among themselves, but interloan more often to the small-

[29]Shirley Baker and Mary Jackson, "Maximizing Access, Minimizing Cost," *Public Library Quarterly*, 1993, no. 3, pp. 3–20.

[30]Valerie Bennett and Esther Dell, "Use of Group 3-Level Memory Telefacsimiles," *Bulletin of the Medical Association*, 1993, no. 3, pp. 265–270.

to medium-sized libraries. The flow tends to go from the large to the small; it is rarely the other way around.

For example, Mackey reports from the Spartanburg County Public Library in South Carolina that the system puts a wanted article into the hands of a user every 4 hours, 365 days of the year.[31] This is the case of a larger library serving a county with several smaller libraries. Other medium- to large-sized libraries have much the same experience, and thus there seems to be a correlation between use and size.

The major drawback to interlibrary loan is its financial implications. First, the larger libraries loan far more than they receive; therefore the system tends to be more costly for them. Second, interlibrary loan as an alternative to buying an item offers problems of fairness, at least when an item is borrowed more than once in a short period of time. Finally, no one is ever certain about the specific cost of an interlibrary loan transaction. There simply are too many variables involved.

A 1993 report of interlibrary loan activities among research libraries found: (1) The major cost of interlibrary loan is staff, about three-quarters of every dollar. (2) The other expenses are communication, photocopying, supplies, equipment, materials delivery, and so forth. (3) More than one-half the ILL requests are done through photocopies rather than transmitting the original.

Budget cuts are making more and more libraries less willing and less able to loan, and more anxious to borrow. "It is our opinion that the current system is reaching the breaking point."[32] Libraries must act in consort to solve the problems associated with interlibrary loan. One significant approach is to shift as much as possible from a library-to-library system to an end-user-to-document-supplier system. This is fine as far as it goes, but in the opinion of one expert it may go too far. Document delivery one to one may mean a threat to the library. While this author doubts it is a serious challenge, it is worth considering: "As corporate, school, and even public libraries continue to shut down across the country, the traditional online industry may be positioning itself to take up the slack if libraries start to fail completely. Commercial search service or library utility executives may just be waiting for *the call*. They probably expect it's only a matter of time before a dean of a small college or a budget cutting city manager calls to ask whether their service would negotiate a fixed-fee combination of database access and document delivery paid for by what is left of the late library's budget. Don't say you weren't warned."[33]

---

[31]Terry Mackey, "Interlibrary Loan: An Acceptable Alternative to Purchase," *Wilson Library Bulletin,* January 1989, pp. 54–56. The county library serves a population of about 250,000.

[32]Shirley Baker and Mary Jackson, "Maximizing Access, Minimizing Cost," *Public Library Quarterly,* 1993, no. 3, p. 8.

[33]Barbara Quint, "The Document Delivery Business," *Wilson Library Bulletin,* September 1994, p. 71.

THE ELECTRONIC BOOK

Up to this point document delivery has been synonymous with periodical articles and related items in newspapers and business or scientific studies. Beyond that, though, the digital text has broader promise and is certainly even more revolutionary for the average person.

In the mid-1990s the Library of Congress launched a program to make all of its holdings (from periodicals and books to recordings and films) available in digital form online. Under the banal name of National Information Infrastructure the revolutionary project's potential for document delivery is quite beyond most people's imaginations. Essentially, though, any book one wishes to read, where the Library of Congress has access, can be called up on a computer screen, read, downloaded, or whatever. The whole world, then, is a personal library.

Another example is the Vatican Library. Working out an arrangement with IBM, the Vatican will make not only printed works, but also manuscripts available online to the world—in full text and with the illustrations and other graphics. What once took a trip to Rome to view will take only a click of a mouse. Similar projects are planned for all research and national libraries.

Meanwhile, on Internet, the by now famous Project Gutenberg is attempting in a more limited way to make books available online—at least those where copyright and royalty demands are not about. There are only a few dozen titles available, but the founder at the Illinois Benedictine College in Illinois has hopes of increasing the number to include all of the classics. The immediate objective is to have 10,000 books in electronic format by 2001. (Information about the project is available from the founder through Project Gutenberg Newsletter, also on the Internet.)

Throughout this text it has been pointed out that by the turn of the century most reference books will be available in electronic format, and many, such as directories and indexes, will be available only in that format.[34] Conversely, the average "read in bed" title or "read for classes" book is likely to be available only in print for many generations to come. There are some compromises.

1. Collections of rather esoteric materials—out of copyright, and therefore free—will become more popular in electronic format. For example, Chadwyck-Healy, an English firm with offices in the United States, has pioneered the "giant" literature database. Three examples, some of which are discussed fur-

---

[34]As a reminder of one of many such reference works discussed in the first volume, consider "bundling" of reference works; for example, the Microsoft Bookshelf includes seven basic reference books on one disc, at $50 to $199. (If purchased in print, they would cost a total of $290.) Visuals and sounds are added for those who wish to look up words or have questions in *The Concise Columbia Encyclopedia*, *The American Heritage Dictionary*, *Roget's II Electronic Thesaurus*, *The World Almanac and Book of Facts*, *Bartlett's Familiar Quotations*, and *The Concise Columbia Dictionary of Quotations and Hammond Atlas*.

ther in this text: (*a*) The English Poetry Full Text Database includes the work of 1350 poets from Anglo-Saxon times to the end of the nineteenth century. Search is by subject, poet, title, phrases, and so on. One may search the texts. (*b*) English Verse Drama covers verse drama from the Middle Ages to the early twentieth century. It has more than 1500 works by 450 authors. (3) Patrologia Latina Database is the full collection of extant Latin prose with, again, full-search capabilities.

Critic Hugh Kenner points out that many of the full-text library classics include poor translations and sometimes even worse editions without notes. "There's also full search and browse ability, but, Lord, how'd you begin to guess what to search for? Or use what you've found."[35] The response to that might be—ask a good reference librarian.

2. Major publishers offer books, including children's works, on CD-ROMs. Random House under the name of Living Books publishes about a dozen children's titles a year. Only very large or specialized publishers are involved because it costs hundreds of thousands of dollars to develop an original CD-ROM book. Also there can be sales resistance at an average of $60 a title as compared with $12 to $15 for a child's book in print. Little of this is of much concern to reference librarians other than the influence these vast selling books have on the publisher's other titles—including reference books, such as encyclopedias, for children and young people. A hypertext, multimedia almanac, or even directory may not be far behind.

3. Customized textbooks, with a wide selection of everything from typefaces and grades of paper to binding, are now available on many university campuses.[36] Locally produced texts, often made up of judiciously selected articles and bits and parts of other books (sometimes along with some multimedia materials) are known as *coursepacks*. Copyright is cleared by receiving standard approvals from publishers and authors.

McGraw-Hill offers Primus, an electronic print-on-demand system for custom textbooks.[37] The professor organizes what is wanted and sends it to the publisher, who then draws upon technology to print out the texts when and as needed. The assumption is that McGraw-Hill has the rights to publish the material, much of which it holds through its numerous publications.

While few reference librarians are concerned with textbooks, it is obviously important to have a record of what coursepacks are currently being employed. Furthermore, the concept has implications for reference publishing. There will be little to stop a library or an individual from ordering an out-of-

[35]"Electronic Books," *Byte*, November 1993, p. 404.

[36]"Textbooks from the Terminal," *Publishers Weekly*, June 13, 1994, pp. 42–44.

[37]As of 1996 several other major publishers were offering books on demand, among these, Cambridge University Press, Marcel-Dekker, and John Wiley.

print book or other unavailable materials in much the same way a student gains access to a home textbook. The publisher will reprint as few as a dozen books on request, and while the unit cost may be higher than printing, say, 5000 copies, at least it is reasonable and within the library budget.

The technological miracle goes beyond the traditional reprint. A local bookstore, library, or even individual will be able to reprint a book as needed. The file will be encoded electronic data, downloaded from online, CD-ROM, or files supplied by individual publishers. The day will come when one may simply order an item from among, say, the 100 million individual titles at the Library of Congress by having it downloaded and printed (or held online or on a CD-ROM, etc.) at a key command. The long-term results of such storage and retrieval by individuals and by librarians is still to be evaluated. Meanwhile, the concept of the coursepack and the quickly printed book to order is an indication of what lies ahead for all reading matter, and for that matter, multimedia from television to CD-ROMs and recordings of music.

MICROFORM

The advent of virtually immediate access to full-text periodicals, book reports, and the like has hardly begun to dent the favorite way to store material. That, of course, is on microform. The majority of libraries have at least some full text, usually full-text image, of periodicals and newspapers in this format. And they will continue to do so because: (1) The other electronic forms only go back to the mid-1980s or early 1990s, while records on microform normally, if wanted, can be retroactive to the first date of publication, say, of a periodical. (2) Microform, at least for now, is less expensive. Not only is the form itself less costly, but so is the hardware needed to use, for example, a sheet of microfiche. (3) Possibly of some importance is that librarians are accustomed to microform as a place to turn for retrospective materials, as are most users over the age of 25. (4) Also, there are over 75 suppliers of microform as compared to no more than a dozen or two of CD-ROMs used exclusively to store older material.

Microform is hardly new, but it has many new applications in the library. It is used more and more to preserve space, to keep bibliographies and other reference aids relatively current, and to provide easy access for users. Microform exists in two formats: the roll and flat transparency or card. The familiar 35-millimeter reel or roll has been in libraries for so long that many librarians and users think only of this form when microform is mentioned. In the flat microform there are several basic varieties or types: (1) Microfiche, or fiche, is available in different sizes, but the favored size is the standard 4 by 6 inches, with an average of 98 pages per sheet. Various reductions may either increase or decrease the number of pages. (2) Ultrafiche, as the name implies, is an ultrafine reduction, usually on a 4- by 6-inch transparency. One card may contain 3000 to 5000 pages. (3) Micropoint is a 6- by 9-inch card that contains up to 100 pages of text in 10 rows and 10 columns.

Most newspapers are available in microform. This is true of the national papers, as well as the local newspapers. Therefore, libraries usually have a special section filled with newspapers on microform.

It is important that the microform or printout edition be the same as the one indexed. All the indexes indicate which edition of a newspaper is used for indexing. For example, in the instructions in the front of the *National Newspaper Index* there is an explanation of the symbols employed to show whether the edition is national, or late city, or whatever. *The New York Times* has a similar explanation for various regional editions.

Ulrich's International Periodical Directory, among others, indicates after each periodical whether or not it is available in microform, and from which supplier. *Ulrich's,* in the first volume, gives the names and addresses of the leading suppliers of microform, as well as publishers.

There is little question that microform will gradually give way to CD-ROMs and online storage. A single CD-ROM or an online magnetic tape or disc will hold the equivalent of hundreds of thousands of roles of microfilm, and almost as many microfiche cards. Whereas now the cost savings are not that apparent, they will be so when more retrospective electronic files and less expensive hardware are available.

SUGGESTED READING

Baker, Shirley, and Mary Jackson, "Maximizing Access . . . ," *Public Library Quarterly*, 1993, vol. 13, no. 3, pp. 3–20. A white paper which introduces new ideas about the present and future of document delivery and interlibrary loan. The outline form is ideal for future discussion. The authors succeed in meeting the goals of the subtitle: "A First Step toward the Information Access Future."

Cargill, Jennifer, ed., *Advances in Library Resource Sharing.* Westport, CT: Mecklermedia, 1992. This is a volume in an ongoing series which appeared first in 1990. The articles and case studies are involved with a variety of cooperative resource-sharing activities.

Everett, Virginia, "U.S. Newspapers Online," *Database*, October/November 1994, pp. 14–25. This is a basic discussion of the subject, and while it includes particulars it is much broader than a simple listing.

Francoise, Hebert, "Service Quality: An Unobtrusive Investigation of Interlibrary Loan in Large Public Libraries in Canada," *Library-and-Information-Science-Research*, Winter 1994, pp. 3–21. A study which investigates the quality of interlibrary loan in Canadian public libraries from the library's and the user's point of view. Measures of interlibrary loan evaluation are reviewed.

Gilmer, Lois, *Interlibrary Loan Theory and Management.* Englewood, CO: Libraries Unlimited, 1993. This is a basic manual on interlibrary loan, and about as good as anyone is likely to find in the 1990s. All facets of the ILL are considered, including even a brief history. A starting point for anyone interested in the subject, and a source of answers for others with specific problems.

Graham, Cornish, "Europe Divided or United? Networking and Document Supply, Now and in the Future," *Libri*, 1994, no. 1, pp. 63–76. This is a fine overview of Europe and the problems of cost and the networks that find and supply documents. The author considers the good and bad features of such services, particularly in terms of the needs of eastern Europe. Much of what is said is applicable to the United States as well.

Harloe, Barbara, ed., *Guide to Cooperative Collection Development*. Chicago: American Library Association, 1994. A 35-page pamphlet, this gives basic tips and advice on how to coordinate "collection development activities across local, state, national, and international boundaries." The appendix is a "directory of selected collection development cooperatives."

Jackson, Mary, "Training for ILL Practitioners," *Wilson Library Bulletin*, 1994, no. 5, pp. 75–76. A department training program is explained as well as guides that will be of help in ILL. The brief article goes a long way to explain the daily work of the ILL librarian. See, too, her article, "Integrating ILL with Document Delivery," in the no. 1, 1993, issue of the *Bulletin*.

Mandelbaum, Judith, "Searching for Photographs in Full Text Newspapers Online," *Database*, October/November 1994, pp. 28–33. The author shows how one may search in the indexes for references to the missing photographs, graphs, and so forth, and then turn to the printed version for the necessary graphics. This is time-consuming and costly, but in most cases (if you are a trained searcher) it works.

Ray, Ron, "A Skeptic's View of the Future for Combined Acquisitions and Document Delivery," *Library Acquisitions*, Fall 1993, pp. 347–351. The author points out that there is a natural confusion between acquisitions of information, that is, reference-oriented materials, and acquisitions of other materials. The former tends to be for individuals, the latter for the community of the library as a whole. Document delivery satisfies immediate demands, while broader acquisitions policies consider the future. He urges one to keep the two missions separate.

Roche, Marilyn, *ARL/RLG Interlibrary Loan Cost Study*. Washington, DC: Research Libraries Group, 1993. The 64-page report contains findings on costs of interlibrary lendings in North American research libraries.

Walters, Sheila, "Commercial Document Delivery: Vendor Selection Criteria," *Computers in Libraries*, October 1994, pp. 14–16. Here is a handy checklist of what to look for and what to do in the commercial document delivery territory. The author shows how to expand interlibrary loan by including commercial document delivery suppliers.

Walters, Sheila "The Direct Doc Pilot Project at Arizona State," *Computers in Libraries*, October 1995, pp. 22–26. Typical of now numerous articles on comparative costs of document delivery systems, this found that OCLC average cost per document was $17.95; RLIN/RLG, $16.50; and UnCover, $11.09. Average turnaround time was 1.3 to 2.6 days. The major problem was poor resolution of documents received.

PART III
INTERVIEW AND SEARCH

CHAPTER SIX
THE REFERENCE INTERVIEW

This chapter, as well as Chapters 7 and 8, is concerned with the heart of reference services. Yet, before embarking on this discussion it is worth considering the state of the interview and the search in many libraries today.

In any medium to large size library, students and laypersons are found clustered around one area of the reference section—the CD-ROM or online terminal. Most believe this is the place to find what is needed. Most have little or no searching skill other than an ability to manipulate digital forms of data as they do home CD-ROM games.

Given a problem, other than where to locate the library bathroom or exit, the unskilled layperson turns to the computer terminal, enters a word or two, and waits for results. True, she or he must first find a database, but this has become almost automatic in libraries where menus indicate one should turn to X or Y database for questions about large categories from "science" to "humanities." Experienced hands realize a fast approach is to use OCLC's *ArticleFirst* where there are some 15,000 periodicals with possible answers to their query. Others may choose the *Expanded Academic Index,* a CD-ROM with some 1500 periodicals, or a related type of mass coverage index.

Easy to follow menus indicate how to extract citations, and as one can draw upon 1500 to 15,000 periodicals for help, material will pop up on the screen which seems to meet the needs of the user. None of this requires much skill, although typing helps.

As there are so many magazines and journals to search, inevitably even the most obtuse or difficult word or phrase will be matched with an article or two. Actually, the results are more likely to number 10 to 100 articles. The citations are printed out and the layperson or student then moves to the periodical section to find the material. (More sophisticated systems indicate if the library has the periodical. Some, too, offer abstracts or full text which makes the searcher's quest even easier.) If the printer has not jammed and the computer has not gone mad, the searcher walks away happy and convinced the quest is a success. Few searchers have any real concept of whether or not the articles truly will be useful.

In one sense the search is complete, and usually without much help from the librarian. The question here is whether or not the search is merely a representation of a search. The quality and the result of the quest lead the searcher to two conclusions: (*a*) there is more to information than most people appreciate; (*b*) if people are to be truly informed they more and more need the assistance of the librarian. This aid requires an interview and a well-planned search, not simply someone pointing the student to the computer terminals. If the librarian is to continue as a professional, interview and search are absolutely necessary to master, to understand, and, above all, to use in day to day service.

An Overview of the Interview

A discussion of the reference interview points up the true nature of reference service. It is an art form with different responses for different people, different situations. Granted, technology, logic, and a knowledge of history are involved; one does have to know information sources, understand the finer points of a given subject, and have an understanding of human foibles—including one's own. Still, when it comes to explaining how to conduct the reference interview or, in fact, when not to engage in conversation, there are no specific rules, no well-beaten paths, no completely sound responses. Almost everything depends on the situation, the individuals, and the particular time and place.

Unfortunately or fortunately, depending on how one views such matters, the reference interview can be discussed, dissected, and deconstructed without making much difference for the individual involved in the process. Too often the rules and the suggestions are as broad as they are banal. Qualities that constitute the good interview tend to be inherent in the personality of the librarian who instinctively knows which move or word is appropriate, or whether withdrawal is suitable. A draconian personality is going to have problems with a well-meaning patron. Anyone ruffled by puzzles is not likely to be happy in the interview. On the other hand the self-confident, calm, and responsible librarian will search for opportunities to converse with people about their reference problems. Ostensibly one is born to be a good conversationalist, or not; but even the best and most self-sufficient interviewer can learn from those who have experienced the seduction and the horror of the interview. And that is what this chapter is about.

Interview and Mediation

A few years ago Catherine Ross and Patricia Dewdney outlined approaches to the reference interview.[1] In less than three pages they presented twelve problems put by slightly nervous librarians, with as many practical, sound answers. "Why do people ask general questions when they really want something very specific?" "What about users who ramble on and never get to the point?" "Isn't body language important?" The queries are familiar to anyone who has worked at a reference desk. Speaking from experience, common sense, and appreciation of human differences Ms. Ross and Ms. Dewdney give concise answers. Both the good-natured, sometimes puzzled questions by the conscientious librarians and the sound response point up the joys and the headache of the reference interview.

Although the reference interview is the subject of this chapter, it is not necessarily that commonplace. Most questions hardly need a long discussion between the librarian and the client. At the same time, the ever-growing masses of information require someone who can help the user find what is needed. The reference librarian as mediator is synonymous with the interview. Also, the interview represents a broader issue—that of communication between the librarian and the user. The librarian should be concerned with communication rather than with the particulars of a one-to-one interview.

One may discount the importance of the reference interview, but even critics realize how important it is that the librarian understand the patron's needs, even if they are only directional. It becomes more complex when the new technologies literally cry for explanation. Call it what you will, but the poor user who cannot get the terminal to function desperately needs to talk with the librarian. Conversation, interview, discussion—no matter how it is labeled—is as essential in today's library as any resource.

The reference interview, which takes place between the librarian with expert knowledge and the layperson in need of information, is a form of communication. Obvious, to be sure, but consider the etymology of *communicate*. The word derives from the Latin to "impart," "participate." Other key meanings associated with the word communicate include "share," "convey," "reveal," "exchange," and "express." A person who fails to "participate" in a discussion is not communicating, unless it is in the sense of a nonverbal signal for disdain or stupidity, for instance. Communication does not necessarily have to be verbal.

Still, key words are the heart of the reference interview. The librarian must appreciate fully the human meaning of *impart, participate, share, convey,* and *reveal.*

---

[1]Catherine Ross and Patricia Dewdney, "Reference Interviewing Skills: Twelve Common Questions," *Public Libraries*, Spring 1986, pp. 7–9. The questions were put to the authors by working librarians concerned with communication problems and the reference interview.

A current, perhaps common, denominator of the computer search is that it reveals, but fails other tests of communication.

A 1995 study produced for the U.S. Department of Education found that managers consider "attitude" the most important factor, followed closely by "communication skills,"[2] when evaluating a potential employee. Much the same might be said in considering the reference interview. A successful interview implies an open attitude on the part of the librarian as well as sometimes extraordinary communication abilities.

Nothing quite ensures the success of the interview as much as experience. No article, no book, no bit of personal advice can be as instructive as an hour or two fielding questions. In the beginning weeks or months it is advisable to seek advice from others who have had the same experiences, the same frustrations. Granted, not even the most practiced librarian is necessarily an expert on the interview, but at least she or he has been there and survived, and even the worst interviewer can give suggestions on how to succeed.

Setting the Stage

"I have always been of the opinion that a man should know either everything or nothing. 'Which do you know?' 'I know nothing, Lady Bracknell!' I am pleased to hear it. I do not approve of anything that tampers with natural ignorance." This invaluable maxim from the heart of Oscar Wilde's play *The Importance of Being Earnest* sets the scene for the typical reference interview.

On one part of the stage is the reference librarian who knows "everything." On the other side, the student or adult who knows "nothing." Outside the library they are neither omniscient nor ignorant, but both are caught in a position where this is the assumption. Trying to pinpoint the exact question, to locate the precise type and amount of information needed, requires considerable knowledge and experience. Meanwhile, the person asking the question seems perfectly superfluous to the undertaking. One can hope the particular drama may be brightened by allowing the user a trifle more to say. The librarian should not be in the role of Lady Bracknell, applauding, as she does, "natural ignorance."

Granted that the user and the librarian are not stupid, and both are involved with the question and the interview, the experienced reference librarian still knows:

> The librarian is at a disadvantage in the encounter. Librarians must ask themselves at least eight fundamental questions with each reference transaction—Did the patron ask a non-question? Did the patron ask the question correctly? Did the patron understand the question and the range of answers sufficiently to pose the ques-

---

[2]"National Survey," *The New York Times*, February 20, 1995, p. A13. The survey pointed up the lack of necessary skills taught to future workers in public schools.

tion? Did I hear the question correctly? Do I have the tools to answer this query? Did I understand the question? Did I read the tool correctly? And is the tool accurate? The issues must be faced with each question and there is nothing we can do about that except to remember that it is up to the librarian to ask or answer these questions, and there is nothing we can do to eliminate them.[3]

At times certain types of people make it necessary to modify the standard responses, the standard decisions, as to whether to launch an interview. For example, individuals who are normally uneasy in conversation find it difficult to ask the librarian for assistance. At the same time the need is so great that they have to overcome their reluctance. Experience indicates that the shy person is more likely than most to open the interview with a statement such as "I know this is a stupid question." The librarian should be careful not to humiliate the shy individual asking the question.

Despite major efforts to woo people to the reference desk, many simply resist such assistance. This reaction is due to many things besides being shy: (1) lack of understanding of what the librarian will, or will not, do, that is, whether one may expect maximum service or minimal directions to a reference source; (2) prior training in school, and particularly in grade and high school where the focus is on the user learning self-help methods rather than relying on the librarian; (3) prior unfortunate experiences with librarians which may keep an individual from asking for help.

The psychological human barriers are beyond count. Who, for example, feels free to ask a question when staff members are engaged in idle chatter with one another or when the librarian appears either too timid or too domineering to offer assistance? Also, the language and cultural barriers, from library jargon to the inability of the librarian to appreciate the patron's use of signals, may be confusing.

WHO NEEDS AN ANSWER?

To interview or not to interview more often than not depends on the individual's needs rather than on the type of overt question. Following are examples of the types of people who do or do not need assistance and an interview:

1. The individual who requires only a minimum of help, often to find the copying machine or catalog, and who is in the library primarily for pleasure not for study. This person rarely, if ever, needs the assistance of a reference librarian.

2. The "moderate" information seeker who may have a question once or twice a year about a practical measure such as how to find stock market quotations or how to lay a tile floor. Here a reference librarian may be of assistance,

[3]Jack Hicks, "Mediation in Reference Service . . . ," *The Reference Librarian,* 1992, no. 37, p. 58.

if only in evaluating the probable level of difficulty of the material to satisfy the reader.

3. The student who, at any age, is involved with finding just the right amount and type of information to complete a paper, prepare a speech, or pass a test. An interview is usually desirable.

4. The serious researcher who needs specialized materials as well as specialized assistance in locating data for business, scientific, or scholarly reasons. An interview is a major consideration, although in a few cases the researcher may wish to conduct the search (manual or online) without assistance other than directional help.

Outside these four categories of reference service users (and nonusers) there are variations:

5. The traditional self-educated individual, once a standard type, but rapidly becoming more the exception than the norm. Here a person uses the public library as an informal university to attain competency in everything from good speech and writing to philosophy and business. At one time, particularly before World War II and mass college education, this person was well known in libraries. Today this person is more of a shadow (some would say a cliché) than an individual seeking knowledge. This is not to discount the importance of such service, although most of these people may be classified in (2) above, that is, moderate information seekers or, possibly, students or researchers.

6. Then there is the "group" type of person who joins a "great books" discussion group and attends films, lectures, and the like sponsored by the library. Before or after attending one of these activities, the person may wish information from the reference librarian about the subject(s) under consideration.

Satisfactory Service

Just how satisfactory is reference service in a library? Questions such as those below set the stage for understanding what the average individual requires. Informally or formally, what type of answers would one get to the following questions?

1. How difficult was it for you to find someone to help you, and how long did it take before a reference librarian had the time to discuss the problem with you?

2. Did you feel comfortable, or did you feel like you were imposing on the time and the good nature of the librarian?

3. Did the librarian seem to take an interest in your problem?

4. How much time and effort did the librarian take to understand precisely what you were looking for, as well as the type of information you needed?

5. At this point, did the librarian find what you needed, or did the librarian indicate how you could find the data yourself? Which of these two approaches do you prefer, that is, do you want an answer, or do you want someone to help you find what is needed?

6. Did the library have what you needed? Was there enough of it, and was it in the form you required, that is, a book rather than an article, a CD-ROM citation rather than a photocopy of a print index page, and so on?

7. If the material you needed was not in the library, what steps were taken to help you either find alternative sources or obtain the material from another source?

8. Did the librarian follow up and ask if you needed more or less data? Were you asked if what you received was satisfactory for your particular purposes? Was the user encouraged, as a matter of fact, to continue to ask the librarian for clarification and help?

Study the Successful Users

A more thorough, rewarding approach to understanding user satisfaction and problems is suggested by a working librarian who studied people who are always successful in their reference encounters. The librarian identified common client techniques which result in consistent satisfaction with reference service. The most common user factor is attitude. "What counts is not the attitude of the librarian alone but rather more importantly that of the client. Clients insist on, and get, the proper data to fulfill their needs and they accept nothing less."[4]

In the study of the successful library patron, it was found that they knew how to conduct a reference interview from the other side of the desk. The patron shares certain skills:

1. Assumes a personal relationship with the librarian.

2. Assumes ownership for the transaction.

3. Is always prepared to accept the information provided and then evaluate the data.

4. Comes as prepared as possible—tries never to pose a question in a vacuum.

[4]Ibid.

5. Is persistent, stopping the query only when he or she has all the information needed.[5]

Enter the Computer

There is another aspect to this, and that concerns just how helpful the librarian is to the client in using the new technologies. Is the librarian helpful with CD-ROMs and, where available, the online library catalog?

If the librarian agrees to find the answer, there is hardly any need for the user to learn the complexities of a CD-ROM terminal/monitor/printer. Be that as it may, most libraries do not have the professional help for complete service. The user must learn to find basic data at a terminal. Many people, and particularly those who realize help from reference librarians is limited, embrace the computer terminal and its avenue to CD-ROMs or online reference sources. Unless they are young and have had experience with computers at home and in school, most do need at least some limited assistance.

Is advice on which keys to push, or which clicks of the mouse are necessary, really a reference interview? The question is important for three pragmatic reasons: (1) Does the individual really understand how to get from the question to, say, an abstract on the terminal monitor? (2) If the individual has knowledge of the technology of searching, is there an equal appreciation of the various levels of searching sophistication? (3) Will the individual be able to objectively determine whether the first two or three citations printed out or viewed are what is needed?

If the answer is no to any of these three questions, then the reference interview, or some form of basic instruction and assistance, is required.

When an online search is needed, the reference interview is usually built into the process—at least where the librarian is the mediator. Rapid developments of online searching by laypersons may seem to point to the elimination of the middle person. That is true if only an undifferentiated citation or two is required in a relatively short amount of time. It is *not* true, as it is *not* true for a CD-ROM search, when discrimination is the object.

In most libraries, though, the online search continues to be done by the librarian to save time, money, and frustration. When the decision is made to employ an online search, librarians ask the individual to fill out a preliminary form on which the question is stated. Sometimes this is done simply, but other times it is suggested that the user write a brief "narrative" in which the question is framed. For example, in one model of the form the following is requested: name and address of the user, title and purpose of the search, terms and the synonyms likely to be used in connection with the topic, list of important people in the field, and, sometimes, a note on maximum cost.

[5]Ibid., p. 59.

The use of the preliminary interview-search form is almost universal, simply because it saves valuable time. The form forces the user to consider the question and to be precise in its formulation. A similar form for any reference interview would no doubt improve all types of searches. The form also serves as a good departure point in formulating and negotiating new vocabulary as the librarian and patron work together.

Sometimes a research "expert" will present the librarian with a list of key words rather than the hoped-for "narrative." One problem with the list of key words is that the words may not be acceptable to the system. Often they do not take into account the interactive features of the computer search. It is always best to have a broad understanding of what is needed, not simply what the user sees as the major and minor terms. At the same time one does not want to dismiss this kind of assistance. It is better to have a user who is interested than one who expects the searcher to do everything.

Online searching is improved—if only in cutting the length of time needed to search—when there is a separate and quiet section for the interview and the search itself. Even though a ready-reference search may take no more than a minute or two, and can be done in a typical, busy reference situation, the in-depth online quest may run from 50 to 70 minutes. One can imagine how much longer this can take when it is done in the middle of the normal chaos at the reference desk.

Enter OCLC's FirstSearch

So much for the past, for the traditional online search aided by the librarian. With the advent of OCLC's FirstSearch and the opportunity for laypeople to make their own online searches without bankrupting the library reference budget, matters have changed. Another element in that change has been the widespread development of online consumer services (such as America Online) and the even more widely used avenues on the Internet. Anyone who navigates these by now common information highways knows the ins and outs of online searching, if not always the best routes.

Just as many students and laypersons embrace CD-ROMs because they eliminate the need for a mediator, for a librarian, much the same has happened with the introduction of public online searching. Somehow it is comforting for many people to sit down in front of a terminal and weave in and out of the information traffic jams without help or driving instructions.

The paradox is obvious. Whereas complex information technology requires considerable skill, the average library client is set free by CD-ROM and online searches to find his or her own way with a minimum of background, a minimum of skills. Many love this situation, prefer it to the sometimes humbling experience of having to ask for help.

The average user is going to crash, time and time again. What may be worse, the same user will walk away from the wreck convinced that there has been no accident, that the drive for information was a complete success. Experts and people wise enough to understand the complexities of information will usually want the assistance of a librarian. Furthermore, they may need help not only with databases, but also with the various technologies involved.

Perhaps all of this will resolve itself when the masses of information overwhelm even the most confident of the uninitiated. But for now the reference librarian must at least offer to be a mediator.

REFERENCE LIBRARIAN AS MEDIATOR

> The problem is that so far only half the information revolution has been delivered to us: the access and the volume. The other half is reducing the flood to a meaningful trickle. The people who make the money are going to be the ones who make the filters and the off switches.[6]

This is hardly a new insight, although it becomes an increasingly important aspect of information as the next century approaches. If librarians are not in "the business" for "the money," they certainly should be the experts who design and act as filters, as the "off switches," as mediators between users and masses of undifferentiated data.

The role of mediator is as important as any assumed by the reference librarian. It is impossible to assume the role unless a reference interview, with its follow-up, takes place. Those who argue that the reference interview is not necessary, or moribund, or even dead, are obviously unaware of the rapid developments in information which make that interview more important today than it ever was in the past.

> Many of the functions now performed in all libraries . . . functions such as document identification, document delivery, overdue notices, interlibrary loan, even cataloging—will become increasingly computerized and clerical. We have little professional future in these transactions. Our future is in the process of proactive reference work, of information intermediation, aimed not at validating a library policy but at the specific and unique needs of the person who just contacted us. And what that person needs may or may not simply be a book or even an article. However, whatever it is, that becomes our job.[7]

If, in the past, the primary role of the library was to collect and organize information, today the focus is more on how to access and filter data. Information is no longer confined to a single library. It is available on a global scale. The

[6]Quoted in *Newsweek,* February 27, 1995, p. 76.

[7]Herbert White, "The Reference Librarian as Information Intermediary," *The Reference Librarian,* 1992, no. 37, p. 34.

ideal is to collect all of the world's information and make it available to all of the world's people. More than ever the primary purpose of the reference librarian is as mediator.

Mediators for Online Information

The massive loading of facts into a magnetic tape, on a CD-ROM, or on the head of a pin demonstrates easy storage. The problem that remains is how to find the precise fact needed. Mechanical aids, from searching for key words to juggling phrases and mastering boolean logic, improve speed and accuracy of retrieval. Still, the same problem that one has when one digs through piles of books and journals persists. What is relevant? Furthermore, is the author, publisher, journal, editor, and so forth reliable?

One may applaud the triumph of the electronic networks that bring the word of one person (i.e., through bulletin boards, e-mail, electronic journals, newsletters, etc.) to another without interference of a middle person (i.e., an editor), but a major difficulty remains. What is useful, marginally useful, and a total waste of time? Furthermore, among that which appears to be useful, what is current, objective (where necessary), accurate, and specific to a need? Out of the piles of printouts in any hour of a 24-hour period what is worthwhile, even entertaining to read? The person is entirely on her or his own. It may take more time to wade through the material than one has patience or hours in a day.

Some believe everyone has the right to publish and read or view what is out there. One may publish anonymously or pseudonymously. The responsibility for putting out information is that of the individual. The catch of this information boiling up from the bottom is twofold: First, the responsibility to select and choose shifts from the publisher, the editor, and the author to the reader. Second, lacking any checks on information, how can the reader know what to read?

The advantage to having someone filter out the garbage or the material of no interest to a particular individual is obvious. For example, newspapers, magazines, and books are directed to specific audiences. This process relies on editors (i.e., mediators) skilled enough to recognize what is needed by X or Y.

Experience teaches the reader which magazine, newspaper, or for that matter television broadcast is of appeal. The individual may discount a good deal of what is printed or reported visually and orally, may even mistrust the media as a whole, but will inevitably, at a minimum, rely on mediators to filter out what is not important.

Need for information mediation is apparent. Recognition of this may come slowly to the library profession, but not to people anxious to make money from the process. A partial solution is to develop software that will filter out what is not needed. All major and some lesser-known firms are at work on such projects. Some are in place, such as an e-mail screen to put priority tags on the messages and a program to select by subject certain types of news stories for the computer reader. DIALOG and other vendors of databases have for some time now helped the searcher by showing how often key words appear in given indexes. Similar efforts are being developed which are more sophisticated and take into consideration word placement, word emphasis, and other elements to indicate relevancy of given articles.

Librarian-User Interactions

It is not always easy to serve as a mediator. Problems present themselves:

1. The user has less than total confidence either in the knowledge of the librarian about the subject or the ability of the librarian to translate the question into a suitable response. (Answer: The properly carried out reference interview should allay both fears. Also, the interview should make it clear that the librarian can go beyond the specific knowledge of the user to embrace other, related fields.)

2. The user has mixed feelings about the quality of the collection. (Answer: Not only should a reference librarian serve as the middle person between information and the client, but in order to do this well the librarian must ensure the quality of the collection. The process of collection development—from pamphlets to online services—is a necessary parallel to mediation. In a day of increasingly tight budgets and equally expensive and diverse new technologies, the collection policy itself is a mediation between the possible and the desirable.)

3. The user looks to the reference librarian for assistance at an elementary level consistent with the user's education, cultural background, and so forth. (Answer: When meeting needs, when building and developing reference collections, the librarian must keep in mind that not everyone is a graduate of MIT or a local university. Most people come from diverse backgrounds and educational and economic levels of the community. Their needs will differ. The librarian should judge the same potential material in a different way when, say, trying to gather books in a multicultural area.)

4. The user may not want to ask for everything in case the librarian proves to be censorious, either directly or indirectly. Here the librarian as mediator is the villain in the piece, or so thinks the user. This all too common feeling or attitude explains why so many students welcome online searching and CD-ROMs where they can go around the librarian and directly to the computer terminal to do their own searching. This end run avoids what they all too often see as a conflict with the librarian. (Answer: Mediation is more than a word. It is an operating principle of the reference librarian who, when deciding what is best for X or Y patron, must at the same time be diplomatic, kind, objective, and neutral. This is a given. Period.)

THE REFERENCE INTERVIEW—STEP BY STEP

Years of experience, volumes of articles, and numerous books prescribe certain definite steps in the reference interview. Although it is a highly individualized form of communication, there are certain steps that many find useful.

The rule of the successful interview is in four parts: (1) Obtain the greatest, most precise information about what is needed. (2) Understand at what level the material is needed and how much is required. (3) Complete the interview, and arrive at the necessary key data, in as short a period as possible. (4) Maintain a good relationship with the person asking the question.

It is absolutely imperative that the librarian have all the facts necessary to answer the question. How is this done at the average reference interview? Three or four points will help: (1) Ask enough questions to make certain the user's question is understood in dimensions of what is or what is not required. (2) Try to keep the patron on the verbal track and do not let distractions interrupt the clear goal of clarifying the question. (3) Where appropriate use open-ended questions which encourage the user to expand on needs rather than respond with "yes" or "no." (4) Be sure to talk the language understood by the user. On one hand this may be simple street talk, on another it may be a conversation filled with technical jargon. (5) Where there is any doubt, be sure to ask questions about, for example, the length of the required response or the need to consult books or journals or both.

No question should be dismissed as trivial, soporific, or banal. There are a few occasions when a question does not deserve attention, although the librarian should make an effort to be polite, or at least not attempt to strangle the person on the other side of the desk. For example: "Do men who habitually wear a hat increase the probability of baldness?" "Can you find a book which will confirm that somewhere in a field in northern New York State there used to be a sign saying 'Please do not throw stones at this notice?' " "Where can I find a biography of either Beavis or Butthead?" Actual questions, mind you; but can even these be dismissed as trivial or banal? There are times when the librarian must make critical decisions without help from textbooks.

1. What Is the Question?

> What users need is not necessarily what they say they need, and certainly not always what they say they want. We should not blame them for that inaccuracy. Users bring with them preconceptions about the library, about us, about what we are capable of doing, and about what we are willing to do.[8]

First, foremost, and always the purpose of the reference interview, even if it only takes a moment, is to clarify the question. For example: "A patron . . .

[8]Ibid., p. 33.

demanded a book called 'Oranges and Peaches', but really wanted Darwin's 'Origin of the Species.' Another wanted to know the complete history of garbage. What, inquired one, is the weight of a 747? What was John Lennon's eyesight? What is the membership of the Mickey Mouse Club? Where do egg cartons come from?"[9]

Infinite pains should be taken to understand the question. This implies, too, an equal effort to understand the needs of the individual and how much or how little information is required to satisfy the question.

Experienced reference librarians know that the original question put to them by a user is rarely the *real* question. Different people, with equally different needs, phrase their queries in different ways. The librarian who has a tolerance for ambiguities and vagueness will follow a simple, direct route to a possible answer. For example, when the query is vague, the librarian may not try to get more information through the interview, but will look for a basic broad subject approach which is likely to meet the needs of the user.

In a school or academic library setting, the normal reason for asking a question is related to an assignment. The student wishes to know where to locate a reference work or needs serious help finding material for a paper or talk. Teachers will want more refined sources, although essentially they are in quest of the same types of answers. "To summarize, the student does not go through all possible ways to phrase a question rationally nor does the librarian rationally pick the best answer. In the reference process, the two participants try to elucidate their frameworks and try to merge the two. A successful answer is when the two come to a common understanding."[10]

The greatest variety and type of queries are put to the public librarian. Clients are not only students and teachers, but laypersons of different ages and backgrounds who may wish to gather information for practical purposes. Questions may range from how-to and self-help problems to business, scientific, or research decisions.

A distinct advantage of the e-mail request for information is the necessity for the user to write out what is needed, much as in a person-to-person interview with a librarian before an online search. The person with the question uses terms familiar to herself or himself and, if a subject expert, terms employed in the subject. Given this type of specific information, the librarian is usually able to make up for the lack of interpersonal communication. Also, of course, there is nothing to prevent the librarian from phoning or using e-mail to clarify this or that point. "Using electronic mail to request reference service may . . . be

[9]*The New York Times*, February 13, 1992, p. B11. These are queries put to New York libraries. People sometimes muddle words and word order; for example, the request of a fifteen-year-old: "Is there a saying that goes, 'Hope springs a turtle?' "

[10]Felix T. Chu, "Reference Services and Bounded Rationality," *College & Research Libraries*, 1994, no. 5, p. 459.

beneficial to the process as it forces users to think about and then state their information needs in formal, written form. . . . Interactive real time communications (perhaps using chat/talk modes) and/or follow-up contacts (through electronic mail) may also be necessary."[11]

2. Essential Information

One purpose of the reference interview, whether it be brief or long, is to help the librarian answer search questions.

The first piece of essential information is whether the query needs only a quick, easy answer, or requires a number of complex steps which may take from 5 to 10 minutes or longer. One judges this, at least after a bit of experience, almost intuitively. For example, when the librarian is asked the birth date of Mathias Grunewald, the answer may be found quickly in any general or art encyclopedia. The same query becomes complex when the person wants details on the painter's work, the *Isenheim Altarpiece*.

Beyond determining if the question requires a single, quick answer, or more of a search, the librarian wants to learn:

a. What kind of information is needed? For example, if the query is about flying saucers, does the user want a definition, a history, an illustration, a news story, a confirmation—or what?

b. How much is needed—a simple fact, a book, or a mass of material? How much information does the user already have about the topic? (It helps to know this in order to avoid duplication.)

c. How is the information going to be used—for a talk, to answer an idle question, as a beginning for research?

d. What degree of sophistication is required—a beginning article or an advanced monograph?

e. How much time does the user wish to spend (1) finding the information and (2) using the information? Obviously, if each is a short amount of time, then one ends up with a small amount of essential data.

f. When is the information needed? Is there a definite deadline?

3. Isolating and Correcting the Question

The librarian must be able to classify the type of question being asked. The exact nature of the query may be brought out by a few courteous questions. For ex-

[11]Eileen Abels and Peter Liebscher, "A New Challenge for Intermediary-Client Communication: The Electronic Network," *The Reference Librarian*, 1994, no. 41/42, pp. 190–191.

ample, if a user asks for airplane magazines, the librarian might point to the rack, or might respond with: "The airplane periodicals are over there, but we could give you more specific information about airplanes in some other sources we have. Do you want anything in particular, or do you just want to look at the airplane magazines?"

Often the patron may confuse the issue and give the wrong clues about the information needed. For example, in seeking an author, the user may have the name spelled incorrectly, or in seeking the source of a quotation, the user may misquote the passage. The librarian must then hope that the quotation is accurate at least in terms of subject matter so that a subject search may be launched. The librarian may recognize an error in information, a wrong spelling, a misconceived notion about a subject. He or she may then suggest other possibilities, while trying to discover, through courteous cross-questioning, another approach to the query. Often a single clue obtained this way will give enough information to correct the mistake in the query.

When working with students, the librarian sometimes finds it helpful to ask to see the teacher's question in writing or to see an outline of the material. The librarian may have enough personal knowledge of the subject to make mental corrections of user errors and go on with the search for materials.

4. Question Summary

In any interview, no matter how short, it is wise to summarize the question or the facets of the question. The client may then correct or modify the librarian's response. For example, "If I understand you correctly. . . . Let's be sure I understand you correctly. . . . In summary, you wish. . . ." All these are openers for the librarian who then goes on to state the query as succinctly as possible. If the interview is lengthy or complex, it is wise to occasionally offer such summary statements to help clarify matters.

The art of restating and paraphrasing the main points of the interview, in order to achieve a maximum of mutual clarity, is difficult. It requires not only that one listens, but also that one uses memory and common sense. The process will fail if the librarian too often summarizes, repeats, or forgets what went before.

5. Open and Closed Questions

In the analysis of the reference interview, one is confronted with the open and closed question. The *open* query is general and one which begins with a broad topic. The respondent replies in his or her own words. Example: "What do you consider the primary elements of a good reference interview?"

The *closed* question is restrictive and normally calls for an equally specific reply. Example: "Do you think that the reference interview is useful or not useful?"

One talks of open and closed questions both in terms of the person asking the question and the librarian's response. The patron may begin a discussion with a closed question: "Do you have Henry Smith's *Tropical Flowers?*" "Where is the *Readers' Guide?*"

The closed question may be answered in one of two ways. Either take the query at face value and locate the specific item or, in the reference interview, attempt to change it over to an open query. For example, the person looking for the *Readers' Guide* can be told it is on the second table from the left. End of interview. Changed to an open query, the question would go a step further. "Can I help you find something specific?" or "There are other general indexes which may help, too. Do you have a specific question?"

Also, where online searches and CD-ROMs are available, the librarian may wish to point out that the quest for material in the *Readers' Guide* may be had electronically. If the user is interested, the librarian is then launched into another set of questions. The first is simply: "Are you familiar with the online (and/or CD-ROM) system?" Here a "yes" answer should be opened up because there is much more than a yes or no reply to that type of query.

As much depends on the methods of the librarian as on how the queries are labeled. A friendly, open person can ask a series of closed questions, but by her or his manner imply that the user is free to counter not only with answers, but with questions, too. Someone less skilled may bring the interview to a disastrous end with closed questions, but have no better luck with the open-query approach.

No matter how the gambit is analyzed, the best advice in the reference interview is to turn a tight yes and no discussion into a relaxed conversation about the topic. If this can be done with either closed or open approaches, then that is fine. The result is what is important, not how one classifies the questions.

INTERVIEW PROBLEMS

In any discussion of communication in general, and the reference interview in particular, the participants are likely to split into two or three groups. One is firmly convinced that most of the rules can be learned through proper courses, workshops, study, and the like. This is a persuasive argument for anyone who believes in education, but indications are that more lip service is paid to this than to any real effort on the part of teachers, students, or working librarians to implement it. The normal approach is to dismiss the interpersonal communication experts with a shrug and point out the attitudes of the second group: that the interview is more of an art than a science.

The third group admits that both sides in the communication controversy are right; that the interview is both an art and a science. While this author is more inclined to bend toward the interview as "a performing art," this is not to discount the importance of a clear understanding of the research and findings connected with interpersonal communication.

If an interview is in order, and the subject appears to be relatively complex and requires equally complex sources, it is best to give a few moments over to friendly conversation about the subject as well as the individual's need for materials. This is both relaxing and revealing. It tends to put the user at ease and the end result may be a more cohesive statement of the question.

Views of the Librarian and the User

The user must assume that the librarian is competent, and the librarian, in turn, must assume that the user can make his or her needs clear. The relationship can shift when either party recognizes a lack of certain skills or understanding in the other. The librarian should go into a more patient, slower gear; but the user may shift into a high degree of impatience. The natural reluctance of some highly skilled experts to trust their queries to a librarian, whom they usually view as a generalist, is due in no small part to the presumed low status of the librarian.

Conversely, some librarians take a less than heroic view of the frustrated user. For example, a few years ago an experienced reference person wrote a tongue-in-cheek article on, yes, "the stupid question" and how it can be handled. In reality, few would have the temerity to call any question stupid, particularly if personal experience is recalled in a bank, airport, store, or dentist's office. Now and then every one of us asks questions that are less than brilliant but which appear quite sane, natural, and necessary to us.

> I think it's a healthy exercise to put yourself in the patron's place every now and then—imagine the nerve it must take to approach a total stranger to ask a question about something that really matters to you. And if the question does sound stupid—if someone asks "Is this the reference desk?" immediately after you've answered the phone "John Jones, reference desk, can I help you?"—then empathize, empathize, empathize. Maybe the caller is so wrapped up in formulating a question that he or she didn't even hear what your stock phone response was.[12]

Mutual respect is called for in any interview situation. It is imperative if the question is to be understood. As anyone knows who observes a dialogue, most of the early discussion involves establishing a relationship that can be neutral, friendly, or downright hostile. This helps to establish a context for the question-interview–search-answer. The context, or "setting," allows the parties in the transaction to clarify for each other such important aspects of the relationship as the degree of urgency of the request, the limits of the help to be provided,

---

[12]Mark Plaiss, "Stupid Reference Questions," *Library Journal*, October 15, 1985. See, too, the letters to the editor which followed for several months. Also Charles Anderson, "Stupid Questions," *RQ*, Summer 1986, p. 433.

and the amount of intimacy that both parties may be willing to share in working toward closure of the transaction.[13]

Interview Interactions

Most people who approach a reference librarian with a question expect to like the librarian, or at a minimum, not dislike the individual who is about to help them with a problem. Students in particular tend to be no more than indifferent, but even the most blasé can be at least focused if the query is more than a "where" or "what" ready-reference or directional query. The secret of rapport is the attitude of the librarian. One should appear relaxed, yet secure in the knowledge that an answer is a relatively easy matter. Interest and at least a dash of sympathy help, as does the occasional smile, nod, and word of encouragement.

Even brief encounters require another person, and often the individual putting the question, to shape an interaction. Everything from dress, age, and tone of voice may encourage good or bad feelings by the librarian. While attention to both verbal and nonverbal cues are necessary, the wise librarian maintains a certain distance and neutrality. If the student, for example, complains about the "stupid assignment" (a common comment in all types of libraries), the librarian might comment: "Well, that can be a real problem," without actually evaluating the quality of the assignment.

It is not always easy to show even a shadow of empathy with an individual who, for good reason or not, simply reminds you of figures from a Bosch painting or an MTV commercial. Here one of two moves is appropriate. Either shift the person to another librarian who may be a trifle more sympathetic, or respond as openly and as positively as appropriate. Unfortunately the world is made up of some people who are moderately or completely antisocial, and yet need assistance. It is moments like that which test the librarian's true professional self.

Difficult People

Otherwise calm librarians sometimes panic at the idea of the reference interview. There is no reason to be nervous. It is a ripping good exchange which tends to be more pleasant than painful. On the other side of the reference desk it may be a different matter.

The difficult patron takes many forms. Still, there are common characteristics of types:

---

[13]Beth Hockey and Brian Nielsen, "Linguist Analysis of Reference Transactions," *Library Software Review*, May–June 1988. The researchers recommend that the design for a computer system which will answer questions must get around the lack of human contact between the person posing the question and the machine with the answer.

1. *Indefinite.* "I want something on whales" or "What's the value of property in this town?" Generalities, vague concepts, and sometimes just plain lack of intelligence accounts for the indefinite question. Conversely, patrons may be indefinite because they are not sure what they are seeking, more or less asking. At any rate, the best approach is to turn from open to closed questions. Force the user to focus. "Whales? Is this for a class paper?" "Yes." "Do you want to know about all whales, or just those in the Pacific?" Whatever method is used, at the end the librarian should have a more specific notion of what is required.

2. *Anger and hostility.* Here the individual may be as angry with the need to ask the question (for a child, for a paper in school, for a mistake) as with the librarian for being there to reply. Tone of voice, attitude, and type of question give this away without much need for analysis. The best way to handle this type of hostility, at least in the reference situation, is to ignore it as much as possible. Also, one should take plenty of time to reassure the individual that the librarian is there to help, not to do battle.

3. *Lack of focus.* The questioner may be confused and unable to focus on what is really wanted. Unless a person is suffering from dementia, this may simply be another case of feeling indefinite about what is wanted. More likely, though, the person lacks a command of the language in general and a specific subject area in particular. The librarian should try to formulate the question in easy-to-understand language. At the same time the librarian should indicate there is plenty of time and the nervous user should relax enough to have a gentle conversation about needs.

Those are only three of scores of what might be termed descriptors of difficult patrons. Everyone has a favorite complaint. Possibly the worst is the totally removed individual who has no sense of other people, who believes the librarian is there to serve, no matter how foolish or long-winded the question. This type requires patience, and according to some librarians, a help to the exit.

Talkers, who refuse to listen either to themselves or to the librarian, are another common headache. Normally, too, fast talkers are interested in everything except the question. Here, again, the way out is to try to rephrase the query with a closed question. "It seems to me you need something on automobile registration?" or "Am I mistaken in thinking you are really looking for a guide to automobile registration?"

INTERVIEWING TECHNIQUES

Everyone has his or her own personal approaches to the reference interview and, if they work, this is fine. On the other hand there is a consensus that certain attitudes and feelings can be useful, even for the most experienced librarian. Among the most frequently mentioned:

1. Listening

Listening is a major consideration in the interview. Nothing is more important than to pause, listen, and look attentive. However, doing so is *not* all that simple, and aside from making a genuine effort to listen, the reference librarian should be aware of a few of the subtle, but vital, aspects of the process.

There is a difference between *passive* listening and *active* listening. The former requires no skill. One simply lets the other person talk, interjecting at reasonable times an affirmative sign that one is indeed listening. Active listening at the reference desk includes not only hearing what the other persons says, but also evaluating and summarizing the message so that it can be acted on.

2. Approachability

One circumstance which is neither special nor unique, but all-important in the reference interview, is the matter of approachability. The librarian should appear willing to give assistance.

Essentially one must be sensitive to the needs of others, open to relaxed and free discussion about a problem, and able to overcome sometimes subtle conflicts between oneself and the person asking the questions. One should have a strategy for dealing with arrogant and shy persons. In order to do this, one need not be a saint but only aware of the positive and negative aspects of one's own communication patterns. This can be learned in numerous ways, from workshops, to maintaining a diary of a day's activities, to asking users what they consider the positive and negative aspects of a given interview.

The personality of the librarian is the major variable in any discussion of the reference interview and the larger matters of communication and approachability. Although there is no definitive superperson profile available against which to measure the average librarian's degree of personality and communication skills, common sense tells one that the ideal is somewhere between the stereotype (little old gent in tennis shoes) and the twenty-first-century information robot. Short of intensive psychoanalytical help, someone who is naturally shy is not going to be the best reference librarian, any more than the person who is confident to the point of arrogance. The average "social animal" will do nicely, particularly when he or she brings a glimmer of self-understanding to the mastering of the reference interview. Also, recognize that exposure of personality is fraught with danger for both the patron and the librarian. That danger cannot be avoided, but it should be recognized.

There is even a test to take to determine one's approachability. The test, somewhat tongue in cheek, asks the respondent to gauge such things as facial expression and methods of handling negative comments. One of the 29 test queries might be enough to reveal a librarian's true personality in relation to reference work: "Do you look toward each potential library user as a: (1) new adventure? (2) learning experience? (3) pain in the neck? (4) service which must be rendered?"

A good interviewer will keep out of the foreground—a lesson all too few professional interviewers of celebrities master. Fortunately, it is a better-understood maxim by reference librarians. The librarian should know as much about the subject as possible, but plainly try to shake off the urge to let the person with the question recognize the depth of his or her knowledge.

3. Verbal and Nonverbal Cues

As the author Robert Kelly puts it: "Our memory banks are flooded with 10,000 images like scraps of silent movies . . . but the words are lost, or just shadows of a sound. . . . We know people by knowing what they do."[14] And a good part of this knowledge comes from gestures, facial expressions, or the very stuff that makes up that memory bank of 10,000 images.

According to researchers, verbal signals are only about 10 percent of the message at the reference desk; the remaining 90 percent consist of signs. Nonverbal signals suggest anger, sarcasm, intimacy, whining, or whispering as well as fixed messages regarding age, build, or dress.

The concept goes back to Darwin's classic work *The Expression of the Emotions in Man and Animals* (1832). Some research predates Darwin. Along the way and into the twenty-first century a considerable amount of nonsense about the subject as well as a few serious contributions have been published.

In the latter category researchers find, contrary to expectation, that certain facial expressions can be universally recognized from western Germany to western Sumatra. Some of these are contempt, fear, surprise, disgust, and happiness. What are the universal signs of contempt? Typically contempt is expressed by tightening a corner of the month, cocking the head to one side, and looking down the nose. Signs of anger include glaring, clenched jaws and furrowed brows, and tightly pressed-together lips.

Nonverbal cues are obvious in many situations. Gregariousness or being overly shy are apparent to almost anyone, and when either is recognized the reference librarian acts accordingly in the structure of the reference interview. Conversely, one can become too confident and assume it is possible to read subtler clues from an expression or gesture. "For example, people who gesture a lot and look you in the eye are perceived to be dominant. . . . But this is not the case. . . . It's actually the reverse."[15] Studies indicate most books on teaching nonverbal cues are worthless or, at best, of minimal assistance in the reference interview. None is absolutely required reading, and the librarian should do only

[14]Robert Kelly, "Mortality Tale," *The New York Times Book Review*, October 3, 1993, p. 11.
[15]"Non Verbal Cues to Personality . . . ," *The New York Times*, September 17, 1991, p. C9.

what is natural. To act from a sense of duty rather than a sense of friendly interest is to undermine the whole process.

Gestures should be kept to a minimum, and one should not mimic what the user is doing, for example, putting hand to chin when the user does so, and so forth. The tone of voice may also be considered a nonverbal cue, and it is wise to keep it even, although a little excitement when one makes a discovery is useful. Attempt to mask irritation or downright anger by keeping the proverbial "straight face," and, again, an even tone of voice. Look interested, and be interested, in what the person is saying. Do not turn away when it seems time to end the interview. Let the user make that decision, although subtle guidance is acceptable.

Other aspects of the nonverbal in the reference interview are obvious to almost anyone who engages in a normal conversation with a friend or even with a stranger at a party. A smile is welcome, but a frown is enough to turn away all but the totally insensitive. One talks in a relaxed manner and does not rush headlong into the discussion or insert awkward stops so the other person is not sure whether to fill the space or be quiet.

4. Dress

A method of placing people in well-understood social and behavioral slots is to evaluate them in terms of dress. Presumably, a person dressed as though from the pages of a fashion magazine is more likely to be receptive to intelligent conversation and assistance than the same-aged person dressed like a refugee from an MTV rock-and-roll band. Add to this judgment such details as body odor, posture, height, and weight, and one becomes a kind of amateur Sherlock Holmes. Unfortunately, too many times the evaluation is wrong. Unless the librarian is omniscient a safe rule is to evaluate individuals in terms of their questions not by the cut of their clothes.

Ideal Behavior

What is the ideal behavior of the perfect reference librarian? First, include a quick, interested smile when the person approaches the desk. Make eye contact, but do not try to stare the person down. Try to keep gestures to a minimum and speak in a relaxed tone. Throughout the interview, speak, listen, and clarify and above all else give the person asking the question your full attention.

Generally, it is not appropriate to consciously use nonverbal gestures. Still, in the course of a truly friendly interview a bit is appropriate. Again, though, much depends upon the librarian and the patron. For example, an admiring gaze will indicate to the patron the question is one the librarian has longed to hear for years. Other appropriate cues, the tilt of the head, a brief look of fascinated approval of the query and the way the person is putting it to you, and a smile are guaranteed to establish the proper atmosphere. Where appropriate, the arm touch may give the person putting the question the feeling that you are paying close and careful attention.

On the other hand another school considers any nonverbal cue a danger, a bad sign, and certainly not in the best of taste. The librarian should be approachable, but make no effort to alter his or her personality to suit the situation.

Primarily be yourself. If this self fits into the rhythm of the reference interview, you are born to the profession. If, at the end of a brief conversation, people rush away from you in horror, it might be better to turn to another part of the library, possibly administration. A dash of humor and a bit of perspective are the best preparations for the reference interview.

SUGGESTED READING

Berinstein, Paula, *Communicating with Library Users*. New York: Special Libraries Association, 1994. This is a 65-page pamphlet used for self-instruction of special librarians. It is useful for any reference librarian in that it is an intelligent, pragmatic discussion of the reference interview in particular and other communication techniques in general.

Chu, Felix, "Reference Service and Bounded Rationality: Helping Students with Research," *College & Research Libraries*, September 1994, pp. 457–461. An excellent example of how to use the reference interview with methods of measuring the results. A major focus is "the ambiguous nature of good and acceptable answers according to students." From the point of view of a university librarian, but much of the wisdom could be employed in other types of libraries.

Hanne, Daniel, "The Uses for Assumptions and Skepticism . . . in the World of the Reference Librarian," *RQ*, Spring 1989, pp. 303–306. The author points out that most librarians are right to be skeptical about the "real" question put to them by a user. Failure to delve further may result in wasted time and total misunderstanding. Examples are given of such futile searches.

Morris, Ruth, "Toward A User-Centered Information Service," *Journal of the American Society for Information Science*, January 1994, pp. 20–30. A study of communication and information needs, this perceptive article analyzes the need to understand the user. Suggestions are given on how to measure satisfaction, and how to tailor information delivery to meet specific needs. See, too, the detailed bibliography.

Morrison, James, *The First Interview*. New York: Guilford Press, 1993. While this explores the various techniques of the medical interview, much of the general advice is applicable to the reference interview; for example, see Chapter 3, Developing Rapport, and Chapter 10, Control of the Later Interview.

Redlich, Barry, "Refining the Art and Music Reference Interview," *New Jersey Libraries*, Summer 1993, pp. 28–30. An outline of interviewing techniques "used by the staff that may also be used as guidelines for other libraries." While directed to music questions, much of what is outlined will be useful to others.

Ross, Catherine, and Patricia Dewdney, "Reference Interviewing Skills: Twelve Common Questions," *Public Libraries*, Spring 1986, pp. 7–9. Here is a three-page article which sums it up. The questions are as current today as they were when this article was published, and are just as likely to puzzle librarians another ten to twenty years from now. The answers are marvelous and suggest the delights of the interview.

Rubin, Rhea, "Anger in the Library," *The Reference Librarian*, 1990, no. 31, pp. 39–50. The author discusses the rise in displays of anger, particularly at the reference desk, where the patron is upset about some real or imagined wrong. Rubin gives good advice on how to handle the "difficult" individual, and why the librarian should try to check his or her own anger. See too: Beth McNeil and Denise Johnson, eds., *Patron Behavior in Libraries*. Chicago: American Library Association, 1995. This handbook by 15 experts provides answers to issues such as how to handle the angry patron and how to deal with the mentally ill, the homeless, and the like.

Smith, Lisa, "Evaluating the Reference Interview," *RQ*, Fall 1991, pp. 75–81. An intelligent, practical view of the reference interview and its real, as contrasted with its theoretical, importance in reference services. The author concludes that evaluation is necessary and helpful, but only at a highly personal level where peer review is employed as the evaluator.

CHAPTER SEVEN
RULES OF THE SEARCH

In reference services there are two basic types of searches, both dictated by format. The first is the manual search, or the search of printed materials. The second is the computer-assisted search (i.e., online or on CD-ROM). The searches have much in common, yet are different enough to warrant separate treatment.[1] No matter which type is used, finding the needed information is more important than the process. And the process varies. One librarian may favor a type of "guerrilla warfare"; another may be more comfortable with a considered, logical plan; a third may use both approaches.

The search is an integral part of the reference interview. Despite efforts to analyze, chart, and teach by numbers, it can be as subjective and intuitive a process as the interview itself, and just as complex.

An analysis of the search reveals that it may take one or two different, sometimes simultaneous, paths. The first concerns the thought processes of the librarian. The second concerns the actual steps the librarian takes once the thought processes have been triggered. For example, some searching is almost automatic in that the librarian knows from practice where to look. But sometimes considerable thought may be given to the question and to the source of its answer. Once the mental process has evolved, the actual search is then a matter of locating materials in given forms. Obviously, even the simplest thought process requires a follow-through to a source and an answer.

---

[1]Both types of searches are considered in the first volume of this text, usually in conjunction with a specific reference work. Here an effort is made to present an overview rather than the particular points of searching.

Attributes of Skilled Searchers

What makes a reference librarian a skilled searcher? More important, what attributes contribute to the ability to determine what is "best" or "better" information in a particular situation? What, in fact, determines success or failure as an information mediator, the person between the mass of data and the specific needs of an individual?

In general, the advice of a survivor of the Donner party (where most were killed by storms as they tried to cross the Sierra Nevada in 1846–1847) seems applicable: "Never take a cutoff, and hurry along as fast as you can." Shortcuts and cutoffs in a storm, as in a search, can be useful, but normally they lead to disaster. It is far better to approach the search in a methodical fashion.

The ideal search expert will have: (1) An understanding of details with an appreciation of logic and be blessed with a fine to excellent memory. (2) Enthusiasms and interest in what the search is all about. (3) An understanding of individual needs, which is another way of saying the person should have fine communication skills. (4) Self-esteem and confidence. This is important when the librarian comes to make decisions about what is or is not needed by the individual. The person with the question must sense that the librarian is knowledgeable. (5) Finally, an ability, like the survivors of the Donner party, to be able to admit a wrong trail was taken, and it would be best to go back and begin again. An able searcher is willing to admit error and has the ability to make equally quick changes.

Aside from personal qualities, the individual must have: (1) A firm knowledge of a subject field(s). This implies constant reading, constant attention to new developments, and these days constant conversations, often over the Internet or similar networks, with others in the field. Only a subject expert—the librarian—can deal with confidence with another subject expert—the user. Here one is talking about users who are doing research,[2] not students who may have wandered in from a recent class assignment. Both deserve similar attention, but the expert will make more demands. (2) A firm knowledge of technology—particularly where the search is conducted using an electronic data source. Experience is most important. Constant reading and double-checking on new developments is equally necessary.

---

[2]Only a small percentage of professional researchers use the library, and even a smaller group use it for serious work. Furthermore, only a minority are seeking primary sources. Most are seeking data to validate an existing hypotheses, whether they be in science or the social sciences or humanities. Finally, like all students and laypersons, the majority want to be assisted, not instructed, while in the library. Obviously a few do want to search databases, but in practice most put their assistants to the task, particularly where there is no reference librarian in the wing. See a series of articles in *The Chronicle of Higher Education 1990–1993* by E. C. Ladd and S. M. Lipset on faculty, research, and teaching. See, too, C. B. Osburn. *Academic Research* (Westport, CT: Greenwood Press, 1979).

SEARCH STRATEGY

The search strategy a librarian employs depends primarily upon the nature of the inquiry. In their broadest terms, the inquiry and the search may be divided into two types. (1) If the inquirer seeks specific data, as in the case of a ready-reference query, the goal is predicted, and the search strategy can be laid out in a methodical, step-by-step fashion. A standardized pattern of routine movements can be prescribed, the purpose being to include, or exclude, certain alternatives. (2) A more in-depth inquiry, as in the case of a specific search-or-research query, requires an investigative type of strategy. Faith in routine must be replaced by faith in insight.

Consider the difficulties of the librarian assisting an individual to find information. Much of the search strategy is conducted by the librarian at a subconscious level; for example, while the interview is progressing, the librarian is matching needs with sources—rejecting some, accepting others. The librarian's fundamental effort is to match the query and the library system's resources.

The search process generally begins with an interview, no matter how short. Once the librarian has received the message and has understood the question, if only tentatively, the next logical step is to match that question with the source(s) most likely to yield the answer. If someone asks for information on Tom Jones and knows this Jones is serving in Congress, the librarian sifts through a series of mental signals: Congressman, important personage—*Who's Who in America*. If the question concerns the literary figure Tom Jones, the signals are different: literature, Henry Fielding—encyclopedia for Fielding, *Masterplots* for summary of *Tom Jones*, and eighteenth-century literary criticism. If the reference is to the singer, then the signal is to an appropriate index, which may be anything from *Access* (which lists more music magazines than *Readers' Guide*) to *Magazine Index* to *Popular Periodicals Index* to more specific music sources and *Biography and Genealogy Master Index*. And so the process goes. Matching the question with the logical source is as complex as the needs of the user. Depending on the sophistication of the user's needs, one source may be used, or a more complex source, or even several sources may be needed.

The advent of numerous electronic databases and abstracting services has made the task somewhat easier in that one does not have to dash about the library seeking likely reference books. Still, sitting before a terminal and monitor, the same question remains: Which source is the best for the needed information?

Despite the most rational type of searching pattern, serendipity and browsing may be equally effective, or certainly affect the manual or computer search. As one browses, for example, one learns index terms, the scope of the subject, and basic terminology. Often, too, the primary writers in the field become evident.

Search Process

Whether one turns to a printed almanac or an online full-text abstracting service, the basic principles of the search process are much the same:

1. The query is first analyzed and clarified through the reference interview. One determines the type of question asked, the parameters to be established (i.e., purpose, scope, time span, amount of material, level of material, etc.), and the source(s) or system(s) where the necessary information is likely to be found.

2. In the case of the majority of ready-reference queries, a source usually comes readily to mind. The source is consulted, and the answer is given.

3. In the case of search-and-research queries (and more difficult ready-reference questions), it is necessary to consider numerous sources. At this point, a likely source is usually one of two major possibilities:

a. Bibliographies, indexes, the library catalogs are consulted, that is, not sources of answers in themselves but access points to answers. Thanks to electronic databases this is by and large the most favored path by today's reference librarian.

b. Form or subject sources are referred to, from standard reference books to magazines, newspapers, vertical-file material, and a given subject area on the shelves. In most situations, because the searcher is not entirely sure of the avenues for an answer, **(a)** will be a first choice as a source.

4. Generalizations about both the manual and the computer-aided search are in order. Where bibliographies, the catalog, and so forth, are to be searched it is best to determine likely subject headings or primary words which may be located in an electronic database search. A helpful aid at this point is to list key words most likely to be appropriate for such a search. A choice of action must then be made. The searcher may

a. Broaden the search in terms of the subject headings and key words.

b. Narrow the search.

c. Select more specific, or less specific, subject headings, or key words.

d. Find more appropriate terms.

5. Through steps 3 to 4, there should be some type of dialogue between the user and the librarian. Or the dialogue may follow later when likely material is gathered. At any rate, adjustments in terms of which data can be used, which are peripheral, and which are useless, must be made throughout the total search process.

6. At this point other decisions must be made:

a. A judgment has to be made about the relevance of the data to the specific question put by the user.

b. If there is too little material, the librarian must decide in what order to search other sources.

c. If nothing can be found, the librarian must decide whether to try new or modified approaches, to give up, or to suggest to the user other resources (i.e., other libraries, interlibrary loan).

d. In any case, the librarian must determine how much more time can be given to answering the question.

Were the search process always this neat, the problem would only be one of finding specific sources or entry points to those sources. In practice, however, the librarian may decide that a given reference book or CD-ROM has the answer but not be able to find it; turn to another similar title but not find it; go to a bibliography but not find it; go to a CD-ROM index, find it, but then discover the articles are too broad for the user; return to the index but not find additional materials; go to another print index—and on and on until the patience of either the librarian or the user has worn out. In most situations this does not happen, but it can.

One may argue that the online or CD-ROM search is a real joy in that the index is always there, at least if the years needed are covered by the database. There is a possible search problem. Given the ease of using, say, *Magazine Index* on CD-ROM versus the need to find an elusive printed index, both the user and the librarian will prefer to use the CD-ROM. The user may be willing to accept material which is approximate, if not precise. Why? Because it is so much easier to find on a CD-ROM than in the manual search. This situation is likely to occur when someone is looking for background data, and is not too concerned with specific dates, places, names, and so forth.

THE SEARCH AND PROBLEM SOLVING

As stated before, the librarian is subconsciously clarifying questions and locating probable sources of information. In the average reference situation, each of these steps may be going on almost simultaneously. At any rate, rare is the librarian who consciously diagrams each step and moves neatly from square to square. Once the circuit of matching the question with possible sources is closed, however, the librarian must have a strategy for finding the information itself. The strategy may involve no more than taking out a volume of an encyclopedia or looking up information in a CD-ROM index or in the library catalog. On the other hand, it may involve a more extensive search that leads to dead ends and frequent returns to "Go."

The search process is strongly governed by the objectives and the philosophy of the reference service. If the service is minimum, that is, primarily one of helping the user find citations and possible sources, the librarian's search is really directional. The user will be advised to search X index or Y reference book or to look under P subject heading in the catalog. The user may even be counseled to try another department in the library or another library. These days the user may simply be urged to sit down at the computer terminal and try to figure out how to find a citation from that same *Magazine Index*. Younger people, accustomed to such things, are delighted. Older people (say over twenty-one years of age) may be completely baffled. Even the minimalist reference librarian may have to help the user get started.

If the service is middling or moderate, the librarian will go to the index, catalog, or reference source and help the user find what is desired.

If the service is maximum, the librarian will collect the information and follow through by gathering added citations and sources until satisfied that the user has enough material to answer the question. These days, too, maximum service means helping the user with the CD-ROMs, either through instruction or actually securing the citations for the user, or both.

Automatic Retrieval

Memory is one of the vital keys to a reference librarian's success. The librarian's memory may be filled with facts, but what is really significant is that the librarian has the ability to recall a specific reference work in terms of how it matches the question at hand. Librarians are capable of a considerable amount of this "automatic retrieval" of information. The automatic retrieval operates whenever the reference librarian knows (1) the solution or answers to a specific question or problem or (2) has an unvarying, simple rule for finding the answer.

In the case of (1), this may be no more complex than knowing the name of the mayor of the city or the population of the state. Obviously, there is no need to consult any reference aid except memory. In the case of (2), which occurs more frequently in daily reference service, the librarian knows a simple operation or procedure that is guaranteed to find an answer.

Both basic processes, memory and learning procedures, serve the reference librarian as they serve all of us, but for a reference librarian, learning the procedures is essential. And the procedures are more complicated than mastering the multiplication table. Some examples will suffice:

1. The same search procedure can be learned and used time and time again to find the answers to questions about prize winners. The technique for learning the Pulitzer Prize winner for 1995 is the same as that for finding the name of the Nobel Prize winner for 1985.

2. Once one learns to find the distance between New York and San Francisco, it is easy to apply the same procedure in finding the distance between San Francisco and Tokyo.

3. The procedure for finding the first line of a verse using "love" is the same as that for finding the first line of a verse using "hate."

4. The procedure for finding X book in the library is the same as that for finding Y book.

The same techniques or set of rules (sometimes referred to in the literature as "algorithms"), once learned, will automatically generate answers to the same set of questions or queries. The answers can be looked up or retrieved by what are essentially the same automatic techniques used when one masters any set of rules, from those for multiplication to those for boiling an egg.

Much—possibly too much—of reference work is no more difficult than any other automatic process, given these essentially automatic methods of deriving answers for certain types of questions. The librarian simply masters a group of rules and equivalent sources for finding answers. This becomes a subconscious process, almost a reflex action. If, for example, someone asks for the name of the secretary of the treasury, one would turn automatically to the *United States Government Manual*. Should the librarian suspect the post has been filled recently, the reference work would be *Facts on File* or an online check of a current newspaper. Matching the question with the probable source of an answer is no more difficult than knowing how to shift gears in a car, provided, of course, one is a trained driver.

In general, completely automatic techniques for handling questions are limited to answering directional and some ready-reference queries—and possibly some search queries involving no more than finding a group of documents. Research queries are rarely that easy to answer automatically.

The Trial and Test Search

In a very real sense, the search strategy is tantamount to making a hypothesis and then testing its validity through the search. For example, the answer to the question should be found in Y source (hypothesis). Y source is found, but the answer is not there. If it is not in Y, it is not likely to be in B, but it will probably be in C (hypothesis). A check of C proves the answer is there, and the hypothesis is correct. In initiating the search, the librarian can list all the possibilities, attach a success-probability function to each, and solve the problem by selecting what seems to be the best source(s) for the answer.

The formulation and the testing of any hypothesis presupposes a careful analysis, but in practice how often is this really done? If the librarian is left out of the search process, the average user is more likely to browse (or, as one student put it, "cruise") the collection until something likely turns up. It may not be the best source, but it is a *source,* and it at least serves the purpose, no matter how poorly, of answering the question. Even the librarian may conduct a cruise, although usually with a little more direction. For example, a biographical query may simply lead the user to the biography section in the reference section or the general collection in the hopes of finding what is needed without further effort. A question about a quotation may take the librarian, with no other thought about other possible sources, to books of quotations or a CD-ROM quotation database.

This is not to say that browsing is not beneficial; in fact, with proper direction it may be a very legitimate search process. It needs only a minimum of thought or planning, and it can be modified as it goes along to produce the desired results.

The ability to solve the problem, that is, carry on the search process, depends not only upon the librarian's existing knowledge of the collection and the question, but also on changes in that existing knowledge. The librarian begins the process by mentally testing and validating or invalidating given hypotheses and then accepting one hypothesis and testing it against the possible source. In a ready-reference question this may be quite enough, but if the source fails to provide an answer, the librarian learns to discount the hypothesis and, perhaps, the form for this type of query. Instead of an almanac, a yearbook may be more useful. This decision requires reorganizing the problem in terms of new hypotheses and building upon the state of knowledge existing when the question was first posed.

Throughout the search procedure the librarian is making decisions as to whether or not this process, this source, or this bit of information will be relevant to solving the problem of X question. One should not go "full steam ahead" on a request that has been translated into the terms of the information system without testing those translated terms first. After a partial search, it will be discovered whether the subjects chosen are adequate, or if there is a need for adjustment and refinement.

TRANSLATION OF THE QUESTION

Once the librarian has isolated, understood, and clarified the question, the next logical step is to "translate" the query into the form required by the available information system.

Form

Essentially, a basic step in translation is to isolate the form(s) for possible answers. The average television viewer or newspaper reader will translate the question— "Where can I find tomorrow's weather forecast?"—in terms of form and find the answer by turning to the paper or switching on the weather forecast. In another situation, the question, "Where can I find the difference between the meaning of weather and climate?" would result in the translation of the query into the form of, say, a dictionary entry or an encyclopedia entry.

Of course, the translation of either question might be in terms of a human resource. "What's the weather tomorrow?" we ask the weather forecaster.

"What's the difference between weather and climate?" the librarian asks the geographer.

Either question, too, might be translated in more depth. For example, the query changes if put by an airline pilot or by a geographer who wants a definitive explanation of weather and climate. In either case, the translation will be in more sophisticated forms, such as daily weather maps or scientific journal articles.

The most obvious type of translation occurs during a librarian's self-questioning: "Is the answer most likely to be found in a book, a pamphlet, a periodical, or a government document? Is an online database an even better source?" This decision is usually based on the depth and timeliness of information sought, as well as on the sophistication of the user. Another decision is based on knowledge of the collection or awareness of what is involved in obtaining materials from another library. For example, a library may have a good pamphlet collection, but the librarian who has not used the collection often may fail to consider it when a particular question is asked. Also, the librarian who realizes that technical materials on a given subject are well covered in a nearby library has the advantage of several options: go to the phone for an answer, or refer the user to the other library, or borrow the needed materials.

In the majority of ready-reference queries, as well as most search-and-research questions, the isolation of the form is probably the easiest bit of translating. And perhaps it is too easy. For example, a "typical" librarian who has grown accustomed to equating certain queries with biographical sources, or specific standard sources, often overlooks equally excellent or better forms.

Subject

The next most decisive and generally the easiest translation of a specific question to the library system is made by isolating the subject field. Queries about where to find information on "X member of Congress," or "Y American baseball player" will take little translation. The librarian will automatically go to the biographical section. The "where" or "what" query, by definition, inevitably leads to a subject classification. Queries such as "What is the cost of living in New York City?" "What is the formula for water?" and "Where is the capital of Alaska?" inevitably lead to related subjects, whether statistical data or chemistry handbooks or geographical sources.

All these queries, though, are at a simple, telegraphic level where a connection between query and subject is self-evident. Problems arise when the subject is not clear or, more likely, when the librarian's knowledge of the subject field is too general or too inadequate to translate the query into a meaningful source.

What happens when the question is clear enough, but the librarian is uncertain what salient part of a large subject area should be tapped? If, for example, the user wants material on the classical theory of unchecked population growth, the librarian, in an interview situation, might try to gain a more specific insight into the needs of the user. But if the needs cannot be expressed in any more definitive terms, what next? The obvious answer, if the librarian happens to know of Thomas Malthus, is to begin either with his works or with essays about Malthus. Lacking that subject knowledge, the librarian will move from the known, population and population growth, to the unknown. The subject might be checked in a general encyclopedia for the historical background or in a subject encyclopedia. Inevitably the name of Malthus will appear. The librarian should then find subject material on Malthus and the Malthusian theory. If this does not prove satisfactory, a search of the encyclopedia (or for that matter, the catalog or any general bibliography concerned with population) will provide other key subject terms to consider.

These steps follow the old tried-and-true principle of moving from the known to the unknown. Obviously, this presupposes an understanding of the general parameters and the vocabulary of the subject. Lacking this, the librarian should return to the negotiation of the meaning of the question with the inquirer.

Success depends on a thorough knowledge of the library's classification systems, from cross-references in catalogs and indexes to storing and shelving systems. For example, the librarian may realize that a query has to do with the history of computers in business but be unable to make the association between the subject and the likely subject heading in the catalog or the place the material might be on the shelf—perhaps under business history, technology, or an important name in computer development.

The reference librarian must be able to move comfortably from the general subject to the specific subject. This presupposes a thorough knowledge of close subject classification, and the imagination to move about in related subject areas. For example, if nothing can be found about the history of computers in business under the subject of computers, the librarian should then move instinctively to the broader area of history or general works on technology. If the material is not available in the given library, the librarian must also know what bibliographies and union lists to consult in order to obtain it from another library.

A thorough knowledge of the general collection is presupposed here, primarily because the query may be answered not by scouring the usual sources but by looking in a standard biography, history, or manual in the circulating collection.

Time

The element of time as related to a spatial situation is fairly well determined in the question "Where can I find the per capita income of America?" The answer is going to be from a current, not a historical, source. The question "What was the per capita income of America in 1860?" uses the same relation, but obviously leads the librarian to a different era.

Sometimes, though, the time element is not clear. For example, when the user says, "I want something on the history of New York," she might be given a general history of New York City, but more likely something on a certain period. A request for "something on President Clinton" must be narrowed down in terms of today or yesterday, his term as governor, his term as president, or his private life.

Once the time element is determined, it is relatively easy to move to corresponding sources, that is, if the library has those sources. One of the major problems in almost all but the largest libraries is timeliness. Retrospective sources are probably to be found in considerable number in libraries, but the question which demands information that was generated yesterday, the day before yesterday, a week ago, or even a month ago will pose definite problems for many of them. Of course, in libraries with access to online services the time element can be solved rather easily. The problem, though, is cost—at least for the present.

Language

In the United States, in all but the largest libraries the collection is essentially in the English language. True, libraries serving Hispanic communities may have a number of Spanish titles, but by and large the reference section will be in English—as will, by the way, most of the electronic databases. In large libraries, though, the librarian obviously must know whether the inquirer can handle French before including an article from a French periodical among the sources.

The level of reading comprehension is another aspect of language which must be considered. The specialist will be satisfied with one source, the amateur with quite another, and the young student with a third. The difficulty arises with the adult user who may be better educated or less educated than the librarian suspects, so the librarian should try to determine the comprehension level of the user first.

Availability

It seems obvious that the librarian cannot produce materials which are not in the library. But—and this is important—the right source may be precisely determined, although unobtainable. Everyone is familiar with the common situation of locating an article in an index and then going to the shelf and discovering that the library does not subscribe to the magazine, or, more likely, that the magazine is there but the particular issue is missing, or that the issue is there but someone has cut out the article. One advantage of the online or CD-ROM index is that the citation to a journal will usually indicate whether or not the library has that journal. Another approach is that even where the title is not in the library, the librarian may be able to order the article(s) directly from the index vendor at the same computer terminal. The factor of availability is often more important than recognized. Ready accessibility, as countless studies have found, is a major factor in determining what type of information is used.

When the question is of the search-and-research type, and not the ready-reference variety, the emphasis tends to change. Here, instead of looking for a simple answer or an extremely limited amount of material, the librarian is seeking the highest-possible number of relevant and pertinent documents for the user's information requirements. This situation shows the importance of the use of bibliographical aids and adds the further challenge of matching the question with the access language of such aids.

ACCESS LANGUAGE OF THE INFORMATION SYSTEM

The librarian must know the control and access language of the collection and reference sources chosen. This means an appreciation of indexing and cataloging subject terms; it also implies a knowledge of the classification scheme of the collection, the location of reference books on the shelves, even the place where, say, the ERIC microfiche are filed. It certainly implies an understanding of how to find electronic databases. In this broader, more general context the language of the information system is more directional than conceptual.

The directional language is probably the most familiar one to the average library user, particularly the user who either does not want to bother the reference librarian or has little faith in the librarian's ability to locate needed answers and information. Usually such a patron simply finds a section of materials—books, magazines, documents, and so forth—which may answer his or her needs and commences to browse. In order to do this, though, the user must understand the language of classification or at least have learned through experience where the needed materials are located. That these materials happen to bear significant classification numbers may mean little to the user.

The normal library-reference pattern of access by way of the language of the information system begins with specifics such as author and title, which, if accurate, afford exact entry through the catalog, index, abstract, or bibliography. Here, in fact, there is really no translation. Lacking a specific entry, the librarian must translate the query into a subject form which the catalog, index, abstract, or bibliography will accept.

The librarian should not hesitate to confess ignorance of the meaning of certain terms. If it is obvious that the user cannot help (particularly true in the case of students who may be as puzzled as the librarian by a teacher's specific wording), the terms should be checked in a general dictionary, encyclopedia, or standard work on the subject. A dictionary will suffice for definitions, but an encyclopedia may be necessary for an overall view, especially when the question involves a matter of judgment. For example, in order to understand a request for material on hydrometers, a dictionary definition of "hydrometer" may be sufficient. However, if the question is "What is the dividing line between legislative matters of policy and executive matters of administration?" a dictionary definition of the terms will be of little help, and a quick check of an encyclopedia article on government may clarify the question.

Common failures at this level may come from misunderstanding and from failure to grasp the meaning of the terms. The user's mispronunciation may indicate one word, when the user actually had another term in mind; for example, the pronunciation "neurglia" for "neuralgia." Or the user may spell a term, name, or event wrong and delay the search. This is particularly true when information on persons or places is sought. The difficulties of the situation are apparent in the cooperative reference service when a request is channeled to a central library for material on china or seals. The requestor must clarify whether "china" is the country or the dishes, and whether "seal" is the animal or the signature sign. Context of the words may or may not make the proper selection apparent.

Searching Bibliographies and Indexes

About 50 to 80 percent of all manual or electronic searches of catalogs and indexes are by subject. Such subject searches usually lead to selecting books or articles or, in the case of the catalog, finding the shelf location of books in order to browse through the area of interest. Normally this search is limited to one place; that is, the librarian or user goes no further than a single subject heading.

The catalog is the starting point for many searches. Here one expects to find author, title, and subject analyses of materials available in the library. The catalog limits the search to subject headings assigned by the cataloger. Linkage is indicated by "see" and "see also" references. This has its limitations, although it has the advantage of specificity.

Key Words

At any rate, to return to the librarian who is helping the mystified user, one excellent approach to subject headings that might be appropriate for the search is to check the key words. When the key word is not found in the index or catalog, synonyms should be sought in the various subject-heading and authority lists, which are part of every library system.

The key word analysis is helpful when first writing down the question. This is hardly necessary for most ready-reference queries, but where it appears there will be some difficulty in translating, or where the search promises to be a relatively long or difficult one, the librarian (or the inquirer) should phrase the question, in writing, as clearly as possible. This obviously forces either party to think about exactly what is being sought. In this, one is not particularly influenced by the logical and linguistic constraints of the system.

RULES OF THE GAME

Over the years, reference librarians, through experience more than through scientific analysis or theoretical considerations, have compiled useful approaches to searching. Some of these are of the limited "how-we-do-it" type, but many others are of considerably more universal interest. Some applicable techniques are listed here.

1. When you know the answer is in a source, it usually is. There are times—and we have all had them—when, after checking all the possible places for an answer, one source stands out as the most likely key to the problem. But a check of the source did not help. Take heart: The answer is there; it will just take some proper "page-shaking" before it falls out. Admittedly, this course will occasionally fail, but if it does, the fault lies not in chance, but in your choice of source.

2. Depend on no one's prior research for accuracy or completeness. This involves fellow staff members. Although the staff members of your department are renowned "good guys" and have never led you astray, the moment one of them hands you a question and specifies that A, B, and Z have already been checked, believe them not. It may happen that they speak the truth; it will, however, not always occur that way. Of course, if they have followed all the rules set forth here, trust can be extended—halfway.

3. Keep a list of where you have looked. On a long question it is folly to try to remember all the sources checked and the results of each search. It is doubly foolish to expect to transfer all this negativeness to the next researchers and expect them to remember it too. So mark, somewhere, the source checked and the result.

4. Take your time. One professional librarian twice selected the correct reference source but overlooked obvious answers because she was in too great a hurry. In another case, the key information from the patron was obtained but the librarian did not take sufficient time to examine it. Lack of time to interview and to consult sources appeared to be another major cause of professional failure.

5. Try various entry points. The subject approach is the most common, but consider the name of an author or an organization. Normally the author search is limited to those with some knowledge of the field, but it does no harm to ask the user (where appropriate) if the name of an author or organization is known.

Time to Reply

How long does it take to answer a query? There is no definitive answer; some general replies can be made based upon experience and study. Most ready-reference questions can be answered in a matter of minutes, and 90 to 95 percent of them may be answered in under 5 minutes. Search and research questions may take from a few minutes to hours, or even days.

How much effort and time should the librarian take to answer a difficult question? A major constraint is the policy of the library. The library may have a written policy in which specific time limits are outlined, or there may be an unwritten understanding about the time per question.

An equally important aspect of the time element is what some call the "irritation quotient"; that is, just how long should the user be asked to wait for an answer? Potential irritation can be curbed at the beginning if the reference librarian indicates approximately how long the user should expect to wait for an answer.

In a related matter, everyone is familiar with the sometimes long wait for an interlibrary loan item, the necessary wait in line until the librarian is available, the wait which culminates at the reserve desk only to find the wanted item is gone, and so on, and so on. Not all of this, of course, is the fault of the librarian, but he or she should be aware that time is a very important factor in influencing the use or nonuse of the library.

When to Quit

Another major aspect of the time factor is deciding at what point one should give up the search. When the librarian concludes that the limits of the library's resources have been exhausted, the user should be referred to a larger library or to one with specialized materials. In smaller libraries the most frequent referral is to the state library; larger libraries may be part of a system or network that includes resources of public, college, or university libraries in the immediate area.

Search Failures

Other than those caused by lack of system resources, failures may be attributed to two basic flaws in the search process itself. The first, and most inexcusable, is a simple lack of the librarian's interest in either the user or the user's question; if an answer cannot be found immediately, a less conscientious librarian might call the search to a halt before it actually gets started. The second, and more common, failure is a lack of communication between the librarian and the user. At times the user cannot communicate in terms the librarian can translate into possible keys to an answer, and neither the librarian nor the user is sure what is being researched. The librarian may either misunderstand the query or accept the query at face value, without determining whether the user has given all the vital information or even the correct information. Another cause of search failure is the librarian who misses an obvious, but unexpected, answer.

Some questions cannot be answered, at least by the librarian at a given time with a given collection. These difficult questions often are filed under such descriptors as: librarian's tears, fugitive file, PDQ file, or Sisyphus file. "A sisyphean file prevents continual and often ineffective labor such as that performed by Sisyphus."[3]

THE ANSWER

Infatuated—some would say intoxicated—with the ability to retrieve millions of facts, a librarian may forget the essential point to all of this: how the information is used. The average manual print search is not likely to turn up more than essential data. Harness the computer to the search, and the results can be overwhelming. This leads to essential questions about results.

It is not enough just to locate a piece of the data, a source, or a document. There should be some kind of subsequent evaluation, interpretation, or clarification on the part of the librarian. This should be as much a professional duty as the interview and the search itself, although always with two considerations: (1) A user who does not want assistance should not have it forced upon him or her. (2) There are numerous times, as in most ready-reference queries, when the answer speaks for itself. One hardly need take time to explain, "Yes, the population of Zewa is truly 323,000."

Unfortunately, in the average situation the librarian only points out the reference sources (from online indexes to encyclopedia articles) and leaves the relevancy of the material to the individual. In the optimal situation the librarian helps determine the base relevancy. Several factors will help focus on the right answer for a particular individual's need.

Level of Inquiry. The librarian is often able to determine the level of sophistication of the material required by weighing the age, experience, and immediate needs to the user. The judgment is made before the actual search is begun; the librarian is not likely to start looking for material on nuclear power

---

[3]"The Exchange," *RQ,* Spring 1989, p. 306. Sisyphus, in the Greek legend, was required to roll a huge stone up a hill to the top. Since it constantly rolled down again, his task was everlasting, that is, his was an endless, maddening job.

for a scientist in the children's section. When the material has been found, the librarian, again in consultation with the individual, should be able to suggest what sources are too detailed or too technical and what sources are not detailed or technical enough.

Amount of Information Required. This is the quantitative side of the level of inquiry. The amount of information needed will depend, of course, on the proposed use of the materials. A student preparing a paper for a junior high school class in history will need considerably less material than a student on the graduate level at a university.

Dumping. The information or materials required cannot just be dumped in the user's lap, but must be introduced step by step as the patron goes through a certain pattern of behavior. A wide variety of potential sources should be offered wherever possible, but only in some logical, easy-to-understand order.

Where there is little or no control the user may suffer from the excellence of the search, that is, too much material is retrieved and dumped on her or him.

Clarity. When citations rather than data or materials are presented, how much does the user understand? In this situation it is important that the librarian follow through with explanations, as needed, of the different kinds of references (from books to articles and reports), of abbreviations of journal names, and of any unusual terms or library jargon. In fact, the librarian should exhibit a general willingness to help with an explanation of any questionable matter.

Location. Where is the periodical or book located? It is not enough for the librarian to suggest the catalog. The librarian should help the user find the references, an act which in itself provides an opportunity to point out that material not in the library may be produced through interlibrary loan.

User-Anticipated Answers. An unhelpful answer may be anticipated, and accepted, by the user for a number of reasons. Thus, the essential question-negotiation process of the interview is negated. The odds are that the user will go away not with the *desired* answer but with an answer shaped by the anticipation of little or no real help from the librarian. In this case the patron's preconceived notions have cut short the reference interview.

The type of answer anticipated by a user is usually revealed in the phrasing of the question. Such phrasing is dependent upon a given situation or individual, but some good examples are found in these common situations.

1. *Time.* The user thinks: "The librarian has only a little time to help me." The user then says to the librarian: "I have to have an answer in the next 5 minutes."

Another version of this situation occurs when the user either believes the librarian is saying or actually hears the librarian say: "I have only 5 minutes to assist you, so please keep the request simple."

The result of this anticipated time difficulty is that the user either is confused or, more likely, frames a question to elicit a quick, simple answer.

2. *Form.* The user thinks: "The librarian is helpful when it comes to suggesting periodical indexes or magazines, but is likely to refer me to the catalog if I ask for more extensive materials. The user then says to the librarian: "I need something out of a magazine."

One may reverse the thought process; that is, the user does want a book, but only a short, easy-to-read title. Rather than ask the librarian for an easy book, the user says: "I'd like a magazine article, not a book."

The result of this conflict is that the user may end up with nothing, or several books, or the wrong periodical articles.

3. *Clarity.* The user thinks: "In the past I have been able to get current material without waiting, so, while I would like some background material, it will be faster to ask for recent books or magazines." The result is a good current book which might not help, although in the process of finding the book on the shelves the librarian may indicate where similar books of an older copyright date are located.

The solution to the difficulties is dialogue, which can build a mutual trust and understanding between the librarian and the user. Another solution is found in subsequent follow-up by the librarian. If a source has been indicated, the librarian should try to discover whether or not the source was adequate. Where the actual data or documents are retrieved by the librarian an effort must be made to determine if these materials are precisely what is needed or wanted.

The point is that providing information is not the final step. In the best of all situations the librarian is as involved with the answer as in finding the answer; and this concept is in need of development. The step after the information is located may be the most important phase of the entire search process, particularly when the librarian is working with a user who has only a vague notion of what is needed. This category, of course, includes almost any student or layperson who is involved with more than a ready-reference question.

LIBRARIAN AS MEDIATOR

Throughout this text it has been stressed time and time again that the future of reference work will be in helping the beginner and the expert alike in finding critical, essential data. The librarian will be a mediator between masses of useless information and specific bits which the user requires. "The issue for the next century will not be one of format. We will use all sorts of formats, and they will matter only to the extent to which they are the most useful. The issue will be one of protecting the client against garbage."[4]

There are so many people and organizations feeding the insatiable information networks that data overload is causing psychological burnout. Mechanical methods, now being introduced, filter out the good from the bad, the indifferent from the important, but the computer programs to date are too broad to be of much real value. For example, they may eliminate items by date or by format (book, journal, report), include only items from specific journals, and so forth. The discrimination point is helpful, but much too broad.

Faced with a stack of bricks, which ones are best for building a mansion or a doghouse? The experienced mason knows. A good manager knows how to select the few papers that will really assist in the operation of the business. Technology has brought us more data than anyone or any organized group needs. It remains for the humble individual to choose and to select.

The problem for future historians examining the twentieth century will be the plethora rather than the patchiness of information. That plethora can be partly dealt with by new technologies such as digital storage or by selection. It is in selection that the reference librarian makes the greatest contribution. Selection not only of reference works—from almanacs to online computer services—but selection of what those items bring to the surface of the information pool.

Commercial Services

All of this is hardly a revelation. Anyone working with information knows the importance of dams and spillovers. Consider some examples of commercial interest in how to pick and choose data, how to mediate between the user and the flood of information.

AT&T's Personal Link Services (being refined at the time of this writing) employ software which automatically gathers and processes information for the user. Someone interested in telephone stock, for example, could program a software agent which would search specific subject and news databases each night and present a compilation of all telephone news in the morning.

There are numerous private firms that offer information-filtering online service—for a price. Aimed at executives who can pay for someone to pick the gems out of the information garbage, the services are available from an increasing number of concerns from Dow Jones News/Retrieval (Dow Vision) to CompuServe (Executive Service Option). Costs range from $1500 a month (Dow Jones) to $40,000 a year for 10 users. Obviously, the sophistication of the service differs somewhat from $120 a year to $40,000 a year. Still, the purpose,

[4]Herbert White, "Is Anyone Still Training the Circus Animals?" *Library Journal*, February 15, 1995, p. 136.

no matter what the cost, is the same. And here one wonders just how different these are from free assistance by many librarians. That question waits to be resolved as the so-called filtered information services develop through the 1990s.[5]

So-called agent-based systems are on the horizon for not just a few, but for everyone with major searching habits. Pioneering work in this field, as indicated, limits itself to filtering tasks that are predictable, repetitive, and relatively simple. In most software there is a specific agent for each specific task. "The system learns about its user's habits, interests, and behaviors with respect to that task." The catch is that it will take a massive number of agents to even come close to making decisions a single, experienced reference librarian can make in seconds. And even under the best of circumstances, few agent-driven systems are likely to be right more than 80 or 90 percent of the time. A good reference librarian can hit the 100 percent target every time, and with telling accuracy.[6]

SDI Filters

Then there is SDI (selective dissemination of information), and its close relative, "electronic clipping service." Actually, they both serve the same purpose: to filter out and reduce information to essentials for individuals. They differ only in method.

With the computer and database(s), the user or the librarian establishes a profile of needs and interests. This is "fed" into the computer's clipping service and at regular intervals the user receives citations, abstracts, and, in some cases, full articles about evolving issues and topics. Most of the large vendors from DIALOG and NEXIS to DataTimes provide the clipping service. Also, there are several smaller firms with this as a focus.

Consider DataTimes' Passport (personalized automated search service). It is typical of all services in results if not techniques. The user establishes a profile of interests. Once this is done, about 300 databases are searched daily—including over 100 newspapers. Articles matching the user's profile are faxed or mailed to the user on the same day. Delivery systems vary with each system. The cost of a full-text article delivered averages about $5 per article. It is less for a simple citation.

DIALOG's Alert service begins with a menu, or a questionnaire, for the user which, when answered in full, determines the shape of the profile. A similar pattern is followed by Dow Jones News/Retrieval's CLIP and NEXIS.

All of the commercial services are expensive and primarily geared for business and for agencies where clipping services are useful. Actually, the librarian

---

[5]Hunter McCleary, "Filtered Information Services," *Online,* July 1994, pp. 33–42. A good overview of a developing marketing strategy with a brief discussion of representative firms.

[6]Scott Berkun, "Agent of Change," *Wired,* April 1995, p. 177. This is an interview with MIT Professor Pattie Maes who is working on prototype systems among which is a Usenet news group filter program.

may establish a much simpler method of SDI for individuals who come into the library by simply tagging articles or specific titles in indexing services for browsing by the user. OCLC's First Search ArticlesFirst (discussed elsewhere) is a good example.

If a commercial service is considered viable, then the librarian must ask certain evaluative questions: The librarian's first decision is to find which services offer the databases. Second, is there a wide range of options for material from a simple citation or headline to the full text? Third, how often does the system monitor databases—daily, weekly, and so forth? Fourth, what is the type of delivery, and are there options, that is, fax, print, and so on? Fifth, is the final product easy to read, easy to follow? Sixth, comparison of cost is a factor, but the last one on the list as the costs are much the same for all of the services.

SUGGESTED READING

Ewing, Keith, and Robert Hauptman, eds., "The Reference Librarian and Implications of Mediation," *The Reference Librarian*, 1992, no. 37. The role of the librarian as mediator between information and ultimate use is considered in depth. Both the practical and ethical questions of the process are discussed. Experienced librarians and teachers offer various points of view on a role which becomes increasingly important for today's reference librarian. A must read for the student who wonders if there is more to reference work than directing someone to a CD-ROM or the bathroom.

Kuhlthau, Carol, et al., "Validating a Model of the Search Process," *Library and Information Science Research*, 1990, vol. 12, no. 1, pp. 5–31. The authors explain a six-stage model of the search process established for students in a school library. They ask if the model may be applicable to other types of libraries. They find the process does "hold for a large, diverse sample of library users." While technical, the article indicates search patterns the student will find useful in studying a subject.

Piternick, Anne B., "Decision Factors Favoring the Use of Online Sources for Providing Information," *RQ*, Summer 1990, pp. 534–543. The University of British Columbia library school professor explains the factors that determine whether the librarian turns to printed or online sources. (Here *online* is used to embrace CD-ROMs as well as traditional electronic services.) As she points out, "making choices between printed and online sources is not a simple task," although this perceptive article does much to indicate steps to solve the dilemma. A related article: W. M. Havener, "Answering Ready Reference Questions: Print versus Online," *Online*, January 1990, pp. 22–28.

Richardson, John, *Knowledge-Based Systems for General Reference Work*. New York: Academic Press, 1995. An expert and professor explains in easy-to-follow terms the intricate paths "of original research that advances our understanding of the reference professional's knowledge." Highly practical examples are given as well as advice on shifting "toward the procedural knowledge of reference work." While hardly a beginner's text, it should be required reading for anyone involved with research and reference services. Highly recommended. Note: Portions of this book have appeared elsewhere as articles.

Rowley, J. E., and D. R. Butcher, "The Search/Information Interface Project 2: Manual and Online Searching," *Journal of Information Science*, 1989, vol. 15, no. 2, pp. 109–114. An English team studies the output of a number of searchers performing the same search. The differences between the manual and online search are considered, and the various factors that contribute to search success are studied.

CHAPTER EIGHT
COMPUTERIZED REFERENCE
SEARCHES

A majority of academic, public, school, and special libraries today offer some form of computerized reference searching. The emphasis in the mid-1990s is on the CD-ROM and related approaches from online to tapes. Generally they are easy to use, and they have appeal for both laypersons and librarians. In many ways the digital index has taken the place of the printed indexes, and particularly the general or much-used subject indexes.

Typically, a user wanders into the library in search of material for a paper ("I'd like one or two SHORT articles."); or background data of a practical type ("Can you find me something EASY TO UNDERSTAND on back trouble?"); or, on occasion, specific research ("Can you help me find background material on the evolution of war in the Balkans?") Computerized searching is ideal for the average client's typical "one or two items" query. Most users are able to sit down at the computer monitor and extract at least two or three current citations. Since many services now offer lengthy abstracts, the total citation, with abstract, may more than fulfill the need of the average student or adult. On the other hand, the queries about the Balkans and the bad back may (and should) require the assistance of a trained reference librarian. In the case of the bad back the librarian will have to determine the proper sources to use for easy-to-understand information; and in the Balkan query the librarian will have to help focus closer on what is needed. In each case, the electronic database is a great help.

The necessary elements for electronic searching include: (1) *Hardware*, which is the personal computer, the CD-ROM drive, the fax, the modem, and so forth. Even a cursory glance at library and computer magazines will keep one abreast of the hardware. Only one thing is certain about it—within a short time

201

it will become outdated and even obsolete. (2) *Software,* which makes it possible to retrieve information from the database.

The actual search will depend upon the platform, contents of the database, and cost (if any). Once the system and the database are selected the search request can be entered. The results are then reviewed for modification—usually to narrow or widen the process.

What follows is an overview of a complex type of searching. It is not meant to teach one how to search. Furthermore, there are numerous detailed guides, including those from vendors and publishers, for specific searching.

Manual or Computer

When does one turn to a computer or to a printed source for a reference response?

Most ready-reference queries are answered more efficiently in a ready-at-hand printed work. For example, it is easier to determine the height of the Empire State Building in an almanac or architectural handbook than by searching for the answer in, say, a general CD-ROM or online database. Where a simple answer is called for, the print source is usually best. One turns to a computer when the "simple" turns out to be complex.

Someone who needs one or two articles on a subject may find it faster at a computer terminal. Certainly, too, anyone looking for material in depth from an index is better served at the terminal.

Unfortunately, laypeoples' love affair or hatred of technology helps make the decision. If it is love, it is the computer. If it is hate, it is the printed volume. All too often this simple answer is overlooked.

Given access to computer-assisted searching and a reasonably adequate hardcopy reference collection, one can arrive at some general conclusion about which medium to use: (1) Where an online search is called for there rarely is need to augment it with a manual search. The exception is where retrospective material, not found in the database, is needed, or where another index is necessary but not available online. (2) Where a CD-ROM search is used, the same situation arises. Generally, the CD-ROM material will be enough in itself, but there are times when a manual search is needed to augment the computer-assisted search.

Confusion arises when one turns from a manual to a computer-assisted search. Some common problems: (1) The subject headings may not be the same in the printed and the machine-readable version. (2) Dates of coverage differ, with the printed work normally going back many more years than the computer database. Most databases, for example, are retrospective only to the mid-1980s, although the printed index may go back twenty or more years beyond the computer cutoff. (3) The online search will likely have more current materials available than the printed source. (4) A number of search strategies are available with a computer, but with printed work the search is normally confined to a specific time period, and then by author or by subject.

Which type of search provides the best results for the user? There are so many variables that it is difficult to come to any general conclusion. First and foremost, the skill of the reference person is a major factor. An expert reference librarian will outperform the beginning computer searcher. And vice versa.

Database Knowledge

The librarian must have a thorough knowledge of the database, and must be able to quickly ascertain such things as period of coverage, type of materials considered, and frequency of updating.

There are about a dozen widely used databases out of a possible choice of over 6000. Either on CD-ROM or online, public and academic reference librarians are more likely to search (in rough order of such use): Psychological Abstracts, ERIC, ABI/Inform, MLA (Modern Language Association), MEDLINE, Dissertation Abstracts International, Social Sciences Citation Index, PAIS, Newspaper Abstracts and the GPO Monthly Catalog. Clients, on the other hand, are likely to confine searches to much more general databases such as those offered by The H. W. Wilson Company (i.e., Readers' Guide, Applied Science and Technology Index, etc.) or Infotrac (from Magazine Index to Newspaper Index). And where available they will use OCLC's First Search choices such as ArticlesFirst and the various catalogs.[1]

Various systems and software allow the searcher to: (1) search databases within a given large subject area and (2) find out how many times a key word(s) appears in each of the databases. Many systems permit the user to type in the key word and see how often it appears in 20, or fewer, related databases.

There are useful mnemonic devices for the trained searcher, but of limited use to laypersons. First one must choose the proper broad subject area, which is not all that difficult; but then one must decide among the databases simply in terms of number of potential citations. The quantitative approach is helpful, to be sure, but qualitative aspects are more important. These can be known only to the person familiar with the vendor and the databases offered. For example, is it better to use a database with 3026 entries for "nuclear waste" or one with 30 or 3? It depends on what is indexed, the situation, and, more important, how familiar the searcher is with the given database(s).

Matching the question with the source(s) of response is a primary contribution of the reference librarian. How long will the librarian be needed for this task? It depends. If the technology experts are correct, the matching of question with source(s) will be done virtually automatically in the near future. "The user

---

[1]*Online*, March 1992, p. 27. The choices represent a single survey, but are much the same no matter where or when the survey is conducted—at least for the general reference situation.

will not have to know the difference between DIALOG and NEXIS and CompuServe—the system will simply guide him to the correct information, performing the search without showing the complicated database selection process or search strategies. . . . The [librarian] will be there to assist, and to dive in deeper or retrieve the rest."[2] This sounds fine, but everything depends on the software. To date the promise has been considerably more than what has been delivered, at least in the area of substituting a software agent for a skilled librarian.

CD-ROM versus Online

Some believe CD-ROM is only a stopgap format between the librarian and information. They point to the fact that the successful consumer information systems, from Prodigy to America Online, offer online services. Eventually online will be not only more efficient than CD-ROMs, but also probably less expensive and easier to use.

Meanwhile, and for at least five to ten years, the CD-ROM is preferred in reference service because: (1) It can run without a charge per minute, and as of now is less expensive than online. Users can spend time in front of a computer terminal without fear of running the library into debt. (2) Thanks to simplified searching methods, the CD-ROM is a good choice for the average beginner, student, or layperson. (3) It gives an end user the sense of being in control of a search without needing a library specialist to hover nearby.

Comparing the role of online and CD-ROM in a library is a treacherous business because of the numerous variables. Still, it seems safe to conclude that

1. The average layperson and student learn how to do CD-ROM searching. More and more indexes are available for patron search on CD-ROM or an equivalent.

2. Public and school libraries rely almost completely on CD-ROM searches. (Larger public research libraries are the exception.)

3. Academic libraries use both CD-ROM and online, with the majority of students found at the CD-ROM terminal. Faculty with research projects will combine both but are more likely to prefer the online search and the help of an experienced librarian.

4. Specialized libraries where information is needed almost immediately, and where cost is not a major factor, prefer the online search.

[2]Fiona Mellor-Ghilardi, "The Information Center of the Future," *Online*, November/December 1994, p. 9.

THE SEARCH

Despite lack of standardization of databases and software, there are some basic search patterns that are relatively common to all.

Most vendors-publishers-distributors offer two or three levels of search difficulty. The beginner starts one place, the expert another. The difference between beginner and expert is measured in accuracy, relevancy, and the time it takes to search.

Searching techniques at a computer terminal, as many information experts know, began in the 1970s with the advent of the windows and pull-down menus. The software, with a companion mouse, revolutionized searching methods. As a part of Apple computers, Microsoft's Windows, and many others, the menus are a vast improvement over the earlier command-line interface. Here one had to memorize a series of steps in order to do anything from turning on the computer to employing boolean logic. Menus changed all of that, and while searching is far from easy at the more refined, advanced stages, at least it is within the grasp of the average individual.[3]

The system is not perfect, and particularly falters with Internet connections and searching. While Microsoft launches a more sophisticated Internet access system, other companies seek interfaces which will be easy for even the most confirmed "computer-search dummy" to use. Forerunners are the so-called geographical interfaces which depict objects on the screen from the real world, rather than animations or drawings. The text-and-icon systems, as employed by most of the consumer networks such as America Online, are constantly revised. For example, one company offers three-dimensional photographs of the user's work space (with a card file, printer, desk, etc.). The images are clicked on when needed.[4]

The essential commands for a beginner are much the same as for an expert: (1) Decide which database to search. (2) Select key words. These are rarely subject headings, but are words familiar to the individual looking for data. An experienced librarian would try to use assigned subject headings or a combination of key words. (3) Enter these, or other commands, at the terminal, and accept, widen, or narrow the search. (4) Examine the results. (5) Print out the citations and, if available, abstracts.

---

[3]NEXIS/LEXIS, for example, offers Company Quick Check where users can choose from a variety of icons to select company information, names of officers, financial statements, and so forth. The software automatically selects the appropriate source(s).

[4]The catch to the icons as keys to searching commands is that they are metaphors and, therefore, subject to various emotional responses by the viewers. Some may think one set of images cute, another too simple and banal. Photographs, that is, physical space metaphors, are understood by almost everyone and quite easy to master. However, this is far from perfect and will make at least a few people uncomfortable.

Even a beginner soon learns how to limit or expand a search, and often the "limit" keys are found as part of the software. What many beginners do not understand is that the first three or four records may not be the best, may not, in fact, be of any real use at all. This misunderstanding often results in search and retrieval of periodical articles of little or no value. At the point where the user begins to weigh what to use, the librarian should be at hand to help the user determine relevancy.

Searching Patterns[5]

While software differs, by now the major publishers and vendors have established certain well-defined searching patterns. Four examples will make the point. In searching Information Access Company databases, as with The H. W. Wilson Company offerings, and many other general and wide-subject databases, there are two to three distinct paths. The easy path is for the beginner and requires little or no knowledge of searching. There may be a middle path for more seasoned searchers, but all systems have the sophisticated road for the experienced searcher.

1. The first path is for the beginner or the impatient individual who does not want to master search patterns. IAC calls it ES or Expanded Search. Other vendors/publishers have similar titles. No matter the finer points of searching, these simple systems depend on the user typing in key words that are subject headings or are part of the title, abstract, article, and so forth. Simple boolean logic may be used as well. The catch is that not all parts may be searched, for example, IAC's simple approach does not allow key word access to the entire entry. (Conversely, the same tape mounted in an OPAC does give complete searching possibilities.) IAC's more sophisticated searching pattern, again duplicated by competitors, is called EF and has numerous built-in search options which permit the experienced user to narrow or widen the pattern.

2. America History and Life on CD-ROM offer another search pattern. It has two menu screens. A general search screen includes the most searched fields from subject to title. The subject field allows free-text searches of titles, descriptors, and abstracts. The mechanics are typical. One simply moves a cursor to highlight the desired field. One types the search term and as the search progresses the total number of hits for each term is displayed. A combined total then appears. One may call up individual citations.

The advanced specific search menu, among other things, allows browsing the term field index. This, in turn, permits a more sophisticated approach by suggesting related terms.

[5]See the first volume of this text for specific search patterns for specific reference works. What is suggested in this section is a pattern followed by many publishers and vendors.

3. PAIS on CD-ROM has the "browse" or "search" menus—again a typical approach. In the browse mode the user can enter subject headings or key words, author, title, and so forth. When an item appears on the monitor, a shift of the cursor to the item brings up the citation (which in this case can be either brief or full). Where the search mode is employed there is a subdivision between "expert" and "novice." With the latter the searcher may use boolean logic, as can the expert. Again, the difference is sophistication. The expert search opens the possibilities of using two-letter field tags, combined sets, truncation, and limitations.

4. The citation indexes, such as the Social Science Citation Index, have the direct, easy search by words in titles, authors, and the like. Beyond that, the more important search is for cited references. Here one can find, at a moment, how many times an author or a paper has been cited. One goes to the more advanced menu, selects "citation," and then the user types in the author's last name. This opens up a dictionary window with a list of these names, and initials. The user finds the name, moves the cursor, and then goes through a variety of steps—clearly explained by the publisher—which will give the needed number of citations.[6]

Differences on a Theme

There are numerous broad differences in searching, particularly when one switches from one type of database to another. For example, consider:

1. *Searching Mosaic/Web on Internet.* The appeal of Mosaic, and similar software, is that one simply clicks words or images on a computer screen to call up text, sound, image, or all. In a Web document there are three pieces of information which are part of that document: (*a*) the address of the place where the information is located, that is, the server; (*b*) the address of the particular document on that server; (*c*) the protocol, that is, the language the host computer must use to retrieve the document. One clicks the desired highlighted word or phrase. The server finds the document and sends it to the user. Displayed on the screen, the document may indicate other information available from pictures to sound. Depending on the MHz (megahertz) power modem and other hardware, the message(s) may arrive in seconds, or the user may have to wait for minutes, even longer. Sometimes the channel is so overloaded that the reaction time may take an hour or more, if at all.

2. *Multimedia CD-ROMs.* Searching a multimedia CD-ROM varies with the software, but basically most follow a pattern. If the disc is an encyclopedia or a keyboard, a mouse allows the user to interact with what you put on the screen. Among the options offered for fairy tales is "themes." Click this on and

---

[6]For detailed information on searching ISI citation indexes, see Martin Courtois and Judith Matthew, "Tips for Searching . . . ," *Database*, June 1993, pp. 60–65.

a list of related themes in the encyclopedia comes up. Click "ogres" and a list of stories in which an ogre is a hero appears as well as, with another click, an animated cartoon of a rhyme complete with music and voice. If the user now types in a brief note on country or language gained from another text, the user has added to the database. Activities change the multimedia text in two ways: The user makes additions and if she or he saves the data of the earlier search she has created an individual record. The encyclopedia text has not been altered, but a new record has been produced.

User Searching

Where a simplified menu approach is used, few users have any great difficulty. True, they have to be introduced to the computer, but beyond a basic short lesson, the system is simplicity itself. Or is it? Where a straightforward search for a few citations is required, yes. Once the search gets complicated, once a decision has to be made about just how many indexes to search (manually, online, or on CD-ROM), then the librarian is a welcome guide.

When CD-ROM is employed and time is not a factor, the client may flounder about and experiment until some type of answer is reached. This is particularly true where the layperson is operating the system without help from the librarian. When the user turns to the online search, every moment (or search) is costly and inevitably the librarian is involved. There may be exceptions where, for example, the searcher is as qualified at the computer as in the subject area. This is rare.

Misunderstanding is likely to happen in the best of situations. For example, even when the computer keyboard employed for the local catalog is clearly marked, a user may try desperately to find an article in a magazine or, vice versa, employ a CD-ROM to find *Tarzan of the Apes* in the library. At this point the librarian is called in to help, often after a great waste of time and effort on the part of the confident layperson searcher.

Pressed for time, the average reference librarian can do little more than give basic instruction on how to mine information from an electronic database. Usually, too, the librarian is there to answer specific problems—whether it be how to sign off and get to another database or clear the paper from the printer. Beyond that the user may well believe that the successful capture of four or five citations more than meets the need. Well, yes and no. For the average high school or college student where experience is more important than relevancy, the casual hands-on approach is probably good enough. Granted, it could be much better with help from the librarian, with, indeed, the librarian doing the search. Beyond the semester paper, beyond instruction on basic electronic database searching, the average student is served, if not well.

In matters of research, from material for a master's thesis to review of welfare problems in X or Y community, the individual's search is not enough. More is required. Much more, and it is here that only an experienced searcher and experienced reference librarian will do. The problem is that average individuals looking for this in-depth information will possibly have the false idea that they can get it for themselves. Why? They have had hands-on experience as students, and that seemed to go well enough. The pity is that the users are too frequently misled into believing all electronic databases are alike and easy to use.

Helpful Search Features

Despite the lack of standardization of databases and software, there are certain common features, at least for most. These include:

1. *Function keys.* Almost all systems allow the user to press a function key on the PC keyboard which will serve as a command. For example, "F8" may mean print out, or start a new search, or change files, or . . . well, it depends on the system. In some, one presses "alt," that is, all fields, and when the fields appear presses the proper key for title, author, and the like. What is badly needed is a standardization of the function keys. This is particularly obvious to anyone who searched one system with the help of such keys and then turned to another where "F8" now is a command for changing the file rather than modifying a search.

2. *Find.* Most database searches use the FIND command to find key words, subject headings, a combination of sets, add restrictions, and the like. After that is a DISPLAY list which gives an abbreviated list of citations, usually in chronological order, with author, title, and date of publication. Where this order, or another, is not used many programs allow for the use of a SORT command which sorts the citations by date and name of author. One may limit the search by specifying book, periodical, recording, or other publication type.

3. *Proximity.* Once the desired term (or author) is selected, the user-friendly system allows one to see words in the neighborhood of the primary term (author). The person can then move up or down, or select, usually by number, one of the terms. Where a new term is desired this is typed in and, where needed, the neighborhood of other terms in the dictionary is shown again.

4. *Special features.* Almost every electronic database offers special features for searching. These help short-circuit often repeated cycles. For example, NEXIS has the "focus" feature. This offers a shortcut for modifying the search, which explores different aspects of related topics and limits key word searches to titles and topics. In reverse, one may broaden the key word search to every phrase in the full text.

5. *Help.* All systems have a help command. At a point where there is confusion, one presses the help function key and text will appear on the screen. Options for getting in-depth advice about a given situation are usual. The help may be extremely basic or relatively complete and complex. It all depends, once again, on the system employed.

Often more helpful, particularly for difficult situations, is the ability to phone an 800 number for direct advice from a skilled individual rather than from a machine. All good services offer this type of assistance, particularly online.

EXPERT SEARCHING

A successful search requires precision, timeliness, and, most important, relevancy. Only a trained searcher will attain these qualities and goals. Even though the principle of the search is getting easier, the actual search is growing more complex. This is so because of the increasing number of choices. Where once the searcher could choose among only a handful of databases, now selection can be made from among hundreds. And along with the multiplicity of choices, there is an equal confusion of commands. Each database, or group of databases, tends to have separate searching patterns that must be mastered.

Even when one is familiar with the process of searching, there are numerous factors involved. One must get connected to the system in order to be able to search the material. One must be able to master commands in order to draw out what is needed. Finally, one must have an appreciation of what can and cannot be found in a given database. And so on.

It may be true that many of the same problems exist in a manual search. The essential difference is that one is dealing with traditional books and periodicals, not with an unfamiliar, some would say "unfriendly," machine.

In searching electronic databases many of the same rules for searching print sources are in place. This is particularly true for necessary preliminary steps:

1. Be sure the question is understood. For online searches it is a common practice to have the user write down the specific question, often with key words and subject areas. Similar advice may be given the individual using a CD-ROM.

2. Know which database to use and the form that is needed. Subject content comes first. After that, consider if the user is going to do the search. If so, then use a CD-ROM (where possible) to allow the user the time and experience needed. If not, and if the CD-ROM format does not cover what is needed, an expert librarian can search the databases more efficiently.

Expert Searching

Both the expert and beginner will use menus and other simple searching patterns, but turning now to the professional reference librarian, consider other possible, more difficult, yet satisfying routes.

Expert searching, while it follows many of the steps familiar to beginners, differs in an important respect. Usually the experienced searcher skips over the novice menus and suggestions and goes to the sophisticated search pattern. The result is a fast, relatively inexpensive, and exact search.[7]

Since so many databases have so many peculiar approaches, the wise searcher follows several rules: (1) Commands will be second nature for the "basic" online databases which may be used daily. This may be from 5 to 10 sources, but usually no more. (2) The searcher will know how to limit and expand results in a particular database. (3) Familiarity with subject headings and particularly the thesaurus employed by the database will result in more precise hits than simply using key words. At any rate, a command of synonyms is imperative. (4) Use the particular features offered by a vendor-publisher-distributor.[8]

Success or failure of an expert search depends on two primary factors: the software and the skill of the searcher. "Good online searching is not a trick. . . . It is a more complex process that benefits from interaction, intuition, and an understanding of how the computer is processing the information."[9]

Documentation. Any good online or CD-ROM system will include instructions, or documentation, in the form of a manual. One might argue that ideally no such manuals should be necessary since the system explains itself through a series of menus, automatic actions and reactions, and useful "help" signals when needed. Or, again ideally, the search is simple enough to be summarized in a half page or so. To date none of this is possible, and therefore the manual is required.

Actually, of course, most laypersons simply follow the menu on the screen or rely on a flip chart rendering of search commands. Few have the patience to search a manual. On the other hand, few librarians will rely on basic instructions when much more sophisticated and, in the end, simpler and more accurate searches may be performed with a thorough knowledge of the system's operational patterns.

Modifying the Search. Normally there are three basic search modifications: (1) There is too much material. (2) There are too few citations. (3) Related data are required, which means entering more search terms. A fourth possibility is that the search topic was wrong. The results are so far off that the search must

---

[7]For a detailed explanation of these and other steps, see Carol Tenopir, "Eight Tips for Cost-Effective Searching," *Library Journal*, October 1, 1992, pp. 65–66. The steps illustrate the problem with giving detailed information on searching—several of them have been superseded by searching advances and changes in software. Still, the basics are sound.

[8]For example, see Donna Dolan, "Crossing Database Lines: DataStar's CROS Feature," *Online*, March 1993, pp. 56–59.

[9]Carol Tenopir, "Overcoming the Black Box Syndrome," *Library Journal*, June 1, 1994, p. 38.

be recharted. Beyond that, trouble arises because the wrong commands were given and . . . well, almost anything can happen until the librarian is familiar with the database's eccentric approaches to information.

There are two basic reactions to the need to modify. The beginner or amateur wipes the screen clear and simply begins again by entering new words, new commands. The expert librarian calls up the various search commands, from connection search terms and words to changing levels of search, by using the system's usually unique set of orders.

Boolean Logic. The magic key to limiting or expanding computer-assisted search is boolean logic. This is just another way of saying one can search for a key word and then expand or limit the search. Boolean logic is named after George Boole (1815–1864), who used three operators (plus, times, and minus) for combinations of logical statements. Essentially, it is a method of combining terms in searches, particularly since very few searches are begun using only a single term.

Boolean logic often appears to be more complicated than it actually is. Put in elementary terms:

1. The operator "OR" (A or B). The use of the disjunctive "or" is simply a way of asking for more and more material. In common speech, one is more likely to use "and"; for example, "I want material on science courses and science instruction and science units." But in a search this is translated into "science-courses *or* science-instruction *or* science-units." Actually the user wants any article containing any one of the terms, and so the "OR" operator is employed.

2. The operator "AND" (A and B). The "OR" alone tends to be too inclusive for most searches, so the librarian is likely to resort to the "AND" operator which restricts searches, causing retrieval only of documents containing the specified terms tied to each other and "AND." In the search for science materials it would now be documents with "science-courses *and* science-instruction *and* science-units," that is, a document would have to contain all these words or descriptors to be retrieved. The use of the logical conjunctive "AND" will narrow and clarify the search.

3. The operator "NOT" (A and not B) or (A–B). A third boolean connector is "NOT" where it is noted that a term must *not* appear anywhere in the document. Here one would say, "Give me college and library, but *not* college library circulation." The terms are limited even further. The computer is asked to locate only "college libraries," not "junior college libraries."

The obvious problem with boolean logic is that it employs concepts which seem to contradict ordinary English. AND normally means you want more, that is, "I'll take one orange *and* an apple and a grape." But in boolean logic it means less. OR normally signifies "I'll take this *or* that," but in boolean logic it means you will take both this and that.

A major test of the worth of any database or system is whether or not it allows boolean searching. All too often this is not the case with CD-ROMs. Here one is limited to key words and subjects, but without the benefits of expansion or limitation, at least in a simple, direct fashion.

This explains why it is often said that laypersons prefer the lack of complications in searching on CD-ROM. They are happy when there are only a few steps that are explained through a menu system. The problem, of course, is that they rarely get all they might from the CD-ROM database, or they get less-than-precise information.

Search Aids after Boolean

Until the mid-1990s the primary method, in fact the only method for sophisticated searching, was by use of boolean logic. Boolean was the accepted approach to almost all searches on all systems. This changed as the need for easier approaches to gathering information became apparent. And while boolean will likely remain the preferred method for sophisticated, difficult online searches, there are creditable alternatives online. For example: (1) *Congressional Quarterly's* use of the Personal Librarian's Search Engine. (2) DIALOG's Target. (3) Mead's Free Style. (4) WESTLAW's WIN.

These search aids provide relevance. Enter one word or a string of words and the software searches the database(s) for how many times the word(s) appears in a document, as well as the document's length. The citations are then displayed in order of relevance—normally about 25 to 50 items. An example of this is DIALOG's Target. As an advertisement points out: "You don't enter search terms in the traditional boolean . . . format. Simply choose your database and enter Target followed by one or more key search terms. You'll get a list of up to fifty high quality hits, ranked by the number of times your search term appears. The best sources rise to the top. The bull gets cut."[10] The ad claims that this will cut search time and cost. A similar system, with different commands, is offered by Mead Data Central as Free Style and can be used in searching NEXIS.

This may appear easy enough, but there are numerous "catches" to the beginner. The major one is the "false drop," that is, the turning up of numerous irrelevant and useless citations. "In a statistical system, hard-to-pinpoint false drops are likely to occur if the system doesn't match for common phrases. For example, if a searcher inputs *New York, Compton's MultiMedia Encyclopedia* and WESTLAW's WIN will recognize that as a phrase. DIALOG's will treat each term independently (unless the searcher explicitly enters the phrase with quotes

---

[10]*Library Journal,* June 1, 1994, pp. 8–9.

"New York") and find some articles that only have "new" and others that only have "york."[11]

Search Problems. Depending on the database and software, a major stumbling block for a sophisticated search is the numerous rules and requirements for entering search queries. Typically, for example, each system (or group of databases from a given vendor or publisher) will have particular rules for spacing of words, use of parentheses, and periods and commas. Compound words and phrases, segments, order of commands, keystrokes, limiting searches, are other elements that tend to differ from database to database.

The software includes or does not include certain features and components. For example, one software program may offer searching by years, by languages, or by ISSN numbers. Another may have only one, or none, of these. In another the file is arranged chronologically. Fields (from author and title to source) are available, but in what order? Are there enough access points, or (sometimes) too many for the beginner or the expert?

Other examples: The searcher in quest of a personal name is faced with a variety of search patterns, depending on the software. What command do you give when there is more than one spelling for a name, or you don't know the precise spelling? (Usually it is "thoms OR toms") but the command may be different, right down to spacing. Does the first or last name come first? How do you distinguish *the* John Smith from 100 other John Smiths? (Usually the command allows you to give the name with a modifier such as birthday, date of death, profession, etc.) One common way around this confusion is to call up the dictionary list of names in the file and select the wanted name(s).

The examples of what many consider anarchy in searching software, have several rays of hope. First and foremost, a given vendor tends to use the same search software for almost all databases. Consequently without even examining a new SilverPlatter release (i.e., a CD-ROM) the user knows it will have the same search pattern. This is generally true for the other electronic database vendors.[12]

The challenge of competition from online consumer systems—from CompuServe to Prodigy—has forced the traditional online systems such as DIALOG to simplify searching patterns. Now, and in the future, these large systems will work toward ease of use by not only librarians, but also laypersons. Windows,

---

[11]Tenopir, loc. cit.

[12]Carole Schildhauer, "The Ten Commandments of Quick and Dirty Online Searching (on DIALOG), *Library Journal*, October 1, 1992, p. 65. In 7 of her 10 commands the author of the brief, 150-word listing stresses the necessity of knowing the quirks of a given database or vendor's systems. If nothing else, the rules point out the need for standardization, expert searching, and individual, experienced search style. Little of this is of interest to the layperson who simply wants an answer; but it is of considerable help to the would-be professional searcher. In the same space (i.e., pp. 65–66), see Carol Tenopir's related essay, "Eight Tips for Cost-Effective Searching," for online searching.

for example, will become part of DIALOG. Furthermore, rates for the large vendors will be lowered to compete with the home services.

Full-Text Searches

Most databases permit the user to search the full text of the abstract or, in some cases, the full article. Here one must understand the difference between a *controlled vocabulary* search and a *free-text* search. A controlled vocabulary exists where subject headings, or descriptors, are assigned. In a manual search, if one wants to know what subjects have been used, a list of subject headings, such as the ones published by the Library of Congress or Sears, is consulted.

Matters are somewhat different for the computer search. While Library of Congress subject headings may be consulted, the searcher is more likely to depend upon a thesaurus. Many of the databases, although not all, have their own specialized thesaurus. Here the field of possible terms is more limited than in the Library of Congress lists, certainly more specialized, and less likely to depend upon numerous synonyms.

The advantage of a controlled vocabulary is that the user may immediately check the subject headings used by the indexer. For example, if someone wants material on the aged and insomnia, she or he turns to a list of subject headings or to a thesaurus and finds that X database uses the term "elderly" for the aged; "geriatrics" is a related term, and "sleep disturbance" is used along with insomnia.

The free-text approach may be more scattered and less precise, but it does have such advantages as being able to locate terms—new expressions and descriptors—not yet in the indexer's vocabulary. Command of a broader group of terms, in turn, may lead to more articles and less reliance on the skill of an indexer.

Useful as a free-text search may prove, the best type of database is one that offers both a free-text and a controlled-vocabulary approach. A database constructed without any editing or intellectual effort at input (i.e., without controlled vocabulary) requires considerable expertise on searching—it becomes more an art than a science.

While free-text searching is common online, it is not so usual with CD-ROM systems. Few allow this subtle type of search, at least where the quest is for key words in more than a title or an abstract. Few allow the user to delve into the full text of the article. Again, this is an argument for using online systems, especially when in-depth searching is required.

Since every word in the language is a potential search term, one of the most common mistakes made by new searchers who are not librarians is to rely completely on free-text, natural-language search strategies. Oddly enough, the trained librarian goes the other way and tends to rely too much on controlled vocabulary.

In the real search there is no specific way to know (other than through experience) which method is best. Where there is a choice, it is usually wise to use a combination of controlled vocabulary and free-text searching.

Even the best computer searches are subject to some of the same problems associated with a manual search. The greatest difficulty is with catchy headlines and jargon which disguise what is needed. For example, someone looking for material on Exxon in *The Wall Street Journal* chooses to search headlines. This is usually a fast and efficient approach. Not always, though. Material on Exxon is entirely missed when the headline reads "Rogue Knocks over the Big Boys," a piece on the oil company without any reference to its name in the headline. The solution is to search for the company name in the text.

Correct spelling is another difficulty. One may search without any luck for material on "Ragan" instead of the proper spelling, Reagan; or fail to find material on the drug company Hoffmann-LaRoche, Inc., because the entry is simply Hoffman LaRoche, without the hyphen.

Expert Search Devices

Experienced searchers have individual approaches, but most agree there are several devices that speed the search and cut costs. While they follow the steps just outlined, they may do it in an abbreviated fashion.

At this point searchers turn to the computer for what is known as a "quick and dirty search." Let Robert Wagers go on from here:

1. Compose a "quick and dirty" search with a few terms, the logical operators and no more than one adjacency operator. This "briefsearch" format has been useful for intermediaries and offers the advantage of using a small number of terms and operators. It is important that the user-searcher understand that this is a *trial* search. He is to use the information he finds to modify this search effectively.

2. Display results in a trial format for evaluation. Most database systems offer a format which provides some evaluative information (titles, lead paragraphs, index terms). Users should be instructed about using this information to determine how well they are doing, and they should also be taught how to modify their searches.

3. Modify the search with one or two simple changes. I would limit the modifications to the following: adding terms to represent a concept, using another form of the terms for a concept (index phrases), or eliminating or intersecting a concept. Other changes may be necessary, but these three should be enough for the user to handle initially.

4. Print final results in a format containing all the necessary fields.[13]

[13]Robert Wagers, "Can Easy Searching Be Good Searching?" *Online*, May 1988, p. 79. Several years on and the advice remains sound.

Search Evaluation

There are many ways to evaluate the effectiveness of a computer search, not the least of which is the satisfaction of the user. In the early days a measure of satisfaction involved the focus on cost and how efficient the search was in terms of getting the maximum results for the fewest dollars. This remains a factor, particularly in terms of the abilities of the search analyst and the measurement of that person's skills. Other evaluative points include:

1. For the most part, the more citations, the more likely the search is to be a success. The catch is that one can simply give the user nearly everything on the subject which would introduce a swamp into the proceedings.

2. Librarians who spend more time in an interview and in preparing a search statement do better than those who are sloppy about such standard procedures.

3. The more manuals, guides, and so on, at hand, usually the better the search.

4. Practice makes perfect, that is, the more hours searched, the better the searcher.

5. Librarians who do searching in a separate location away from the reference desk do higher-quality searches.

FUTURE SEARCHING PATTERNS

Ultimately the computer search will be done verbally, without use of keyboard, menus, icons, or whatever. By the mid-1990s there were several tentative steps in that direction. WESTLAW's LawTALK and WESTLAW's WIN allow the user to carry on an entire search of legal materials without touching the keyboard. Training takes place when the user acquaints the computer with his or her voice by reading *Alice in Wonderland*. Where the voice command is not understood or more is needed the screen displays a menu of choices. An impressive added feature—by simply saying "Go to Word Perfect" the computer is set up to take a letter or other document.

Logical searching is done within the software after the natural-language command is entered. The result is a listing of relevant documents in which the user is most likely to find what is needed. The system cancels unimportant words such as "Search out data on medical malpractices" "search out data" and "on" would be canceled and the system would seek out how many times medical malpractice appeared. Beyond that it is up to the individual to decide what, specifically, is required among the first 20 or up to 100 citations; and, more important, be able to formulate a clear, unambiguous question with as few extraneous words as possible. The system works well because it covers a small field (i.e., law) which has its own easily recognized terminology. So-called plain English in a wider subject area has yet to be tested for a given search system.

In 1995 the competitor, NEXIS/LEXIS, offered a similar service for LEXIS, the law database.

Working toward the ultimate user's delight, IBM and Compton's New Media by 1995 were developing speech commands for searching CD-ROMs. A user may say, for example, "Show me everything on the American Civil War." Speech-recognition patterns having been established for that voice, the screen gives up the appropriate information furnished by keys or by clicking a mouse. In time, users may not only search, but also dictate notes about their research into the computer for ultimate printout as a finished report.

The notion that "electronic robots" or "intelligent software agents" will match question with source(s) and, in some minds, go the next step and indicate which is or is not relevant for finer points of the query, is highly desirable. Experience indicates what is desired may not be immediately possible, particularly if costs are factored into the dream of a mechanical reference robot. Be that as it may, it is certain that the basics of matching question and source will be worked out electronically. Equally, it is certain a reference librarian with more skills will need to be on call to refine the search and, more important, to help when the computer fails.

SUGGESTED READING

Jeng, Ling Hwey, et al., "Designing and Managing Online Searching Instruction," *Journal of Education for Library and Information Science*, Fall 1994, pp. 337–340. A poll of teachers shows the various methods and approaches to teaching online searching. Along the way the results indicate "online searching is not merely an extension of reference activities."

Kim Park, Taemin, "The Nature of Relevance in Information Retrieval . . . ," *Library Quarterly*, 1993, no. 3, pp. 318–351. Just what is "relevance"? The author offers a model which reflects the "nature of the thought processes of users who are evaluating bibliographic citations." The user's satisfaction with relevance depends on numerous factors, other than objectivity.

Lancaster, F. W., et al., "Searching Databases on CD-ROM . . . ," *RQ*, Spring 1994, pp. 370–385. The subtitle explains the purpose of this study—"A Comparison of the Results of End-User Searching with Results from Two Modes of Searching by Skilled Intermediaries." The results are predictable. "The users . . . found only about a third of the really important items."

Marchionini, Gary, *Information Seeking in Electronic Environments*. New York: Cambridge University Press, 1995. Here is a lucid, considered text on the theory and practice of searching for information at a computer. The University of Maryland professor has a thorough knowledge of both the problem of and the potential solution to computer searches. Particularly useful for the numerous suggested strategies and the intellectual approach to gathering information. Highly recommended for both beginners and would-be experts.

Michel, Dee Andy, "What Is Used during Cognitive Processing in Information Retrieval and Library Searching? Eleven Sources of Search Information," *Journal of the American Society for Information Science*, August 1994, pp. 498–514. This is a technical article reporting on an effort to explain the ins and outs of searching. The examples and suggestions are useful for the more advanced student.

Norris, Carol, and Mark Ellis, "End-Users and Database Searching," *Library Hi Tech*, 1990, vol. 5, pp. 95–104. This is a "selected annotated bibliography" on the subject of variations on searching. While the focus is the end-user, much of the material is applicable to various other aspects of computer searching. It is *not* dated.

Schamber, Linda, et al., "A Re-examination of Relevance . . . ," *Information Processing and Management*, 1990, no. 26, pp. 755–776. Another view of what constitutes relevance for a particular group. The authors offer a "dynamic, situational definition" which is hardly applicable for all situations, but at least sets up a methodology.

Secrets of the Super Searchers. Wilton, CT: Online Inc., 1994. "The accumulated wisdom of 23 of the world's top online searchers" is found within this collection. Topics cover everything from the reference interview and finding the right databases to the strategy of the search itself. A useful guide, particularly for those with a bit of experience in searching.

Sullivan, Michael, et al., "End-Users, Mediated Searches, and Front End Assistance Programs on DIALOG . . . ," *Journal of the American Society for Information Science*, January 1990, pp. 27–42. In a controlled study the author found that laypersons making their own online searches did as well as librarians, as least after some training. The training was on either a menu system or a native command system. The searchers were doctoral students, able and willing to search on their own, as well as afford the effort. There is considerable detail about differences between the end-user groups and the mediated controls.

Walker, Geraldine, *Online Retrieval*. Englewood, CO: Libraries Unlimited, 1993. A lucid and intelligent guide for beginning searchers online. In addition to the basic "how-to-do-it" material, the text is laced with theory and queries to challenge accepted notions of searching.

Zimmerman, Donald, and Michael Muraski, *The Elements of Information Gathering*. Phoenix, AZ: Oryx Press, 1994. The subtitle narrows the manual, *A Guide for Technical Communicators, Scientists, and Engineers*. The first section on strategies for starting an information search is of value to anyone, as is the second section on how to organize the material of the search. The third and fourth sections are more technical and for the specific audience noted in the subtitle.

PART IV
INSTRUCTION AND
POLICIES

CHAPTER NINE
BIBLIOGRAPHICAL INSTRUCTION[1]

A reference librarian finds happiness in the pursuit of an answer. Most laypersons are unhappy because under the barrage of data they make wrong choices. "Even in controlled situations individuals make choices which are persistently and painfully wrong, and which require the intervention of a paternalist figure to correct." This, in turn, implies the average individual "needs to be able to trust the social networks in which we are embedded."[2]

Given the hypothesis that most people make incorrect choices, for almost as many reasons as there are individuals, it seems only rational that the librarian intervene and attempt to help make the correct decisions concerning everything from the proper article or book to the appropriate CD-ROM to search for a paper on economics, choice, and happiness. The reference librarian hopes to ensure choices that are more often than not the correct choices.

In an ideal library there would be a librarian to answer any query. In particular, the question that requires assistance in interpreting and deciding what is an appropriate, complete, and accurate response needs a mediator. Usually a librarian is *not* available to mediate. Therefore, two primary avenues are open: (1) Hire more reference librarians by cutting back on hours and other services. This is rarely acceptable. (2) Lacking librarians, give the hapless user enough instruction in the use of the library to at least better the odds that he or she will

---

[1]In addition to the term "bibliographical instruction" or BI, other descriptors are found in the literature. Among these: "user education," "library instruction," "educating users." "Computer instruction," "CD-ROM and online instruction," and so forth have been added as part of the descriptor of service in many libraries.

[2]"Choice Does Not Pave the Road to Happiness," *Guardian Weekly*, November 14, 1993, p. 21.

make the right choices. This second avenue is the rationale for much biblio-graphical instruction.

Most users, it can be argued from experience and observation, wander in and out of a library and rarely need assistance. Given a notion, for example, where the periodicals are located, or where to find biographies they will do fine on their own with or without a catalog or, for that matter, a librarian. Most are capable of making at least an elementary search at a CD-ROM terminal, just as they are able to search for basic materials in any printed general index, such as *The Readers' Guide to Periodical Literature*. The majority of people require only a minimum of help because they need only a minimum of information.

Librarian as Technician

The real, all too often unexamined, argument is that most people need a min-imal amount of information *only* because this is all they expect. Having learned that they must dig out their own answers, they have little reason to address a li-brarian. Would more data be useful? Would a librarian's assistance be helpful? Probably yes, but because of economic restraints and some librarians' attitudes about service, few libraries test the information waters with a user.

Much of this is going to change in favor of more service for the client. As electronic retrieval becomes widespread, as searching becomes more sophisti-cated, as greater amounts of data become available, more help will be required by the layperson from the librarian. Both as a technologist, who understands hardware and software, and as an information expert, the librarian will become increasingly necessary.

Once the client understands that he or she can turn to the librarian for explanation of everything from the best software, say, for a home computer to the best article from a popular magazine the librarian will fulfill a necessary role in a community which too often tends to dismiss librarians as clerks.

Technicians, particularly in America, are honored. By choice or by shove, librarians working with computers have become those honored technicians. This same group, by the way, rarely spends much time teaching. They help and solve problems.

Service and Education

Bibliographical instruction is incompatible with the concept of helping and solv-ing problems for the individual. The reference librarian can do one or the other, at least consistently, but not both. To attempt to give answers to questions, to solve computer problems while insisting on teaching the user to solve his or her own information and technical problems, is to confuse the client. Furthermore, it ultimately defeats the role of the library as an information resource.

Granted, school libraries and some parts of public library service may have bibliographical instruction built into their programs, and granted, both may be accomplishing an educational service (although that is debatable), "Adult patrons are not in the public library to be educated, unless they tell you specifically that is why they are there. They are usually there to be served . . . and pointing them in the general direction of a stack section . . . is not reference work."[3]

There are the two basic arguments. One group, and by and large the most vocal, favors bibliographical instruction. They argue that it is a necessity, and is important to the overall education of the individual (particularly in school and academic libraries). They follow a historical tradition that goes back to the nineteenth century.[4] Librarian as educator is, simply put, a key part of being a professional librarian.

The other group, including this author, opposes formalized instruction, but certainly agrees that it should be given *if asked.* Opposition is based on the familiar argument that you cannot even begin to teach someone enough to make correct decisions about complex information sources, much less every changing technological information advance.

Information mediation is a highly skilled profession, and one that takes much education and more experience to master. It cannot be taught to an indifferent student or a layperson who has an extra 5 or 10 minutes while wandering around the library. Nor can it be mastered even when there are formal courses for laypersons on the use of the library and its resources. It is as foolish as it is unfair to laypersons to believe one may elucidate, explain, and otherwise teach a skill of such depth and importance in a matter of minutes or over a few single credit course hours. To think this can be done is to deny the profession. It is to substantially cheat the individual who walks away firm in the knowledge that he or she knows the library and its resources.

False Battle Lines

There is no need to draw a battle line between those who advocate bibliographical instruction and those who say it is impossible, and not even advisable. No matter what a librarian may believe theoretically, action is dictated as much

[3]Herbert White, "The Reference Librarian as Information Intermediary," *The Reference Librarian,* 1992, no. 37, p. 26.

[4]Bibliographical instruction became an important part of public library service in nineteenth-century America. Librarians considered it necessary for people seeking self-education. The role of teaching dominated the library profession from the early public libraries well into the period after the Second World War. It continues to this day with no lack of enthusiasm. For an excellent, relatively short summary of the history of bibliographical instruction (along with an impressive bibliography), see Mary F. Salony, "The History of Bibliographic Instruction," *The Reference Librarian,* 1995, no. 50/51.

by the librarian's personality, willingness to help (or not to help), and a conviction that every situation is different.

If it appears that a patron might benefit from instruction, then it should be given. If not, normally it is simpler to find the answer for that individual. For example, a bright student with a need for background reading on the common cold, may appreciate a brief lesson on how to use the *Readers' Guide* or the *Index Medicus*, probably on CD-ROMs. One with less interest or less apparent concern about sources may prefer simply to be given a popular magazine piece or an encyclopedia article. Questions prompt different responses. Few librarians are likely to launch a lesson on the use of the *World Almanac* when they can quickly find the answer to how many Americans go to college by referring to the *Almanac*. Ready-reference questions usually do not require bibliographical instruction.

Much, too, depends on the type of library. Academic and school libraries put considerable emphasis on bibliographical instruction. They see it as part of the broader education of the student. Public libraries give little time to instruction because few laypersons really want to be told how to use an index. The exception is the teaching of how to search at a terminal using CD-ROM or online. This requires basic understanding of technology and search patterns. With more CD-ROMs in public libraries, the role of bibliographical instruction has taken on an added dimension. The librarian should be as familiar with the technology as with the electronic databases themselves. Ideally, the librarian should be able to help and advise on hardware and software—both in the library and at the user's home.

In the course of a day the reference librarian will answer questions about where this or that is located, or how to use this or that index, or explain the process of digging out this or that piece of information. No working reference librarian is against helping the patron master basic library procedures. Knowledge of how to use the catalog and how to search a CD-ROM index is useful for those who are interested. This type of help (or call it instruction) is as much a part of being a professional librarian as a doctor's explanation of a test to a patient, a mechanic's display of a damaged part and how it was replaced, or the carpenter's reassurance about need while adding up a bill. Conversely, doctors, mechanics, and carpenters are not compelled to teach the layperson their professions or trades.

There is much to be said for allowing the user, no matter what age or position, to determine whether (1) information is wanted, or (2) instructions are wanted, or (3) a combination of both is desirable.

Instruction Benefits

Anyone who wanders into a library for the first time realizes whether it is "user friendly," "detached," or "hostile." Librarians claim the first descriptor, while students often turn to the last two. There are as many reasons for these attitudes as libraries and librarians. A basic one is misunderstanding about the goals of the library. The historical, theoretical purpose is known to everyone; but the average individual with individual needs is more concerned with how easy it will be to find X or Y book, an article, or, these days, a computer terminal. At this point a friendly face, a gentle smile, an appearance of authority can ease the situation and can, indeed, turn what was until that moment a hostile place into a friendly spot.

Bibliographical instruction, it might be argued, is offered to persuade the individual that the library is there to help. Assistance will be given gracefully with an appreciation for particular needs. Even the most vocal foe of instruction will agree on the necessity of making the library hospitable.

BASIC APPROACHES

Where bibliographical instruction is employed, there are several approaches. Most instruction is turned toward explaining a different library resource, usually with the catalog coming first, followed by exercise on how to find and read citations and abstracts from CD-ROM or print indexes. The usual next step is to familiarize the user with much-used reference sources. This may be little more than to point out where they are found in the library or they may be rather extensive exercises in searching.

Instruction in CD-ROMs, Internet, and online searches and the like offers new challenges. Whereas it is a given that younger people are comfortable at a computer terminal, this is hardly proven. Actually, the computer terminal in the library is often different from the game-playing laptop at home. Sometimes involved searching patterns (even with simplified menus) will dismay the otherwise confident child of the computer age. He or she may be just as put out as older brothers and sisters who had to master the use of print indexes. Incidentally, any working reference librarian will testify that from time to time the most sophisticated computer-oriented student will confuse the OPAC and the CD-ROM terminals and look for a given book in ERIC rather than in the library catalog.

Instruction Methods

Libraries have several traditional instruction methods:

Orientation Tours. Certainly the most familiar type of library instruction is the orientation tour of the library. This may or may not be directly involved with reference services, although traditionally a reference librarian is likely to be in charge of such a program.[5]

In academic and school libraries the instruction is established along set patterns. The librarian, at a given time(s) each year, indicates the major points of interest, explains the rules and regulations, and leaves the library groups with the feeling that, when in doubt, one should ask the librarian. This may be supported by audiovisual programs and printed guides. The printed guides, which may be general (i.e., "A Self-Guided Tour of Your Library") or specific (i.e., "Selected Resources of Anthropology") are normally prepared by reference librarians. If the library is large, some type of floor plan or map should be supplied. The presentation should follow a logical sequence, usually along geographical lines from the time the person walks in the front door until he or she walks out.

The public library may have the same type of aids, but usually more modest goals. Instead of giving detailed instructions, there will be simple, easy-to-follow notes about how long a book may be kept out, where the circulation desk is located, and the like. The tours are more likely to be informal and held on a one-to-one basis when someone requests information about the library. Some public libraries work closely with schools, hold planned tours, and do have specific material for elementary and secondary school users.

The obvious problem with the orientation tour is that it tends to be superficial since it is brief, and is therefore often forgotten. Despite the fact that the tour does not seem to provide any lasting educational experience, it accomplishes at least three goals: (1) The tour makes the individual more comfortable in the library. (2) The tour encourages the individual to ask for help. It should at least make the patron realize that the librarian is a cooperative human being. (3) The tour allows the librarian to have some concept of the problems and difficulties faced by those who first enter a library. If used properly, orientation may do much to improve library service, such as placing the reference desk in a better location, putting up directional signs, or making circulation practices a bit easier to understand.

Exercises on the catalog, that is, OPAC (online public access catalog), are common. They range from a handout for the student and a 5 to 10 minute lecture on the catalog to structured small-group activities with specific problems and explanations.

Formal Courses. There is little question that the most effective type of bibliographical instruction is tied to a teaching program. This may be done formally with short courses of a general nature, or in lectures tied to the specific

---

[5]Mary DuMont and Barbara Schloman, "The Evolution and Reaffirmation of a Library Orientation Program in an Academic Research Library," *Reference Services Review,* Spring 1995, pp. 85–93. A candid analysis of a typical library orientation of the library, along with other methods of instruction. The authors conclude, despite some modifications, that "library orientation . . . continues to serve as the foundation of the library's instructional program."

research needs of the would-be historian or social scientist. Depending on the situation, the course or series of lectures may be the jurisdiction of the teacher or the librarian, or a combination of both. Today it tends to be the latter.

Where possible, the formal courses should be required. If not required, two things may happen: (1) Instruction will not reach the very ones who need it the most and are not motivated to use the library. (2) The librarian, often uncertain of the size and interest of the class, may take a less-than-enthusiastic interest in preparation.

The actual structure of the course varies. Guides that give tips on structure and methods are available. Theories of learning are important, at least at the sophisticated level of instruction. There is no shortage of help. Suggestions can be found in any treatise on bibliographical instruction. See, for example, the section on teaching methods and planning in the *Sourcebook for Bibliographic Instruction,* described in the "Suggested Reading" section at the end of this chapter.[6]

ELECTRONIC DATABASES AND INSTRUCTION

Pros and cons of bibliographical instruction have changed in two important ways over the past five to ten years. First, and most important, the introduction of technology, and particularly CD-ROMs, has forced a reevaluation of the process. Second, cultural diversity, with an emphasis on audiences from various backgrounds, has raised the pedagogical imperative that such instruction is necessary. This seems particularly true in the academic setting where parts of a pluralistic student body desperately need assistance.

Cultures from many different parts of the world, as well as sections of the United States, do find one thing in common. They are familiar with the notion of electronic databases, if not always on how they operate. This gives the instructor a bit of common ground for all students.

Written guidelines should be debated, drawn up, and approved by reference staff concerning computer and electronic database instruction. "In addition to prioritizing certain products and patrons, consideration should also be given as to whether discs duplicate printed materials or locally mounted databases, and on which terminals the software should be loaded. Here as well, policy on CD-ROM instruction could be spelled out." Also "written guidelines are useless unless a reference interview reveals the scope and depth of a student's assignment. Librarians must be sure that such a search is appropriate before

---

[6]There are countless articles on the subject of learning theories. See, for example, Diane Porak et al., "Teaching Method . . . ," *RQ,* Summer 1994, pp. 484–495. This is a superior overview. Note, too, the references for more reading on the same subject.

agreeing to commit resources. The degree of assistance required by the patron should also be obtained; such assistance may have to be delayed."[7]

Instruction Steps

There are two basic electronic database preinstruction steps:

1. The individual seeking an answer to a question should be "interviewed" (if only in a few words and few seconds of time) concerning his or her needs. Not everyone can or should use the new technologies. The interview will determine whether the individual should then go on to a computer terminal or use other reference materials.

2. At a minimum, anyone who is going to use a CD-ROM or online service should pose three essential questions: Does the individual know which index or source to search? Does the individual understand how to conduct a minimum search? Does the individual understand the results of the search? In the context of failure to receive a satisfactory response to any of these queries, the person should be helped by the librarian.

If interest continues, the librarian should be able to tell the individual that informal or formal courses are available to master the basics of electronic database searching. This presupposes that such instruction is at hand.

Aside from search problems, the librarian should be handy to answer queries about the computer terminal, software, and any other technical aspect in which the user is interested. Normally, this is no more than helping clear a paper jam, negotiating how to print out a citation, or, more likely, explaining how to turn off or on the computer terminal monitor. Rarely, for example, does the librarian explain the technical aspects of a network, or what computer the user might wish to purchase for home use in order to best tap information facilities. Even more unusual is to have someone call from home for assistance in a program that failed, a disc that won't operate properly, and so forth. Granted, this type of information is given by computer centers and by manufacturers, but one suspects it might be better given by the experienced librarian.

Beyond the immediate, the library should offer courses on technology, computers, networks, and so on. These may be formal or informal, but should be available for interested clients. One may argue that this is being done in universities today through computer center staffs, but it is more logical to have the instruction focused in the library. Certainly, too, public and school libraries should offer such courses.

Is Nanny Necessary?

On the other side of the CD-ROM new technologies argument, there is a group that deplores what Michael Gorman dismisses as a "terribly nannyish attitude"

---

[7]Charles R. Hixon, "CD-ROM and the Undergraduate: Reference and Instruction at Risk," *Reference Services Review*, Fall 1993, p. 34.

by reference librarians. The user who wishes to use a CD-ROM should be free to do so. Incomplete or otherwise flawed searches must be determined by the individual, not by the librarian. "As librarians, we should be rejoicing in the fact that technology has brought us systems that are so well received and so heavily used. . . . The best systems are those that can be used by the reasonably intelligent, if uninstructed, user. . . . Many [bibliographical instruction] programs owe the existence and success to the 'user hostile' nature of the systems about which they teach. Replace those systems with others that are truly 'user friendly' and the whole purpose of [instruction] is called into question."[8]

In calling for the dismantling of all bibliographical instruction, Gorman strikes an optimistic note: The library "will be service oriented and will strive to provide the services that users want rather than the services that we believe they ought to want."[9] The catch, of course, is that few people have any idea of what they want or need until they want or need a solution to a current problem.

Fundamental Instruction

Typically, where more than minute-to-minute help is offered, a formalized approach to mastering CD-ROMs (and related technologies) is given in three or four steps. First, there is a lecture and a demonstration. The latter often involves the students as well as the instructor with simple searching problems. Next, there may be visuals, videos, and other suitable methods of demonstrating the search process. Finally, there is the computer tutorial where the individual student, or a group of students, is given hands-on instruction.

Basic instruction and continued reiteration of basics are important. In addition, the teacher must give continued reassurance that the beginner is doing the right thing. "Searchers need continuous motivation to prevent them from quitting."[10] Generally, only time and experience will make the layperson truly comfortable at the terminal. Beyond searching mechanics is the content. Content is more important, at least for the average person, than either the how-to-do-it or theoretical aspects of searching.[11]

There are almost as many CD-ROM instruction exercises as teachers, librarians, and students. For example, at random from several articles: (1) Exercises in boolean logic, with particular emphasis on the use of "and" and "or." Rarely do the searching techniques become more complicated. (2) A sheet on

[8]Michael Gorman, "Send for a Child of Four or Creating the BI-Less Academic Library," *Library Trends*, Winter 1991, p. 355.

[9]Ibid., p. 357.

[10]Carol Tenopir, "The Emotions of Searching," *Library Journal*, September 1, 1994, p. 136. In other words, the librarian must consider the human elements involved with mastering the search. See, too, "For Further Reading" at the end of Tenopir's study.

[11]This approach to CD-ROMs is widely considered in the literature. One of the better articles, which is a summary of teaching methods as well, is Dorothy Davis, "A Comparison of Bibliographic Instruction Methods on CD-ROM Databases," *Research Strategies*, Summer 1993, pp. 156–163.

which the student explains the question and then attempts to outline key words for searching. More advanced groups become familiar with controlled vocabulary, subject headings, and so forth. (3) Search strategies at the computer terminal. All students are given a single question and then asked to deliver the printouts of three to a half dozen "best" citations.

Internet

More libraries, of all types, are offering patrons access to the Internet. In some cases the individual wandering into the library is familiar with the system, but usually a modest amount of instruction is necessary.

Three approaches are favored and none is unique. In the approach used most often the individual is given a hands-on, short course of instruction with the "footnote"—if "you get confused, let me know." After the workplace one-to-one instruction, a short workshop for interested users is most often employed. Beyond that instruction of a longer, more methodical nature is offered. This is rare because of the same old problem of time and lack of teaching skills, particularly for librarians who themselves have difficulties on the Net.

Often the Internet protocols are explained. This may be done through brief courses, lectures, seminars, and the like. The common experience in Net instruction is the necessity of providing more advanced Internet training. These advanced workshops concentrate on locating and searching specific sources.

Still, the most frequent type of instruction is at the terminal itself when the bewildered user turns to the working librarian for an answer to a question. The queries may vary from which key to push, to the meaning of a "Gopher," to a more sophisticated query about a specific search pattern. Younger learners tend to prefer this immediate type of puzzle-solving instruction to the more structured workshops or courses.[12]

INSTRUCTION EVALUATION[13]

After many years of trying to teach people of varying ages and backgrounds how to use the library, the essential question remains unanswered: Has it worked?

---

[12]There are all too few articles on teaching the Internet in the standard bibliographical instruction setting. Some worth considering, often with references: Marcos Silva and Glenn Cartwright, "The Design and Implementation of Internet Seminars," *Education for Information,* June 1993; Pamela McLaughlin, "Embracing the Internet," *Bulletin of the American Society for Information Sciences,* February/March 1994; and, in the same issue, Susan Kendall, "Internet Training." See also Nina Stephenson and Deborah Willis, "Internet In-Service Training . . . ," *The Reference Librarian,* 1994, No. 41/42, p. 217. This offers a good overview of current instructional practices.

[13]See the final chapter of this text for general evaluation suggestions. How to evaluate instruction is of great interest, and much has been written on the subject. See, particularly, *Evaluating Bibliography Instruction* (Chicago: American Library Association, 1983); and the chapter on evaluation in *Sourcebook for Bibliographic Instruction* (Chicago: American Library Association, Association of College and Research Libraries, 1993).

No one knows for sure, as few librarians have had either the time or the knowledge to follow up the instruction with evaluative studies. Efforts to evaluate the effectiveness of library instruction indicate that there is value in the process. Inevitably, success is tied to an academic credit-bearing course on library instruction and not to informally structured encounters between the librarian and the user. Difficulty with evaluation involves lack of time and, to a lesser extent, lack of skill. The result tends to be specific evaluations of narrow areas of instruction and, as often as not, is only a step or two above the anecdotal.[14]

A relatively common attribute of all bibliographical instruction evaluation is anxiety. Understandably, librarians, like most people, are anxious when their work is quantified and qualified. Few librarians are eager to systematically evaluate their effort, although almost all are willing to have suggestions about bits and parts such as the proper hour, the proper place, the topics to cover, and so forth.

Evaluative Methodologies

There is consensus that, aside from the obvious evaluation of the success or failure of instruction, the pattern of the study must consider the type and the depth of materials and skills covered, teaching methods employed, and attitudes of both those giving and receiving the instruction. In an effort to focus instruction, the second edition of *Model Statement of Objectives for Academic Bibliographic Instruction*[15] stresses the need to teach conceptual knowledge about the library, not simply how to read a call number or understand a citation. Put another way, the ultimate end of instruction is that the individual feel comfortable and be able to move from point X or point Y in research to asking a librarian for help when necessary.[16]

How is the librarian (far from being an experienced teacher or educator) going to do what few others can accomplish, that is, measure a student's conceptual understanding? The lack of people addressing the near-impossible problem of measurement indicates its difficulty. Few who support the idea of instruction have any real notion of how to judge whether it works or not.

A time-effort-efficiency study would be of value to answer one recurrent library-patron problem: Is it, indeed, faster and more economical for the librarian to search the needed material online, on a CD-ROM, or in print for the user? Or is it wiser to show the user how to find his or her own information,

[14]For example, see Craig Gibson, "Accountability for BI Programs . . . ," *The Reference Librarian*, 1992, no. 38, pp. 99–108; and Donald Barclay, "Evaluating Library Instruction," *RQ,* Winter 1993, pp. 195–202.

[15]Chicago: American Library Association, Association of College and Research Libraries, 1991.

[16]Frequently, studies find that the majority of people, particularly students, are uncomfortable in a library. If instruction eases this anxiety and response, then few would argue with its value. See, for example, Constance Mellon, "Library Anxiety," *College & Research Libraries*, March 1986, pp. 162–163.

even when this consists of basic instruction in the use of CD-ROM retrieval at a computer terminal? If, for example, 300 people a day have questions that can be answered at a terminal with access to a dozen or so general and specialized online or CD-ROM abstracting and indexing services, would it cost less simply to have librarians at many terminals finding proper responses? In most cases the client would ask the question, leave and return in an hour, a few hours, or a day for the printed responses from the CD-ROM or online source.

Conclusion

No matter what the justification, from philosophy of reference service to lack of staff, laypersons and students will be finding their own answers for years to come. One may argue that the librarian should offer to find the necessary data, and at a minimum serve as a mediator between the data and the user's requirements. This is the goal, but meanwhile the librarian must make do with what is available. Facts conspire against the ideal: (1) Inadequate budgets, limited staff, and new technologies cut back on good service. (2) Given the situation where the user must, at least sometimes, find information, then it is absolutely necessary that some instruction in library use be given—if only a printed map of the shelving arrangement. (3) The new technologies require considerably more: "The growing volume of questions engendered by the availability of CD-ROM products illustrates that most students gladly welcome reference assistance." Without assistance the novice at a computer terminal will "often produce myriad value-zero citations, references that are unavailable, inappropriate, ultimately unreadable, or irrelevant to the student's information needs."[17]

It is hardly a surprise, but the majority of university students have only a vague notion of what to expect from an electronic database search. Most search with little or no understanding of what is involved or how to do the search. And yet, the majority are satisfied with sometimes less than precise results. Result is all. Accuracy seems secondary. This is hardly the type of conclusion any reference librarian would wish for a student's search, no matter how sloppy. The question, as Gorman raised earlier in this chapter, is: "How prevalent and important is this type of search result?" Is the reference librarian a "bothersome nanny" who has too little faith in the ability of students to find what they need without instruction, without direct help from the librarian?[18]

In the best of all possible library and information worlds this type of questioning would not be necessary or even helpful. Unfortunately, today the tech-

---

[17]Hixon, op. cit., p. 32. In quoting several studies, Hixon notes that one out of every three citations found by a student at a terminal is of no use, and 40 percent of students fail to understand the full meaning of the citations. Commonly used library and computer terms mean nothing to laypersons.

[18]Patricia Wallace, "How Do Patrons Search the Online Catalog . . . ?" *RQ,* Winter 1993, pp. 239–252. This is a fascinating study with suggestions on how bibliographical instruction for online searching might be augmented and improved.

nology is far ahead of the average user's needs. Mediation, or so this author believes, is necessary. Without it few people will really find what they specifically require. On the other hand, perhaps instruction will help bring us closer to the best of all possible library information worlds. The jury is out.

SUGGESTED READING

Behrens, S. J., "A Conceptual Analysis and Historical Overview of Information Literacy," *College & Research Libraries*, July 1994, pp. 309–322. An excellent essay on the background and the present and future of bibliographical instruction. Citations are such that the reader can follow the history of the concept. A basic article.

Bessler, Joanne, "Do Library Patrons Know What's Good for Them?" *The Journal of Academic Librarianship*, May 1990, pp. 76–85. The author urges reference librarians to shift their interest from instruction in use of the library to more and better service. Her dim view of bibliographical instruction is commented on by six other librarians. Most seem to agree, if only in part, with her conclusion.

Bodi, Sonia, "Teaching Effectiveness and Bibliographic Instruction," *College & Research Libraries*, March 1990, pp. 113–119. An experienced reference librarian and teacher examines the various approaches to bibliographical instruction. She is primarily involved with improving the process and offers some practical steps that any librarian might follow.

Edwards, Sharri, "Bibliographic Instruction Research," *Research Strategies*, Spring 1994, pp. 68–78. This is a listing and "analysis of the journal literature from 1977 to 1991" on the subject. Emphasis is on teaching research techniques.

Feinman, Valerie, "Bibliographic Instruction," *Computers in Libraries*, January 1993, pp. 63–67. Here the focus is on teaching the use of computers and related technologies. Practical advice for almost any situation.

Fisher, Jean, and Susanne Bjomer, "Enabling Online End-User Searching," *Special Libraries*, 1994, no. 4, pp. 281–291. Librarians often lack the time to instruct users. Most employees are interested in learning online searching since they can use it as an immediate tool. The authors explain how to set up such a training program, as well as how to develop it over time. Contracting out basic teaching is suggested.

Jacobson, Frances, and Michael J. Jacobsen, "Representative Cognitive Learning Theories and BI . . . ," *Research Strategies*, Summer 1993. pp. 124–137. A discussion of how teaching online searching to beginners is a major step forward in bibliographical instruction. Theoretical aspects are given as well.

Jakobovits, Leon, and Diane Jakobovits, "Measuring Information Searching Competence," *College & Research Libraries*, September 1990, pp. 448–461. A technical approach to bibliographical instruction, this raises research issues not often found in articles. Techniques are shown, too, on searching methods. While the style is a bit hard to follow (one of the authors is a professor of psychology and is more familiar with jargon than with library use), the conclusions are valid enough.

Kuhlthau, Carol, *Teaching the Library Research Process,* 2d ed. Metuchen, NJ: Scarecrow Press, 1994. A manual to be used with secondary students, this is a better-than-normal guide for the student on how to use the library. Various activities are suggested to improve the learning process in the typical school media center. Many of the approaches for teaching are as applicable to beginning college students as for those in high school.

Lancaster, F. W., et al., "Searching Databases on CD-ROM," *RQ,* Spring 1994, pp. 370–386. The dean of evaluation reports on a study that compared results by users working alone and then with intermediaries. In one article Lancaster shows evaluative techniques as well as strategies for improving searches by users.

"Library Orientation and Instruction 1990 . . . ," *Reference Services Review*. This is an annual feature in the journal and is an annotated listing of materials dealing with bibliographical instruction. The review has been published since 1974 and is by and large the most valuable bibliography on the subject. Division is by type of library.

Martin, Lynne M., ed., "Library Instruction Revisited: Bibliographic Instruction Comes of Age," *The Reference Librarian*, 1995, no. 50/51. An impressive collection of points of view on bibliographical instruction in the mid-1990s. The contributors present university and college solutions to the difficult problem.

Mood, Terry, "Of Sundials and Digital Watches . . . ," *Reference Services Review*, Fall 1994, pp. 27–32, 95. An elegant plea for the librarian to become a professional and answer questions rather than make a gigantic effort to educate the user in the process. "It is time to replace that model [of bibliographical instruction] with one in which the librarian actually does the search."

Pitkin, Gary M. *The Impact of Emerging Technologies on Reference Service and Bibliographic Instruction*. Westport, CT: Greenwood Press, 1995. About one dozen experts on technology, libraries, reference services, and bibliographical instruction combine forces to look into the future. Their findings indicate that instruction needs a "new paradigm based on the imperative that no faculty member should teach and no student should graduate without being fully information literate." No one will argue with this point. The real point of discussion pivots on how to achieve this goal.

Prorak, Diane, et al., "Teaching Method and Psychological Type in Bibliographic Instruction," *RQ*, Summer 1994, pp. 484–495. Various methods of bibliographical instruction in an academic library setting are used for equally various types of people. Conclusion: "No significant relationship was found between students' scores and teaching method or personality type." But, the teachers prefer small groups because "we did not see any of the small group method students fall asleep during class." The references are current and useful.

Reed, Lawrence, "Locally Loaded Databases . . . ," *RQ*, Winter 1993, pp. 266–273. A discussion of the need for expanding bibliographical instruction to include the new electronic resources. The author examines the students' search skills and the methods of teaching. He suggests a new instruction model for many academic libraries.

Rettig, James, "The Convergence of the Twain or Titanic Collision? BI and Reference in the 1990s Sea of Change," *Reference Services Review*, Spring 1995, pp. 7–20. The dean of reference reviewers explores how the new technologies, particularly in reference services, have changed the purpose and scope of bibliographical instruction. The task of BI is to learn what the average user needs in order to survive among online searching, CD-ROMs, and the equal shortage of librarians. See, too, the bibliography for an overview of reference and instruction today.

Salisbury, Lutishoor, "Integrating Technology in Reference Services," *Library Administration & Management*, Summer 1994, pp. 162–172. A practical approach to the use of bibliographical instruction in reference services sections where it is necessary that students learn to understand the new technologies.

Sourcebook for Bibliographic Instruction. Chicago: American Library Association, Association of College and Research Libraries, 1993. A pamphlet, produced by the Bibliographic Instruction Section of the Association of Research Libraries, this provides practical advice and guidance for instruction at the academic library level. The five chapters describe the basic approaches, with a dash of theory as well. Note, too, the "Recommended Reading" section.

CHAPTER TEN
REFERENCE SERVICE POLICIES
AND EVALUATION

Traditional reference service depends on good library management and planning. The administration's policies must provide for everything from adequate new reference works to the latest computer systems. Without such aids, reference questions cannot be answered.

Reference librarians are usually not involved with daily administration. But they are concerned with the many policies and administrative goals that include aspects of personnel, professional development, and hiring of new employees. These are normally in written, sometimes published, policy statements prepared jointly by staff and administrators. The policy reflects the day-to-day activities of the library staff.

The individual library's written policy statement should incorporate certain basic considerations:

1. *A statement of purpose* which includes goals and objectives, not only of the reference process but of the library (and the system) as a whole.

  a. The goals and objectives must be discussed in terms of the reality of budget, political process, staff, space, and so forth.

  b. More important, the goals must be understood by all; that is, the librarian should be able to explain the purpose of the proposals, and if they are not practical or logical, the goals should be reexamined.

2. *A statement defining the broad strategy* that will be followed to reach the goals and objectives.

    a. There should be a thorough analysis of "present time," that is, precisely what is going on at the current time in the reference process.

    b. There should be a plan, with due consideration of cost, personnel, overall library goals, and so on for future development and growth.

    c. Finally, there should be periodic evaluation of the movement(s) toward future time. And in the light of the evaluation, the general and the specific strategies should be modified or even dropped in favor of new approaches.

Purpose of Policy and Procedures

The purpose of the policy and procedures is to state guidelines for providing reference service in order to ensure a uniform standard of service of the highest-possible quality consistent with available resources. Reasons for having a policy are almost as numerous as the librarians who draw them up, but essentially:

    1. The drafting or modification of a policy requires some appreciation of the overall goals, purposes, and direction of reference service. The systematic analysis of service given, or not given, helps formulate these necessary objectives.

    2. Standards are established, not only for service but also for such things as building of the collection, handling of interlibrary loan materials, and preparation of correspondence.

    3. A better view of the audience served (or not served) is achieved by considering objectives and standards. Obviously, neither can be analyzed without a careful study of library patrons.

    4. Levels of service must be considered, that is, just how much assistance is to be given to help the user find information or in actually finding the information for the user?

    5. Without a view of the world beyond the scope of the reference desk, services may become less than ambitious, locked more into routine and daily expediency than addressed to long-range needs of the individual and the community the librarian hopes to serve.

    6. Policy statements are developed to resolve controversies such as why the microform staff cannot do all the threading of film readers or why advance notice of class assignments is necessary.

    7. The policy serves as a touchstone of continuity for new staff and helps refresh the memory of veterans who may need a guide for rarely occurring problems.

    8. Since there usually are not enough staff members for ideal service, the statement establishes priorities in the hierarchy of services.

9. And this leads to probably the most useful aspect of the policy statement: It serves to clarify, if not always answer, nagging queries about the limits of service that the librarian faces daily. For example, a good policy should consider (to name only a few) such things as: (*a*) What type of material is considered "reference" material and what does this mean in terms of use, circulation, storage, and so forth? (*b*) Who is served first? The person standing at the desk or the person with a question on the phone? (*c*) What should be done when a person wants legal, medical, or consumer advice? (*d*) Are the rules different for children, young people, and adults?

Why No Policy Statement?

Not all libraries have such policy statements and, in fact, these policy statements are probably rare in small- to medium-sized libraries with equally small staffs. But even in larger libraries there is some opposition to written policies. There are numerous reasons, both expressed and unexpressed, for the showing of less-than-enthusiastic interest in a codified policy. Commonly expressed reasons are:

1. Formulation is a time-consuming and sometimes costly business and, in a period of short staff and small budgets, the time and money are better spent elsewhere.

2. Often even the most detailed statement will not answer *every* problem.

3. Procedures and policies must change in response to need, technology, and so on, and there is little point in trying to codify them.

4. Even with a procedure on policy statement, few staff members will bother to use the statement and will rely primarily on experience and advice from peers to solve problems.

Even with written policies, there are decisions that librarians must make throughout their careers. It is with some of these concerns, from ethics to gaining professional status, that the remainder of this chapter is concerned.

ETHICS AND THE REFERENCE LIBRARIAN

Many years ago one critic summarized the proper attitude of the reference librarian toward everything from war and peace to the proper way to lay a kitchen floor: "No politics, no religion, no morals."[1] A reference librarian should be objective, and while assisting an individual to find information, should make no judgment on the advisability of answering the query.

Over the years librarians have come up with ethical problems. The "Statement of Professional Ethics," which is the guideline of the American Library As-

---

[1] D. J. Foskett, *The Creed of a Librarian* . . . (London: Aslib, 1962), p. 10. The piece may be dated, but the creed goes on and on and on.

sociation, helps answer some ethical problems. The following should be found in all reference policy statements. The guidelines cover the major points of ethical consideration:

> I. Librarians must provide the highest level of service through appropriate and usefully organized collections, fair and equitable circulation and service policies, and skillful, accurate, unbiased, and courteous responses to all requests for assistance.

> II. Librarians must resist all efforts by groups or individuals to censor library materials.

> III. Librarians must protect each user's right to privacy with respect to information sought or received, and materials consulted, borrowed, or acquired.

> IV. Librarians must adhere to the principles of due process and equality of opportunity in peer relationships and personnel actions.

> V. Librarians must distinguish clearly in their actions and statements between their personal philosophies and attitudes and those of an institution or professional body.

> VI. Librarians must avoid situations in which personal interests might be served or financial benefits gained at the expense of library users, colleagues, or the employing institution.[2]

Library Record Confidentiality

Confidentiality and privacy are of growing concern to reference librarians now that the Internet, and all it implies, is in place. Also, the daily use of electronic databases often requires logging in and logging out, which may be necessary but is a danger to confidentiality. Often there is a managerial conflict between the necessity of keeping records and the expectation of the user for protection of his or her privacy. At the same time, the American Library Association, among others, has gone on record in favor of privacy of reference transactions.

As an experienced reference librarian points out, the question may be more theoretical than real. Very few outsiders ask for a user's records. At the same time while students do not expect confidentiality, faculty members assume as much. Much the same situation seems true in school and public libraries, that is, younger people do not think about the question and adults automatically assume records are confidential. The American Library Association believes tradition and education support the librarian who honors confidentiality. The ex-

[2]"Statement of Professional Ethics" (Chicago: American Library Association, 1991). These are often incorporated into other guidelines by the ALA. (The ALA encourages the wide distribution of the guidelines, and they may be used without formal permission from that organization.) See, too, "Standards of Ethical Conduct . . ." which outlines the standards for special collection librarians. Many of these are applicable to reference librarians and are found in *The Whole Library Handbook 2* (Chicago: American Library Association, 1995), pp. 453–456.

pectation of privacy is such that the majority of the library profession—law or no—observe the confidentiality rule. Courts support the library claim to confidentiality even though it is not a formalized law.

In summary, librarian Rosemary DelVecchio puts it this way:

> The very nature of our dual roles, as the protector of information access and as a responsible member of the community in which we live, will, doubtlessly, keep confidentiality of the patron and the librarian's accountability in the world of grayness. There is no solution without losing personal integrity or professional standards. The Codes of Ethics, even if corollaries are added, can only be seen as a guiding light in the gray fog until they become legal standards. Until then, and even after, the librarian must use a mixture of instinct, tact, discretion and common sense at the reference desk.[3]

Reference Accuracy

Past studies indicate that, about 50 percent of the time, a reference librarian either will give a wrong answer or an incomplete answer, or refer the user to a wrong source, or make no effort to answer the question at all. For the most part, the studies are based on unobtrusive tests.[4] Some typical questions are put to a given group of librarians (usually in different libraries of the same type). One may grant that not all studies are objective, or even well constructed. Still, the alarming aspect of reference accuracy is that even when librarians know they are being tested, they may not do much better than librarians unaware of the study.[5]

Reference staffs correctly answer about 50 to 55 percent of the questions put to them by the public. The responses by some librarians, as it would be by any group whose professional skills are questioned, are: (1) It is not true, at least in my library. (2) It may be true, but the testing methods were flawed enough to make it doubtful. (3) The questions posed hardly measure the real abilities of the reference librarians. (4) The interpretation of the results is flawed.[6]

[3]Rosemary DelVecchio, "Privacy and Accountability at the Reference Desk," *The Reference Librarian*, 1992, no. 38, p. 139.

[4]See Thomas Childers, "Measuring the Difficulty of Reference Questions," *RQ*, Winter 1991, pp. 237–243.

[5]There is less in the literature in the mid-1990s on reference accuracy than in the 1970s and 1980s, possibly because so much attention has been turned to the new technologies. Still, there is no reason to think matters have improved much. For an overall view of such studies see Jo Bell Whitlach, "Unobtrusive Studies . . . ," *College & Research Libraries*, March 1989, pp. 181–194; Kenneth Crews, "The Accuracy of Reference Service," *Library and Information Science Research*, 1988, no. 10, pp. 331–335; particularly, Thomas Childers, "Evaluative Research in the Library . . . ," *Library Trends*, Fall 1989, pp. 250–267; as well as Peter Hernon and Charles R. McClure, *Unobtrusive Testing and Library Reference Services* (Norwood, NJ: Ablex, 1987).

[6]Patricia Hults, "Reference Evaluation: An Overview," *The Reference Librarian*, 1992, no. 38, p. 143.

Another fascinating aspect of less than thorough service is the attitude of the public served. "Patrons continue to rave about our performance. User surveys . . . [find] that an overwhelming majority of patrons are highly satisfied . . . frequently surpassing the 90% satisfaction high."[7] The conclusion is that a better approach to evaluating reference services would be to examine the whole process, not simply answers to a few questions.

Laypeople using the *General Periodical Index* or *The Readers' Guide to Periodical Literature* on CD-ROMs generally are happy with the results, but unaware of any flaws in their searches. This is a standard response to numerous surveys and studies in both public and university libraries. Consensus among users is that the CD-ROMs are much preferable to the old, standard print versions of general indexes.[8]

A group at Illinois State University ran a typical unobtrusive study. Conducted as it was by experts in the field, including E. W. Lancaster, it is interesting to see the variations. Questions were put person to person, not over the telephone as is usual in such studies. It was all done within the single library . . . again, out of the ordinary. The questions were put to librarians at different times in the library by paid student assistants. A total of 190 transactions were studied, and a standard scoring method was employed.

Several conclusions were drawn: (1) Partial or incorrect answers were provided or suggested more than 40 percent of the time. About 50 percent of the time the answer was complete and correct, or a student was shown a source where the answer was complete and correct, or the student was shown several sources with the same end results. (2) Types of questions (from ready-reference to search) did not affect either attitudinal scores for the librarian or accuracy. (3) "Answering a question correctly and completely was not a good predictor of how well the students in this study perceived they were being treated. Conversely, librarians who project positive images do not necessarily answer questions with the highest accuracy."[9]

Freedom of Information and Censorship

Although the American Library Association (ALA) has clearly and properly taken a stand on the side of "intellectual freedom," censorship remains a persistent and pressing problem in all libraries at all levels of service. The ALA

[7] David Tyckoson, "Wrong Questions, Wrong Answers," *The Reference Librarian*, 1992, no. 38, pp. 153–156. The experienced reference librarian and teacher then goes on to plead for a more complete method of evaluation. It is a winning argument.

[8] Jennifer Blackburn, *Retrieval Results of Unassisted Searches of Two General Periodical Indexes* (Kent, OH: Kent State University, 1993). MLS research paper. (ERIC: ED 367339.)

[9] Cheryl Elzy et al., "Evaluating Reference Service in a Large Academic Library," *College & Research Libraries*, September 1991, p. 12. This is a thorough study which might serve as a model for others of its type.

moves vigorously against the threats of the censor, and it is an ongoing issue discussed among librarians year in and year out.[10] Two or three points are worth stressing.

The discussion of censorship must always include a look at the misguided individual who wishes that all reference works (including dictionaries) with four-letter words were removed from circulation. Political groups often lobby for the removal of books with opposing views. A more insidious type of censorship is that of the publisher who withholds a reference work because it may inflame opinion or, more frequently, because it will not make enough money although valuable.

The censor rarely invades the reference section. Few judges of American morality have much to say about indexes and bibliographies, but ready-reference titles might be another thing again. Take, for example, *Homemade Grenade Launchers, Home-Built Claymore Mines, The Ultimate Sniper,* or *Get Even: The Complete Book of Dirty Tricks.* While not routinely purchased for the reference section, all are in *Books in Print* (or were in the early 1990s) and sell nicely. Three of the largest publishers of this type of guide to violence and crime—Delta, Paladin Press, and Loompanics Unlimited—report sales of a total of 700,000 books in 1993, or about double the number of the five previous years.

The genre is not new, or necessarily confined to criminals on street corners. Bruce Easley, for example, is the author of *Biz Op: How to Get Rich with Business Opportunity Frauds and Scams.* The author has been featured on many talk shows and his books appear regularly in the larger bookstores.

In or outside the reference section the natural question is: "Should the library buy such titles?" A more refined point is that if the books are purchased, should they be limited to the reference section? This type of query, which deserves an answer, depends on the individual library and the community. Librarians may concede that there are times when a "how-to-do-it" reference work, no matter how popular, should not be in the library. Is this a violation of the sacred creed of freedom to read? It is. The author's particular view is that there should be no censorship. Any book or any form of communication which does not violate the law should be available to the individual who makes the request.

The reference librarian need not recommend, for example, the by now famous *Anarchist Cookbook* (with sales of over 2 million), which was published in 1971 and has plans for making pipe bombs, among other things. On the other hand if X or Y wants the book, it should be available. Needless to add, not all

---

[10]The ALA has an office in Washington, D.C., dedicated to "intellectual freedom," and numerous members of the ALA staff are involved with the subject. Note, too, the various ALA committees, as well as the prestigious ALA Intellectual Freedom Award. For details on their stand see almost any issue of *Library Literature* and, to be sure, the *ALA Intellectual Freedom Manual* which is updated from time to time and contains official actions of the ALA against the censor.

working librarians agree with this point, no matter how they defend the freedom to read.

A refutation of censorship might be that few criminals ever use a library, and the only real way that crime pays in a library is to write a book about it. And evidence indicates strongly that few criminals get their ideas from reading matter, whether it be pornography or how-to-do-it manuals.

Networks and Censors

While censorship of reference books, for the most part, has not been a serious problem, a more difficult situation presents itself with the international flow of data over computer networks. Even the most liberal of civil libertarians recognizes the difficulties involved with international networks. If nothing else, the reference librarian should be aware of the flash point discussions concerning the pros and cons of network censoring.

One legal method of evaluating material is to measure it against contemporary community standards of what is decent or obscene. The law is difficult to enforce in a nation with television, newspapers, magazines, and other forms of communication. It is impossible to enforce in a system, such as Internet, which scans the globe. A basic community standard in New York, for example, may not be the same for New Delhi or for other points in the world. One may pass bills that ban indecent or criminal matter on the Internet, but the high cost of running down the elusive "publisher" will more than make the law unenforceable. "Requiring network providers to monitor what goes out over their systems is unworkable—it's like asking the phone companies to monitor what's uttered in billions of conversations. The only way that you can really control content is to cripple the whole network."[11]

The plus side of the inability of any one person or country to censor material is that it opens the world to the clarion call of freedom. (Of course, the assumption is that the country involved has enough computers and laptops to spread the message.) On a minus side it equally opens up the world to hate and harassment on a scale not yet possible to envision.

An individual may press slander, libel, and harassment charges against another individual on the Internet. Who is to find the person or group of persons? Once found, say, in a far off part of the globe, who is to press charges?

The lesson for reference librarians is relatively simple. Leave this flow of information alone. Any effort on the part of the librarian to police or monitor what goes in and out of a library computer terminal is to ask for problems. One may post required legal rules, as done for copyright at the photocopying ma-

[11]*Newsweek*, February 27, 1995, p. 29.

chine, but beyond perfunctory measures, the librarian should leave regulations, if required, to the government.

Consumer Network Censors

Consumer networks tend to police their own systems and rely on customers to report problems on the cyberspace frontier. America Online, for example, has shut down several feminist discussion groups because "it was concerned that the subject matter might be inappropriate for young girls."[12] Objectionable words are censored on Prodigy. The perennial problem presents itself, that is, has America Online the right to muzzle feminists, or Prodigy to decide what is an "objectionable" word?

The kind of "information" some believe is a driving force, if not the primary force, behind the popularity of the consumer online services is chatter.[13] The services foster matchmaking and sexy chitchat. At any given time users can log onto a discussion area, use an assumed name, and play out fantasies with others. While all of this is fair adult entertainment, the problem is that the consumer networks, as well as Internet, are available to schoolchildren.

But sex chatter is hardly the only area for consideration. Internet's Usenet provides messages hardly found on school library shelves. Detailed bomb making, suicide methods, drug recipes, and even hacker advice on how to break into telephone systems and cash machines are part of the mix. While consumer networks have managed to censor and check some material objectionable for children and objected to by consenting adults, this is almost impossible on the Internet. So when a librarian or teacher contemplates bringing the Internet into public schools the situation is essentially all or nothing. Educators protect themselves by policy statements and, often, by having parents sign consent forms for their children to use Internet.

The phrase "information wants to be free" is heard often on Usenet discussion groups. The American Library Association admits the situation is extremely complex, particularly for school libraries, and in the mid-1990s was studying its position on electronic communications and freedom of speech. Meanwhile, as one critic puts it: "Losing the Internet in schools just because of

[12]"Censors Become a Force," *The New York Times,* June 29, 1994, p. 1. Freedom has its network price. In mid-1994, for example, a California couple was convicted of sending images of bestiality and sexual fetishes over an Internet bulletin board. The decision was made despite the fact that the bulletin board was not free ($99 a year) and tried to screen out children and teenagers. As critics put it, "The case bodes ill for any American computer system that carries any sexually related material at all." "Couple Convicted of Pornography," *The New York Times,* July 31, 1994, p. 15.

[13]This conclusion is a consensus among online watchers, for example, see any column of John Dvorak in *PC Magazine* as well as online directories. *The Internet Yellow Pages* (New York: McGraw-Hill, 1994) provides a full nine pages on sex-related news groups. This is more space than given any other topic. See, too, David Taylor's Guide to Social Networks available on the Internet.

some information on it—and we're really talking about a small percentage of total information—it's a pretty bad investment. If a student was smuggling dirty pictures in their science textbook, would we take away all the science text-books?"[14]

Hackers and Crackers

Another aspect of library ethics concerns the role of the hacker and cracker and information. The hacker tries to figure out how any code of data operates, and drops it at that.[15] The cracker not only discovers how a database operates, but "cracks" into it, sometimes for nefarious purposes. The distinction may not always be clear, but hackers are the ladies and gentlemen of the information highway, while the crackers are the crooks and thieves.

There is danger in the ability of an unscrupulous for-profit cracker to find the key to germ warfare, secret weapons, and confidential government studies.[16] In 1995, for example, a few Russian salespeople began peddling plutonium to the world. This is a less than appealing practice for those trying to check the atom bomb. At a more mundane level, crackers can intercept, read, and even change content of e-mail.

While neither the hacker nor the cracker is likely to take up headquarters in a library, the reference librarian should be aware of their existence. Steps should be taken to block anyone having unauthorized access to library files, whether they be public or private.

Book Theft

Another type of crime is of more than academic or passing interest. This is the theft of library books. Usually it is a volume of an encyclopedia or a reference work in which an individual has found the answer to a school assignment. A "classic" case of theft was reported in England where "a bookworm stole 42,000 volumes for his private library over a 30 year period." The thief explained "I like having the books and using them." Among the acquired books, taken for

[14]Education section, *The New York Times*, November 6, 1994, p. 23.

[15]Technical wizardry marks the hacker who breaks into private networks and computer systems. Stealing software and data by mastering the password and route to private materials, the computer addict ranges from young teenagers to experienced adults. Few to date are involved with such mundane things as library networks or access to standard information databases.

[16]"Cyberspace's Most Wanted Hacker Eludes FBI Pursuit," *The New York Times*, July 4, 1994, p. 1. The hacker in question is the person who, as a teenager, broke into the North American Air Defense Command computer, foreshadowing the 1983 movie *War Games*.

the most part out in a bag or simply thrown out a library window, was not one, but two sets of the *Britannica*."[17]

QUESTION OF FEES

Nothing generates more discussion than the question: "Should information continue to be free from a library, and particularly from a public library which has a tradition of free access to information?" On the "yes" side are the advocates of equality who point out, correctly, that patron fees simply widen the gap between the "information rich" and the "information poor," between the middle classes and the underclasses. On the "let's charge, at least for use of the latest information technologies" side, one argues the logic that without added income the library will not be able to provide the new technologies to anyone—rich, moderately well off, or poor.

Those who consider fees viable admit: "The complex issues comprising the fee service topic involve questions of who pays for what services, what is paid, how payment is made [indirectly through partial tax support or by direct payment tied to amount of use], where payment is made, when payment is made, and how the payment relates to direct and indirect costs of offering the services."[18]

Despite the rationalization for fees, despite the almost universal application of some type of fee structure, the fact remains that fees severely limit the use of reference service. People who pay fees are those who (1) have no other choice, which is not often, or, more likely, (2) those who have funds from outside sources to pay the fees. The majority who do not pay feel the information is hardly worth it, or, more likely, simply do not wish to pay the fees.

The answer to fee or no fee depends on a vast number of variables, all of which rest on two premises: The library does, or does not, offer free information to one and all. The public has a right, or no particular right, to equal access to the newest information technologies.

The author of this text feels no one should have to pay fees for standard services, including access to the new technologies. Individuals who wish added services, meaning anything which the library does not ordinarily do for an individual or group, may be expected to pay to cover, at least, the added expenses.

---

[17] *The Times Literary Supplement*, June 17, 1994, p. 16. The thief was sentenced to fifteen months in jail. The thief explained that he stole the books not for profit, but to surround himself with them because they were more reliable than people. The case aside, theft is a major problem in all libraries and the subject of numerous articles, several monographs, and so on. Space does not permit giving it the attention it deserves.

[18] Peter Young, "Changing Information Access Economics," *Information Technology and Libraries*, June 1994, p. 105. This is a long, well-considered article which offers both points of view about fees, and comes down on neither side. See pp. 106–108 for points, both pro and con, on fees.

Of course, it is never that simple in that someone must define "standard" and "does not ordinarily." And, as indicated, there are other variables, both emotional and financial, that make it difficult to resolve the question.

COLLECTION EVALUATION

The reference librarian from time to time must step back from the evaluation of individual sources and evaluate the collection as a whole. Thanks to rapid document delivery, networking, and interlibrary loan, the problem of collection evaluation has both eased and become increasingly complicated. It is easier as availability of fewer titles is needed directly on the shelves. Electronic databases, which eventually will replace most printed works in the reference section of the library, have helped ease the necessity for concerns about space and shelving.

At the same time, the potential availability of so much (at a sometimes undetermined cost) has made collection development complicated. For example, is it better to purchase X periodical, or have it available on a CD-ROM, or simply order bits of it from a document delivery organization, or forget it entirely? Similar puzzlers must be asked of the majority of reference sources, at least where networking (from the local area network to OCLC and Internet) is available.

Collection evaluation is a study in itself, but reference source evaluation has three parts. First, the librarian decides what type of reference materials—books, periodicals, electronic databases, and so forth—to buy. Second, the librarian studies reviews and where possible the reference works themselves. The material is then accepted or rejected. Third, periodically the whole collection is examined to evaluate its overall quality and whether it is keeping up with the users' changing needs.

Librarians must continue to raise and answer the quality question because what may be adequate one year may be less than desirable the next. There are several points to consider in evaluating quality: (1) What is the optimum size of the collection for the particular library? (2) What type of materials should it contain, for example, should there be more emphasis on science than social science? (3) What are the cost considerations?

Additional factors to weigh include: (1) Who is going to use the collection, and will even the largest (or smallest) collection be suitable? (2) If a certain type of material is required this year, will the users' needs change so that a different type will be necessary the next year? (3) What resources are available from nearby libraries, and how much can service be improved through interlibrary loan document delivery and use of databases? (4) If the budget must be cut, which type of material should be given more or less consideration?

Number and Type

Since answering reference questions may involve the resources of the whole library, and, for that matter, libraries and collections elsewhere, it is difficult to zero in on the precise type of materials to be evaluated. Normally, one concentrates on reference books per se. These are the titles that are dutifully marked as such, are listed in such annotated standard guides as *Guide to Reference Books*, and are categorized and reviewed by such services as *Library Journal* and *Choice*. Beyond that, the librarian will want to evaluate the serials collections (an obvious and integrated part of the indexes and abstracting services); the government documents and how they are treated; and, in more and more cases, the number and type of databases used directly or indirectly for reference service. One should consider the collection as a whole, as well as its parts.

Experience recommends shortcuts. Almost any survey of holdings finds that the reference collection (or, for that matter, any tested subject sections in that collection) which meets standards for both retrospective and current holdings accurately reflects the quality of the library as a whole. That is to say, if the reference collection, or a representative part of it, is good, the library is likely to be good. At times this test fails, as in a library where the rest of the staff is not of the caliber of the reference librarians, but these instances are unusual.

The next consideration concerns the number of reference works a basic collection should have, the number to be added each year, the number to be weeded, the number of dollars necessary for acquisitions, and so forth. Ideally, there is sufficient money to acquire everything that is needed, as well as materials on the periphery of need, but this is rarely the case. So some indication of numbers should be useful, some quantitative guide helpful.

Unfortunately—some would say fortunately—national or even regional standards or figures do not exist. Determining the optimum size of a collection within a library involves so many variables that an attempt to set one standard would be meaningless. There are negative answers to some questions that may be helpful: (1) Is there an ideal size for any given type of library? No. (2) Can one work out a ratio between size of the reference collection and the rest of the collection? No. (3) Can one develop a useful figure by working out a ratio of the number of librarians and the number of potential users? No. (4) Can one determine the size of the collection by applying any statistical methods? No. (5) Is there a correlation between the size of the collection and the degree of successful reference performance? Yes and no, depending on who does the study.

Still, there are some rough guidelines for establishing the optimal minimum and maximum size of a good reference collection, including print and electronic formats. Generally, the best test of the right size is a simple one: Does this library have the amount of material to answer the reference questions that are usually asked? If the majority of questions are answered quickly and correctly by the available collection, then it is the optimum size. Simple observation and experience are the key to this evaluation exercise, and there are some practical hints on what to observe:

1. When a book or other source must be borrowed or when a librarian must call another library for information from a work not in the library, then purchase should be considered. When the source is needed more than twice in a single month, the work should be purchased—if, of course, funds are available.

2. When the users cannot find what is needed, then purchase of more titles should be considered. Here, of course, one must count upon interviews, questionnaires, and observations for answers to the frustration. A simple technique, which also helps establish contact between librarian and user, is to ask people periodically if they are managing to find what they want.

3. Both large and small libraries keep their collections updated and growing in size through purchases. When deciding what to buy, one may rely on reviews from *Choice* (about 500 reference titles considered each year), *Library Journal* (about 400 titles), and more specialized works. There is also the *American Reference Books Annual,* which annotates about 1500 to 1800 publications.

4. Keep track of unfilled requests. How many times and for what type of works did the library have to refer to another library? If, for example, X title is consistently used, but is not in the library, one suspects it would be a good idea to purchase the title. This is the case where periodical statistical checks can be most useful. What journals or articles, for example, had to be requested on interlibrary loans for *x* period of time to fulfill reference requests?

By now it should be apparent that determining the proper number of reference titles is more of an educated gamble than a statistically accurate measure. The variables help to explain the reluctance of individuals, committees, or even the American Library Association to assign numerical guidelines to size in the acquisition process.

Intrinsic Quality

Throughout the first volume of this text, various rules and suggestions were given about evaluation of reference titles in general and those categorized by form. When one evaluates a whole reference collection, this type of judgment is vital.

The mechanics of evaluating a collection in terms of quality include three tested procedures:

1. Isolate a representative list of *retrospective titles,* and check to see if these are in the library. The list is considered statistically representative of a fair sampling for large libraries when chosen from a random sampling of titles in *Guides to Reference Books,* or for smaller libraries when chosen from titles in *Reference Sources for Small and Medium Sized Libraries.* In the former case, a list of about 450 to 500 titles would be available, whereas in the latter situation, the list would be no more than 100 titles. The library with a majority of these titles is likely to have a good collection.

2. A more accurate approach is to isolate two or three *subject areas,* particularly those areas of most interest to people who use the collection, and check availability of representative titles. In this case, a list of titles taken from the same sources cited above would include titles in the subject area. A similar technique is applicable when one turns to even more specialized bibliographies such as *Sources of Information in the Social Sciences.*

3. Isolate titles, again using lists, to check the *timeliness of the collection.* Here one might take a representative sampling from *American Reference Books Annual* for the past year, the list of reference titles that appears in *Library Journal,* or a list of titles in the six or seven library journals (or specialized subject journals) for the past six months.

Online, CD-ROM, and Other Digital Formats

As content and purpose is much the same, whole electronic database collections may be evaluated in a similar manner to print collections. The obvious difference is format and cost. In addition, the library should determine how many databases should be available, which vendors should be represented, how much should be charged (if anything), how many librarians should be on duty to offer such services, whether there should be online training for laypersons, and so forth.

Budget

Few reference librarians are directly involved with the preparation of the library budget. However, two points must be made:

1. As many have observed, the budget is a statement of the ultimate goals, policies, and services of the reference section. It is a current view of where things stand, of just how much importance the library places on reference service. Furthermore, budget line items show the part of reference services (from personnel to online searching) deemed most important.

2. The reference librarian will be asked to recommend what is and what is not needed for the next fiscal year. Although not directly involved with the figures (i.e., with where the money comes from), the librarian at least is concerned with what it will mean not to get a particular request. Furthermore, librarians are the ones who must implement what is implied in the budget. Managing the budget is the concern of every reference librarian.

WEEDING

A constant ongoing aspect of reference source evaluation is the weeding process. Weeding is the removal of information sources from the reference collection. There are various ways of determining whether a particular work should be ranked as obsolescent or of little value to the reference librarian.

What follows concerns primarily printed titles, which remain of major importance in the reference collection no matter what the future may hold for electronic formats. At this time there are few libraries with so many CD-ROMs that weeding electronic databases is a consideration.

1. Study the use of the title. This can be determined by a survey of how often the book is off the shelf. (Circulation records can be studied to see which books are checked out most frequently, but this is rarely the case in the reference section.)

2. Timeliness is often a factor, although not always. A source "ages" in the sciences and social sciences in only one to five years, although in the humanities sources can last up to twenty-five years or longer.

Weeding is a cost-efficient method of ensuring needed new space and keeping the collection efficient for use. Weeding is a delicate process. Conceivably, any book, pamphlet, CD-ROM, magazine, newspaper, or other written material can have reference value, particularly for the historian or anyone else concerned with social mores and records of the past. To discard such a work is akin to destroying the past. For example, one of the most difficult research problems is to locate materials in local newspapers of the nineteenth century.

Anyone who has sought contemporary opinion or statistical data or a biography of a little-known figure knows that there is no limit to the material that may be found in older reference works, certainly in books from both the general and the specific reference collections. Many of these older reference works, such as the early editions of the *Encyclopaedia Britannica*, are now classics, and are invaluable sources of material found nowhere else.

Understanding these warnings, there is still a need for judicious weeding. Libraries are always short of space, and this is particularly true in the reference section. Weeding clears the shelves of little-used, or sometimes never-used, materials. Actually, few works are discarded in larger libraries. They are sent off to storage. Smaller libraries cannot afford this luxury, and the material is often systematically removed.

Guidelines for Discarding

Each library must establish its own general and specific guidelines for discarding materials. As is true of acquisitions, each library has its own peculiar needs, its own type of users. It is important to weed materials to meet the needs of those users, not the standards established in a text or at another library.

With that word of caution, some general criteria may be suggested:

Timeliness. Most of the reference titles that are used for ready reference have to be up to date. Older titles may be helpful historically, but are of little value for current material.

Reliability. Data and viewpoints change, and the changes must be reflected in the reference collection. Yesterday's reliable explanation of a given event or phenomenon may not apply today.

Use. Needs change from generation to generation, and yesterday's valued reference work may no longer be used by today's reference librarian, today's user.

Physical condition. Books wear out and must be either discarded or replaced with new editions.

Later editions. Most popular reference works go into several editions, and it is normally pointless to maintain earlier editions when the latest edition of a standard work can be obtained. Another linked consideration: duplication of materials. Perhaps a title was unique four or five years ago, but today there are more recent, even better titles in the field. In that case the older title may be discarded.

Language. Sometimes a foreign language work may be discarded because no one is using it. It may have been purchased at a time when the particular language was important to the library's users.

To make a wise selection of what should be discarded requires:

Thorough knowledge of the collection. The librarian should know how the work is used and by whom. Should a particular work be totally eliminated, should a new edition be purchased, or should a similar work be considered? These are all questions that vary from situation to situation and can be answered only by the librarian working closely with the collection and the public.

Knowledge of other resources. A librarian needs to understand the collections of regional and national libraries. Is at least one copy of what you propose to discard in a local or national collection for use at some later date? Obviously a much-used work, such as a ten-year-old copy of the *World Almanac,* need not be checked. But any material that is purely local (particularly pamphlets and material without lasting value), anything more than fifty years old, and any items about which there is a question regarding use or value should first be cleared with the larger libraries in the region. Such an item may appear shabby and of little use, but may prove to be a unique copy.

Older works worth keeping. One must remember that age does not necessarily dictate whether a work is discarded. No worthwhile reference collection lacks, for example, a copy of the dated *Encyclopedia of the Social Sciences* or the mass of bibliographies and other guides that were published a number of years ago and are still basic works.

Encyclopedias. Maintain as many older editions as space allows, *but* try to obtain a new edition at least every five years, and preferably every year.

Almanacs, yearbooks, manuals. These are usually superseded by the next edition or the succeeding volume. Nevertheless, as the information in each is rarely duplicated exactly (new material is added, old material deleted), it is wise to keep old editions for at least five years, preferably ten years.

Dictionaries. In a sense, these are never dated and should never be discarded unless replaced by the same editions. An exception might be the abridged desk-type dictionaries. The unabridged works and those devoted to special areas are of constant value.

Biographical sources. Again, the more of these and the more retrospective the sources, the better. Only in a few select cases should any be discarded.

Directories. Like yearbooks, almanacs, and other such works, these are frequently updated, and the older ones (five to ten years) can generally be discarded safely.

Geographical sources. Inexpensive atlases may be safely discarded after five to ten years. More expansive, expensive works are invaluable. In fact, many gain in both research and monetary value over the years.

Government documents. Never discard these if they are part of a permanent collection. Discards should be considered where material is used only peripherally for pamphlet files. However, be particularly careful to check local and state materials before discarding.

In the subject areas, it is relatively safe to assume that except for botany and natural history, science books are generally dated within five years. The recurrent yearbooks, manuals, and encyclopedias may be discarded as new editions are obtained. In the humanities, discarding should rarely take place unless the material is quite obviously totally dated and of no historical or research value. In the social sciences, timely or topical materials may be considered for discard after one to five years.

EVALUATION OF REFERENCE SERVICES

What constitutes ideal reference service? The answer is a high score in five areas: personnel performance, collection development, introduction of new technologies and reference services, evaluation of services and personnel, and administrative capacities. This section is concerned primarily with services and personnel. It seems a suitable way to end a text in that the text is written by and for librarians.

Speaking from experience, reference librarians inevitably point out that happy librarians are those with good salaries and fair hours. Beyond the obvious: (1) There should be an intelligent division of labor so that, for example, x number of hours on the reference desk or instruction with CD-ROMs is balanced with x number of less strenuous hours. (2) Continuing education, particularly in the new technologies, is an absolute must. (3) Specialization should be recognized and rewarded. The librarian who becomes an expert on computers and electronic databases or in anthropology or in eighteenth-century criticism is a valuable asset at a reference desk. (4) There should be some scale to measure overwork, burnout, and the hazards involved with the constant pressure of serving the public. The library should not wait until the librarian becomes ill or has to quit to recognize the stress factors in the job.

An experienced reference librarian wants evaluative answers to questions such as these: (1) "What is the role of paraprofessionals in providing reference service and what are the limits, if any, on the services they can provide effectively?" (There is a measured difference between the professional and the nonprofessional. Much depends on personality, education, and attitude between the two.) (2) "How much of a difference do the actions of reference personnel make?" (Most people only rarely use the services of a reference librarian. Why? Generally, the answer seems to be that they expect little, and in too many libraries the expectations are real.) (3) "What factors do users weigh most heavily in judging the effectiveness of reference service?" (That's easy. The major factor is a satisfactory answer to their question. The problem is what is "satisfactory." Is the average person expecting too much, or too little? Probably, too little.[19]

Library Evaluation

There are numerous reasons for the evaluation of reference libraries. Some are literally required to meet demands of accrediting groups or administration directives. Some are traditional: The evaluation is built into routine study of practices, the revision of the library policy manual, or management studies. Others are economical: Cuts or failure to increase budgets means scaling back services. Which services are to be cut, modified, and so on? Even without budgetary threats, the best system is one which is operated efficiently within standard budget requirements. This, in turn, factors into the purchase of new technologies, the place of the library in the economic changes in networks, and so forth.

The most common evaluation is relatively nonstructured and informal. Routine assessments of reference service are built into the annual activities of the staff. Unfortunately this has the drawback of putting too much emphasis on

---

[19]James Rettig, "Reference Research Questions," *RQ,* Winter 1991, p. 169. The questions are Rettig's, the tentative answers are from the author of this text.

collected data and too little on qualitative measurements. It requires less effort, less staff time, and certainly less commitment, for example, to gather statistics on how many people use CD-ROMs than the degree of their satisfaction.

Evaluation results are usually measured against national standards for school, public, and university libraries.[20] (All of these are available from the American Library Association, and tend to be modified from time to time.) Then, too, in an age of networks and electronic communication, the library will be measured against other libraries of equal size, in similar communities, and with the same purpose and budget. Measurements vary from those that are more concerned with how many questions were answered (outcome measures) to measures that evaluate the ability to deliver this or that service in x or y amount of time. Still, no matter what standard or group of measurements employed, the goal is to use evaluative systems suitable and practical for the particular library. To impose a scale that may meet the needs of national managers but not those of the local reference librarians is to impose chaos on any study. Before assessment tools are employed, there must be an understanding of what tools will or will not work in the particular library.

Generally the methodology employed and the tools used depend on the local library and what one is trying to discover about services. The purpose of the research study must be carefully decided and outlined. Failure to do so, if nothing else, may result in an endless add-on type of study that starts at no particular point and can never seem to reach a conclusion.

An expert, Jo Bell Whitlach, outlines the four basic steps for effective studies of reference services:

1. Defining the purpose of the research and obtaining agreement from library staff involved in the research. An important consideration is the value of the research for library decision making: Will the study provide information useful in improving library services?

2. Providing concise statements of study goals and objectives and the information that is needed.

3. Selecting appropriate methodologies related to study objectives; this requires a careful analysis of the strengths and weaknesses of possible methodologies.

4. Collecting and analyzing the data.[21]

EVALUATION METHODS

Over the past twenty-five or thirty years the amount of material on reference service evaluation has risen dramatically. This is due to two factors: (1) short-

---

[20] *Standard for Community, Junior and Technical College Learning Resource Programs* (Chicago: American Library Association, 1990). This is only one example of the standards available for almost any type or size library. See the American Library Association catalog of publications.

[21] Jo Bell Whitlach, "Reference Services: Research Methodologies for Assessment and Accountability," *The Reference Librarian*, 1992, no. 38, p. 17.

age of librarians, and (2) increased technological aids. As a result there are several more steps and results to evaluate.

Essentially any process can be analyzed in four or five steps. The first step is to determine the purpose of the evaluation, its goals, and precisely what one hopes to learn. Second, use a comparative ruler to measure the situation as it exists against a more ideal situation or against local or national standards. Third, decide which methods should be used to gather the necessary information and data. Fourth, determine how the methodology is to be carried out, that is, who is going to do what, at what cost, and under what time limits. After these preliminaries, one proceeds with the process, gathers the information, and makes any necessary modifications to the methodology. Finally, the results have to be analyzed, and conclusions must be drawn from the results to assist in understanding and possibly changing the situation which is under study.

The process of evaluation requires both subjective and objective methods, attitudes, and approaches. Emphasis should be, and tends to be, on objective methodology. There may be an almost mystical faith in the scientific method and in objective data, but the fact remains that it produces results. Scientific results convince governing bodies to provide more funds and persuade skeptics that improvements in service might be useful. At the same time, it is ridiculous to assume that a cumulation of statistical data on, say, how often people use the dictionary, will give anything more than just that—data—and will provide very little information about the quality of the collection. It is imperative that the objective studies have a fine focus and that they be balanced by subjective observations and analyses.

There are a number of desired or necessary qualities in evaluative instruments. Effective methodology should (1) demonstrate validity; (2) demonstrate reliability; (3) utilize the natural setting; (4) assess multiple factors in the reference process; and (5) include sufficient input, process, and outcome factors so that cause-and-effect relationships become apparent. In addition, the use of a standardized form to collect and report data should (6) utilize an adequate and unbiased sample; (7) provide for comparing data; (8) provide for timeliness of results; and (9) provide for interpretability.

Today most evaluations are conducted either by the library staff or by consultants. The staff usually performs evaluations, primarily because there are limited funds for outside help. On occasion, academic faculty, usually from a library school, will study the library for a scholarly research effort. In such a situation, the library tends to be only one of a larger group that is studied and the specific evaluative techniques and findings may or may not be applicable to the particular library studied.

There is much more to the evaluation of reference services than data on successfully answered questions. The components of reference evaluation would go like this: One must look at (1) *answering success* based on obtrusive, expert judgment, librarian or patron report, or unobtrusive study; (2) *the cost* and tasks involved with reference services; (3) *the reference interview* and how reference questions are classified for the search; (4) the quality of the *reference collection,* including new technologies from CD-ROMs to Internet access; (5) the quality of the staff.

EVALUATIVE TECHNIQUES AND METHODS

The most common approach for analyzing the reference process is the *obtrusive* method. Unfortunately, the descriptor is accurate enough: It means that everyone is well aware of the "obtrusive" presence of people, questionnaires, interviews, and the like used in the study.

Since this is the most-used approach, there are scores of examples in the literature. They include checking how long it takes an individual or a group of librarians to answer a set of questions and determining what methods are employed in selection of reference works or choice of databases in an online search. Other examples are found throughout this chapter.

The obtrusive method has the drawback of putting the subjects on their guard. With this method it is absolutely necessary to use easy-to-understand questionnaires and interview techniques, carefully explaining ambiguous statements. Most important, the librarians must be aware of the purpose and goals of the study, understanding that there is no hidden agenda, no secret threat.

If the objective methodology is carefully explained, the librarians will not be threatened by thinking the administration is trying to find a reason to dismiss them, to check their advancement, to increase the speed of answering questions, or of having a hidden motive behind the study. The real objective is to improve reference services, but how many librarians are able to believe this when they feel threatened? Of course, the good administrator should be able to calm such fears, but where there is a lack of faith in leadership, there will probably be problems with such evaluation techniques.

Unobtrusive Techniques

The *unobtrusive* approach is, as the name indicates, a method by which the subjects are not aware they are being evaluated. Usually, the unobtrusive test is divided into the factual query ("What is the height of the Empire State Building?") and the bibliographical question ("Who published *Death of a Salesman?*"). Surrogate information users, either directly or over the telephone, query the librarian who is unaware that an evaluation is under way. The method has become increasingly accepted. It is by far the most-used methodology for evaluating services today.

A simplified example of unobtrusive testing: 12 public libraries of various sizes and in various locations are visited by students with only one question. (The more usual unobtrusive test uses a battery of queries of various types.) The query in this instance is "What do you have on John Major?" All the libraries visited have the basic sources to afford a correct answer, for example, *Who's Who, The New York Times Index,* and the *Readers' Guide* or *Magazine Index.* None of the reference librarians queried know the students' real purpose—that a test is under way. This is the first and most basic requirement for unobtrusive studies. The students have a list of points to observe and to comment on at convenient stages of the study or, if possible, at the conclusion. The students report back on several aspects of reference service given—the reception, the management of a reference interview, how the search was conducted, and, of course, the answer.

The methodology, although simplified, fulfills the need to test for: (1) the right, wrong, or incomplete answer; (2) the proper use of the reference interview, if used at all; (3) search strategies employed and reference works consulted; (4) the use of referral, where necessary, to another point in the library or to another library; and (5) the general attitude of the librarians. Some claim that an unobtrusive approach is not only better, but it does less internal harm because the staff simply does not know it has taken place.

Combining obtrusive and unobtrusive methods, experts have come up with new evaluation techniques and new jargon. The combination is known as *outcome studies,* that is, studies which evaluate the outcome of a reference transaction.

Surveys

Polls and surveys are as much a part of America as MTV, politics, and the automobile. Rarely a week goes by that a group of well-known masters of the query do not report on still another facet of American life. Librarians are familiar with the methodologies employed, and know the protests which are heard if the poll goes against X or Y group's ideas. (The questions are inconsistent with the answer. The questions point to only one acceptable answer. The survey failed to consider . . . and so it goes.) Criticism, right or wrong, is heard every time a survey is run. "Simply put, it means that the manner in which the questions are asked (worded, ordered) greatly impacts upon the way people perceive and respond to them. Beyond problems stemming from the way respondents reply is the way in which those responses are interpreted."[22]

What is the point of all this for librarians? Surveys are a help, but not the complete answer. Surveys may be used in evaluative studies of service, but with some consideration of their lack of reliability. Finally, unless a cursory study, the survey should be checked and edited by someone who is an expert in such matters. The reference librarian might turn to a reference source for the name(s) of such a person in the community.

[22]Anthony Walsh, "All the World Is Data," *The Reference Librarian,* 1992, no. 38, p. 47.

Sampling

Sampling is a method of selecting a random or specific portion of the population and is used in opinion polls, market research, television popularity, and the like. The method is useful in analyzing aspects of reference service, such as the kinds of reference questions posed by users.

Records should be maintained on questions asked of the service: How many were there? How were they answered? Who asked them? But if done too frequently, the amount of paperwork will take time away from providing service. A better approach is to sample every few months. Some libraries pick two or three days a month every three or four months, and on those days record complete information on the reference queries made. This type of sampling, without interfering with the regular conduct of the reference service, indicates basic trends and, if done in a complete fashion, will show user satisfaction or lack of satisfaction.

The sampling technique is employed, too, for questioning users. The usual procedure is to select blocks of time in a day, week, month, or even year and sample user reaction by means of a questionnaire.

Interviews

The personal interview is often a key part of a survey. Here the person making the evaluation sits down with the librarian and in a structured way tries to determine, through the discussion or interview, the character of reference services, and in some cases, the abilities of the librarian. Both evaluations, of course, might be considered in an interview.

Individual interviews will show how the librarian with a low batting average for questions analyzes the query. In contrast, how does the librarian with an excellent record do the same? Do librarians think of various approaches, sources, and interview techniques, or are they stuck in the proverbial question-and-answer rut? Is success due to education, natural verbal ability, intelligence, energy, knowledge, intuition—or what? We now have only a vague notion of the success profile. Individual interviews and analyses of the data could yield solid answers.

A more common type of interview is one in which the reference services user is asked about the success or failure of those services. The responses are less than trustworthy often because the users believe they will be supporting the librarian by giving what they think are "correct" answers or they think the answers really do not matter.

As an evaluation tool, an interview usually takes place between the reference librarian and the interviewer and between the interviewer and individual users of reference service. Others, of course, can be questioned, from the head librarian to the nonuser. There are great advantages to interviews as an evaluating technique, particularly when the interviewer has training and is able to clearly differentiate fact from fiction, opinion, and bias. The drawbacks result when the respondent and the interviewer are at odds, when the respondent is inhibited by oral questions, when the interviewer intimidates the respondent, and when the respondent is trying to make a good impression. Still, when handled skillfully, an interview will often reveal information that can be obtained in no other way.

The available guides to evaluation describe a rather traditional interview methodology:

1. Ask a sampling of students about their ease in obtaining sources.

2. Talk with a sampling of students and faculty to gain insight into their satisfaction with services.

Interviews do work and do produce information, but there are so many variables, and they are so time-consuming, that the technique is rarely used.

Observation

"I could tell by the way he left the reference desk that he was not happy with the answer." "The reference interview seemed to go well." "There never is anyone at the reference desk." "No signs, no indication of where to find the reference people."

All of the above are based on observation. The first two are subjective observations of reference librarians in action. The last two are observations of fact. Of the four statements, the last two are the more valuable because they are observable conditions. The statements illustrate the rewards and the possible witchhunt aspects of simple observation of people's actions and structured conditions.

Given the problem of observation, an ultimate requirement is that it be systematically channeled by measures which will ensure accuracy and eliminate, as much as possible, the human factor. This is done in most library studies, particularly where an unobtrusive study is made of reference services.

Quantitative Studies

In quantitative studies the librarian is dealing with statistical data or with known quantities that may be changed and measured by variations on a system, practice, goal, and so forth. For example, one may measure the number of referenda questions asked, and vary results and evaluation by using one reference librarian instead of two and changing the hours of the questions, the place of the questions, the amount of time, and so on. No matter what is done, it can be measured quantitatively.

The usual employment of quantitative data is in measuring circulation, hours, number of questions asked, number of users, and so forth. Here the raw numbers can be juggled and studied, but at least the numbers are accurate. This is particularly true today as most libraries employ computers to keep track of everything from circulation to reserve items to number of cards issued.

In one typical study, for example, quantitative measures revealed: "That our staff answered 553,143 reference questions in 1991, up 100,486 over the previous year. Thirty-nine percent of these questions were fielded at the Main Library, with the Business Department ranking as the busiest department, with 46,567 questions. The Social Science and Science-Technology Departments answered over 30,500 questions each and four of the branches did as well."[23]

Given the raw data of quantitative studies, the librarian may use them for almost anything from annual reports to justification for hiring more staff. Internally, too, the figures are useful as explained by the counted reference questions in the previous example. Information on figures concerning queries assist in collection development. Librarians "can explore which parts of the reference collection get the most use and perhaps buy more circulating materials on those subjects; they can document the days of the week and the hours of those days which are the busiest so that additional staff can be assigned. These statistics and others can also be used to show the need for additional staffing or redeployment. The same statistics, in harder economic times, can help the managers come up with new ideas for needed self-service pathfinders for patrons, reallocation of responsibilities among librarians, clerks, and pages alike, although still within the confines of their job descriptions, and even physical rearrangement of certain areas to accommodate heavy patron use."[24]

Quantitative measurement is preferable for most managers and many librarians because it does deal with data and not the problematic area of quality. It is, for example, much easier to count reference questions or the number of people who use CD-ROMs daily than to ascertain the quality of the answers and the quality of the layperson searches. As White puts it: "What we measure is not quality but quantity, as typified in academic libraries by holdings, and in public libraries by circulation. The most successful transaction is perceived to be the one that leads the user out the door with the greatest number of items; but I restate the obvious when I note that this is at best an educational and never an informational value system. Under the latter, less information, provided it is the correct information, is almost always preferred."[25]

[23]Jane Pinkston, "Assessment and Accountability at Toledo-Lucas County Public Library," *The Reference Librarian*, 1992, no. 38, p. 47.

[24]Ibid.

[25]Herbert White, "The Reference Librarian as Information Intermediary," *The Reference Librarian*, 1992, no. 37, p. 30.

Qualitative Studies

Where the librarian measures the "quality" of this or that, the human factor must be taken into consideration. The advantage of such a measure is that it covers various elements of the real world. The problem is that there often is a lack of detachment, of objectivity, which can thwart the best-constructed qualitative evaluation.

Usually the unobtrusive qualitative study is favored to evaluate personnel. And this is discussed in the next section.

EVALUATING LIBRARIANS

Almost without exception a set of procedures exist for evaluating and guiding reference librarians, as for all employees of the library. Certain elements are found in personnel policy statements. There usually is some indication of the daily activities of the reference librarian from number of hours at the reference desk to duties in collection development.

The primary benefit of a written personnel policy statement can be summarized in one word—fairness. Policies may or may not work, depending on who wrote them and who interprets them, as well as on the given sense of understanding or misunderstanding between parties involved.

Recognizing the vagaries of human nature, the usual policy statement is general. It rarely spells out what to do when one librarian takes exception to the rules governing Monday evening hours. At the same time given policy sections can be quite specific, for example, the salary scale and antidiscrimination clauses.

The literature on reference service runs over with surveys which attempt to draw an accurate personal profile of the happy, successful reference librarian. Much of the statistical fallout is predictable: (1) Daily contact with all types of people requires an interest in conversation, and enthusiasm for helping. (2) The librarian is confident without being aggressive. (3) The librarian is imaginative, creative, and able to make quick turnarounds when either the question or the response has been misinterpreted. (4) The librarian has a memory for details and is able to follow clues with the skill of a Sherlock Holmes.

Evaluation Forms

Normally the library has evaluation forms that are filled out by the librarian's immediate supervisor. A self-evaluation is less often used, but can be useful. Performance ratings tend to get particular attention during the early months and years of a reference librarian's employment, but they probably should be used in later years too. "Probably" because it depends on the type of library, the administrator, and the librarian among other things. If at all possible, there should be mutual agreement among all parties involved on the types of evaluation employed for testing the experienced librarian.

Peer Evaluation[26]

There are different approaches to discovering whether or not a reference librarian has one or all of the required magical qualities. Peer evaluation is a useful technique to improve reference services, but as the process implies it has rewards as well as dangers. The results are based on the day-to-day activities of the reference librarian. Evaluation is by peers and peer groups who, literally, watch the librarian in action. Criticism may be mild ("Not advisable to turn a pencil in your hand during the interview") to highly critical ("Never seems to listen to the person with the question") to praise ("Demonstrates an unusual ability to get on with patrons"). The rewards are improved service and, under most circumstances, a happier reference librarian.

The obvious pitfall is that the system smacks of the "self-improvement" approach whereby peers point out, often with politically correct attitudes, what is wrong with the person being evaluated. Another problem with this approach, as with any in which the qualifications of the individual are tested, is that the focus is often on shortcomings. And this carries over from the individual to studies of the library as a whole.

> We always seem to focus on the shortcomings of individual librarians. But the problem is more extensive: it is in fact institutional and endemic to the profession. There is a more important flaw in almost all of these studies: the tests assume that a librarian's competence assures delivery of competent service. The profession must learn that competence and delivery of service, though intertwined, are not the same thing. Testing and measurement as used by the profession have been almost a textbook example of feeding the disease to the patient as a cure.[27]

Competency Measures

The competencies of the reference librarian may be measured in numerous ways, although the most telling test is simply how well questions are answered. Other equally major tests:

1. Is the librarian keeping up with new technology, for example, with CD-ROM, online searching, Internet, and so forth?

[26]An example of peer evaluation at its best, with few of the difficulties encountered: J. P. Kleiner, "Ensuring Quality Reference Desk Service: The Introduction of a Peer Process," *RQ,* 1991, no. 30, pp. 349–361.

[27]Jack Hicks, "Mediation in Reference Service . . . ," *The Reference Librarian,* 1992, no. 37, p. 51.

2. What knowledge does the librarian have of reference and related sources?

3. How well does the librarian negotiate the reference interview, the search, and the analysis of the results?

4. Does the librarian have a positive attitude about people and the reference process? Kindness, tenacity, patience, and determination are only a few of the required personal and intellectual traits.

Performance Measurement

Using statistical data to measure satisfaction of user with reference service, the time it takes to answer a question, the number of questions answered, and cost per query in performance analysis tends to be favored more by managers than by working librarians. To be judged against a preset scale seems more appropriate for the performance of a worker on a production line than for a professional. Today it rarely works or has the cooperation of staff.

Such measurement not only lacks support, but also is costly and time-consuming. And trying to determine the worth of a reference section by how many questions are answered in a given time is too crude a method to produce any effective evaluation.

Reference librarians will agree that some measure of performance is needed. The difficulty is ascertaining the measures to employ. The simplistic, numerical approach is not enough because it may give a totally misleading picture of service.

In a discussion of how managers may evaluate research-and-development results in industry, a team of management consultants offers advice that applies to evaluating reference services and librarians as well: (1) Focus should be on measuring outcomes, not personal behavior. Every reference librarian has a personal approach to service. This should be honored as long as the behavior does not interfere with the natural flow of daily activities. (2) Make the measurement system simple. The best systems are based on the collection of data on six to eight key indexes. (3) Make the measurement as objective as possible. Industry techniques may differ from those appropriate to libraries and librarians, but the foregoing three golden rules are applicable to any method of measurement.

Stress at the Reference Desk

Working with, talking with, and helping people are by definition stressful situations. Even under the best of circumstances reference work requires a lot of concentration and energy, and a reference librarian may be forgiven for the occasional thought that being alone on an island might not be a bad idea. And when the library is noisy and the person asking a question is less than cooperative, then true stress sets in.

What causes stress for the reference librarian? Or another way of putting it, is there anything that does *not* cause stress at the reference desk? It depends on the situation, the personality of the librarian, and a dozen other variables. Still, one may generalize. Although meeting interesting people is one of the positive aspects of the job, rude patrons are a major stress. While the variety of reference work is enjoyable, the workload can be hectic. And there is never enough time. Problem solving and learning are major benefits, and yet anyone who has worked at a reference desk has experienced a nagging sense of inadequacy. Often, a question refuses to be isolated so that it has a specific meaning, and once it is clarified, the resources available do not give a current, correct answer. In other words the challenge and the stimulation are always there, but so is the stress.

Reference Burnout

Experienced reference librarians have written about stress and reference "burnout." Increasing demands on the librarian result in this all-too-familiar fatigue syndrome.

There are as many ways to meet the burnout problem as there are librarians and libraries. A few common approaches: (1) Every seven or so years the librarian is given a sabbatical or time off to relax in some other aspect of the profession. (2) More assistance is given at the reference desk by paraprofessionals who can field the 60 to 70 percent of questions that are no more than directional and occupy an inordinate amount of the reference librarian's time. (3) The actual number of hours at the reference desk is limited, and often rotated. Some find the average of 15 to 20 hours too much, and they should be given the opportunity to do other tasks. (4) Continuing education that includes everything from online searching to philosophy helps. (5) Finally, but very important, the supervisor should be open to the librarian's suggestions on how to avoid burnout. Anything that is reasonable should be considered.

SUGGESTED READING

Aluri, Rao, and Mary Reichel, "Performance Evaluation," *Journal of Academic Librarianship*, 1994, vol. 20, pp. 145–154. The authors oppose performance evaluation and point out that it results in destroying staff morale while achieving almost nothing in the way of information for administrators. A system can be tested in this way, but not individuals.

Baker, Sharon, and F. W. Lancaster, *Measurement and Evaluation of Library Services*, 2d ed. Arlington, VA: Information Resources Press, 1991. A basic work, this is the first place to turn for information on the process of evaluation. Lancaster is the expert of experts in this field. His coauthor is not far behind. (See also Lancaster, below.)

Blandy, Susan, Lynne Martin, and Mary Strife, eds., "Assessment and Accountability in Reference Work," *The Reference Librarian,* 1992, no. 38. From "research methodologies" to "account-ability" a major group of experts in the field of evaluation of reference services (1) point out the practical steps with such evaluation, (2) explain the possible pitfalls and the problems, and (3) cover virtually every conceivable situation where evaluation is needed. A must for anyone considering evaluation of collections or services. Note the current bibliography.

Brown, Janet, "Using Quality Concepts to Improve Reference Services," *College & Research Libraries,* May 1994, pp. 211–219. While this is a study of an evaluation system employed at Wichita State University, most of the study is applicable to evaluation in other academic settings. Well written and particularly practical.

"Continuing Education for Reference Librarians," *The Reference Librarian,* 1990, no. 31/32. The com-plete issue is given over to what graduate librarians should continue to do to improve their capabilities. Suggestions on everything from online searching to the role of multiple networks are considered. The dozen or more articles, by experienced librarians and teachers, also offer many practical tips for the working reference person.

Crawford, Gregory, "A Conjoint Analysis of Reference Services . . . ," *College & Research Libraries,* May 1994, pp. 257–267. Another effort, another plan to evaluate reference service in aca-demic libraries. Despite the awkward name, it has definite possibilities for determining, for example, how satisfied the users are with certain procedures.

Garrett, Marie, "Applied and Professional Ethics: Resources for Research," *RQ,* Summer 1990, pp. 397–403. The author lists books and periodicals that deal with ethics and moral issues. This guide to the literature of ethics covers several professional fields, and much of it is applica-ble to librarians and also to those who put questions to librarians about ethical matters.

Jahoda, Gerald, and Frank Bonney, "The Use of Paraprofessionals in Public Libraries for Answering Reference Questions," *RQ,* Spring 1990, pp. 329–331. A careful study of why and how para-professionals are employed with suggestions as to what they should and should not do.

Koster, Gregory, "Ethics in Reference Service," *Reference Services Review,* Spring 1992, pp. 71–80. A description of where to find information on ethics in reference service. Suggestions are given on the best way to teach the subject. Case studies and codes of conduct are examined.

Lancaster, F. W., *If You Want to Evaluate Your Library,* 2d ed. Urbana, IL: University of Illinois, Grad-uate School of Library and Information Science, 1993. The dean of evaluation shows the practical steps necessary to judge a library. There is a section on reference services and ref-erence work is mentioned throughout the lucid text. The first choice for evaluation.

Larson, Carole, "Developing Behavioral Reference Desk Performance Standards," *RQ,* Spring 1994, pp. 347–349. An objective look at performance standards as found at the University of Nebraska. The article shows how the process was organized and carried out, apparently to the satisfaction of the staff.

Lowenthal, Ralph, "Preliminary Indications of the Relationships between Reference Morale and Performance," *RQ,* Spring 1990, pp. 380–393. Turning to reference staffs in four public li-braries, the author finds that where morale is high the chances of getting a complete and accurate answer are much better than when the staff is dissatisfied. Although further study may be needed, the premise seems sound.

Phillips, Steven, *Evaluation.* London: Library Association, 1993. One of a series of library training guides for British librarians, this concise 58-page outline is an excellent introduction to prin-ciples and practices. Well organized, the 10 sections move from an introduction and an ex-planation of the need for evaluation to a final checklist. There is a concluding group of use-ful forms.

Research in Reference Effectiveness. Chicago: American Library Association (Reference and Adult Ser-vices Division), 1993. A series of papers on evaluation of reference services. As most of the papers are by working librarians, the suggestions are practical and applicable to almost any reference situation.

Slote, Stanley, *Weeding Library Collections*, 3d ed. Edgewood, CO: Libraries Unlimited, 1989. A basic text on weeding, Slote's book gives precise rules on the subject. Equally helpful are examples drawn from 40 different types of libraries. Required reading for anyone involved with weeding problems.

Tyckoson, David, "Wrong Questions, Wrong Answers," *The Reference Librarian*, 1992, no. 38, pp. 151–174. Subtitled "Behavioral vs. Factual Evaluation of Reference Service," this perceptive article explains both the necessary conditions for good reference services and how they are to be evaluated. Clear, practical, and in itself almost enough for any reference librarian to judge performance.

Van House, Nancy, et al., *Measuring Academic Library Performance*. Chicago: American Library Association, 1990. A detailed discussion of the methods of measuring services, including reference work. The book is highly pragmatic and even includes forms and other materials that can be used in measurement. Much of the advice is applicable to other types of libraries.

Westbrook, Lynn, "Evaluating Reference: An Introductory Overview of Qualitative Methods," *Reference Services Review*, Spring 1990, pp. 73–78. A thoughtful discussion of the methods of evaluation from observation and interviews to surveys and unobtrusive testing. Written for beginners, the expert author assembles the advice in an easy-to-understand fashion and makes an excellent case for qualitative evaluation.

INDEX

Abbott, Tony, 116
Abels, Eileen, 167*n*
ABI/INFORM, 68, 123, 127, 134, 136, 203
Abstracts, in electronic sources, 40
Academic Abstracts Full Text Elite, 128
Academic American Encyclopedia, 81
Academic libraries, 8
   and bibliographical instruction, 226
   CD-ROMs and online sources used in, 204
   and Internet, 91
   orientation tours of, 228
   readings on, 25
Academic Research, 180*n*
Access language of information systems,
      190–192
Acquisitions, and document delivery, 150
Addison-Wesley, 32
ADONIS, 134, 137–138
Advanced Document Delivery System, 136
Advertising, online, 33
   on consumer networks, 80
   and full-text document delivery, 123
   on Internet, 92–93
AIDS information, 111–112*n*
ALA (*see* American Library Association)
ALA Intellectual Freedom Manual, 243*n*
Alert, 198
Alliance of Library Networks, 73
Almanacs, weeding of, 254
"Alternative Career Directions for
      Librarians," 53
Aluri, Rao, 266
America: History and Life, 206
America Online:
   and censorship, 245
   and copyright, 46
   cost of, 111
   The New York Times on, 130
   rating of, 81*n*
   searching system used by, 205
American Chemical Society, 123
American Civil War, The, 37
American Library Association (ALA):
   and censorship, 242–243, 245
   and confidentiality of library records,
      240
   and intellectual freedom, 243*n*
   library standards from, 256
   on networks, 61
   "Statement of Professional Ethics" of,
      239–240
   (*See also* Choice; *RQ*)
American Library Directory, 73*n*
American Reference Books Annual, 250, 251
AMIGOS, 74
Anarchist Cookbook, 243
Anderson, Charles, 170*n*
Apple Computer, 83, 85
Applied Science and Technology Index, 203
Archie, 106
ArchiGopher, 110
Ariel, 134
ARL (Association of Research Libraries), 131,
      144
ARL/RLG Interlibrary Loan Cost Study, 140*n*
Article Clearinghouse, 140
Article Express International, 137
ArticleFirst, 68, 132, 153, 199, 203
ASAP, 80
ASCII formatting, 123*n*
Association of Independent Information
      Professionals, 54

Association of Research Libraries (ARL), 131, 144

Asynchronous transfer mode, 115

AT&T Corporation, 83, 111*n*

AT&T PersonaLink Services, 197

Auletta, Ken, 56, 86

Authority of reference sources, on Internet, 96, 112–113
  and frequently asked questions, 106

Authors (*see* Copyright)

Baker, Russell, 116

Baker, Sharon, 266

Baker, Shirley, 144*n*, 145*n*, 149

Bane, Adele, 86

Barclay, Donald, 233*n*

Baroudi, Carol, 117

Basch, Reva, 39, 39*n*

Behrens, S. J., 235

Bennahum, David, 111*n*

Bennett, Scott, 48*n*

Bennett, Valerie, 134*n*, 144*n*

Benson, Allen, 117

Bentley, Stella, 39

Beowulf, 110

Berinstein, Paula, 176

Berkun, Scott, 198*n*

Berne, Ellen, 101

Bernstein, Richard, 20–21

Berreby, David, 56

Bessler, Joanne, 235

BIB (RLIN Bibliographic File), 70

Bibliodata Full Text Sources Online, 131

Bibliographical instruction, 223–236
  basics of, 227–229
  for electronic sources, 226, 229–232, 234
    readings on, 235–236
  evaluation of, 232–234
  in formal courses, 228–229
  history of, 225*n*
  about Internet, 232
  with orientation tours, 227–228
  pros and cons of, 224–227
  readings on, 235–236

Bibliographical networks, 61, 65–76
  and document delivery, 132–134
  and interlibrary loans, 142–144
  MELVYL, 72, 134
  regional and state networks, 73–75
  uses of, 65–66
  WLN, 72, 74

(*See also* CARL; OCLC; RLIN; *other specific networks*)

Bibliographical utilities (*see* Bibliographical networks)

Bibliographies, searching of, 191

Bibliothèque Nationale, 84

BI-L, 100, 100*n*

Biographical sources, weeding of, 254

Bird Info Network, 99

BITNET, 106

Biz Op: How to Get Rich with Business Opportunity Frauds and Scams, 243

Bjomer, Susanne, 235

Blackburn, Jennifer, 242*n*

Blandy, Susan, 267

Bob software package, 36

Bodi, Sonia, 235

Bonney, Frank, 267

Book Industry Study Group, 5

Book Industry Trends, 56

Bookmarks, 105

Books:
  electronic books, 37, 146–148
  future of, 54–55
  U.S. sales and reading of, 5–6
  violence and crime guides, 243–244
  (*See also specific works*)

Books & Periodicals Online, 131

Books in Print Plus, 41

Boole, George, 212

Boolean logic, 212–213

Bowker (R. R.) Company, 137*n*
  search software from, 41–42

Braid, J. A., 120*n*, 125*n*

Braun, Eric, 117

Britain (*see* United Kingdom)

British Library, 70, 110

British Library Document Supply Centre, 133, 134

Broderbund, 32

Brown, Christopher, 104*n*

Brown, Janet, 267

BRS (*see* CDP)

Bruwelheide, Janis, 56

BUBL (Bulletin Board for Libraries), 99, 106

Buffalo Free-Net, 77

Bulletin Board for Libraries (BUBL), 99, 106

Bulletin board systems, 90, 98–99
  (*See also* Listservs; Usenet)

Burnout of librarians, 266

Burrow, Gale, 86

Burwell Directory of Information Brokers, 53–54
Bush, Vannevar, 34, 56
Business:
  and e-mail, 103
  and Internet, 111
Business ASAP, 128
Business Periodicals Global, 128
Business Periodicals Index, 139
Butcher, D. R., 199

California Library Authority for Systems and
    Services (CLASS), 74
California State Library, 70
Campbell, Peter, 30*n*
CAPCON, 74
Cargill, Jennifer, 149
CARL (Colorado Alliance of Research
    Libraries), 72, 74
  and document delivery, 133
  Magazine ASAP from, 128
  UnCover of, 72, 132, 133, 150
Cartwright, Glenn, 232*n*
Cassidy, John, 24
Cataloging, with RLIN, 71
CDP, 78
  and document delivery, 136, 139
CD-Romance, 52
CD-ROMs, 29–30
  books on, 147
  cost of (*see under* Cost of reference sources)
  currency of, 41
  and document delivery, 135, 137–138
    full-text document delivery, 123, 127,
    130
  ERIC on, 41, 68
  evaluation of, 41–42
  future of, 55*n*
  image quality of, 42
  on networks, 42, 61
    wide-area networks, 79–80
  for OCLC access, 68
  periodicals on, 52, 127
    Newsweek Interactive, 122*n*
  popular titles, 33–34
  publishers and vendors of, 32, 41–42, 50
  and reference interview, 160
  searching of (*see under* Searching electronic
    sources)
  (*See also* Electronic sources [*for general
    information*])
CD-ROMs in Print, 34*n*

Cello, 109*n*
Censorship, 242–246
Cerf, Vinto, 94*n*
Chadwyck-Healy, 146–147
Chemical Abstracts, 137
Chemical Journals, 123
Chemistry, and full-text document delivery,
    123
ChemSearch, 79
Childers, Thomas, 241*n*
Choice, 39, 250
Chronicle of Higher Education 1990–1993,
    180*n*
Chu, Felix T., 166*n*, 176
Cisler, Steve, 87, 102*n*
CitaDel, 70, 71, 133
Citation indexes, searching of, 207
City University of New York, 75
CLASS (California Library Authority for
    Systems and Services), 74
Clement, Gail, 117
Clinton administration, 103–104
CLIP, 198
Collection evaluation, 248–254
College education, 5
Colorado Alliance of Research Libraries (*see*
    CARL)
Commerce Net, 90
Commercial networks (*see* Consumer
    networks)
Communet, 77
Communicating with Library Users, 176
Communication networks (*see* Networks)
Community information center, 22–23
Community networks, 8, 77
Compact disc–read-only memory (*see* CD-
    ROMs)
Company bulletin boards, 99
Company Quick Check, 205*n*
Competency measures, 264–265
Complete Internet Companion for Librarians, The,
    117
Compton's Interactive Encyclopedia, 213
Compton's New Media, 32, 36, 218
CompuServe, 81, 82
  "clipping" services on, 104
  as information mediator, 197
  Magazine ASAP from, 128
  Presidential Discussion Forum on, 104
  rating of, 81*n*
Computer ASAP, 129

Computers:
  and desktop publishing, 49–50
  home use of, 6
  personal computers, 36
  prevalence of, 116*n*
  and television, 83–86
  (*See also* CD-ROMs; Databases; Electronic
    sources; Networks; Online sources)
Computers in Libraries, 97
Confidentiality of library records, 240–241
Congressional Quarterly, 213
Consumer networks, 61, 80–83
  and censorship, 245–246
  charges by, 79
  "clipping" services on, 104
  and e-mail, 103*n*
  and Internet, 108
    and World Wide Web, 109
  searching of, 161
  (*See also specific networks*)
Consumer Reports, 81
ContentsFirst, 68, 70, 132
Controlled vocabulary searching, 215–216
Copyright, 46–49
  and document delivery, 141
  and networks, 63
  readings on, 56
Copyright Clearance Center, 48, 137*n*
Copyright Primer for Librarians and Educators, The,
    56
Cost of reference sources:
  of CD-ROMs, 33–34, 42, 44, 45
    books on, 147
    vs. online sources, 204
  of interlibrary loans, 144, 145
  of online sources, 44–46
    vs. CD-ROMs, 204
    newspapers on, 130
    periodicals on, 128, 129
  of other electronic sources, 44–46
    commercial services as information
      mediators, 197
    consumer networks, 81–83
    for document delivery, 125, 133–141,
      150
    electronic clipping service, 198
    information brokers, 53
    Internet, 110–112
    OCLC and RLIN, 71–72
    vendors' fees for network access, 79
Coursepacks, 147–148

Courtois, Martin, 89*n*, 207*n*
Cox, Jennifer, 110*n*
CQ Washington Alert Service, 134
Crackers, 246
Crawford, Gregory, 267
Creed of a Librarian, The, 239*n*
Crews, Kenneth, 241*n*
Crime and censorship, 243–244
Criminal Justice Abstracts, 45
Cromer, Donna, 100*n*
Cuadra, Carlos, 31
Currency of reference sources:
  and document delivery, 141–142
  of electronic sources, 40
    CD-ROMs, 41
    vs. printed sources, 202
  hierarchy of, 12
  and searching, 189
  and weeding, 252
Customized textbooks, 147–148
Cyberliteracy, 63–64
Cybernetics, 62*n*
Cyberspace, 62–63

Dante Project, 99
Dartmouth College, 99
Darwin, Charles, 174
"Data discman," 37
Data Times, 129, 198
Database, 97
Database site licenses, 80
Databases:
  on Internet, guide to, 97
  licensing of, 48
  searching of (*see* Searching electronic
    sources)
  vendors' guides to, 78–79
  (*See also* CD-ROMs; Electronic sources [*for
    general information*]; Online sources;
    specific databases)
DataStar, 78
  and full-text document delivery, 129,
    130
  Magazine ASAP from, 128
Davis, Dorothy, 231*n*
D'Elia, George, 25
Dell, Esther, 144*n*
Delphi, 83
Delta, 243
DelVecchio, Rosemary, 241
Democracy on Trial, 25

Demographics:
  of library users, 20
  trends in, 4–5
Desktop publishing, 49–50
Deutsch, Peter, 98*n*
Dewdney, Patricia, 155, 176
Dewey, Patrick, 39
DIALOG, 61
  charges by, 44*n*, 79
  copyright payment system of, 48
  and document delivery, 126, 135
    full-text document delivery, 129
  electronic clipping service from, 198
  and Internet, 96
  and Knight-Ridder, 72, 78
  Magazine ASAP from, 128
  newspapers from, 129, 130
  and regional networks, 73–74
  searching system of, 42, 164, 213, 214–215
DialOrder, 129, 135
Diaz, Karen, 95*n*
Dickinson, Gail, 39*n*
Dictionaries, weeding of, 254
Dictionary of Computer Words, 98*n*
Dillon, Patrick, 56
Directories, weeding of, 254
Directory of Directories on the Internet, 117
Directory of Electronic Journals, Newsletters, and
    Academic Discussion Lists, 117, 131
Disadvantaged, as library users, 19–21
Discovering Authors, 32
Discussion groups, 90
  (*See also* Listservs)
Dissertation Abstracts, 45
Dissertation Abstracts International, 203
DOCLINE, 144
Document delivery, 48, 119–150
  basics of, 124–126
  and bibliographical networks, 132–134
    OCLC, 132–133, 136, 150
    RLIN, 133–134, 150
  and CD-ROMs, 135, 137–138
    full-text document delivery, 123, 127,
      130
  from commercial firms, 134–138
    DIALOG, 126, 129, 135
    Information Access Company, 123, 129,
      130, 134–136
    vs. interlibrary loans, 139–141
    NEXIS, 128, 129, 139
    UMI, 123, 126–128, 133, 134–136, 140

cost of, 125, 133–141, 150
  definition of, 124*n*
  and electronic books, 146–148
  evaluation of, 138–142
  and information brokers, 52–54
  in microform, 148–149
  off-site document delivery, 132–138
  readings on, 149–150
  and technology, 125–126
  and vendors and publishers, 124*n*, 125, 135,
    138
  (*See also* Fax for document delivery; Full-text
    document delivery; Interlibrary loans)
Dolan, Donna, 211*n*
Dorrance Joan, 25
Douville, J., 39
Dow Jones News Online, 128–129
Dow Jones News World Report, 128–129
Dow Jones News/Retrieval, 78, 79, 129, 130,
  197, 198
Dow Jones News/Retrieval—Enhanced/TEXT,
  129
DuMont, Mary, 228*n*
Durniak, Barbara, 140*n*
Dvorak, John, 245*n*

Easley, Bruce, 243
Eastern Massachusetts Regional Library
  System, 101
Easynet, 60
EBSCO:
  and document delivery, 127, 134–136
    full-text document delivery, 123
  hybrid databases from, 128
  search software from, 42
EBSCOdoc, 136
Echo, 38
Economic Bulletin Board, 99
Education:
  multimedia used in, 34–35
  and networks, 59
    readings on, 86, 87
  and OCLC CD-ROMs, 68
  in U.S., 5, 6–7
  and videoconferencing, 85
  (*See also* Bibliographical instruction;
    Literacy)
Education Resources Information Center (*see*
    ERIC)
Edwards, Sharri, 235
Electronic books, 37, 146–148

Electronic clipping service, 198
Electronic journals, 51–52, 121
Electronic Journals Online, 68
Electronic mail (*see* E-mail)
Electronic sources, 15–16, 29–150
　and bibliographical instruction, 226,
　　229–232, 234
　　readings on, 235–236
　and collection evaluation, 251
　and copyright, 46–49
　cost of (*see under* Cost of reference sources)
　currency of, 40
　　of CD-ROMs, 41
　　vs. printed sources, 202
　documentation for, 211
　electronic books, 37, 146–148
　electronic journals, 51–52, 121
　evaluation of, 39–46
　　readings on, 56
　manuals for, 43
　multimedia sources, 34–35
　organization and contents of, 40–41
　periodicals on (*see under* Periodicals)
　vs. printed books, 54–55
　readings on, 56–57
　and selective dissemination of information,
　　16
　(*See also* CD-ROMs; Computers; Databases;
　　Electronic books; E-mail; Full-text
　　document delivery; Games and
　　entertainment; Networks; Online
　　sources; Searching electronic sources;
　　specific services, publishers, vendors, and titles)
*Elements of Information Gathering, The: A Guide for
　Technical Communicators, Scientists, and
　Engineers*, 219
Ellis, Mark, 219
Ellsworth, Jill, 82
Elsevier, 123, 138
Elshtain, Jean, 25
Elzy, Cheryl, 242*n*
E-magazines, 50–51
E-mail:
　and consumer networks, 80
　free, 33
　for interlibrary loans, 143
　and Internet, 90, 91, 102–104, 114
　and Listservs, 100
　and networks, 63
　over Prodigy, 83
　for reference service requests, 166–167

Encyclopedias:
　on consumer networks, 81
　weeding of, 254
Engineering Information, 134
Engineering Societies Libraries, 137
England (*see* United Kingdom)
Engle, Mary, 117
English Poetry Full-Text Database, The, 147
English Verse Drama, 147
Entertainment (*see* Games and entertainment)
EPIC, 68, 71, 133
ERIC, 203
　on CARL, 72
　on CD-ROM, 41, 68
　cost of, 45
　searching of, 32
　on state network, 75
ESL Information Services, 137
Estienne, Henri, 30
Ethernet, 60
Ethics, and reference librarians, 239–247, 267
Europe:
　document delivery in, 150
　teletext in, 84
European Community, 13
Evaluating Bibliography Instruction, 232*n*
Evaluation, 267
Evaluation of reference services (*see under*
　　Reference services)
Everett, David, 139*n*, 143*n*
Everett, Virginia, 149
Ewing, Keith, 199
Eworld, 83
Excite, 107
Exec-PC, 99
Expanded Academic ASAP, 128
Expanded Academic Index, 134, 153
*Expression of the Emotions in Man and Animals,
　The*, 174

Facts on File, 32
Facts on File, 72
Fair use, 47, 48
FAQ (frequently asked questions), 105–106
Favier, Jean, 30*n*
Fax for document delivery, 133, 134, 136, 137
　by interlibrary loan, 142, 143
Fax Research Services, 134
Faxon Company, 136
Faxon Finder, 136
Faxon Research Services, Inc., 136

Federal Whistleblower's BBS, 99
FEDLINK, 74
Feinman, Valerie, 235
Fiber optic technology, 113*n*
Fiche, 148 (*see* Microfiche)
File transfer protocol (FTP), 94
Find SVP, 53*n*
First Interview, The, 176
First Service Network, 56
FirstSearch, 45, 67–70, 87, 133, 161, 203
   (*See also ArticleFirst; ContentsFirst*)
FirstSearch-L, 100–101
*Fiscal Directory of Fee-Based Information Services in
   Libraries, The*, 54
Fisher, Jean, 235
"Flaming," 103, 117
Florida International University, 117
Folio Corporation, 137*n*
Foskett, D. J., 239*n*
Foster, Erin, 102*n*
Foster, Stephen, 9*n*
France, teletext in, 84
Francoise, Hebert, 149
Franklin Electronic Publishers, 37
Free Style, 213
Freedom of information (*see* Censorship)
FreeMark Communications, 33
Free-nets, 77
Free-text searching, 215–216
Frequently asked questions (FAQ), 105–106
Frum, David, 25
FTP (file transfer protocol), 94
Full Text Sources Online, 121*n*, 131
Full-text document delivery, 119–132
   guides for, 130–132
   and hybrid databases, 126, 127, 128
   and Internet, 124
   nature of, 122–124
   and newspapers, 129–130
   and online sources, 127–129
   of periodicals, 121–122
   steps in, 124

Gabbard, Ralph, 56
Gainor, Larry, 102*n*
Galbraith, John Kenneth, 3
Gale Directory of Databases, 38*n*, 130–131
Gale Guide to Internet, 97
Gale Research Inc., 32
Games and entertainment, electronic, 33–34
   on Internet, 90

   on World Wide Web, 109
   with virtual reality, 35
Games & Entertainment on CD-ROM, 34*n*
Garrett, Marie, 267
Gasaway, Laura, 49*n*, 56
Gateways, 60
General Electric Information Service, 83
General Periodicals on CD-ROM, 128
Genie, 83, 104
Genuine Article, The, 135, 137, 140
Geographical interfaces, 205
Geographical sources, weeding of, 254
Get Even: The Complete Book of Dirty Tricks, 243
Gibson, Craig, 233*n*
Gibson, William, 62
Gigabit Testbed Initiative, 115
Gilmer, Lois, 149
Glavash, Keith, 140*n*
Glimpses of Heaven, Visions of Hell, 57
Global Networks, 86
*Global Voices, Global Visions: A Core Collection of
   Multicultural Books*, 25
Gopher, 104–105
Gorman, Michael, 54*n*, 230–231, 234
Gornick, Vivian, 102*n*
Government Printing Office, 70
Government sources:
   on Internet, 99, 111
   weeding of, 254
GPO Monthly Catalog, 203
Graham, Cornish, 59*n*, 120*n*, 150
Great Britain (*see* United Kingdom)
Greek literature, on CD-ROM, 30
Grolier, Inc., 32
Guardian Weekly, 113
Guide to Cooperative Collection Development, 150
Guide to Reference Books, 250
Guides:
   to Internet and World Wide Web, 97, 107,
      117
   to online sources for full-text document
      delivery, 130–132
   vendors' guides to databases, 78–79
   to violence and crime, 243
Gunter, Linda, 86

Hackers, 246
Handicapped, reference services for, 21
Hanne, Daniel, 176
Hapgood, Fred, 86
Harasim, Linda, 86

Harloe, Barbara, 150
Hauptman, Robert, 199
Havener, W. M., 199
Health (*see* Medicine and health)
Health ASAP, 128
Health Net, 84
Hernon, Peter, 241*n*
Hicks, Jack, 157*n*, 264*n*
High Performance Computer Act, 113
High-definition television, 30
Hixon, Charles R., 230*n*, 234*n*
Hockey, Beth, 171*n*
Home-Built Claymore Mines, 243
Homemade Grenade Launchers, 243
Hooked, 108*n*
House Government Operations Committee, 99
Hubs, 60
Hull, Theodore, 117
Hults, Patricia, 241*n*
Hybrid databases, 126–128
Hypertext, 34
    readings on, 56
    and World Wide Web, 108–109
Hypertext, 56

IAC (*see* Information Access Company)
I&R (information and referral services), 22–23
IBM Corporation, 36, 82, 110, 127, 146, 218
If You Want to Evaluate Your Library, 267
Illinois Benedictine College, 146
Illinois State University, 242
Illiteracy (*see* Literacy)
Illustrations, and full-text document delivery, 123
Impact of Emerging Technologies on Reference Services and Bibliographic Instruction, The, 236
Income distribution, 4, 7
    readings on, 25
Indexes:
    on CD-ROMs, 127
    and document delivery:
        from bibliographical networks, 132–133
        full-text document delivery, 126–129
    searching of, 191
Indiana University, 110
Information:
    access to, 12–13
    as commodity, 30–31
    glut of, 16–19, 31–32, 115
        and librarians as mediators, 163–164, 196–197

    and library users, 13–16
    packaging of, 9–12
    (*See also* Reference services; Reference sources)
Information Access Company (IAC):
    CD-ROMs networked by, 42, 80
    and document delivery, 127, 134–136
        full-text document delivery, 123, 129, 130
    hybrid databases from, 128
    searching of databases from, 42, 206
Information and referral services (I&R), 22–23
Information brokers, 52–54
Information highway (*see* Electronic sources; Information superhighway)
Information Marketplace, 137
Information on Demand, 140
Information search, retrieval, and delivery (ISRD), 142*n*
Information Seeking in Electronic Environments, 218
Information services (*see* Reference services)
Information sources (*see* Reference sources)
Information superhighway, 61–65
    (*See also* Electronic sources; National information infrastructure)
InfoStore, 136, 140
InfoTrac, 128
InfoTrac Articles, 136
InfoTrac 2000 Delivery System, 136
Institute for Scientific Information (ISI), 135, 137
Insurance companies, and Internet, 93
Interactive advertising, 93
Interactive television, 83–86, 93
Interlibrary loans, 119, 124*n*, 132, 133, 142–145
    cost of, 144, 145
    vs. document delivery, 125
        from commercial services, 139–141
    readings on, 149–150
    and technology, 126
International reference sources, 13
    bibliographical networks, 65
Internet:
    access to, 106–108
    advertising on, 92–93
    anonymous remailer on, 48
    authority of reference sources on, 96, 112–113
    basics of, 95–96
    as bibliographical network, 66–67

and censorship, 244
and community networks, 77
congestion on, 113–114
and consumer networks, 80–83
cost and management of, 110–112
and e-mail, 90, 91, 102–104, 114
and frequently asked questions, 105–106
future of, 63, 115
and Gopher and Veronica, 104–105
guides to, 97, 107, 131
hazards of, 94
history of, 92
in information gathering, 15
and local area networks, 76
MELVYL on, 72
OCLC on, 68
popular uses of, 33
Project Gutenberg on, 146
publishing on, 50–51
readings on, 86, 87, 116–118
and reference services (*see under* Reference
    services)
searching on (*see under* Searching electronic
    sources)
and SilverPlatter Information, 32
slowness of, 113
Uncover on, 133
users of, 90–91
and vendors, 96, 108
(*See also* Bulletin board systems; Listservs;
    Usenet; World Wide Web)
Internet Access Providers, 108n, 114n
Internet Connections—A Librarian's Guide, 117
Internet Directory, The, 117
Internet for Dummies, The, 117
Internet Hunt, 100
Internet in a Box, 108n
Internet Multicasting Service, 90n, 111
Internet World, 97, 108n
Internet Yellow Pages, The, 245n
Internet's World on Internet, 116, 131
Interviews, to evaluate reference services,
    260–261
"Invisible college," 15–16
ISI (Institute for Scientific Information), 135,
    137
ISRD (information search, retrieval, and
    delivery), 142n

Jackson, Mary, 139n, 142n, 144n, 145n, 149,
    150

Jacobson, Frances, 235
Jacobson, Michael J., 235
Jahoda, Gerald, 267
JANET (Joint Academic Network), 106
Jeng, Ling Hwey, 218
Jenkins, Simon, 55n
Jesudason, Melba, 25
Johnson, Denise, 177
Johnson, Mary, 100n
Joint Academic Network (JANET), 106
Journals (*see* Periodicals)
Juno Online Services, 33

Kaestle, Carl, 25
Kanton, Andrew, 102n
Katz, Bill, 25
Kelly, Robert, 174
Kendall, Susan, 232n
Kenner, Hugh, 147
Key words, in searching, 191–192
Khali, Mounir, 125n
Kibbee, Jo, 99n
Kim Park, Taemin, 218
Kinder, Robin, 89n, 117
Kinnucan, Mark, 139n
Klassen, Tim, 117
Kleiner, J. P., 264n
Knight-Ridder Information, Inc., 72, 78, 133
    (*See also* DIALOG)
Knowledge-based systems, 57
Knowledge-Based Systems for General Reference Work,
    199
Kohl, David, 87
Koster, Gregory, 267
Krol, Ed, 89n
Kuhlthau, Carol, 199, 235
Kurosman, Kathleen, 140n

Ladd, E. C., 180n
LaGuardia, Cheryl, 35n, 39
Lancaster, F. W., 218, 235, 242, 266, 267
Landow, George, 56
Lane, Carol, 39
Languages, and searching, 189
Lanier, Don, 117
LANs (local area networks), 75–77
Larson, Carole, 267
Lasch, Christopher, 25
Law (*see* Copyright)
LawTALK, 217
Leach, Ronald, 120n

Leonard, David, 56
Levine, John, 117
LEXIS, 78, 137*n*, 205*n*, 218
Librarians:
  as educators, 224–225
  and ethics, 239–247, 267
  evaluation of, 263–266
  and information brokers, 53–54
  and information superglut, 16–19
  and Internet, 97–98, 114
  interviews of, to evaluate reference services,
    260–261
  as mediators, 155–157, 158–159, 162–164,
    196–197, 199
  and networks, 64–65
  and problems with patrons, 170–172
  stress among, 265–266
  as technicians, 224
  (*See also* Bibliographical instruction;
    Reference services)
Libraries:
  budgets of, 7–8
    and collection evaluation, 251
    and interlibrary loans, 144–145
    readings on, 25–26
    (*See also* Cost of reference sources)
  and copyright, 46–48
  evaluation of, 255–256
  fee-based services from, 54
  as information brokers, 54
  as information mediators, 17–19
  and networks, 60, 61, 64–65
    Internet, 91
    local area networks, 75–77
    regional and state networks, 73–75
  orientation tours of, 227–229
  roles of, 4
  theft of books from, 246–247
  U.S. use of, 7
  users of, 13–16
    readings on, 24–26
  (*See also* Academic libraries; Interlibrary
    loans; Librarians; Reference services;
    specific libraries)
*Libraries and Copyright: A Guide to Copyright Law in
  the 1990s*, 56
Library Alliance, 131
Library consortium, 61
Library Journal:
  Internet column in, 89*n*
  reference titles in, 251

reviews in, 250
  of electronic sources, 39
Library of Congress:
  and document delivery, 141
  and national information infrastructure,
    146
  subject headings of, 215
  Vatican Library and Renaissance Culture
    from, 110
  (*See also National Union Catalog*)
Library of Congress Information System
  (Locis), 105
Library of Congress Marvel, 105
LibRef-L, 100
Licensing of databases, 48, 128
Liebscher, Peter, 167*n*
Lipset, S. M., 180*n*
Listservs, 100–101, 103
  Communet, 77
Literacy, 5
  computer literacy, 63–64
  and library use, 7
  and poverty, 3
  readings on, 25
  and searching, 189
Literacy in the United States, 25
Local area networks (LANs), 75–77
Locis (Library of Congress Information
  System), 105
Loompanics Unlimited, 243
Los Angeles City Public Library, 110
Los Angeles Times, 130
Lowenthal, Ralph, 267
Lycos, 107

Mac, 108*n*
Mackey, Terry, 145
Maes, Pattie, 198*n*
Magazine Articles Full Text, Select, 128
Magazine Articles Summaries Full Text Elite,
  128
Magazine ASAP, 122*n*, 128
Magazine Express, 128
Magazine Index, 72, 203
Magazine Index Plus, 80
Magazines (*see* Periodicals)
Magazines for Libraries, 39
Magnetic tape, and document delivery, 124*n*
Malthus, Thomas, 188
Mandelbaum, Judith, 150
Manuals, weeding of, 254

MARC (machine-readable cataloging), 67, 69, 70, 71
Marchionini, Gary, 218
Marcus, John, 43*n*
Martin, Lynne M., 236, 267
Massachusetts Institute of Technology (MIT), 86, 126–127
Masters of Deception: The Gang That Ruled Cyberspace, 57
Matthew, Judith, 207*n*
Maule, R. William, 87
MBone (Multicast Backbone), 115
McClure, Charles R., 241*n*
McCure, Jim, 49*n*
McGill University, 106
McGraw-Hill, 147
McLaughlin, Pamela, 232*n*
McLeary, Hunter, 198*n*
McLuhan, Marshall, 55
McNeil, Beth, 177
Mead Data Central, 78, 137*n*, 213
  (*See also* NEXIS)
Measurement and Evaluation of Library Services, 266
Measuring Academic Library Performance, 268
Medicine and health:
  and Health Net, 84
  Oklahoma state network for, 75
  telemedicine, 85
MEDLINE, 32, 41, 203
Meeting Community Needs with Job and Career Services, 25
Mellon, Constance, 233*n*
Mellor-Ghilardi, Fiona, 204*n*
MELVYL, 72, 134
Merriam-Webster's Collegiate Dictionary, 37
Michel, Dee Andy, 218
Michelin travel guides, 37
Michigan Library Consortium (*see* MLC)
Microfiche, 148
Microform, 148–149
Micropoint, 149
Microsoft Bookshelf, 146*n*
Microsoft Corporation, 32, 36, 79*n*, 82, 109*n*, 205
Microsoft Network (MSN), 82, 115
Milheim, William, 86
Miller-Lachmann, Lyn, 25
Minitel, 84
MIT (Massachusetts Institute of Technology), 126–127
MIT Media Laboratory, 86

MLA, 203
MLC (Michigan Library Consortium), 74
Model Statement of Objectives for Academic Bibliographic Instruction, 233
Molin, Sandra R., 87
Mood, Terry, 236
Morgan, Keith, 99*n*
Morris, Ruth, 176
Morrison, James, 176
Mosaic, 98, 108*n*, 109, 110, 207
MSN (Microsoft Network), 82, 115
Multicast Backbone, 115
Multiculturalism, and reference services, 19–21
  readings on, 25–26
Multimedia Mail, 83
Multimedia sources, 34–35
  readings on, 56
  searching of, 207–208
  and videoconferencing, 85
  and virtual reality, 35–37
  (*See also* Hypertext)
Multimedia Technology from A to Z, 56
Muraski, Michael, 219
Murdoch, Rupert, 83, 90
Music, and OCLC CD-ROMs, 68–69
Music Library: Musical Sound Recordings, 68–69

NAILDD (North American Interlibrary Loan/Department Delivery), 142*n*
Naked in Cyberspace: How to Find Personal Information Online, 39
National Academy of Sciences, 59
National Center for Supercomputer Applications, 59, 109*n*
National Commission on Libraries, 91*n*
National information infrastructure, 61, 115, 146
National Information Infrastructure Advisory Council, 92*n*
National Library of Medicine, 41, 70, 100, 112*n*, 144
National Newspaper Index, 149
National Research and Educational Network (NREN), 59, 92*n*, 113
National Science Foundation, 111
National Union Catalog, 67*n*, 69, 105
Native American Multimedia Encyclopedia, 32
Natural information networks, 75
Navigator (Netscape Navigator), 107, 109*n*
Necromancer, 62

Negroponte, Nicholas, 86
NetFirst, 68
NETLINET (New England Library
    Information Network), 68
Netscape Communications Company, 107,
    109*n*
Netscape Navigator, 107, 109*n*
Networks, 59–87
  CD-ROMs on, 42
  and censorship, 244–246
  community networks, 8, 77
  and cost of reference sources, 44–45
  and libraries, 60, 61
  local area networks, 75–77
  readings on, 57, 86–87
  regional networks, 73–74
  and sharing, 61
  state networks, 74–75
  and television, 83–86
  types of, 60–61
  and vendors, 77–80
  wide-area networks, 79
  (*See also* Bibliographical networks;
    Consumer networks; Information
    superhighway; Internet; *other specific
    networks*)
New England Journal of Medicine, The, 52
New England Library Information Network
    (NETLINET), 68
New York City, income inequality in, 4*n*
New York Public Library, 24, 70, 110
New York State Education and Research
    Network (NYSER Net), 75
New York Times, The, 130, 149
News Corporation, 83
News Exchange, The, 84
Newsletter Database, 130
Newsletters, full-text document delivery of,
    130
Newspaper Abstracts, 75, 203
Newspaper Index, 203
Newspapers:
  in microform, 149
  on online sources, 122, 129–130
    on consumer networks, 81
    and full-text document delivery, 123
Newspapers Online, 131
Newsweek, 81, 122*n*
Newsweek Interactive, 122*n*
Newswire ASAP, 130
NEXIS, 78, 137*n*

and document delivery, 128, 129, 139
  electronic clipping service from, 198
  Magazine ASAP from, 128
  newspapers from, 129, 130
  Newsweek and *Time* on, 122*n*
  searching of, 205*n*, 209, 213
Nielsen, Brian, 171*n*
Nielsen Media Research, 90
Nonprint materials:
  on OCLC, 67*n*
  searching for, 150
Norris, Carol, 219
North American Interlibrary
    Loan/Department Delivery
    (NAILDD), 142*n*
Notess, Greg R., 108*n*, 114*n*
Novell, 127
NREN (National Research and Educational
    Network), 59, 92*n*, 113
Nuckolls, Karen, 104*n*
NYSER Net (New York State Education and
    Research Network), 75

Obtrusive evaluation of reference services, 258
OCLC (Online Computer Library Center),
    67–72
  cost of, 71–72
  and document delivery, 132–133, 136, 150
  and interlibrary loans, 142–143
  vs. other bibliographical networks, 72
  searching of, 42, 67–68, 69–70
  (*See also ArticleFirst; ContentsFirst; FirstSearch*)
OhioLink, 87
OHIONET, 74
Oklahoma, state network in, 75
O'Leary, Mike, 39
Omni, 81
On Internet, 121
OnDisc/NEWSPAPERS, 130
O'Neill, Molly, 38
Online, 97
Online Computer Library Center (*see* OCLC)
Online 100, The, 39
Online Retrieval, 219
Online sources:
  addiction to, 38–39
  and copyright, 48–49
  cost of (*see under* Cost of reference sources)
  evaluation of, 42–43
  and full-text document delivery, 127–129
  guides to, 130–132

and librarians as mediators, 163–164
newspapers on, 81, 122, 129–130
periodicals on, 51–52, 121–122, 127–129
popular use of, 38–39
searching of (*see under* Searching electronic
    sources)
(*See also* Databases; Electronic sources [*for
    general information*]; Networks; *specific
    services, publishers, vendors, and titles*)
Online Union Catalog, 68, 69
OPAC (online public access catalog), 228
OPAC directory, The, 72
ORBIT-QUESTEL, 78
O'Reilly & Associates, 91*n*
Orenstein, Ruth, 121*n*, 123
Osburn, C. B., 180*n*
Outcome studies, 259
Outsourcing, 119*n*

Pacs-L (Public Access Computer Forum), 100*n*
PAIS, 203, 207
Paladin Press, 243
Palmer, Eileen, 134*n*
Palmer, Joseph, 67*n*
Paraprofessionals in library work, 255
    readings on, 267
Passport, 198
Patrologia Latina Database, 147
Patron Behavior in Libraries, 177
Peer evaluation, 264
Performance measurement, 265
Periodicals:
    and document delivery, 125–129, 130–146
    on electronic sources, 121–122
        on CD-ROMs, 127
        on consumer networks, 81
        electronic journals, 50–52, 121
        on online sources, 127–129
    Internet information in, 97
Periodicals on Disc, 127
Personal computers, 36
Personal Librarian's Search Engine, 213
Philips, Kevin, 3–4
Phillips, Steven, 267
Photocopying, and copyright, 47
Pinkston, Jane, 262*n*
Piternick, Anne B., 199
Pitkin, Gary M., 236
Plaiss, Mark, 170*n*
"Politically correct," 20–21
Polly, Jean, 87, 102*n*

Porak, Diane, 229*n*, 236
Portable Family Doctor, The, 37
Postman, Neil, 115*n*
Predicasts, 123, 129
Presidential Discussion Forum, 104
Press (*see* Newspapers; Periodicals)
Primus, 147
Princeton Survey Research, 116*n*
Prison libraries, 21
Privacy of library records, 240–241
Prodigy, 80–83
    and censorship, 245
    Los Angeles Times on, 130
Project Gutenberg, 146
PROMT, 123
ProQuest, 127, 128
Psychological Abstracts, 203
PsycInfo, 75
Public Access Computer Forum (Pacs-L), 100*n*
Publishers:
    books-on-demand from, 147–148
    on CD-ROM and online, 50–51
    of CD-ROMs, 32, 41–42, 50
    desktop publishing, 49–50
    and document delivery, 135, 138
    searching of databases from, 206–207
    small press publishers, 50–51
    vs. vendors, 77
    (*See also specific publishers*)

Quality and Value in Information Services, 39*n*
Quantitative studies of reference services,
    261–262
Quicktime Conferencing, 85
Quint, Barbara, 119*n*, 145*n*
Quittner, Joshua, 57

Radio, on Internet, 90*n*
Ray, Ron, 150
Readers' Guide to Periodical Literature, 44, 139, 203
Reading, in U.S., 5–6
    (*See also* Literacy)
Ready-reference questions:
    and bibliographical instruction, 226
    and Internet, 95, 101
    and printed vs. electronic sources, 202
Redlich, Barry, 176
Reed, Lawrence, 236
Reed Elsevier, 134, 137
"Reference Books Bulletin" (in *The Booklist*),
    81*n*

Reference interview, 153–177
  basics of, 154–157
  and librarian as mediator, 155–157,
      158–159, 162–164
  problems in, 169–172
  readings on, 176–177
  satisfaction and success in, 158–160
  and searching electronic sources, 160–162
  steps in, 165–169
  techniques of, 172–176
  and types of users, 157–158, 159–160
  (*See also* Bibliographical instruction)
Reference librarians (*see* Librarians)
Reference questions:
  accuracy of librarians' answers to, 241–242
  in evaluation of reference services, 258–259,
      261–262
  and reference interview, 165–169
  and searching reference sources, 181–183
  "translation" of, 186–190
  (*See also* Ready-reference questions)
Reference services:
  accuracy in, 241–242
  and censorship, 242–246
  and collection evaluation, 248–254
  ethics of, 239–247, 267
    and confidentiality of library records,
      239–240
  evaluation of, 254–266
    and librarian evaluation, 263–266
    methodology of, 256–258
    readings on, 266–268
    techniques of, 258–263
  fees for, 247–248
  and gathering and packaging information,
      9–12
  information and referral services, 22–23
  information brokers, 52–54
  and Internet, 94–118
    access points for, 106
    basics of, 95–96
    and bibliographical instruction, 232
    and bulletin boards, 99
    and document delivery, 124, 136–138
    and e-mail, 103–104
    evaluation of, 112–114
    and frequently asked questions, 106
    and Gopher and Veronica, 105
    guides to, 97
    and Listservs, 100–101
    readings on, 116–118
    and role of librarians, 97–98

  and Usenet, 102
  and World Wide Web, 109–110
  and multiculturalism, 19–21
  and networks, 64–65
    bibliographical networks, 65–66
  and nonlibrary users, 21–23
  policies and procedures for, 237–254
    and policy statements, 237–239, 263
    readings on, 266–268
  readings on, 24–26
  for special groups of users, 19–21
  telephone service, 23–24
  (*See also* Bibliographical instruction;
      Librarians; Libraries; Reference
      interview; Reference questions;
      Reference sources; Searching reference
      sources)
Reference Services Review, 236
Reference sources:
  availability of, 189–190
  "bundling of," 146*n*
  and collection evaluation, 248–254
  home use of, 6
  international reference sources, 13, 65
  "invisible college," 15–16
  language of, 189
  weeding of, 251–254, 268
  (*See also* Cost of reference sources; Currency
      of reference sources; Electronic
      sources; Government sources; Guides;
      Indexes; Libraries; Publishers;
      Reference questions; Reference
      services; Searching reference sources;
      specific works)
*Reference Sources for Small and Medium Sized
      Libraries*, 250
Regional networks, 73–74
Reichel, Mary, 266
Reily, Richard, 6
Research in Reference Effectiveness, 267–268
Research Libraries Information Network (*see*
      RLIN)
Resource Sharing and Information Networks, 87
Rettig, James, 25, 236, 255*n*
Reviews:
  for collection evaluation, 250
  of electronic sources, 39
Revolt of the Elites, The, 25
Rheingold, Howard, 57, 92*n*
Rice University Rice Info, 105
Richardson, John, 57, 199
Risher, Carol, 49*n*

RLG (*see* RLIN)
RLIN (Research Libraries Information
    Network), 70–71
  cost of, 71–72
  and document delivery, 133–134, 150
  and interlibrary loans, 142
  vs. other bibliographical networks, 72
RLIN Bibliographic File (BIB), 70
Roche, Marilyn, 140*n*, 150
Roger, Eleanor Jo, 25
Ross, Catherine, 155, 176
Ross, Lance, 49*n*
Routers, 60
Rowley, J. E., 199
RQ, 39
Rubin, Rhea, 177

Safire, William, 62*n*
Salisbury, Lutishoor, 236
Salony, Mary F., 225*n*
Sampling to evaluate reference services, 260
SAT scores, 5
Schamber, Linda, 219
Scheppke, Jim, 7*n*
Schildhauer, Carole, 214*n*
Schloman, Barbara, 228*n*
School libraries, 8
Science, and Internet, 96
Science Citation Index, 45
Scribner's (Charles) Sons, 32
Scribner's Writers' Disc, American Authors, 32
SDI (selective dissemination of information),
    16, 198–199
Seabrook, John, 117
Search services (information brokers), 52–54
Searching electronic sources, 40, 201–219
  basics of, 205–210
  by beginners, 153–154
  and bibliographical instruction, 226,
      229–232, 234
    readings on, 235–236
  bibliographical networks:
    with indexes vs. tables of contents,
        132–133
    OCLC, 42, 67–68, 69–70
    RLIN, 70
  with boolean logic, 212–213
  CD-ROMs, 41–42, 208
    and bibliographical instruction, 231–232
    free-text searching, 215
    future of, 218
    multimedia CD-ROMs, 207–208

  vs. online sources, 204
  and reference interview, 160, 161
  from SilverPlatter Information, 42, 214
  consumer networks, 80
  cost of, 45
  and database knowledge, 203–204
  evaluation of, 217
  expert searching, 210–217
  full-text searches, 215–216
  future of, 217–218
  hardware for, 201–202
  helpful software and database features in,
      209–210
  Internet, 94–96, 107–109, 205, 207
    with Gopher and Veronica, 104–105
    World Wide Web, 108–109
  with nonboolean search aids, 213–215
  online sources, 42–43
    vs. CD-ROMs, 204
    from DIALOG, 213, 214–215
    from H. W. Wilson Company, 42, 206
    from Information Access Company, 42,
        206
    newspapers on, 130
    NEXIS, 205*n*, 209, 213
    periodicals on, 129
    and reference interview, 160–162
  patterns used in, 206–208
  vs. printed sources, 202–203
  problems in, 214–215
  readings on, 218–219
  and reference interview, 160–162
  and vendors' database guides, 78–79
  (*See also* Hypertext)
Searching reference sources, 179–199
  and access language, 190–192
  and attributes of searchers, 180
  failure in, 193–194
  printed vs. electronic sources, 202–203
  and problem solving, 183–186
  process of, 182–183
  readings on, 199
  results of, 193–195
  strategy of, 181–183
  time for, 193
  tips for, 192–193
  and "translation" of reference questions,
      186–190
  (*See also* Bibliographical instruction;
      Searching electronic sources)
Sears Roebuck, 82
Secrets of the Super Searchers, 39, 219

Seiden, Peggy, 104*n*

Selection and Evaluation of Electronic Resources, 39*n*

Selective dissemination of information (SDI), 16, 198–199

Serials (*see* Newspapers; Periodicals)

Servers, 60

Sex and censorship, 245

Shaffer, Howard, 38

Sherman, Barry, 57

Silicon Snake Oil: Second Thoughts on the Information Highway, 118

Silva, Marcos, 232*n*

SilverPlatter Information, 32
   CD-ROM wide-area network of, 80
   cost of reference sources from, 44, 45
   search software from, 42, 214

Simon & Schuster, 32, 35

Sisyphus, 194

Site licenses, 128

Slatalla, Michelle, 57

Slote, Stanley, 268

Small press publishers, 50–51

Smart cards, 37

Smith, Lisa, 177

Smith, Wendy, 54*n*

Social Sciences Citation Index, 203, 207

Social Sciences Index/Full Text, 127

Society:
   disadvantaged in, 19–21
   income distribution in, 4, 7, 25
   and library use, 3–5
   and multiculturalism, 19–21, 25–26
   and networks, 63–64
   readings on, 24–26

Soc.Libraries.Talk, 101

Software:
   for Internet access and searching, 107–109
   for searching electronic sources, 205–218
   (*See also* Electronic sources)

SOLINET (Southeastern Library Information Network), 74

Somerville, Mary, 26

Sony Corporation, 37

Sourcebook for Bibliographic Instruction, 229, 232*n*, 236

Sources of information (*see* Reference sources)

Sources of Information in the Social Sciences, 251

Southeastern Library Information Network (*see* SOLINET)

Spartanburg County Public Library, 145

Speech recognition, 36, 217, 218

Spiegelman, Art, 38

Spry, Inc., 82, 108*n*

St. Liver, Evan, 25–26

Standards for Community, Junior and Technical College Learning Resource Programs, 256

Starr, Susan, 96*n*

State networks, 74–75

State University of New York, 75

State University of New York OCLC Library Network, 68

Statistical Master Index, 45

Stebelman, Scott, 132*n*

Stein, Bob, 38

Stephenson, Nina, 232*n*

Stevens, Norman, 25

Stoll, Clifford, 116*n*, 118

Stress among librarians, 265–266

Strife, Mary, 267

Stumpers-L, 100

Subjects:
   in searching, 187–188, 191–192, 215
   and weeding, 254

Subscription plans for online sources, 45

Sullivan, Michael, 219

Superdensity CD-ROMs, 30

Survey on Access to Full-Text Electronic Periodical Articles, 140*n*

Surveys to evaluate reference services, 259

Sutherland, John, 29*n*

SVP, 53*n*

Taleb, Mohammed, 110*n*

Target, 213

Taylor, David, 102*n*, 245*n*

Teaching the Library Research Process, 235

Technology (*see* Computers; Electronic sources)

Telemedicine, 85

Telephone service, 23–24

Teletext, 84–85

Television, 30
   and computers, 83–86

"Telnet," 106

Tenopir, Carol, 135*n*, 211*n*, 214*n*, 231*n*

Texaco Corporation, 47

Textbooks, customized, 147–148

Thesaurus for controlled vocabulary searching, 215

Thesaurus Linguae Graecae, The, 30

Thoreau, Henry David, 116

303 CD-ROMs to Use in Your Library, 39
Tidbits, 50–51
Time, 81, 122*n*
Time Warner, 32, 83–84, 86, 90
Trade & Industry ASAP, 129
Tradeline, 129
Transom, 81
Tribble, Judith, 120*n*
TULIP, 138
Tyckoson, David, 242*n*, 268

Ulrich's International Periodical Directory, 131, 149
Ultimate Sniper, The, 243
Ultrafiche, 148–149
UMI, 68
  and document delivery, 123, 126–128, 133,
    134–136, 140
UnCover, 72, 132, 133, 150
United Kingdom:
  and Bulletin Board for Libraries, 99
  JANET in, 106
  teletext in, 84
United Press International, 130
United States:
  educational attainment in, 5, 6–7
  libraries in, 7–8
  reading in, 5–6
    (*See also* Literacy)
  socioeconomics in:
    income distribution, 4*n*, 7, 25
    and library use, 3–5
University Microfilms International (*see* UMI)
University of California, 72
University of Illinois, 109
University of Michigan, 99, 110
University of Michigan Clearinghouse, 105
University of Minnesota, 104*n*
University of Nevada, 104
University of Southern California Jewels,
  105
Unobtrusive evaluation of reference services,
  258–259
Usenet, 82, 100, 101–102
  and censorship, 245
  readings on, 117
Usenet FNews (Fast News Reader), 102
Using CompuServe, 82

Van House, Nancy, 268
Vassar College, 140
Vatican Library, 110, 146

Vatican Library and Renaissance Culture,
  110
Vendors, 61
  of CD-ROMs, 32, 41–42, 50
  database guides from, 78–79
  and document delivery, 124*n*, 125
  and networks, 77–80
    Internet, 96, 108
    regional networks, 73–74
  searching of databases from, 206–207
    (*See also specific vendors*)
Veronica, 104–105
Video Companion, The, 37
Videoconferencing, 85
Violence and censorship, 243–244
Virtual Community, The, 57, 92*n*
Virtual reality, 35
  readings on, 57
Virtual Reality Marketplace, 35*n*
Voice recognition, 36, 217, 218
Voyager Company, 38
VUTEXT, 78

Wade, Nicholas, 86*n*
Wagers, Robert, 216
Walker, Geraldine, 219
Wallace, Patricia, 234*n*
Walsh, Anthony, 259*n*
Walters, Sheila, 150
War Games, 246*n*
Washington State Library, 72
WebAccess, 68
WebCrawler, 107
Weeding Library Collections, 268
Weeding of reference collections, 251–254,
  268
Well, The, 38
Westbrook, Lynn, 268
Western Library Network (WLN), 72, 74
  (*See also* WLN)
WESTLAW, 213, 217
White, Herbert, 162*n*, 225*n*, 262
Whiteley, Sandy, 81*n*
Whitlach, Jo Bell, 241*n*, 256
Whole Internet User's Guide and Catalog, 89*n*
Whole Library Handbook 2, The, 20*n*, 240*n*
Wiant, Sarah, 56
Wide-area networks, 79
Wilde, Oscar, 156
Wiley (John), 123
Wilkins, Walter, 117

Williams, Wilda, 57
Willis, Deborah, 232n
Wilson (H. W.) Company, The, 32
  CD-ROMs networked by, 42
  cost of reference sources from, 44–45
  databases from, 203
  indexes from, on OCLC, 67–68
  searching of databases from, 42, 206
  as vendor and publisher, 77
  WilsonLine from, 78
WIN, 213, 217
Winchester, Simon, 118
Windows, 82, 95
WLN (Western Library Network), 72,
  74

Women, and Internet, 90, 91n
World Wide Web:
  commercial use of, 93
  guides to, 107
  and OCLC, 68
  searching of, 207
  slowness of, 94
  and virtual reality, 35
WorldCat, 67–70

Yahoo, 107
Yearbooks, weeding of, 254
Young, Peter, 247n

Zimmerman, Donald, 219